THE ECONOMICS OF WELFARE:
VOLUME I

T0293593

THE ECONOMICS OF WELFARE:
VOLUME I

ALFRED C. PIGOU

COSIMO CLASSICS
NEW YORK

The Economics of Welfare: Volume I

© 2005 Cosimo, Inc.

For information, address:

Cosimo, P.O. Box 416
Old Chelsea Station
New York, NY 10113-0416

or visit our website at:
www.cosimobooks.com

The Economics of Welfare: Volume I originally published by Macmillan and Co., in 1920.

Library of Congress Cataloging-in-Publication Data
A catalog record for this book is available from the Library of Congress

Cover design by www.wiselephant.com

ISBN: 1-59605-255-4

ANALYTICAL TABLE OF CONTENTS

PART I

WELFARE AND THE NATIONAL DIVIDEND

CHAPTER I

§ 1. The main motive of economic study is to help social improve-ment. §§ 2-3. Economic science will, therefore, be "realistic" rather than "pure"; but not merely "descriptive." § 4. It is very difficult to make its analysis quantitative. § 5. Economic welfare may be defined roughly as that part of welfare that can be brought into relation with the measuring rod of money. §§ 6-9. Instances can be multiplied in which economic causes, that affect economic welfare in one way, affect total welfare in a different way. § 10. Nevertheless there is a presumption that qualitative conclusions about effects upon economic welfare will hold good also of effects upon total welfare. § 11. And reasonably adequate conclusions about effects upon economic welfare can often be obtained by economic science, in spite of the partial and limited character of that science.

CHAPTER II

§ 1. The relation between satisfaction and the money measure is not direct, but is mediated through desires, the intensity of which need not always bear the same proportion to the satisfactions that their fulfilment yields. § 2. For the most part this circumstance is not important. § 3. But for the choice between using resources for the present and for the distant future it is very important. §§ 4-5. Coupled with the fact of individual mortality, it suggests that people are likely to save less and to use up nature's exhaustible stores more quickly than consists with the general interest. § 6. There is a presumption, therefore, against taxes that differentiate against saving. § 7. And in favour of State action to conserve natural resources.

CHAPTER VIII

§§ 1-2. Changes in the distribution of the national dividend in
favour of the poor may be brought about in several ways, the most
important of which is by a transference of purchasing power to
them from richer persons. §§ 3-4. Except in very special circumstances such a transference must increase economic welfare. §§ 5-6.
Particularly in a country where income is distributed as unevenly as
it is in England. § 7. This, however, is not quite the same thing
as saying that a diminution in the inequality of distribution must
increase economic welfare.

CHAPTER IX

§ 1. It may be objected that the consequences of an increase in
the dividend accruing to any group, particularly to a poor group,
discussed in Chapters VII. and VIII. are nullified by reactions on the
numbers of the population. § 2. Even apart from changes induced
by greater wealth in wants and tastes, this thesis is not tenable.
§ 3. And, when account is taken of them, the case for it is further
weakened. § 4. But the fact of migration between countries complicates the issue. § 5. And transferences of income present difficulties.

CHAPTER X

§ 1. The conclusions reached in Chapters VII. and VIII. must now
be reviewed in the light of modern biological knowledge. § 2. That
knowledge warrants the belief that general welfare and economic
welfare alike could be increased by measures restricting propagation
among the obviously degenerate. This belief, however, is additional
to, and does not disturb, our results. § 3. It is sometimes held that
modern biology, by demonstrating the dominant part played by
heredity as compared with environment, has proved economic
inquiries, which are, in the main, concerned with environment, to
be unimportant. Reasons are offered for rejecting this view. §§ 4-6.
It is sometimes held, further, that the advantage to economic welfare
claimed in Chapters VII. and VIII. to result from (1) an increase in
the magnitude and (2) an improvement in the distribution of the
national dividend are cancelled by indirect biological effects.
Reasons are offered for rejecting these views.

CHAPTER XI

PART II

THE SIZE OF THE NATIONAL DIVIDEND AND THE DISTRIBUTION OF RESOURCES AMONG DIFFERENT USES

CHAPTER I

§§ 1-2. The general problem of this Part is to ascertain how far the free play of self-interest, acting under the existing legal system, tends to distribute the country's resources in the way most favourable to the production of a large national dividend, and how far it is feasible for State action to improve upon "natural" tendencies.

CHAPTER II

§§ 1-4. The meaning of the term *marginal net product* is explained. § 5. Marginal social and marginal private net products are distinguished. § 6. As also their respective values.

CHAPTER III

§ 1. In the absence of costs of movement, it can be shown that, provided there is only one arrangement of resources which makes the values of the marginal social net products equal in all uses, that arrangement will maximise the national dividend. § 2. There is difficulty in extending this analysis to differences in degrees of inequality. § 3. In so far as there are costs of movement, the *optimum* arrangement, which is, of course, not so good as the *optimum* arrangement in the absence of costs, is different, and, within limits, indeterminate. § 4. In real life there are likely to be a number of different arrangements of resources, each one of which will make the values of the marginal social net products equal in all uses. Hence, equality of values of marginal social net products does not imply that the national dividend is maximised. § 5. There is here a possible opening for the beneficial use of bounties.

CHAPTER IV

§ 1. Values of marginal private net products are, in general, equal to rates of return. § 2. In the absence of costs of movement,

self-interest tends to make rates of return everywhere equal ; where
there are costs of movement to make them as nearly equal as those
costs allow. § 3. This implies that, except in so far as marginal
private and marginal social net products diverge, anything that
obstructs the free play of self-interest is likely to damage the dividend.

§§ 1-5. In a general way the elimination of obstacles, in the form of
costs of movement or lack of knowledge, to the free working of self
interest is likely to promote equality of returns. But this statement
is subject to qualifications. § 6. It is important to distinguish
between the effects on economic welfare of a real reduction in costs
and those of a mere transference of costs from the persons who control
the movement of resources to the State.

§§ 1-5. The tendency towards equality of returns in different occupations is obstructed by imperfect knowledge, resulting partly from
the character of business accounts, and partly from the general
organisation of business finance. § 6. The intervention of banks,
which naturally look to permanent and not merely to immediate
profit, in the work of promotion may, if other conditions allow, do
something to improve matters. § 7. The control exercised in minor
fields of investment by People's Banks of the Raiffeisen type is a
safeguard against the wasteful employment of borrowed resources.

§ 1. When the units in which transactions are made are large, or
when they are compounded of two factors in a fixed proportion, the
tendency of self-interest to make the rate of returns equal in all
uses is obstructed. § 2. In modern times the size of the unit in
which transactions in respect of capital take place has been diminished
in a twofold manner, partly with the help of the Stock Exchange.
§ 3. The compound character which formerly belonged to this unit
has also, in great part, been eliminated by arrangements which the
great growth of securities adapted to serve as collateral has facilitated.
§§ 4-5. The device of dividing shares into several grades and the
holding of them in their riskiest early age by financiers, who afterwards pass them on, work in the same direction. § 6. In general,
in present conditions, imperfect divisibility in the units of transactions has but little effect.

C̦HAPTER X

§ 1. The relation between marginal private net products and marginal social net products, besides being different in respect of investments in different uses, is also different in respect of investments made under different forms of industrial organisation.   § 2. For some forms do, and others do not, yield a return in the shape of trained capacity among the workpeople engaged in them, as well as a return of commodity products.   § 3. In present conditions investments in Workers' Copartnership Associations and in various kinds of small holdings probably yield a marginal social net product greater than the marginal private net product.   § 4. But the opposite is probably true of investments leading to the "trustification" of industry.   § 5. And possibly, after a point, of investments to promote standardisation.   § 6. It may also be true of investments made in connection with some aspects of "scientific management."

CHAPTER XI

§§ 1-2. Under simple competition investment in any particular industry is carried up to the point at which the marginal private net product of resources there is equal to the marginal social net product of resources in general : and the marginal social net product in the particular industry differs from this to the extent to which it differs from the marginal private net product in that industry.   §§ 3-4. The laws of increasing, constant, and decreasing supply price make assertions about analysis, not about history.   § 5. We must distinguish between increasing, constant, and decreasing supply prices *simpliciter*, and increasing, constant, and decreasing supply prices from the standpoint of the community.   § 6. Decreasing supply price from the standpoint of the community is possible over a wide range.   §§ 7-8. But increasing supply price from this standpoint only in a special case.   § 9. The value of the marginal private net product of investment in any industry is greater or less than the value of the marginal social net product according as this industry conforms to conditions of increasing or decreasing supply price from the standpoint of the community.   § 10. This implies that the value of the marginal social net product is the greater in all industries that conform to the conditions of decreasing supply price *simpliciter* ; but not that it is less in all industries of the converse type.   §§ 11-12. It is possible, by resort to bounties and taxes, to correct the errors of investment consequent, under simple competition, upon divergencies between the values of marginal social and marginal private net products.   § 13. Analogous reasoning suggests that economic welfare might be increased by taxes upon things which are desired for their uncommonness and by bounties on things that are desired for their commonness.   § 14. This analysis is very difficult to apply to practical problems, but it is not, therefore, otiose.

CHAPTER XV

CHAPTER XVI

CHAPTER XVII

CHAPTER XVIII

to different purchasers of ton-miles of transportation, so far as the ton-miles sold to different purchasers are not "jointly supplied." §§ 3-4. The common view that railway services are in large part jointly supplied—that the carriage of copper and the carriage of coal, or the carriage of coal destined for A and the carriage of coal destined for B, over a given piece of line are joint products—is incorrect. § 5. However, some measure of jointness, as, for instance, between out and home journeys, does in fact prevail. § 6. The meaning in concrete form of "the value of service principle" is explained. §§ 7-8. "The cost of service principle" corresponds to simple competition, and "the value of service principle" to discriminating monopoly of the third degree. In general, the former is the more advantageous to the national dividend ; but, as stated in the preceding chapter, circumstances may arise in which the latter is the more advantageous. §§ 9-10. These circumstances, however, are less common than writers on railway economics usually suppose. § 11. Moreover, such benefit as the "value of service principle" is competent to bring about can often be attained more satisfactorily by means of a bounty. § 12. The policy of permitting discriminating charges, subject to the condition that profits are prevented from rising above the normal, is discussed. § 13. Lastly, something is said of zone systems of railway tariffs.

CHAPTER XIX

§ 1. The preceding chapters have shown that, in many industries, neither simple competition, nor monopolistic competition, nor simple monopoly, nor discriminating monopoly will make the value of the marginal social net product of resources invested in them equal to the value of the marginal social net product of resources in general.   We have next to inquire whether this result can be secured by resort to the device of Purchasers' Associations.   § 2. The answer is clearly in the affirmative ; but no inference follows as to the effect on the national dividend, until the comparative advantages in respect of productive efficiency of Purchasers' Associations and ordinary commercial businesses have been ascertained.   § 3. Not much light can be thrown on that matter by historical examples. §§ 4-5. Purchasers' Associations have advantages in respect of production, so far as they save costs in advertisement, are exceptionally well fitted to spread knowledge of the best methods of production among their members, and have exceptionally small need of bargaining and safeguards against fraud. These advantages have led to their successful establishment over a considerable field. § 6. But for various reasons this field is limited, and a study of further remedies for the imperfections of ordinary business forms is, therefore, still required.

CHAPTER XX

§ 1. This chapter is concerned with the general merits of public intervention in industry, including both control and operation, as a remedy for the failures of private enterprise. § 2. For various reasons the experience of the war can afford much less guidance on this

matter than might be expected from it at first sight. § 3. The
problem is essentially the same in industries whose operation does,
and in those whose operation does not require resort to the right of
eminent domain. § 4. The mere failure of private industry, when
left free from public interference, to maximise the national dividend
does not of itself warrant intervention; for this *might* make things
worse. § 5. Certain modern developments have, however, rendered
governmental agencies better fitted for intervention than they were
in former times.

CHAPTER XXI

§ 1. This chapter is concerned with attempts by the State so to
control private monopoly that supply shall be adjusted to demand,
and the national dividend shall, therefore, be as large as it would be
under simple competition. § 2. The policy of maintaining *actual*
competition by refusing to allow rival concerns to combine is discussed. § 3. A second indirect method of control is embodied in
the policy of maintaining *potential* competition. This is worked by
penalising the "clubbing" devices of cut-throat competition, or
destructive dumping, and of boycott. §§ 4-5. The nature and effect
of these "clubbing" devices are explained. § 6. In spite of many
difficulties, it is probable that legislation directed against them, if
carefully prepared, may, at all events, lessen the extent to which
they are employed. § 7. But such legislation, even if successful in
its immediate object, would not serve completely to maintain
potential competition. § 8. The inadequacy of indirect methods of
control makes it necessary to supplement them by direct methods.
§ 9. The policy of encouraging the formation—over against combinations of sellers—of combinations of sellers also possessing monopolistic powers, is discussed. § 10. And the policy of publicity.
§ 11. Control over the terms of sale in monopolised industries
involves a special complication where increasing, but not where
decreasing supply price rules. § 12. War experience affords little
guidance. § 13. Control may be either negative — forbidding
"unreasonable" prices—or positive—establishing maximum prices.
§§ 14-15. The problem of "sanctions" is discussed. §§ 16-20. And
the very difficult problem of settling the basis in accordance with
which the reasonableness of prices shall be determined. §§ 21-25.
Several methods designed to prevent or limit errors on the part of
the price-regulating authority, including the device of sliding
scales, are examined. § 26. There is also, in old-established monopolies, the difficulty that price limitation may disturb "legitimate
expectations." § 27. Moreover, control is necessarily cumbersome
and expensive.

CHAPTER XXII

§§ 1-3. The difficulty of satisfactory public control suggests that
the national dividend might be increased by the public operation
—which is not the same thing as the public ownership—of certain
industries, provided that this would not involve a serious loss of
economy in production. § 4. The experience of the war does not
give much guidance. § 5. The economic efficiency of public and of

THE ECONOMICS OF WELFARE

joint-stock operation of industry cannot be successfully compared by reference to statistics. §§ 6-9. The public operation of industries may assume a number of different forms, and, from the point of view of technical efficiency, it need not be inferior to private operation—particularly controlled private operation. § 10. But, first, under public operation there is a danger that the operating authority may be tempted to maintain its enterprise by the use of unfair extra-commercial methods at the expense of rival enterprises capable of satisfying the same wants more cheaply. § 11. Secondly, under public operation efficiency is likely to suffer through unwillingness to take risks and make experiments. §§ 12-13. Thirdly, efficiency is likely to suffer through the establishment of units of management of an uneconomical size ; though, in industries where the normal state of things is monopolistic competition, public operation is, in this respect, superior to joint-stock operation. § 14. On the whole, apart from a few special exceptions, the proposal for public operation is a live one only where there is monopoly ; and here the case for it, as against that for public control, works out differently in different industries. § 15. When public operation is determined upon for a concern hitherto in private hands, the determination of a proper purchase price presents difficulties. § 16. But, even when a heavy ransom has to be paid to vested interests, it may still be for the general good that a public authority should buy up a private monopoly, in order to stop artificial restriction of output.

PART I

WELFARE AND THE NATIONAL DIVIDEND

CHAPTER I

§ 1. WHEN a man sets out upon any course of inquiry, the object of his search may be either light or fruit—either knowledge for its own sake or knowledge for the sake of good things to which it leads. In various fields of study these two ideals play parts of varying importance. In the appeal made to our interest by nearly all the great modern sciences *some* stress is laid both upon the light-bearing and upon the fruit-bearing quality, but the proportions of the blend are different in different sciences. At one end of the scale stands the most general science of all, metaphysics, the science of reality. Of the student of that science it is, indeed, true that "he yet may bring some worthy thing for waiting souls to see"; but it must be light alone, it can hardly be fruit that he brings. Most nearly akin to the metaphysician is the student of the ultimate problems of physics. The corpuscular theory of matter is, hitherto, a bearer of light alone. Here, however, the other aspect is present in promise; for speculations about the structure of the atom may lead one day to the discovery of practical means for dissociating matter and for rendering available to human use the overwhelming resources of intra-atomic energy. In the science of biology the fruit-bearing aspect is more prominent. Recent studies upon heredity have, indeed, the highest theoretical interest; but no one can reflect upon that without at the same time reflecting upon the striking practical results to which they have already led in the culture of wheat, and upon the far-reaching, if hesitating, promise that they are beginning

3

to offer for the better culture of mankind. In the sciences whose subject-matter is man as an individual there is the same variation of blending as in the natural sciences proper. In psychology the theoretic interest is dominant—particularly on that side of it which gives data to metaphysics; but psychology is also valued in some measure as a basis for the practical art of education. In human physiology, on the other hand, the theoretic interest, though present, is subordinate, and the science has long been valued mainly as a basis for the art of medicine. Last of all we come to those sciences that deal, not with individual men, but with groups of men; that body of infant sciences which some writers call sociology. Light on the laws that lie behind development in history, even light upon particular facts, has, in the opinion of many, high value for its own sake. But there will, I think, be general agreement that in the sciences of human society, be their appeal as bearers of light never so high, it is the promise of fruit and not of light that chiefly merits our regard. There is a celebrated, if somewhat too strenuous, passage in Macaulay's Essay on History : " No past event has any intrinsic importance. The knowledge of it is valuable, only as it leads us to form just calculations with regard to the future. A history which does not serve this purpose, though it may be filled with battles, treaties and commotions, is as useless as the series of turnpike tickets collected by Sir Matthew Mite." That paradox is partly true. If it were not for the hope that a scientific study of men's social actions may lead, not necessarily directly or immediately, but at some time and in some way, to practical results in social improvement, not a few students of these actions would regard the time devoted to their study as time misspent. That is true of all social sciences, but especially true of economics. For economics " is a study of mankind in the ordinary business of life "; and it is not in the ordinary business of life that mankind is most interesting or inspiring. One who desired knowledge of man apart from the fruits of knowledge would seek it in the history of religious enthusiasm, of martyrdom, or of love ; he would not seek it in the market-place. When we elect to watch the play of human motives that are ordinary—that are sometimes mean and dismal and ignoble —our impulse is not the philosopher's impulse, knowledge for the sake of knowledge, but rather the physiologist's, knowledge for the healing that knowledge may help to bring.   Wonder, Carlyle declared, is the beginning of philosophy.   It is not wonder, but rather the social enthusiasm which revolts from the sordidness of mean streets and the joylessness of withered lives, that is the beginning of economic science.   Here, if in no other field, Comte's great phrase holds good : " It is for the heart to suggest our problems ; it is for the intellect to solve them. . . . The only position for which the intellect is primarily adapted is to be the servant of the social sympathies."

§ 2. If this conception of the motive behind economic study is accepted, it follows that the type of science that the economist will endeavour to develop must be one adapted to form the basis of an art.   It will not, indeed, itself be an art, or directly enunciate precepts of government.   It is a positive science of what is and tends to be, not a normative science of what ought to be.   Nor will it limit itself to those fields of positive scientific inquiry which have an obvious relevance to immediate practical problems.   This course would hamper thorough investigation and shut out inquiries that might ultimately bear fruit.   For, as has been well said, " in our most theoretical moods we may be nearest to our most practical applications." [1]   But, though wholly independent in its tactics and its strategy, it will be guided in general direction by practical interest.   This decides its choice of essential form.   For there are two main types of positive science.   On the one side are the sciences of formal logic and pure mathematics, whose function it is to discover *implications*.   On the other side are the realistic sciences, such as physics, chemistry and biology, which are concerned with actualities.   The distinction is drawn out in Mr. Russell's *Principles of Mathematics*.   " Since the growth of non-Euclidean Geometry, it has appeared that pure mathematics has no concern with the question whether the

[1] Whitehead, *Introduction to Mathematics*, p. 100.

axioms and propositions of Euclid hold of actual space or not: this is a question for realistic mathematics, to be decided, so far as any decision is possible, by experiment and observation. What pure mathematics asserts is merely that the Euclidean propositions follow from the Euclidean axioms, *i.e.* it asserts an implication : any space which has such and such properties has also such and such other properties. Thus, as dealt with in pure mathematics, the Euclidean and non-Euclidean Geometries are equally true : in each nothing is affirmed except implications. All propositions as to what actually exists, like the space we live in, belong to experimental or empirical science, not to mathematics." [1] This distinction is applicable to the field of economic investigation. It is open to us to construct an economic science either of the pure type represented by pure mathematics or of the realistic type represented by experimental physics. Pure economics in this sense—an unaccustomed sense, no doubt—would study equilibria and disturbances of equilibria among groups of persons actuated by any set of motives *x*. Under it, among innumerable other subdivisions, would be included at once an Adam-Smithian political economy, in which *x* is given the value of the motives assigned to the economic man—or to the normal man—and a non-Adam-Smithian political economy, corresponding to the geometry of Lobatschewsky, under which *x* consists of love of work and hatred of earnings. For pure economics both these political economies would be equally true; it would not be relevant to inquire what the value of *x* is among the actual men who are living in the world now. Contrasted with this pure science stands realistic economics, the interest of which is concentrated upon the world known in experience, and in nowise extends to the commercial doings of a community of angels. Now, if our end is practice, it is obvious that a political economy that did so extend would be for us merely an amusing toy. Hence it must be the realistic, and not the pure, type of science that constitutes the object of our search. We shall endeavour to elucidate, not any

[1] *Principles of Mathematics*, p. 5. I have substituted *realistic* for Mr. Russell's word *applied* in this passage.

generalised system of possible worlds, but the actual world of men and women as they are found in experience to be.

§ 3. But, if it is plain that a science of the pure type will not serve our purpose, it is equally plain that realism, in the sense of a mere descriptive catalogue of observed facts, will not serve it either. Infinite narration by itself can never enable forecasts to be made, and it is, of course, capacity to make forecasts that practice requires. Before this capacity can be obtained facts must be passed upon by reason. Besides the brute facts, there must be what Browning calls, " something of mine, which, mixed up with the mass, made it bear hammer and be firm to file." It is just the presence of this *something* which is essential to a realistic science as distinguished from mere description. In realistic science facts are not simply brought together ; they are compelled by thought to *speak*. As M. Poincaré well writes: " Science is built up of facts as a house is built of stones ; but an accumulation of facts is no more a science than a heap of stones is a house." [1] Astronomical physics is not merely a catalogue of the positions which certain stars have been observed to occupy on various occasions. Biology is not merely a list of the results of a number of experiments in breeding. Rather, every science, through examination and cross-examination of the particular facts which it is able to ascertain, seeks to discover the general laws of whose operation these particular facts are instances. The motions of the heavenly bodies are exhibited in the light of the laws of Newton ; the breeding of the blue Andalusian fowl in the light of that of Mendel. These laws, furthermore, are not merely summaries of the observed facts re-stated in a shorthand form. They are *generalisations*, and, as such, extend our knowledge to facts that have not been observed, maybe, that have not as yet even occurred. On what philosophical basis generalisations of this sort rest we are not here concerned to inquire. It is enough that in every realistic science they are *made*. As Mr. Whetham, speaking of physics, puts it, any such science " seeks to establish general rules which describe the sequence of phenomena in *all* cases." [2] It is only by

[1] *Science and Hypothesis*, p. 141.
[2] *Recent Developments in Physical Science*, p. 30. The italics are mine.

reference to these general rules that the forecasts, which practice needs, are rendered possible. It is in their fundamental aspect as an organon of laws, and not in their superficial aspect as a description of facts, that the realistic sciences have bearing upon the conduct of affairs. The establishment of such an organon adapted and ready for application to particular problems is the ideal at which they aim.

§ 4. To say this without saying something more would, however, be very misleading. It is not pretended that, at the present stage of its development, economic science is able to provide an organon even remotely approaching to what it imagines for itself as its ideal. Full guidance for practice requires, to borrow Marshall's phrase, capacity to carry out *quantitative*, not merely *qualitative*, analysis. " Qualitative analysis tells the ironmaster that there is *some* sulphur in his ore, but it does not enable him to decide whether it is worth while to smelt the ore at all, and, if it is, then by what process. For that purpose he needs quantitative analysis, which will tell him *how much* sulphur there is in the ore." [1] Capacity to provide information of this kind economic science at present almost entirely lacks. Before the application of general laws to particular problems can yield quantitative results, these laws themselves must be susceptible of quantitative statement. The law is the major premiss and the particular facts of any problem the minor. When the statement of the law lacks precision, the conclusion must generally suffer from the same defect ; and, unfortunately, the task of setting out economic laws in precise form has scarcely been begun. For this there are three reasons. First, the relations which have to be determined are extremely numerous. In physics the fundamental thing, the gravitation constant, expressing the relation between distance and attractive force, is the same for all sorts of matter. But the fundamental things in the economic world—the schedules expressing the desires or aversions of groups of people for different sorts of commodities and services—are not · thus simple and uniform. We are in the position in which the physicist would be if tin attracted iron in the inverse ratio of the cube of its distance, lead in that of the square of its

[1] Marshall, *The Old Generation of Economists and the New*, p. 11,

distance, and copper in some other ratio. We cannot say, as he can of his attractions, that the amount offered or required of every several commodity is one and the same specified function of the price. All that we can say in this general way is that it is *some one* of a specified large family of functions of the price. Hence, in economics there is not, as in dynamics, one fundamental law of general application, but a great number of laws, all expressible, as it were, in equations of similar form but with different constants. On account of this multiplicity, the determination of those constants, or to put the matter broadly, the measurement of the elasticities of demand and supply of the various commodities in which economics is interested, is a very large task. Secondly, this task is one in attacking which the principal weapon employed by other sciences in their inquiries cannot be fully used. "Theory," said Leonardo da Vinci, "is the general; experiments are the soldiers." Economic science has already well-trained generals, but, because of the nature of the material in which it works, the soldiers are hard to obtain. "The surgeon dissects a dead body before he operates on a living one, and operates upon an animal before he operates upon a human being; the mechanic makes a working model and tests it before he builds the full-sized machine. Every step is, whenever possible, tested by experiment in these matters before risks are run. In this way the unknown is robbed of most of its terrors." [1]   In economics, for the simple reason that its subject-matter is living and free men, direct experiment under conditions adequately controlled is hardly ever feasible. But there is a third and even more serious difficulty. Even if the constants which economists wish to determine were less numerous, and the method of experiment more accessible, we should still be faced with the fact that the constants themselves are different at different times. The gravitation constant is the same always. But the economic constants—these elasticities of demand and supply—depending, as they do, upon human consciousness, are liable to vary. The constitution of the atom, as it were, and not merely its position, changes under the influence of environment. Thus the real injury done to Ireland by

[1] Lord Hugh Cecil, *Conservatism*, p. 18.

the earlier English administration of that country was not the
destruction of specific industries or even the sweeping of its
commerce from the seas. "The real grievance lies in the fact
that something had been taken from our industrial character
which could not be remedied by the mere removal of the
restrictions. Not only had the tree been stripped, but the
roots had been destroyed."[1] This malleability in the actual
substance with which economic study deals means that the
goal sought is itself perpetually shifting, so that, even if it
were possible by experiment exactly to determine the values of
the economic constants to-day, we could not say with confidence
that this determination would hold good also of to-morrow.
Hence the inevitable shortcomings of our science. We can,
indeed, by a careful study of all relevant facts, learn *something*
about the elasticities of demand and supply for a good number
of things, but we cannot ascertain their magnitude with any
degree of exactness. In other words, our fundamental laws,
and, therefore, inferences from these laws in particular conditions,
cannot at present be thrown into any quantitatively precise
form. The result is that, when, as often happens, a practical
issue turns upon the balancing of opposing considerations, even
though these considerations are wholly economic, economic
science must almost always speak with an uncertain voice.

§ 5. The preceding paragraph has been somewhat of a
digression. It has now to be added that, just as the
motive and purpose of our inquiry govern its form, so
also they control its scope. The goal sought is to make
more easy practical measures to promote welfare—practical
measures which statesmen may build upon the work of the
economist, just as Marconi, the inventor, built upon the
discoveries of Hertz. Welfare, however, is a thing of very
wide range. There is no need here to enter upon a general
discussion of its content. It will be sufficient to lay down
more or less dogmatically two propositions; first, that the
elements of welfare are states of consciousness and, perhaps,
their relations; secondly, that welfare can be brought under
the category of greater and less. A general investigation of all
the groups of causes by which welfare thus conceived may be

[1] Plunkett, *Ireland in the New Century*, p. 19.

affected would constitute a task so enormous and complicated as to be quite impracticable. It is, therefore, necessary to limit our subject-matter. In doing this we are naturally attracted towards that portion of the field in which the methods of science seem likely to work at best advantage. This they can clearly do when there is present something measurable, on which analytical machinery can get a firm grip. The one obvious instrument of measurement available in social life is money. Hence, the range of our inquiry becomes restricted to that part of social welfare that can be brought directly or indirectly into relation with the measuring-rod of money. This part of welfare may be called economic welfare. It is not, indeed, possible to separate it in any rigid way from other parts, for the part which *can* be brought into relation with a money measure will be different according as we mean by *can*, " can easily " or " can with mild straining " or " can with violent straining." The outline of our territory is, therefore, necessarily vague. Professor Cannan has well observed : " We must face, and face boldly, the fact that there is no precise line between economic and non-economic satisfactions, and, therefore, the province of economics cannot be marked out by a row of posts or a fence, like a political territory or a landed property. We can proceed from the undoubtedly economic at one end of the scale to the undoubtedly non-economic at the other end without finding anywhere a fence to climb or a ditch to cross." [1]   Nevertheless, though no precise boundary between economic and non-economic welfare exists, yet the test of accessibility to a money measure serves well enough to set up a rough distinction. Economic welfare, as loosely defined by this test, is the subject-matter of economic science. The purpose of this volume is to study certain important groups of causes that affect economic welfare in actual modern societies.

§ 6. At first glance this programme, if somewhat ambitious, appears, at all events, a legitimate one. But reflection soon shows that the proposal to treat in isolation the causes affecting one part of welfare only is open to a serious objection. Our ultimate interest is, of course, in the effects

[1] *Wealth*, pp. 17-18.

which the various causes investigated are likely to have
upon welfare as a whole. But there is no guarantee that
the effects produced on the part of welfare that can be
brought into relation with the measuring-rod of money
may not be cancelled by effects of a contrary kind brought
about in other parts, or aspects, of welfare ; and, if this
happens, the practical usefulness of our conclusions is wholly
destroyed. The difficulty, it must be carefully observed, is
not that, since economic welfare is only a part of welfare
as a whole, welfare will often change while economic
welfare remains the same, so that a given change in
economic welfare will seldom synchronise with an equal
change in welfare as a whole. All that this means is that
economic welfare will not serve for a *barometer* or *index* of
total welfare. But that, for our purpose, is of no importance.
What we wish to learn is, not how large welfare is, or
has been, but how its magnitude would be affected by the
introduction of causes which it is in the power of statesmen
or private persons to call into being. The failure of economic
welfare to serve as an *index* of total welfare is no evidence that
the study of it will fail to afford this latter information :
for, though a whole may consist of many varying parts, so
that a change in one part never *measures* the change in
the whole, yet the change in the part may always *affect*
the change in the whole by its full amount. If this
condition is satisfied, the practical importance of economic
study is fully established. It will not, indeed, tell us how
total welfare, after the introduction of an economic cause, will
differ from what it was before ; but it will tell us how total
welfare will differ from what it would have been if that
cause had not been introduced : and this, and not the other,
is the information of which we are in search. The real
objection then is, not that economic welfare is a bad *index*
of total welfare, but that an economic cause may affect non-
economic welfare in ways that cancel its effect on economic
welfare. This objection requires careful consideration.

§ 7. One very important aspect of it is as follows. Human
beings are both " ends in themselves " and instruments of
production. On the one hand, a man who is attuned to

the beautiful in nature or in art, whose character is simple and sincere, whose passions are controlled and sympathies developed, is in himself an important element in the ethical value of the world; the way in which he feels and thinks actually constitutes a part of welfare. On the other hand, a man who can perform complicated industrial operations, sift difficult evidence, or advance some branch of practical activity, is an instrument well fitted to produce things whose use yields welfare. The welfare to which the former of these men contributes directly is non-economic; that to which the latter contributes indirectly is economic. The fact we have to face is that, in some measure, it is open to the community to choose between these two sorts of men, and that, by concentrating its effort upon the economic welfare embodied in the second, it may unconsciously sacrifice the non-economic welfare embodied in the first. The point is easy of illustration. The weak and disjointed Germany of a century ago was the home of Goethe and Schiller, Kant and Fichte. "We know what the old Germany gave the world," says Mr. Dawson in a book published several years before the war, "and for that gift the world will ever be grateful; we do not know what modern Germany, the Germany of the overflowing barns and the full argosies, has to offer, beyond its materialistic science and its merchandise. . . . The German systems of education, which are incomparable so far as their purpose is the production of scholars and teachers, or of officials and functionaries, to move the cranks, turn the screws, gear the pulleys, and oil the wheels of the complicated national machine, are far from being equally successful in the making of character or individuality."[1] In short, the attention of the German people was so concentrated on the idea of learning to *do* that they did not care, as in former times, for learning to *be*. Nor does Germany stand alone before this charge; as witness the following description of modern England written by an Englishman from the standpoint of an Oriental spectator. "By your works you may be known. Your triumphs in the mechanical arts are the obverse of your failure in all that calls for spiritual

[1] *The Evolution of Modern Germany*, pp. 15-16.

insight. Machines of every kind you can make and use to perfection; but you cannot build a house, or write a poem, or paint a picture; still less can you worship or aspire. . . . Your outer man as well as your inner is dead; you are blind and deaf. Ratiocination has taken the place of perception; and your whole life is an infinite syllogism from premises you have not examined to conclusions you have not anticipated or willed. Everywhere means, nowhere an end. Society a huge engine and that engine itself out of gear. Such is the picture your civilisation presents to my imagination." [1] There is, of course, exaggeration in this indictment; but there is also truth. At all events it brings out vividly the point which is here at issue; that efforts devoted to the production of people who are good instruments may involve a failure to produce people who are good men.

§ 8. The possibility of conflict between the effects of economic causes upon economic welfare and upon welfare in general, which these considerations emphasise, is easily explained. The only aspects of conscious life which can, as a rule, be brought into relation with a money measure, and which, therefore, fall within economic welfare, are a certain limited group of *satisfactions* and *dissatisfactions*. But conscious life is a complex of many elements, and includes, not only these satisfactions and dissatisfactions, but also other satisfactions and dissatisfactions, and, along with them, cognitions, emotions and desires. Environmental causes operating to change economic satisfactions may, therefore, either in the same act or as a consequence of it, alter some of these other elements. The ways in which they do this may be distinguished, for purposes of illustration, into two principal groups.

First, non-economic welfare is liable to be modified by the manner in which income is earned. For the surroundings of work react upon the quality of life. Ethical quality is affected by the occupations—menial service, agricultural labour, artistic creation, independent as against subordinate economic positions,[2]

---

[1] Dickinson, *Letters of John Chinaman*, pp. 25-6.

[2] Thus it is important to notice that machinery, as it comes to be more elaborate and expensive, makes it, *pro tanto*, more difficult for small men, alike in industry and agriculture, to start independent businesses of their own. Cf. Quaintance, *Farm Machinery*, p. 58.

monotonous repetition of the same operation,[1] and so on—into which the desires of consumers impel the people who work to satisfy them. It is affected, too, by the influence which these people exert on others with whom they may be brought into personal contact. The social aspect of Chinese labour in the Transvaal and of the attempt by Australian pastoralists to maintain the convict system, as a source of labour supply,[2] had relevance to welfare. So, too, have the unity of interest and occupation which characterise the farm family as distinguished from the town-dwelling family.[3] In the Indian village "the collaboration of the family members not only economises expenses, but sweetens labour. Culture and refinement come easily to the artisan through his work amidst his kith and kin."[4] Thus the industrial revolution, when it led the cottager from his home into the factory, had an effect on other things besides production. In like manner, increased efficiency in output was not the only result which the agricultural revolution, with its enclosures and large-scale farming, brought about. There was also a social change in the destruction of the old yeoman class. The human relations that arise out of industrial relations are also relevant. In the great co-operative movement, for example, there is a non-economic side at least as important as the economic. Whereas in the organisation of ordinary competitive industry opposition of interest, both as between competing sellers and as between sellers and buyers, necessarily stands in the fore-front, and results at times in trickery and a sense of mutual suspicion, in a co-operative organisation unity of interest

[1] Munsterberg writes "that the feeling of monotony depends much less upon the particular kind of work than upon the special disposition of the individual" (*Psychology and Industrial Efficiency*, p. 198). But, of course, the *ethical effect* of monotony must be distinguished from the unpleasantness of it. Marshall maintains that monotony of life is the important thing, and argues that variety of life is compatible with monotony of occupation, in so far as machines take over straining forms of work, with the result that "nervous force is not very much exhausted by the ordinary work of a factory" (*Principles of Economics*, p. 263). Obviously much turns here on the length of the working day. Smart held that "the work of the majority is not only toilsome, monotonous, undeveloping, but takes up the better part of the day, and leaves little energy for other pursuits" (*Second Thoughts of an Economist*, p. 107).

[2] Cf. V. S. Clark, *The Labour Movement in Australia*, p. 32.

[3] Cf. *Proceedings of the American Economic Association*, vol. x. pp. 234-5.

[4] Cf. Mukerjee, *The Foundations of Indian Economics*, p. 386.

is paramount. This circumstance has its influence on the general tone of life. " As a member of a society with interests in common with others, the individual consciously and unconsciously develops the social virtues. Honesty becomes imperative, and is enforced by the whole group on the individual, loyalty to the whole group is made an essential for the better development of individual powers. To cheat the society is to injure a neighbour." [1] In the relations between employers and workpeople in ordinary industry the non-economic element is fully as significant. The *esprit de corps* and interest in the fortunes of the firm, which animate the workpeople in establishments where the personal intercourse of employers and employed is cordial, besides leading to increased production of wealth, *is* in itself an addition to welfare. As large-scale industry extended during the eighteenth and nineteenth centuries, employers and employed became more distant in station, and their opportunities of meeting one another diminished. In the wake of this inevitable physical separation there followed a moral separation—" the personal alienation of the employer from his fellow-men whom he engages to work for him in large numbers." [2] This spirit of hostility was an obvious negative element in non-economic welfare due to an economic cause; and the partial suppression of it through Boards of Conciliation, Whitley Councils and Copartnership arrangements is an equally obvious positive element. Nor is this all. It is more and more coming to be recognised that, if one root of " labour unrest " has been dissatisfaction with rates of wages, a second root, also of great importance, has been dissatisfaction with the general *status* of wage-labour—the feeling that the industrial system, as it is to-day, deprives the workpeople of the liberties and responsibilities proper to free men, and renders

---

[1] Smith-Gordon and Staples, *Rural Reconstruction in Ireland*, p. 240. Cf. the enthusiastic picture which Wolff draws of the general social benefits of rural co-operation on the Raiffeisen plan : " How it creates a desire and readiness to receive and assimilate instruction, technical and general, how it helps to raise the character of the people united by it, making for sobriety, strict honesty, good family life, and good living generally." It has been seen, he says, to produce these effects " among the comparatively educated peasantry of Germany, the illiterate country folk of Italy, the primitive cultivators of Serbia, and it is beginning to have something the same effect among the ryots of India " (*The Future of Agriculture*, p. 481).

[2] Gilman, *A Dividend to Labour*, p. 15.

them mere tools to be used or dispensed with at the convenience of others : the sense, in short, as Mazzini put it long ago, that capital is the *despot* of labour.[1] Changes in industrial organisation that tend to give greater control over their own lives to workpeople, whether through workmen's councils to overlook matters of discipline and workshop organisation in conjunction with the employer, or through a democratically elected Parliament directly responsible for nationalised industries, or, if this should prove feasible, through some form of State-recognised and State-controlled national guilds,[2] might increase welfare as a whole, even though they were to leave unchanged, or actually to damage, economic welfare.

Secondly, non-economic welfare is liable to be modified by the manner in which income is spent. Of different acts of consumption that yield equal satisfactions, one may exercise a debasing, and another an elevating, influence.[3] The reflex effect upon the quality of people produced by public museums, or even by municipal baths,[4] is very different from the reflex effect of equal satisfactions in a public bar. The coarsening and brutalising influence of bad housing accommodation is an incident not less important than the direct dissatisfaction involved in it. Instances of the same kind could be multiplied. The point that they would illustrate is obviously of large practical importance. Imagine, for example, that a statesman

[1] Cf. Mazzini, *The Duties of Man*, p. 99.

[2] Cf. *The Meaning of National Guilds*, by Beckhover and Reckitt, *passim*. "The essence of Labour's demand for responsibility is that it should be recognised as responsible to the community, not to the capitalist" (p. 100). The goal of National Guilds "is the control of production by self-governing Guilds of workers sharing with the State the control of the produce of their labour" (p. 285). The fact that schemes of industrial reorganisation on these lines are exposed to serious practical difficulties, which their authors do not as yet seem fully to have faced, does not render any less admirable the *spirit* of this ideal.

[3] Mr. Hawtrey has criticised my analysis upon the ground that it implicitly makes equal satisfactions embody equal amounts of welfare, whereas, in fact, satisfactions are of various degrees of goodness and badness (*The Economic Problem*, pp. 184-5). There is, however, no difference in substance between Mr. Hawtrey and myself. We both take account of those variations of quality. Whether it is better to say, of two equal satisfactions, that one may in itself contain more good than the other, or to say that in themselves, *qua* satisfactions, they are equally good, but that their reactions upon the quality of the people enjoying them may differ in goodness, is chiefly a matter of words. I have substituted in the present text "the quality of people" for my original "people's characters." [4] Cf. Darwin, *Municipal Trade*, p. 75.

C

is considering how far inequality in the distribution of wealth influences welfare as a whole, and not merely in its economic aspects. He will reflect that the satisfaction of some of the desires of the rich, such as gambling excitement or luxurious sensual enjoyment, or perhaps, in Eastern countries, opium-eating, involves reactions on character ethically inferior to those involved in the satisfaction of primary physical needs, to the securing of which the capital and labour controlled by the demand of the rich would, if transferred to the poor, probably be devoted. On the other hand, he will reflect that other satisfactions purchased by the rich—those, for example, connected with literature and art [1]—involve reactions that are ethically superior to those connected with the primary needs, and still more to those derived from excessive indulgence in stimulants. These very real elements in welfare will, indeed, enter into relation with the measuring rod of money, and so be counted in economic welfare, in so far as one group of people devote income to purchasing things *for* other people. When they do this, they are likely to take account of the total effect, and not merely of the effect on the satisfactions of those people—especially if the said people are their own children. For, as Sidgwick acutely observes: "A genuine regard for our neighbour, when not hampered by the tyranny of custom, prompts us to give him what we think really good for him, whereas natural self-regard prompts us to give ourselves what we like." [2] In these special circumstances, therefore, the gap between the effect on economic welfare and the effect on total welfare is partially bridged. Generally, however, it is not so bridged.

§ 9. There is one further consideration, of the great importance of which recent events can leave no doubt. It has to do with the possible conflict, long ago emphasised

---

[1] Thus, Sidgwick observes after a careful discussion : "There seems, therefore, to be a serious danger that a thorough-going equalisation of wealth among the members of a modern civilised community would have a tendency to check the growth of culture in the community" (*Principles of Political Economy*, p. 523).

[2] *Practical Ethics*, p. 20. Cf. Effertz : "Ce que les intéressés savent généralement mieux que les non-intéressés, ce sont les *moyens* propres à réaliser ce qu'ils croient être leur intérêt. Mais, dans la détermination de l'intérêt le non-intéressé voit généralement plus clair" (*Antagonismes économiques*, pp. 237-8).

by Adam Smith, between opulence and defence. Lack of security against successful hostile attack may involve " dissatisfactions " of a very terrible kind. These things lie outside the economic sphere, but the risk of them may easily be affected by economic policy. It is true, no doubt, that between economic strength and capacity for war there is a certain rough agreement. As Adam Smith wrote : " The nation which, from the annual produce of its domestic industry, from the annual revenue arising out of its lands, labour and consumable stock, has wherewithal to purchase those consumable goods in distant countries, can maintain foreign wars there." [1] But agreement between economic and military strength is ultimate and general, not immediate and detailed. It must, therefore, be clearly recognised that the effect upon economic welfare of the policy which a State adopts towards agriculture, shipping and industries producing war material is often a very subordinate part of its whole effect. Injury to economic welfare may need to be accepted for the sake of defensive strategy. Economically it is probably to the advantage of this country to purchase the greater part of its food supplies from abroad in exchange for manufactured goods, and to keep more than two-thirds of its cultivated land under grass—in which state comparatively little capital and labour is employed upon it and correspondingly little human food produced.[2] In a world of perpetual peace this policy would also probably be advantageous on the whole ; for a small proportion of the population engaged in agriculture does not necessarily imply a small proportion living under rural conditions. But, when account is taken of the possibility that imports may be cut off by blockade in war, that inference need not follow. There can be little doubt that Germany's policy of conserving and developing agriculture for many years at an economic loss enabled her to resist the British blockade in the Great War for a much longer period than would otherwise have been possible ; and, though there are, of course, alternative means

[1] *Wealth of Nations*, p. 333.
[2] Cf. *The Recent Development of German Agriculture* [Cd. 8305], 1916, p. 42 and *passim*.

of defence, such as the establishment of large national grain stores, it is, from a general political point of view, a debatable question whether in this country some form of artificial encouragement should be given to agriculture as a partial insurance against the danger of food difficulties in the event of war. This issue, and the kindred issue concerning materials and industries essential for the conduct of war, cannot be decided by reference to economic considerations alone.

§ 10. The preceding discussion makes it plain that any rigid inference from effects on economic welfare to effects on total welfare is out of the question. In some fields the divergence between the two effects will be insignificant, but in others it will be very wide. Nevertheless, I submit that, in the absence of special knowledge, there is room for a judgment of probability. When we have ascertained the effect of any cause on economic welfare, we may, unless, of course, there is specific evidence to the contrary, regard this effect as *probably* equivalent in direction, though not in magnitude, to the effect on total welfare ; and, when we have ascertained that the effect of one cause is more favourable than that of another cause to economic welfare, we may, on the same terms, conclude that the effect of this cause on total welfare is probably more favourable. In short, there is a presumption—what Edgeworth calls an " unverified probability "—that qualitative conclusions about the effect of an economic cause upon economic welfare will hold good also of the effect on total welfare. This presumption is especially strong where experience suggests that the non-economic effects produced are likely to be small. But in all circumstances the burden of proof lies upon those who hold that the presumption should be overruled.

§ 11. The above result suggests *prima facie* that economic science, when it shall have come to full development, is likely to furnish a powerful guide to practice. Against this suggestion there remains, however, one considerable obstacle. When the conclusion set out in the preceding section is admitted to be valid, a question may still be raised as to its practical utility. Granted, it may be said, that the effects produced by economic causes upon economic welfare are probably, in some measure, representative of those produced on total welfare, we have really gained nothing. For the effects produced upon economic welfare itself cannot, the argument runs, be ascertained beforehand by those partial and limited investigations which alone fall within the scope of economic science. The reason for this is that the effects upon economic welfare produced by any economic cause are likely to be modified by the non-economic conditions, which, in one form or another, are always present, but which economic science is not adapted to investigate. The difficulty is stated very clearly by J. S. Mill in his *Logic*. The study of a *part* of things, he points out, cannot in any circumstances be expected to yield more than approximate results: "Whatever affects, in an appreciable degree, any one element of the social state, affects through it all the other elements. . . . We can never either understand in theory or command in practice the condition of a society in any one respect, without taking into consideration its condition in all other respects. There is no social phenomenon which is not more or less influenced by every other part of the condition of the same society, and, therefore, by every cause which is influencing any other of the contemporaneous social phenomena."[1] In other words, the effects of economic causes are certain to be partially dependent on non-economic circumstances, in such wise that the same cause will produce somewhat different economic effects according to the general character of, say, the political or religious conditions that prevail. So far as this kind of dependence exists, it is obvious that causal propositions in economics can only be laid down subject to the condition that things outside the economic sphere either remain constant or, at least, do not vary beyond certain defined limits. Does this condition destroy the practical utility of our science ? I hold that, among nations with a stable general culture, like those inhabiting Western Europe, the condition is fulfilled nearly enough to render the results reached by economic inquiry reasonably good approximations to truth. This is the view taken by Mill. While fully recognising "the paramount

[1] *Logic*, ii. p. 488.

ascendancy which the general state of civilisation and social progress in any given society must exercise over all the partial and subordinate phenomena," he concludes that the portion of social phenomena, in which the immediately determining causes are principally those that act through the desire for wealth, " do *mainly* depend, at least in the first resort, on one class of circumstances only." He adds that, " even when other circumstances interfere, the ascertainment of the effect due to the one class of circumstances alone is a sufficiently intricate and difficult business to make it expedient to perform it once for all, and then allow for the effect of the modifying circumstances; especially as certain fixed combinations of the former are apt to recur often, in conjunction with ever-varying circumstances of the latter class." [1] I have nothing to add to this statement. If it is accepted, the difficulty discussed in this section need no longer give us pause. It is not necessarily impracticable to ascertain by means of economic science the approximate effects of economic causes upon economic welfare. The bridge that has been built in earlier sections between economic welfare and total welfare need not, therefore, rust unused.

[1] *Logic*, ii. pp. 490-91.

CHAPTER II

DESIRES AND SATISFACTIONS

§ 1. IN the preceding chapter economic welfare was taken broadly to consist in that group of satisfactions and dissatisfactions which can be brought into relation with a money measure. We have now to observe that this relation is not a direct one, but is mediated through desires and aversions. That is to say, the money which a person is prepared to offer for a thing measures directly, not the satisfaction he will get from the thing, but the intensity of his desire for it. This distinction, obvious when stated, has been somewhat obscured for English-speaking students by the employment of the term utility— which naturally carries an association with satisfaction—to represent intensity of desire. Thus, when one thing is desired by a person more keenly than another, it is said to possess a greater utility to that person. Several writers have endeavoured to get rid of the confusion which this use of words generates by substituting for " utility " in the above sense some other term, such, for example, as " desirability." The term " desiredness " seems, however, to be preferable, because, since it cannot be taken to have any ethical implication, it is less ambiguous. I shall myself employ that term. The verbal issue is, however, a subordinate one. The substantial point is that we are entitled to use the comparative amounts of money which a person is prepared to offer for two different things as a test of the comparative satisfactions which these things will yield to him, only on condition that the ratio between the intensities of desire that he feels for the two is equal to the ratio between the amounts of satisfaction which their possession will yield to him. This condition, however, is not always fulfilled. By this statement I do not, of course, merely mean that people's expectations as to the satisfaction they will derive from different commodities are often erroneous. The point is that, even apart from this, the condition sometimes breaks down. Thus Sidgwick observes : " I do not judge pleasures [and the same thing obviously holds of satisfactions other than pleasures] to be greater and less exactly in proportion as they exercise more or less influence in stimulating the will to actions tending to sustain or produce them " :[1] and again, " I do not think it ought to be assumed that intensity of immediate gratification is always in proportion to intensity of pre-existing desire." [2] This consideration obviously has great theoretical importance. When it is recollected that all comparisons between different taxes and different monopolies, which proceed by an analysis of their effects upon consumer's surplus, tacitly assume that demand price (the money measure of desire) is also the money measure of satisfaction, it is apparent that it *may* have great practical importance also. The question whether it has in actual fact great practical importance has, therefore, to be examined.

§ 2. In a broad general way we may, I think, safely answer this question in the negative. It is fair to suppose that most commodities, especially those of wide consumption that are required, as articles of food and clothing are, for direct personal use, will be wanted as a means to satisfaction, and will, consequently, be desired with intensities proportioned to the satisfactions they are expected to yield.[3] For the most general purposes of economic analysis, therefore, not much harm is likely to be done by the current practice of regarding money demand price indifferently as the measure of a desire and as the measure of the satisfaction felt when the desired thing is obtained. To this general conclusion, however, there is one very important exception.

§ 3. This exception has to do with people's attitude toward the future. Generally speaking, everybody prefers present pleasures or satisfactions of given magnitude to future pleasures or satisfactions of equal magnitude, even when the latter are

[1] *Methods of Ethics*, p. 126.
[2] *The Ethics of T. H. Green*, etc., p. 340.
[3] Cf. my "Some Remarks on Utility," *Economic Journal*, 1903, p. 58 *et seq.*

perfectly certain to occur.   But this preference for present
pleasures does not—the idea is self-contradictory—imply that
a present pleasure of given magnitude is any *greater* than a
future pleasure of the same magnitude.   It implies only that
our telescopic faculty is defective, and that we, therefore, see
future pleasures, as it were, on a diminished scale.   That this
is the right explanation is proved by the fact that exactly the
same diminution is experienced when, apart from our tendency
to forget ungratifying incidents, we contemplate the past.
Hence the existence of preference for present over equally
certain future pleasures does not imply that any economic
dissatisfaction would be suffered if future pleasures were
substituted at full value for present ones.   The non-satis-
faction this year of a man's preference to consume this year
rather than next year is balanced by the satisfaction of
his preference next year to consume next year rather than
to have consumed this year.   Hence, there is nothing to
set against the fact that, if we set out a series of exactly
equal   satisfactions — *satisfactions*, not   objects   that   yield
satisfactions—all of them absolutely certain to occur over
a series of years beginning now, the desires which a man
will entertain for these several satisfactions will not be
equal, but will be represented by a scale of magnitudes continually diminishing as the years to which the satisfactions
are allocated become more remote.   This reveals a far-
reaching economic disharmony.   For it implies that people
distribute their resources between the present, the near future
and the remote future on the basis of a wholly irrational
preference.   When they have a choice between two satisfactions,
they will not necessarily choose the larger of the two, but will
often devote themselves to producing or obtaining a small one
now in preference to a much larger one some years hence.
The inevitable result is that efforts directed towards the remote
future are starved relatively to those directed to the near future,
while these in turn are starved relatively to efforts directed
towards the present.   Suppose, for example, that a person's
telescopic faculty is such that he discounts future satisfactions,
which are perfectly certain to occur, at the rate of 5 per cent
per annum.   Then, instead of being ready to work for next

year, or a year ten years hence, so long as a given increment
of effort will yield as much satisfaction as an equal increment
devoted to work for the present, he will only work for next
year so long as the yield of an increment of effort employed
for that year is 1·05 times, and for ten years hence so long
as it is $(1·05)^{10}$ times, the yield of an increment employed for
the present. It follows that the aggregate amount of economic
satisfaction which people in fact enjoy is much less than
it would be if their telescopic faculty were not perverted, but
equal (certain) satisfactions were desired with equal intensity
whatever the period at which they are destined to emerge.

§ 4. This, however, is not all. Since human life is
limited, such fruits of work or saving as accrue after a
considerable interval are not enjoyed by the person to whose
efforts they are due. This means that the satisfaction with
which his desire is connected is not his own satisfaction,
but the satisfaction of somebody else, possibly an immediate
successor whose interest he regards as nearly equivalent to his
own, possibly somebody quite remote in blood or in time, about
whom he scarcely cares at all. It follows that, even though
our desires for equal satisfactions *of our own* occurring
at different times were equal, our desire for future satisfaction
would often be less intense than for present satisfaction,
because it is very likely that the future satisfaction will
not be our own. This discrepancy will be more important
the more distant is the time at which the source of future
satisfaction is likely to come into being; for every addition
to the interval increases the chance of death, not merely
to oneself, but also to children and near relatives and friends
in whom one's interest is likely to be most keen.[1]   No doubt,

---

[1] If k be the fraction of importance that I attach to a pound in the hands of
my heirs as compared with myself, and $\phi(t)$ the probability that I shall be alive
t years from now, a certain pound *to me or my heirs* then attracts me now equally
with a certain pound multiplied by $\{\phi(t) + k(1 - \phi(t))\}$ *to me* then. This is
obviously increased by anything that increases either $\phi(t)$ or k.

If, through an anticipated change of fortune or temperament, one pound after
t years is expected to be equivalent to $(1 - a)$ times one pound now, a certain
$\{\phi(t) + k(1 - \phi(t))\}$ pounds of the then prevailing sort to me then attracts me
equally with $(1 - a)\{\phi(t) + k(1 - \phi(t))\}$ pounds of the now prevailing sort to me
then. Therefore, a certain pound to my heirs will be as persuasive to call out
investment now as the above sum would be if I were certain to live for ever and
always to be equally well off and the same in temperament.

this obstacle to investment for distant returns is partly overcome by stock-exchange devices.   If £100 invested now is
expected to reappear after 50 years expanded at, say, 5 per
cent compound interest, the man who originally provides the
£100 may be able, after a year, to sell his title in the eventual
fruit for £105; the man who buys from him may be able
similarly to get his capital of £105 back with 5 per cent
interest after one year; and so on.   In these circumstances the
fact that any one man would require a higher rate of interest
per annum to induce him to lock up £100 for 50 years than
he would to induce him to lock up the same sum for one year
makes no difference.   But, of course, in actual fact this device
is of very narrow application.   As regards investments, such
as planting a forest or undertaking drainage development on
one's own estate, which can only be accomplished privately, it
is not applicable at all; and, even when investment is undertaken by a company, investors cannot seriously expect to find
a smooth and continuous market for non-dividend paying
securities.

§ 5. The practical way in which these discrepancies
between desire and satisfaction work themselves out to the
injury of economic welfare is by checking the creation of
new capital and encouraging people to use up existing capital
to such a degree that larger future advantages are sacrificed
for smaller present ones.   Always the chief effect is felt
when the interval of time between action and consequence
is long.   Thus, of the check to investment, Giffen wrote:
" Probably there are no works more beneficial to a community
in the long run than those, like a tunnel between Ireland
and Great Britain, which open an entirely new means of
communication of strategical as well as of commercial value,
but are not likely to pay the individual enterpriser in any
short period of time."   A number of other large undertakings, such as works of afforestation or water supply,
the return to which is distant, are similarly handicapped
by the slackness of desire towards distant satisfactions.[1]   This

---

[1] In this connection the following passage from Knoop's *Principles and
Methods of Municipal Trade* is of interest: " To secure an additional supply
of water to a town, ten or more years of continuous work may easily be

same slackness of desire towards the future is also responsible
for a tendency to wasteful exploitation of Nature's gifts. Sometimes people will win what they require by methods that
destroy, as against the future, much more than they themselves obtain. Over-hasty exploitation of the best coal seams
by methods that cover up and render unworkable for ever
worse, but still valuable, seams ;[1] fishing operations so conducted as to disregard breeding seasons, thus threatening
certain species of fish with extinction ;[2] farming operations
so conducted as to exhaust the fertility of the soil, are all
instances in point. There is also waste, in the sense of injury
to the sum total of economic satisfaction, when one generation,
though not destroying more actual stuff than it itself obtains,
uses up for trivial purposes a natural product which is abundant
now but which is likely to become scarce and not readily
available, even for very important purposes, to future generations. This sort of waste is illustrated when enormous
quantities of coal are employed in high-speed vessels in order
to shorten in a small degree the time of a journey that is
already short. We cut an hour off the time of our passage
to New York at the cost of preventing, perhaps, one of our
descendants from making the passage at all.

§ 6. In view of this " natural " tendency of people to devote
too much of their resources to present service and too little
to future service, any artificial interference on the part of
Government in favour of that tendency is bound, unless it
has compensating advantages on the side of distribution, to
diminish economic welfare. Subject to that condition, therefore, all taxes which differentiate against saving, as compared
with spending, must diminish economic welfare. Even without

required. This means that for several years a large amount of capital will
be unproductive, thus seriously affecting the profits of the undertaking and making boards of directors very chary about entering upon any large scheme. . . .
It is almost inconceivable that a water company would have undertaken the
great schemes by which Manchester draws its supply of water from Lake
Thirlmere in Cumberland, a distance of some 96 miles ; Liverpool its supply
from Lake Vyrnwy in North Wales, a distance of some 78 miles ; and Brighton
its supply from the Elan Valley in Mid Wales, a distance of some 80 miles "
(*loc. cit.* p. 38).

[1] Cf. Chiozza-Money, *The Triumph of Nationalisation*, p. 199.
[2] Cf. Sidgwick, *Principles of Political Economy*, p. 410.

differentiation there will be too little saving: with it there will be much too little saving. Property taxes, where they exist, and death duties, obviously differentiate against saving. The English income tax, though it appears to be neutral, in fact, as is shown elsewhere, also does this.[1] The foregoing analysis shows that there is a *prima facie* case for softening the differential element in these taxes. Proposals, therefore, for exempting saved income from income tax, balancing property taxes by heavy "indirect" taxes upon important objects of expenditure, exempting from local rates improvements contributed during the preceding twenty years, and so on, deserve to be carefully weighed. In the construction of a practical tax-system, however, considerations as to what is "fair" between people of different degrees of wealth and as to what is administratively feasible may compel us to accept arrangements which differentiate against savings in spite of our knowledge that such differentiation is in itself undesirable.[2]

§ 7. Our analysis also suggests that economic welfare could be increased by some rightly chosen degree of differentiation *in favour* of saving. Nobody, of course, holds that the State should force its citizens to act as though so much objective wealth now and in the future were of exactly equal importance. In view of the uncertainty of productive developments, to say nothing of the mortality of nations and eventually of the human race itself, this would not, even in extremest theory, be sound policy. But there is wide agreement that the State should protect the interests of the future *in some degree* against the effects of our irrational discounting and of our preference for ourselves over our descendants. The whole movement for "conservation" in the United States is based on this conviction. It is the clear duty of Government, which is the trustee for unborn generations as well as for its present citizens, to watch over, and, if need be, by legislative enactment, to defend, the exhaustible natural resources of the country from

[1] Cf. my *A Study in Public Finance*, Part II. ch. x.
[2] For example, the case against the imposition of equal taxation upon two men, each of whom spends £450 a year, but the first has an income of £1000 and the second an income of £500 a year is, from the point of view of equity, overwhelming.

rash and reckless spoliation. How far it should itself, either out of taxes, or out of State loans, or by the device of guaranteed interest, press resources into undertakings from which the business community, if left to itself, would hold aloof, is a more difficult problem. Plainly, if we assume adequate competence on the part of governments, there is a valid case for *some* artificial encouragement to investment, particularly to investments the return from which will only begin to appear after the lapse of many years. It must, however, be remembered that, so long as people are left free to decide for themselves how much work they will do, interference, by fiscal or any other means, with the way in which they employ the resources that their work yields to them *may* react to diminish the aggregate amount of this work and so of those resources. It does not follow, in short, that, because economic welfare would be increased if a man who now invests, say, one-tenth of his income, *chose* to invest one-half, *therefore* it would be increased if he were compelled by legislative decree, or induced by taxes and bounties, to make this change.

CHAPTER III

THE NATIONAL DIVIDEND

§ 1. GENERALLY speaking, economic causes act upon the economic welfare of any country, not directly, but through the making and using of that objective counterpart of economic welfare which economists call the national dividend or national income. Just as economic welfare is that part of total welfare which can be brought directly or indirectly into relation with a money measure, so the national dividend is that part of the objective income of the community, including, of course, income derived from abroad, which can be measured in money. The two concepts, economic welfare and the national dividend, are thus co-ordinate, in such wise that any description of the content of one of them implies a corresponding description of the content of the other. In the preceding chapter it was shown that the concept of economic welfare is essentially elastic. The same measure of elasticity belongs to the concept of the national dividend. It is only possible to define this concept precisely by introducing an arbitrary line into the continuum presented by nature. It is entirely plain that the national dividend is composed in the last resort of a number of objective services, some of which are embodied in commodities, while others are rendered direct. These things are most conveniently described as goods—whether immediately perishable or durable—and services, it being, of course, understood that a service that has already been counted in the form of the piano or loaf of bread, which it has helped to make, must not be counted again in its own right as a service. It is not, however, entirely plain *which part* of the stream of services, or goods and services, that flows

annually into being can usefully be included under the title
of the national dividend.   That is the question which has now
to be discussed.

§ 2. The answer which first suggests itself is that those
goods and services should be included (double-counting,
of course, being avoided), and only those, that are actually
sold for money.   This plan, it would seem, must place us
in the best possible position for making use of the monetary
measuring rod.   Unfortunately, however, for the symmetry
of this arrangement, some of the services which would be
excluded under it are intimately connected, and even interwoven, with some of the included services.   The bought and
the unbought kinds do not differ from one another in any
fundamental respect, and frequently an unbought service is
transformed into a bought one, and *vice versa*.   This leads
to a number of violent paradoxes.   Thus, if a man hires
a house and furniture belonging to somebody else, the
services he obtains from them enter into the national dividend,
as we are here provisionally defining it, but, if he receives
the house and furniture as a gift and continues to occupy
it, they do so no longer.   Again, if a farmer sells the produce
of his farm and buys the food he needs for his family in the
market, a considerable amount of produce enters into the national
dividend which would cease to enter into it if, instead of
buying things in the market, he held back part of his own
meat and vegetables and consumed them on the farm.   Again,
the philanthropic work done by unpaid organisers, Church
workers and Sunday school teachers, the scientific work of
disinterested experimenters, and the political work of many
among the leisured classes, which at present do not enter,
or, when there is a nominal payment, enter at much less than
their real worth, into the national dividend, would enter
into it if those people undertook to pay salaries to one
another.   Thus, for example, the Act providing for the payment of members of Parliament increased the national dividend
by services valued at some £250,000.   Yet again, the services
rendered by women enter into the dividend when they are
rendered in exchange for wages, whether in the factory or in
the home, but do not enter into it when they are rendered by

mothers and wives gratuitously to their own families. Thus, if a man marries his housekeeper or his cook, the national dividend is diminished. These things are paradoxes. It is a paradox also that, when Poor Law or Factory Regulations divert women workers from factory work or paid home-work to unpaid home-work, in attendance on their children, preparation of the family meals, repair of the family clothes, thoughtful expenditure of housekeeping money, and so on, the national dividend, on our definition, suffers a loss against which there is to be set no compensating gain.[1] It is a paradox, lastly, that the frequent desecration of natural beauty through the hunt for coal or gold, or through the more blatant forms of commercial advertisement, must, on our definition, leave the national dividend intact, though, if it had been practicable, as it is in some exceptional circumstances, to make a charge for viewing scenery, it would not have done so.[2]

§ 3. Reflection upon these objections makes it plain that they are of a type that could be urged in some degree against any definition of the national dividend except one that coincided in range with the whole annual flow of goods and services. But to adopt a definition so wide as that would be tantamount to abandoning dependence upon the measuring rod of money. We are bound, therefore, either to dispense altogether with any formal definition or to fall back upon a compromise. The former policy, though there is more to be said for it than is sometimes allowed, would certainly arouse distrust, even though it led to no confusion. The latter, therefore, seems on

[1] It would be wrong to infer from the above that the large entry of women into industry during the war was associated with an approximately equal loss of work outside industry. For, first, a great deal of war work was undertaken by women who previously did little work of any kind ; secondly, the place of women who entered industry was taken largely by other women who had previously done little—for example, many mistresses in servant-keeping houses themselves took the place of a servant ; and, thirdly, owing to the absence of husbands and sons at the war, the domestic work, which women would have had to do if they had not gone into industry, would have been much less than in normal times.

[2] The Advertisement Regulation Act, 1907, allows local authorities to frame by-laws designed to prevent open-air advertising from affecting prejudicially the natural beauty of a landscape or the amenities of a public park or pleasure promenade. It is not, we may note in this connection, a decisive argument against underground, and in favour of overhead, systems of tramway power wires that they are more expensive. The London County Council deliberately chose the more expensive underground variety for aesthetic reasons.

the whole to be preferable. The method I propose to adopt is as follows. First, in accordance with the precedent set by Marshall, I shall take, as the standard meaning of the term national dividend, that suggested by the practice of the British Income Tax Commissioners. I, therefore, include everything that people buy with money income, together with the services that a man obtains from a house owned and inhabited by himself. But "the services which a person renders to himself and those which he renders gratuitously to members of his family or friends; the benefits which he derives from using his own personal goods [such as furniture and clothes], or public property such as toll-free bridges, are not reckoned as parts of the national dividend, but are left to be accounted for separately." [1] Secondly, while constructing in this way my standard definition of the national dividend, I reserve full liberty, with proper warning, to use the term in a wider sense on all occasions when the discussion of any problem would be impeded or injured by a pedantic adherence to the standard use. There is, no doubt, a good deal that is unsatisfactory about this compromise. Unfortunately, however, the conditions are such that nothing better appears to be available.

§ 4. The above conclusion does not complete the solution of our problem. Given the general class of things which are *relevant* to the national dividend, a further issue has to be faced. For the dividend may be conceived in two sharply contrasted ways: as the flow of goods and services which is *produced* during the year, or as the flow which passes during the year into the hands of ultimate consumers. Marshall adopts the former of these alternatives. He writes: "The labour and capital of the country, acting on its natural resources, produce annually a certain net aggregate of commodities, material and immaterial, including services of all kinds. This is the true net annual income or revenue of the country, or the national dividend." [2] Naturally, since in every year plant and equipment wear out and decay, what is produced must mean what is produced on the whole when allowance has been made for this process

---

[1] Marshall, *Principles of Economics*, p. 524.
[2] *Ibid.* p. 523.

of attrition. To make this clear, Marshall adds elsewhere :
" If we look chiefly at the income of a country, we must
allow for the depreciation of the sources from which it is
derived." [1]   In concrete terms, his conception of the dividend
includes an inventory of all the new things that are made, and
of all the services not embodied in things that are rendered,
accompanied, as a negative element, by an inventory of all the
decay and demolition that the stock of capital undergoes.
Anyone, on the other hand, who had been so far convinced
by Professor Fisher [2] as to hold with him that savings are, in
no circumstances, income, would identify the national dividend
with those goods and services, and those only, that come into
the hands of ultimate consumers. [3]   According to this view,
Marshall's national dividend represents, not the dividend that
actually *is* realised, but the dividend that *would be* realised
if the country's capital were maintained and no more than
maintained.   In a stationary state, where the creation of new
machinery and plant in any industry exactly balances, and
no more than balances, loss by wear and tear, these two
things would be *materially* equivalent.   The dividend on either
definition would consist simply of the flow of goods and
services entering into the hands of ultimate consumers ;
for all new materials at earlier stages in the productive process
that came into factories and shops would be exactly balanced
by the corresponding materials that left them in worked-up
products ; and all newly created machinery and plant would

[1] Marshall, *Principles of Economics*, p. 80.

[2] Professor Fisher himself takes the position that the national dividend,
or income, consists solely of *services* as received by ultimate consumers, whether
from their material or from their human environment.   Thus a piano or an
overcoat made for me this year is not a part of this year's income, but an
addition to capital.   Only the services rendered to me during this year by these
things are income (*The Nature of Capital and Income*, pp. 104 *et seq.*).   This
way of looking at the matter is obviously very attractive from a mathematical
point of view.   But the wide departure which it makes from the ordinary use
of language involves disadvantages which seem to outweigh the gain in logical
clarity.   It is easy to fall into inconsistencies if we refuse to follow Professor
Fisher's way ; but it is not necessary to do so.   So long as we do not do so,
the choice of definitions is a matter, not of principle, but of convenience.

[3] For consistency it would be necessary to exempt new houses that are built
to be occupied by their owners from the category of income and to place them in
that of capital, if a money valuation of their annual rental value is included in
income.

exactly take the place, and no more than take the place, of corresponding machinery and plant that became worn out during the year. In practice, however, the industry of a country is hardly ever in this kind of stationary state. Hence it is extremely rare for the two versions of the national dividend to be *materially* equivalent, and it is impossible for them to be *analytically* equivalent. The question how the choice between them should fall is, therefore, an important one.

§ 5. The answer to it, as I conceive the matter, turns upon the purpose for which we intend the conception to be used. If we are interested in the comparative amounts of economic welfare which a community obtains over a long series of years, and are looking for an objective index with which this series of amounts can be suitably correlated, then, no doubt, the conception which I have attributed to Professor Fisher's hypothetical follower is the proper one. It is also much more relevant than the other when we are considering how much a country is able to provide over a limited number of years for the conduct of a war; because, for this purpose, we want to know what is the utmost amount that can be squeezed out and " consumed," and we do not premise that capital must be maintained intact. The major part of this volume, however, is concerned, not with war, but with peace, and not with measurement, but with causation. The general form of our questions will be : " What effect on economic welfare as a whole is produced by such and such a cause operating on the economic circumstances of 1920 ? " Now it is agreed that the cause operates through the dividend, and that direct statements of its effects must refer to the dividend. Let us consider, therefore, the results that follow from the adoption of those two conceptions respectively. On Fisher's follower's plan, we have to set down the difference made by the cause to the dividend, not merely of 1920, but of every year following 1920 ; for, if the cause induces new savings, it is only through a statement covering all subsequent years that its effect on the dividend, as conceived by Fisher's follower, can be properly estimated. Thus, on his showing, if a large new factory is built in 1920, not the capital establishment of that factory, but only the flow of services rendered by it in 1920, should be reckoned in the dividend of 1920; and the aggregate effects of the creation of the factory cannot be measured without reference to the national dividend of a long series of years. On Marshall's plan this inconvenient elaboration is dispensed with. When we have stated the effect produced on the dividend, in his sense, for the year 1920, we have implicitly included the effects, so far as they can be anticipated, on the consumption both of 1920 and of all subsequent years; for these effects are reflected back in the capital establishment provided for the factory. The *immediate* effect on consumption is measured by the alteration in the 1920 dividend as conceived by Fisher's follower. But it is through total consumption, and not through immediate consumption, that economic welfare and economic causes are linked together. Consequently, Marshall's definition of the *national dividend* is likely, on the whole, to prove more useful than the other, and I propose in what follows to adopt it. The entity — also, of course, an important one — which Fisher's follower calls by that name, we may speak of as the *national income of consumption goods*, or, more briefly, *consumption income*.

§ 6. We have thus achieved a definition which, unsatisfactory as it is, is still reasonably precise, of the concrete content of the national dividend. This definition carries with it certain plain implications as to the way in which that dividend must be evaluated. The first and most obvious of these is that, when the value of a finished product is counted, the value of materials employed in making that product must not be counted also. In the *British Census of Production of 1907* this form of double counting was carefully avoided. The Director described his method as follows: The result of deducting the total cost of materials used, and the amount paid to other firms for work given out, from the value of the gross output for any one industry or group of industries is to give a figure which may, for convenience, be called the "net output" of the industry or the group. This figure "expresses completely and without duplication the total amount by which the value (at works) of the products of the industry or the group, taken as a whole,

exceeded the value (at works) of the materials purchased from
outside, *i.e.* it represents the value added to the materials in
the course of manufacture. This sum constitutes for any
industry the fund from which wages, salaries, rent, royalties,
rates, taxes, depreciation, and all other similar charges, have
to be defrayed, as well as profits." [1] When, however, it
is desired to evaluate the national dividend as a whole,
these allowances are not sufficient. There is no real difference between the flour, which is used up in making bread,
and bread-making machinery, which is used up and worn out
in the process of effecting the conversion. If adding together
the flour and the bread in summing the national dividend
involves double counting, so also does adding together
the machinery and the bread. "Logically," as Marshall
observes, "we ought to deduct the looms which a weaving
factory buys as well as its yarn. Again, if the factory itself
was reckoned as a product of the building trade, its value
should be deducted from the output (over a term of years)
of the weaving trade. Similarly with regard to farm buildings. Farm houses ought certainly not to be counted, nor
for some purposes any houses used in trade." [2] In a broad
general way these considerations can be taken into account by
subtracting from the sum of the values of the net products
of various industries, as defined in the Census of Production,
the value of the annual depreciation, which signifies the annual
cost of renewal and repair of all kinds of machinery and plant. [3]
Thus, if a particular sort of machinery wears out in ten years
—Professor Taussig's estimate for the average life of machinery
in a cotton mill [4]—the value of the national dividend over
ten years will fall short of the value of the aggregated
net product by the value of this machinery. [5] Again,

---

[1] [Cd. 6320], p. 8.

[2] Marshall, *Principles of Economics*, p. 614 *n.*

[3] Cf. Flux, *Statistical Journal*, 1913, p. 559.

[4] *Quarterly Journal of Economics*, 1908, p. 342. The report of the *Census
of Production*, 1907, sanctions the view that an average life of ten years may
reasonably be assigned to buildings and plant in general (*Report*, p. 35).

[5] In industries where large individual items of assets need replacement at
fairly long intervals, it is usual to meet this need by the accumulation of
a depreciation fund built up by annual instalments during the life of the
wasting asset. For machinery which wears out in about equal quantities
every year, Professor Young argues that, provided the renewals and

in so far as any sort of crop wastes the productive powers of the soil, the value of the dividend will fall short of the value of the aggregated net product by the cost of returning to the soil those chemical ingredients that it removes.[1] Yet again, when minerals are dug out of the ground, a deduction should be made equal to the excess of the value which the minerals used during the year had in their original situation—theoretically represented by the royalties paid on their working—over the value which whatever is left of them possesses to the country after they have been used. If "using" means exporting in exchange for imports that are not used as capital, this latter value is zero. If, on the other hand, it means inducing Nature miraculously to transmute the mineral into something possessing greater value than it had in the mine, then, in order to obtain the value of the national dividend from the value of the aggregated net product, we shall need to add, and not to subtract, something. This is sufficient for our present purpose. More delicate issues concerning the precise significance of the notion "maintaining capital intact" are treated in detail in the next chapter.

---

repairs required every year are duly furnished, capital will be maintained intact by that fact alone, and no depreciation fund is necessary (*Quarterly Journal of Economics*, 1914, pp. 630 *et seq.*). It is true that by this method, when the plant has been running for some time, the capital is maintained in any one year at the level at which it stood in the preceding year. But Professor Young himself shows that, in static conditions, when a plant has been established for some time, it will normally be about half worn out (*loc. cit.* p. 632). If half-worn-out plant, that is to say, plant half-way through its normal life—is technically of the same efficiency as new plant, this fact does not injure his conclusion. But, in so far as the efficiency of plant diminishes with age, the case is otherwise. If the capital is to be maintained at the level at which it stood *when first invested*, it is necessary, not merely to provide renewals and repairs as needed, but also to maintain a permanent depreciation fund, to balance the difference between the values of a wholly new plant and of one the constituents of which are, on the average, half-way through their effective life. (Cf. also a discussion between Professor Young and Mr. J. S. Davis under the title "Depreciation and Rate Control" in the *Quarterly Journal of Economics*, Feb. 1915.)

[1] Professor Carver writes of the United States : "Taking the country over, it is probable that, other things equal, if the farmers had been compelled to buy fertilisers to maintain the fertility of their soil without depletion, the whole industry would have become bankrupt. . . . The average farmer had never (up to about 1887) counted the partial exhaustion of the soil as a part of the cost of his crop" (*Sketch of American Agriculture*, p. 70). Against this capital loss, however, must be set the capital gain due to the settlement of the land.

§ 7. It remains to consider the relation between the national dividend as thus evaluated—an addition, of course, being made for the value of income received from abroad—and the money income accruing to the community. On the face of things we should expect these two sums to be substantially equal, just as we should expect a man's receipts and his expenditure (including investments) to be equal. With proper account-keeping this clearly ought to be so. In order that it may be so, however, it is necessary for the money income of the community to be so defined as to exclude all income that is obtained by one person as a gift against which no service entering into the inventory of the national dividend is rendered—all allowances, for example, received by children from their parents. In like manner, if A sells existing property or property rights to B for £1000, the £1000, if already counted as a part of B's income, must not be counted as a part of A's income also. These points are, of course, well understood. But certain further implications are less fully realised. Thus the incomes constituted by old-age pensions and special war pensions must be excluded; though ordinary civil service pensions are properly included, " because these may be said to be equivalent to salaries, and the pension system is only an alternative to paying a higher salary to those rendering existing services and leaving them to look after their own superannuation allowance." [1] There must also be excluded all income received by native creditors of the State in interest on loans that have been employed " unproductively," *i.e.* in such a way that they do not, as loans to build railways would do, themselves lead to the production of services which are sold for money and thus enter into the national dividend as evaluated in money. This means that the income received as interest on war loan must be excluded. Nor is it possible to overthrow this conclusion by suggesting that the money spent on the war has really been " productive," because it indirectly prevented invasion and the destruction of material capital that is now producing goods sold for money ; for whatever product war expenditure may have been responsible for in this way—and a similar argument applies to expenditure on school build-

[1] Stamp, *Wealth and Taxable Capacity*, p. 57.

ings—is already counted in the income earned by the material capital. Yet again, it would seem that income obtained by force or fraud, against which no real service has been rendered, ought not to be counted. There are, furthermore, certain difficulties about payments made to Government. The moneys that governing authorities, whether central or local, receive in net profits on services rendered by them, *e.g.* the profits of the Post Office or of a municipal tramway service, should clearly be counted. What the Treasury receives in income tax or death duties should, on the other hand, clearly not be counted, because this income, which has already been reckoned as such in private hands, is not passed to the Treasury in payment for any services rendered by it, but is merely transferred to it as an agent for the tax-payers. What the Treasury receives in (the now abolished) excess-profit duty and corporation tax, as operated in England, stands, however, on a different footing. It should be counted, because the incomes of companies and individuals were reckoned as what was left *after* these taxes had been paid, so that, if the income represented by them had not been counted when in the hands of the Treasury, it would not have been counted at all.[1] Finally, the main part of what the Treasury receives in customs and excise duties ought, paradoxical as it may seem, to be counted, in spite of the fact that it is already counted when in the hands of the tax-payers and that it is not paid against any service. The reason is that the prices of the taxed articles are pushed up (we may suppose) by nearly the amount of the duties, and that, therefore, unless the aggregate money income of the country is reckoned in such a way that it is pushed up correspondingly, this aggregate money income divided by prices, that is to say, the real income of the country, would necessarily appear to be diminished by the imposition of these duties even though it were in fact the same as before.[2] When the nominal money income of the country has been "corrected" in these various ways, what is left should

[1] Cf. Stamp, *Wealth and Taxable Capacity*, pp. 55-6.

[2] The reason why it is only claimed that the main part, not the whole, of what the Treasury receives under this head should be counted as income is (1) that commodity taxes may not always raise prices by their full amount, and (2) that they may indirectly cause production to contract.

approximate fairly closely to the value of the national dividend (inclusive of incomes from abroad) estimated on the plan set out above.[1]

[1] It should be noticed, however, that one paradox still remains uncorrected by the qualifications set out in the text. If a service, for which hitherto fees have been charged to business men, the fees being of a sort that it is lawful to deduct as a business expense before incomes are reckoned, comes to be provided for and to be paid for by an addition to income tax, the money income of the country is increased, though the real income is unchanged (cf. Stamp, *Wealth and Taxable Capacity*, pp. 52-3). The only way to get rid of this paradox would be to allow business men to deduct the cost of any services which, *if paid for by fees*, would count as a business expense, whether in fact they are paid for by fees or not.

CHAPTER IV

§ 1. THE issue, deferred from § 6 of the preceding chapter, as to the precise significance of "maintaining capital intact" has now to be taken up. We are debarred by the conventions we have adopted from counting as capital durable goods—other than houses—in consumers' hands, in spite of the fact that, so far as giving employment to labour is concerned, a motor car, for example, belonging to anybody other than an owner-driver, is indistinguishable from one belonging to a hiring establishment. This, however, is a secondary matter. For the present purpose the precise content of capital is immaterial. However we define it, it may be likened to a lake into which a great variety of things, which are the fruit of savings, are continually being projected. These things, having once entered the lake, survive there for various periods, according to their several natures and the fortunes that befall them. Among them are things of long life, like elaborately built factories, things of moderate life, like machinery, and things of very short life, like material designed to be worked up into finished goods for consumption or coal destined to be burned. Length of life in this connection means, of course, length of life *as capital* in the industrial machine functioning as a going concern, not the length of life which a thing would enjoy if nobody interfered with it. Coal, for example, if left alone, will last without change of form for an indefinite number of years; but, none the less, the "life" enjoyed by coal in the lake of capital, *i.e.* the period covered between its entrance and its exit, is almost always very short. All things that enter the lake eventually pass out of it again. Some of them pass, so to speak, in their own persons, embodied as material in some finished product, as when cotton yarn emerges as a cloth garment. But exits are not always, or indeed generally, made in the form of a passage outward of the actual elements that originally came in. When coal is burnt in the process of smelting iron, which is to be used eventually in making cutlery, it is the cutlery, embodying the "virtue" of the coal, and not the coal itself, which passes in person out of the lake. In like manner it is, of course, the "virtue" of machines that are worn out in making finished goods, and not the machines themselves, which passes out in person. In one form or another, however, whatever enters also leaves. There is then of necessity always a stream flowing out of the lake so long as it has any contents at all, and in practice there is also always a stream flowing into it. Its contents at any moment consist of everything that has flowed into it in the past *minus* anything that has flowed out. It is theoretically possible to make an inventory of them and also to evaluate them from day to day. When we speak, in connection with our definition of the national dividend, of the need for "maintaining capital intact," *something* is implied about the relation between successive inventories or successive evaluations of the contents of the lake we have been describing. It is the task of the present chapter to make clear what precisely that something is.

§ 2. For our present purpose it is plain that maintenance of capital intact does not require that the money valuation of the contents of the lake shall be held constant. There are certain sorts of change in this valuation to which everybody will agree that, in our reckoning of the national dividend, no attention whatever should be paid. Thus, if in consequence of a contraction in the supply of money in any year, money values all round are substantially reduced, the money value of the stock of capital will contract along with the rest : but nobody would suggest that this should be reckoned when the national dividend is being estimated. Again, Marshall has observed : "The value of the capital already involved in improving land or erecting a building; in making a railway or a machine; 'is the aggregate discounted value of

its estimated future net income."[1] This implies that, if
the general rate of interest rises, the money value of the
stock of capital will, other things remaining equal, be reduced.   Such reductions are irrelevant to the magnitude of
the national dividend.   When the value of particular items in
the capital stock falls because people's taste for the things they
help to produce has declined or because foreign competitors
offer these things at a diminished price, that fall also ought
not, I think, to be deemed relevant; and the same conclusion
holds when the creation of a new item of capital equipment
diminishes the value of an existing item; e.g. when the construction of an electric lighting plant depreciates a neighbouring
gas plant, or when the introduction of a new type of battleship
or bootmaking machine renders existing battleships or bootmaking machines obsolete.   In fact we may, I think, say
quite generally that all contractions in the money value of any
parts of the capital stock that remain physically unaltered are
irrelevant to the national dividend; and that their occurrence
is perfectly compatible with the maintenance of capital intact.

§ 3. It might seem at first sight to follow from what has
been said that the maintenance of capital intact must mean
the maintenance in an unaltered physical state of the inventory
of things lying in the capital lake.   Plainly, if this inventory
is in no way modified, capital is maintained intact in an
absolute sense; and, if some things fall out of the inventory, it
is not maintained intact in an absolute sense.   But, for the
special purpose of this analysis, maintenance of capital intact
does not mean maintenance in an absolute sense.   *Certain* contractions in the physical stock of capital will have to be held
compatible with its maintenance intact, as the phrase is here
understood.   For, it must always be remembered, our concern
is to define the national dividend without parting from the
phraseology made familiar by Marshall.   Thus, suppose that
an earthquake or the onslaught of a hostile nation destroys in
one year half this country's accumulated stock of wealth.   It
would be paradoxical and inconvenient to conclude that our
national dividend was thereby automatically rendered negative.
We must say rather that the loss is a loss on capital account,

[1] *Principles of Economics*, p. 593.

not on income account. In other words, this sort of loss, though, of course, it is incompatible with the maintenance of capital intact in any literal sense, is not relevant to estimates of the national dividend. Hence for our purpose maintenance of capital intact must be *defined* to mean maintenance of it intact, not absolutely, but only when this particular type of loss does not occur.

§ 4. It may perhaps be thought that this opens the way for an endless string of further prevarications; that, for example, the loss of houses by fire or of ships by storm should be put on the same footing as the losses just discussed. That, however, is not so. All disintegrations of capital goods other than catastrophic destructions of the type described in the preceding section are really incidental to the use of them, and are involved in the production of the dividend. This is most obviously true of the ordinary wear and tear which machinery and plant undergo when carrying out their functions. Weathering by lapse of time apart from use is in like case; for a necessary condition of use is subjection to the passage of time. Even the accidents of fire and storm are in like case; for the use of houses implies their subjection to the risk of fire and the use of ships their subjection to that of storm. The national dividend is not truly reckoned until allowance has been made for the replacement of all these types of capital loss. Maintenance of capital intact in our sense is thus equivalent to maintenance in an absolute sense save only that provision must not be made against destruction by " act of God or the King's enemies."

§ 5. We have now reached the conclusion that the maintenance of capital intact for our purpose requires that all ordinary physical deteriorations in the capital stock should be made good. But what exactly do we mean by making good ? When a capital stock deteriorates, *e.g.* through wear and tear, its material components do not disappear from the world, but merely become rearranged in a way that renders them less useful to mankind. Thus what has really disappeared is a physical arrangement embodying a certain sum of values, which we may for convenience measure in money. To make this good there must be added to the capital stock new arrangements of matter embodying a sum of values equal to this sum. Thus, if a machine becomes worn out and has no value at all, we require to add to the capital stock something whose value is equal to that which the machine, had it remained physically intact, would have *now*. The original cost of the machine, whether in real terms or in money terms, is not relevant. Thus it may have cost a thousand pounds to make; but, if its wearing out reduces its sum of values below what it would otherwise have been, not by £1000 but by £500 or by £1500, the replacing machine must have one or other of these values, not the value of £1000. It follows, *inter alia*, that if any piece of capital stock, *e.g.* the equipment of a steel works, has fallen in value in consequence, say, of intensified foreign competition, and if wear and tear depreciates the equipment 10 per cent per annum, to maintain capital intact we need 10 per cent, not of the original cost of the equipment nor of its present replacement cost, but of its present value. If the foreign competition is so strong or if popular taste has turned away from the product made by the equipment so completely that its value has become nil, physical deterioration in it by wear and tear or lapse of time involves no loss of value, and so calls for no replacement. Maintenance of capital intact for our purpose means then, not replacement of all value losses nor yet replacement of all physical losses (not due to acts of God and the King's enemies), but replacement of such value losses as are caused by physical losses other than the above.

§ 6. It is easy to see that different sorts of capital stock undergo losses of this sort—flow out of the capital lake—at different rates. Working capital—materials, coal and so on—usually only has a few months of life in the lake; and fixed capital a life of a number of years, greater or less according to its nature. Hence the annual amount of replacement that is needed to keep £1's worth of working capital intact is much larger than the amount required in respect of a £1's worth of fixed capital. Professor Mitchell quotes some figures which suggest that in the United States the part of fixed capital represented by "movable equipment"—machinery and so on—engaged in industry and agriculture is about equal to the stock of working capital, each being valued at 9000 million pounds.[1] If the normal life of movable equipment be put at ten years and that of working capital at one year, this implies that the annual replacement of fixed capital must, to maintain it intact, amount to 900 and the annual replacement of working capital to 9000 millions—ten times as much. Hence if, in any year, a £100 millions worth of deterioration in fixed capital is made good by adding to the capital stock a new 100 millions worth, not of fixed but of working capital, the value of annual replacement needed in future years to keep the aggregate stock of capital intact will be *pro tanto* increased. In converse conditions it will be diminished.

§ 7. In conclusion a word may be said about the effect of failure to provide sufficient replacement to maintain capital intact. Let us suppose that we start from a condition of stability; that continually for a long time past savings at the rate of 2 million £ per day have been required for maintenance, and have in fact been forthcoming. Something occurs, as a result of which henceforward only 1 million £ will be forthcoming. It is obvious that the level of the lake must fall. But it will not continue to fall indefinitely. For, as a result of the decline in the inflow, the outflow also must diminish, since the progressive fall in the stock of capital involves at the same time a progressive fall in the daily wastage. Presently the outflow will so far decrease that the reduced inflow of 1 million a day suffices to replace it. The contraction in the capital stock thereupon comes to an end and a new equilibrium is established. The period of time that will need to elapse before this happens will depend on the proportions existing initially between capital items of various lengths of life and on such changes as may take place in these proportions during the course of the decline. If the failure to provide replacements is carried to the point that henceforward none whatever are forthcoming, the stock of capital must, of course, eventually disappear altogether. Items with a short remainder of life will become extinct first; then others and yet others. The outflowing stream will diminish to a smaller and smaller trickle,

[1] *Business Cycles* (1927), p. 93.

until, with the demise of the longest-lived item, it and the lake from which it came alike go dry. In this event, however, humanity will take no interest, for the demise of the last capital item will certainly have been preceded by that of the "last man."

CHAPTER V

CHANGES IN THE SIZE OF THE NATIONAL DIVIDEND

§ 1. THE economic welfare of the country is intimately associated with the size of the national dividend, and changes in economic welfare with changes in the size of the dividend. We are concerned to understand, so far as may be, the nature of these associations. To this end an essential preliminary is to form clear ideas as to what precisely changes in the size of the dividend *mean*. It will be convenient, in the first instance, to postulate that the size of that group whose dividend we are studying remains unchanged.

§ 2. The dividend is an objective thing, consisting in any period of such and such a collection of goods and services that flow into being during the period. Since it is an objective thing, we should naturally wish, if we were able, to define changes in the size of it by reference to some objective physical unit, and without any regard to people's attitude of mind towards the several items contained in it. I do not mean that changes in public tastes would be thought of as incapable of affecting the size of the national dividend. They are obviously capable of affecting it by causing changes in the objective constituents of the dividend. I mean that, *given those objective constituents*, the size of the dividend should depend on them alone, and not at all on the state of people's tastes. This is the point of view which everybody intuitively wishes to take.

§ 3. If the national dividend consisted of one single sort of commodity only, there would be no difficulty about this. Everybody would agree that an increase in the size of the dividend should mean an increase, and a decrease a decrease, in the number of units of this commodity. In like manner, if the dividend consisted of a number of different commodities, but the quantities of all of them always varied in equal proportions, there would be no difficulty. The dividend would at any time consist of a certain number of complex units, each of them made up of so much of each commodity, and increases and decreases in the dividend would mean increases and decreases in the number of these complex units.

§ 4. If the national dividend consisted of a number of different sorts of things, the proportion between which was not fixed, but some pre-established harmony made it impossible for the quantity of any one of them to diminish when the quantity of any other was increasing, we should no longer be able to say that the dividend at any moment consisted of such a number of units and at another moment of such another number of units. But we should still always be able to determine by a physical reference whether the dividend of one moment was greater or less than the dividend of another moment: and this, for many purposes, would be all that anybody would need.

§ 5. In actual life, however, the national dividend consists of a number of different sorts of things, the quantities of some of which are liable to increase at the same time that the quantities of others are decreasing. In these circumstances there is no direct means of determining by a physical reference whether the dividend of one period is greater or less than that of another; and it becomes necessary to seek for a definition along other lines. Plainly the definition chosen must be such that, supposing the dividend consisted of one sort of thing only, we should always be able to say that an increase in the quantity of this thing constituted an increase in the size of the dividend. A definition that did not admit of this would be paradoxical. From this starting-point we are led forward as follows. Considering a single individual whose tastes are taken as fixed, we say that his dividend in period II. is greater than in period I. if the items that are added to it in period II. are items that he *wants more* than the items that are taken away from it in period II. Passing to a group of persons (of given numbers), whose tastes are taken as fixed and among whom the distribution of purchasing power is also taken as fixed, we say that the dividend in period II. is greater than in period I. if the items that are added to it in period II. are items *to conserve which they would be willing to give more money than they would be willing to give to conserve the items that are taken away from it in period II.* This definition is free from ambiguity. However the technique of production has altered, —though it has become more costly to make one thing and less costly to make another, though it has become possible to make some entirely new things and at the same time impossible to make some things that used to be made before,—it can yield one conclusion, and one only, as to the effect on the size of the national dividend of any change in its content that may have taken place. If, then, tastes and the distribution of purchasing power were really fixed, there would be nothing to set against the advantages of this method of definition. It would be the natural and obvious one to adopt.

§ 6. As a matter of fact, however, tastes and the distribution of purchasing power both vary. The consequence of this is that our definition leads in certain circumstances to results which, in appearance at least, are highly paradoxical. Thus in period I. tastes are such and such, and in period II. they are something different; in period I. the dividend is a collection C_1 and in period II. a collection C_2. It may happen both that the group with period I. tastes would give *less* money for the items added in period II. than for the items subtracted in that period, and also that the group (of equal numbers) with period II. tastes would give *more* money for the items added in period II. than for the items subtracted in that period. In this case our definition makes C_2 both less than C_1 and also greater than C_1; which is a violent paradox. The only escape from this is to admit that, in these circumstances, there is no meaning in speaking of an increase or decrease in the national dividend in an absolute sense. The dividend decreases from the point of view of period I. tastes, and increases from the point of view of period II. tastes; and there is nothing more to say.[1] It is

---

[1] An exactly analogous difficulty emerges when we attempt to compare the size of the national dividend, as defined above, in two countries. Thus, if the

easy to see that the same paradox may arise, and the same
solution be forced upon us, when the distribution of purchasing
power alters between period I. and period II.   Here again we
can only speak of an increase (or decrease) in the size of the
dividend from the point of view of period I. distribution or
from the point of view of period II. distribution : we cannot
speak of an increase or decrease in any absolute sense.[1]

§ 7. We are thus confronted with the awkward fact that
there are likely to be certain changes in the constitution of
the national dividend, of which it is not possible to say that
they are either increases or decreases in an absolute sense.
Plainly there is serious objection to a definition which leads to
this result.   On the other hand, though it will rarely happen
that a modification of the dividend, which constitutes an upward
(or downward) change of so much per cent from the point of
view of period I., will constitute an equal percentage change from
the point of view of period II., if between these two periods
tastes or distribution have altered, yet it will, we may reasonably
expect, *usually* constitute a change *in the same direction* from

---

German population with German tastes were given the national dividend of
England, they might get less economic satisfaction than before ; while, if the
English population with English tastes were given the German national
dividend, they also might get less economic satisfaction than before.   The
proposed definition would, in these circumstances, compel us to say both that
the English dividend is larger (from the English point of view) than the
German dividend, and also that the German dividend is larger (from the German
point of view) than the English dividend.   It may be added, though the point
is not strictly relevant, that differences in comparative tastes between the
people of two countries can sometimes, though not always, be detected by
statistical methods.   For example, Germans before the war would not eat
mutton though it was a penny cheaper than pork, while Englishmen ate it
readily (Cd. 4032, pp. xlviii and xlix).   Again Germans eat rye bread, whereas
English people eat white bread.   We know that this is not due merely to the
fact that rye bread is relatively cheap in Germany and that Germans are poorer
than Englishmen, because, if it were cheapness alone that was responsible for
the consumption of rye in Germany, there would presumably be a higher
consumption of white bread among better-to-do Germans.   This, however, is not
found.   Hence, we may legitimately infer that Germans have a taste for rye
bread, as against wheaten bread, different from the English taste.

[1] Cf. Dr. Bowley's observation : "The values included in incomes are values
in exchange, which are dependent, not only on the goods or services in question,
but also on the whole complex of the income and purchases of the whole of a
society. . . . The numerical measurement of total national income is thus
dependent on the distribution of income and would alter with it" (*The
Measurement of Social Phenomena*, pp. 207-8).   Cf. also Stamp, *British
Incomes and Property*, pp. 419-20.

the point of view of period II. Most causes, in short, will increase the dividend from both points of view or diminish it from both points of view. Usually, therefore, we can say, without circumlocution or complicated reference to two points of view, that a given cause either has or has not increased the size of the national dividend. The defect in our definition is thus not a fatal defect. Moreover, continued reflection fails to reveal any other definition that is not even more defective. In spite, therefore, of all that has been said, I propose, for the purposes of this volume, to define an increase in the size of the dividend for a group of given numbers as follows. From the point of view of period I. an increase in the size of the dividend is a change in its content such that, *if* tastes in period II. were the same as those prevailing in period I. and *if* the distribution of purchasing power were also the same as prevailed in period I., the group would be willing to give more money to conserve the items added in period II. than they would be willing to give to conserve the items that are taken away in period II. Waiving the distinction, discussed in Chapter II., between desire and the satisfaction that results when a desired thing is obtained, we may state the above definition alternatively thus. From the point of view of period I. an increase in the size of the dividend for a group of given numbers is a change in its content such that, *if* tastes in period II. were the same as those prevailing in period I., and *if* the distribution of purchasing power were also the same as prevailed in period I., the economic satisfaction (as measured in money) due to the items added in period II. is greater than the economic satisfaction (as measured in money) due to the items taken away in period II. From the point of view of period II. an increase in the dividend is defined in exactly analogous ways. From an absolute point of view an increase in the size of the dividend is a change which constitutes an increase from both the above two points of view. When, of two dividends, one is larger from the point of view of one period and the other from that of the other, the two are, from an absolute point of view, incommensurable.

§ 8. Hitherto we have been concerned with groups containing equal numbers.   As between groups of different sizes a direct comparison of dividends would be of little service. We may, however, in imagination reduce the numbers—all classes of persons being treated equally—in the larger group in the proportion required to make it equal to the smaller group, and reduce its money income in an equal proportion. The dividend of the group so obtained may then be compared, on the lines of the preceding analysis, with that of the smaller group.   The result is roughly a comparison of the *per capita* dividends of the two original groups.

CHAPTER VI

THE MEASUREMENT OF CHANGES IN THE SIZE OF THE NATIONAL DIVIDEND

§ 1. THE discussion of the preceding chapter has provided us with a *criterion* by which to decide whether the national dividend of one period is larger or smaller than the national dividend of another period from the point of view of one or other of the periods. But to provide a *criterion* of increases and decreases in the size of anything is not to provide a *measure* of these changes. We have now to study the problem of devising an appropriate measure.

§ 2. Our *criterion* of increase from the point of view of any period being that, with the tastes and distribution of that period, the money demand for the things that have been added to the dividend exceeds the money demand for the things taken away from it, it is natural to suggest that we should employ as a *measure* of increase, from the point of view of the period, the proportion in which the aggregate money demand for the things contained in the dividend of that period (in the sense of the amount of money that people would be willing to give rather than do without those things) exceeds the aggregate money demand for the things contained in the dividend of the other period. A measure of this kind would conform exactly to our criterion. We should have two figures, one giving the change from the point of view of the tastes and distribution of period I. and the other that from the point of view of the tastes and distribution of period II. Plainly, given the criterion decided upon in the last chapter, this is the measure that we should adopt if we were able to do so.

§ 3. Unfortunately, however, this type of measure is

altogether impracticable. In the way of it there stands, as a final obstacle, the fact that the aggregate money demand for the things contained in the dividend of any period, in the sense explained above, is an unworkable conception. It involves the money figure that would be obtained by adding together the consumers' surpluses, as measured in money, derived from each several sort of commodity contained in the dividend. As Marshall has shown, however, the task of adding together consumers' surpluses in this way, partly on account of the presence of complementary and rival commodities, presents difficulties which, even if they are capable of being overcome in theory by means of elaborate mathematical formulae, are certainly insuperable in practice.[1] Even apart from these remoter complications, it is evident that no measure of the kind contemplated could be built up which did not embrace among its terms the elasticities of demand for the various elements contained in the dividend, or, more exactly, the forms of the various demand functions that are involved. These data are not, and are not likely, within any reasonable period of time, to become, accessible to us. Any type of measure which involves the use of them must, therefore, be ruled out of court.

§ 4. Continuing along the line of thought which this consideration suggests, we are soon led to the conclusion that the only data which there is any serious hope of organising on a scale adequate to yield a measure of dividend changes are the quantities and prices of various sorts of commodities. There is nothing else available, and, therefore, if we are to construct any measure at all, we *must* use these data. Our problem then becomes: in what way, if at all, is it possible, out of them, to construct a measure that will conform to the definition of changes in the size of the dividend that was reached in the last chapter? An attempt to solve this problem falls naturally into three parts: first, a general inquiry as to what measure would conform most nearly to that definition if all relevant information about quantities and prices were accessible; secondly, a mathematical inquiry as to what practicable measure built up from the sample information

[1] *Principles of Economics*, pp. 131-2, footnote.

about quantities and prices that we can in fact obtain would approximate most closely to the above measure; thirdly, a mixed general and mathematical inquiry as to *how reliable* the practicable measure, as an index of the above measure, is likely to be.

§ 5. In attacking the first and most fundamental of these issues we have to admit at once that complete success is unattainable. According to the definition of the last chapter, the national dividend will change in one way from the point of view of a period in which tastes and distribution are of one sort, and in a different way from that of a period in which they are of another sort. In order to conform with this, our measure of change would need to be double, being expressed in one figure from the point of view of the first period, and, if tastes and distribution were different in the two periods, in another figure from the point of view of the second period. A measure built up on quantities and prices only cannot possibly answer to this requirement. For, though we may know the quantities and prices that actually ruled in period I., when tastes and distribution were of sort A, and the quantities and prices that ruled in period II., when tastes and distribution were of sort B, we cannot possibly know either the quantities and prices which would have ruled in period I., if tastes and distribution had then been of sort B, or those which would have ruled in period II., if tastes and distribution had then been of sort A. Hence, the utmost we can hope for is a measure which will be independent of what the state of tastes and distribution actually is in either of the periods to be compared, but which will always increase when the content of the dividend has changed in such a way that economic welfare (as measured in money) would be increased whatever the state of tastes and distribution, provided only that this was the same in both periods. Even if the whole of the data about quantities and prices were accessible to us, it would be impossible to construct a measure, based on these data alone, conforming more closely than this to our definition; and, plainly, this degree of conformity is very incomplete.

§ 6. So much being understood, let us turn to the problem

of constructing from full data a measure—we may call it from henceforth the full-data measure—that will conform as closely as possible to the modest ideal specified in the preceding section. What is required is a measure which will show increases in the size of the dividend whenever its content is changed in such a way that, in terms of the money of either period,[1] for a group of given size with constant tastes and distribution, the money demand for the items that have been added is greater than the money demand for those that have been subtracted;[2] or, in other words, that the economic satisfaction (as measured in money) obtained by the group in the second period is greater than it was in the first period. It is not, of course, required that, if, when the excess of economic satisfaction (as measured in money) is E, our measure shows an increase of 1 per cent, it shall, when the excess of economic satisfaction (as measured in money) is 2E, show an increase of 2 per cent. This is not only not necessary, but, in the special case of a dividend consisting of one sort of commodity only, it would even lead to paradoxical results. It is required, however, that, when the excess of economic satisfaction (as measured in money) is E, our measure shall show *some* increase, and that, when the excess of economic satisfaction (as measured in money) is more than E, it shall show a greater increase than it does when the excess is E. This is the framework within which our construction must be made. The problem is to discover what construction will best fulfil the purpose that has been specified.[3]

[1] These words are necessary to take account of the fact that, if the aggregate money income of our group be altered, a second period £ will not be the same thing as a first period £.

[2] It is perhaps well to repeat here in symbols what has been stated previously in words, that, the equation of the demand curve for any commodity being $p = \phi(x)$, the money demand for an increment of h units means, not

$$\{(x+h)\phi(x+h) - x\phi(x)\}, \text{ but } \int_0^{x+h} \phi(x) - \int_0^x \phi(x).$$

[3] Professor Irving Fisher, in his admirable study of *The Making of Index Numbers*, appears to take the view that there is a way of making measures of this sort which is right in an absolute sense, and not merely in the sense that it will yield a measure consonant with the particular purpose which we want the measure to serve. Having examined a great many different sorts of index numbers, he found that, after those suffering from definite defects of a technical sort had been eliminated, the remainder, though formed on widely different plans, gave approximately equivalent results, and concluded : "Humanly

§ 7. In the first of any two periods that we wish to compare any group of given size expends its purchasing power upon one collection of commodities, and in the second on a different collection. Each collection must, of course, be so estimated that the same thing is not counted twice over, that is to say, it must be taken to include direct services rendered to consumers—*e.g.* the services of doctors, finished consumable articles, and a portion of the finished durable machines produced during the year,[1] but not the raw materials or the services of labour that are embodied in these things, and not, of course, " securities." Let us, at this stage, ignore the fact that in one of the collections there may be some newly invented kinds of commodity which are not represented at all in the other. The first collection, which we may call C_1, then embraces x_1, y_1, z_1 . . . units of various commodities; and the second collection, C_2, embraces x_2, y_2, z_2 . . . units of the same commodities. Let the prices per unit of these several commodities be, in the first period, a_1, b_1, c_1, . . .;

---

speaking, then, an index number is an absolutely accurate instrument " (p. 229). Now, the close consilience of the results reached by different methods undoubtedly suggests to the mind that there exists somewhere an absolutely right result to which they are all approximating. But there is, so far as I can see, no real ground for accepting this metaphysical suggestion. Consider the analogy of a measure designed to ascertain the average height of a group of trees. It is easy to find the arithmetical, the geometrical, or any other average of their heights. In many conditions all ordinary forms of average will work out very nearly the same. But this is no proof that there is stored up in heaven an ideal average height different from these and, in an absolute sense, more accurate or truer than any of them. There is a true arithmetical average, a true geometrical average, a true harmonic average; but the concept of an archetypal average right in an absolute sense is, as it seems to me, an illusion. When we want to satisfy a given purpose it is proper to ask : Will the arithmetical or the geometrical average best serve our purpose ? If the two averages happen to be nearly the same, we are in the happy position that it does not much matter should we accidentally choose the wrong one. But we cannot properly say more than this. There is some reason to believe, however, that, when Professor Fisher claims that the choice of the formula for a price index number is independent of the purpose to be served, he is using the term purpose in a narrower sense than mine, and would not disagree with what is here said.

[1] This is necessary in order to conform to the definition of the national dividend given in Chapter III. Had we defined the dividend so that it included only what is actually consumed during the year, no machines would come into it. On our definition we ought strictly to include all new machinery and plant over and above what is required to maintain capital intact, *minus* an allowance for that part of the value of this machinery and plant that is used up in producing consumable goods during the year itself.

and, in the second period, a_2, b_2, c_2. . . . Let the aggregate money income of our group, in the first period, be I_1, in the second I_2. The following propositions result:

1. If our group in the second period purchased the several commodities in the same proportion in which it purchased them in the first period, that is to say, if it purchased in both periods a collection of the general form C_1, its purchase of each commodity in the second period would be equal to its purchase of each commodity in the first period multiplied by the fraction

$$\frac{I_2}{I_1} \cdot \frac{x_1 a_1 + y_1 b_1 + z_1 c_1 +}{x_1 a_2 + y_1 b_2 + x_1 c_2 +}.$$

2. If our group in the first period purchased the several commodities in the same proportion in which it purchased them in the second period, that is to say, if it purchased in both periods a collection of the general form C_2, its purchase of each commodity in the second period would be equal to its purchase of each commodity in the first period multiplied by the fraction

$$\frac{I_2}{I_1} \cdot \frac{x_2 a_1 + y_2 b_1 + z_2 c_1 + \ . \ . \ .}{x_2 a_2 + y_2 b_2 + z_2 c_2 + \ . \ . \ .}.$$

On the basis of these propositions, provided that a certain assumption is made, our problem can be partially solved.

§ 8. If in period II. a single man who had been purchasing a collection of the form C_2, *i.e.* made up of elements in the proportions (x_2, y_2, z_2 . . .), chose instead to purchase a collection of the form C_1, it is certain that his action would leave prices unchanged, so that he could buy the items in his new collection at prices a_2, b_2, c_2, . . . An analogous proposition holds of a single man in period I. who should choose to shift from a collection of form C_1 to one of form C_2. But, when it is the whole of a group, or, if we prefer it, a representative man, who shifts his consumption in this way, it is no longer certain that prices would be unaffected. If the group in period II. shifted from a collection of form C_2 to one of form C_1, it would have to pay, let us suppose, prices a_1', b_1', c_1'. In like manner, if the group in period I. shifted from a collection of form C_1 to one of form C_2, it would have to pay prices a_2', b_2', c_2'. The assumption referred to at the end of the preceding section is that $\{x_1a_1' + y_1b_1' + z_1c_1' + \ldots\}$ is equal to $\{x_1a_1 + y_1b_1 + z_1c_1 + \ldots\}$ and that $\{x_2a_2' + y_2b_2' + z_2c_2' + \ldots\}$ is equal to $\{x_2a_2 + y_2b_2 + z_2c_2 + \ldots\}$. This means that the group in period II. could then, if it chose, buy as much of a C_1 collection, in spite of the shift of prices caused by its decision to do this, as it would have been able to do had that decision caused no shift of prices; and that an analogous proposition holds of the group in period I. If all the commodities concerned were being produced under conditions of constant supply price, the above assumption would conform exactly to the facts. In real life, with a large number of commodities, it is reasonable to suppose that the upward price movements caused by shifts of consumption would roughly balance the downward movements; so that, in general, our assumption will conform approximately to the facts. It is important to remember, however, throughout the following argument, that this assumption is being made.

§ 9. Let us begin with the case in which both the fractions set out in § 7 lie upon the same side of unity; they are either both greater than unity or both less than unity. If they are both greater than unity, this means that our group, if it wishes, can buy more commodities in the second period than in the first, whether its purchases are arranged in the form of collection C_1 or in that of collection C_2. Hence the fact that in the second period it chooses the form C_2 proves that the economic satisfaction (as measured in money) yielded by what it then purchases in the form C_2 is greater than the economic satisfaction (as measured in money) that would be yielded by a collection of the form C_1 larger than the collection of that form which it purchased in the first period.[1] A fortiori, therefore, it is greater than the economic satisfaction (as measured in money) that would be yielded by the actual collection of the form C_1 which it purchased in the first period.

[1] This proposition and the results based upon it depend on the condition that our group is *able* to buy at the ruling price the quantity of any commodity which it wishes to buy at that price. When official maximum prices have been fixed, and people's purchases at those prices are restricted, either by a process of rationing or by the fact that at those prices there is not enough of the commodity to satisfy the demand, this condition is, of course, not realised. During the Great War the situation was further complicated by the fact that the legal prices were often departed from—at least in Germany—in practice.

But, since tastes and distribution are unaltered, the economic satisfaction (as measured in money) that would be yielded by the actual collection C_1 in the second period is equal to the economic satisfaction (as measured in money) that was yielded by the actual collection in the first period. Hence, if both our fractions are greater than unity, it necessarily follows that the economic satisfaction (as measured in money) yielded by the collection C_2 bought in the second period is greater than the economic satisfaction (as measured in money) yielded by the collection C_1 bought in the first period. By analogous reasoning it can be shown that, if both the above fractions are less than unity, the converse result holds good. In these circumstances, therefore, either of the two fractions

$$\frac{I_2}{I_1} \cdot \frac{x_1 a_1 + y_1 b_1 + z_1 c_1 \cdots}{x_1 a_2 + y_1 b_2 + z_1 c_2 \cdots} \text{ or } \frac{I_2}{I_1} \cdot \frac{x_2 a_1 + y_2 b_1 + z_2 c_1 + \cdots}{x_2 a_2 + y_2 b_2 + z_2 c_2 + \ldots},$$

or any expression intermediate between them, will satisfy the condition, set out in § 6, which our measure is required to fulfil as a criterion of changes in the volume of the dividend.

§ 10. In the above circumstances, therefore, the condition we have laid down does not determine the choice of a measure, but merely fixes the limits within which that choice must lie. The width of these limits depends upon the extent to which the two fractions differ from one another. In some conditions there exists between them a relation of approximate equality. Thus, during the later nineteenth century, the dominant factor in the Englishman's increased capacity to obtain almost every important commodity was one and the same, namely, improved transport; for a main part of what improvements in manufacture accomplished was to cheapen means of transport. In other conditions the difference between the two fractions is considerable. Illustrations that would be directly applicable might perhaps be found. I must content myself, however, with one drawn, not from an inter-temporary comparison of two states of the same group, but from a contemporary comparison of the states of two groups. This illustration is only relevant to the present purpose on the unreal assumption that English and German workmen's tastes are the same and that their purchases differ solely on account of differences in

their income and in the prices charged to them. It is
taken from the Board of Trade's Report on the *Cost of Living
in German Towns*. The Report shows that, at the time when
it was made, what an English workman customarily consumed
cost about one-fifth more in Germany than in England, while
what a German workman customarily consumed cost about
one-tenth more in Germany than in England.[1] If, then, the
letters with the suffix 1 be referred to English consumption
and prices, and those with the suffix 2 to German consumption
and prices,

$$\frac{x_1a_1 + y_1b_1 + z_1c_1}{x_1a_2 + y_1b_2 + z_1c_2} = \frac{100}{120}, \text{ and } \frac{x_2a_1 + y_2b_1 + z_2c_1}{x_2a_2 + y_2b_2 + z_2c_2} = \frac{100}{110}.$$

§ 11. Though our condition, in the class of problem so far
considered, only fixes these two limits within which the measure
of dividend changes should lie, considerations of convenience
suggest even here the wisdom of selecting, though it be in
an arbitrary manner, some one among the indefinite number
of possible measures. When we proceed from this class of
problem to another more difficult class, the need for purely
arbitrary choice is narrower in range. It sometimes happens
that one of the above two fractions is greater than unity and
the other less than unity. Then it is clear that both of them
cannot indicate the direction in which the economic satisfaction
(as measured in money) enjoyed by the group has changed.
In the second period, let us suppose, the group's later
income commands a larger amount of the collection of form C_2
than its earlier income commanded; but it commands a smaller
amount of the collection of form C_1 than its earlier income
commanded. In these circumstances common sense suggests
that, if the fraction

$$\frac{I_2}{I_1} \cdot \frac{x_1a_1 + y_1b_1 + z_1c_1 + \dots}{x_1a_2 + y_1b_2 + z_1c_2 + \dots}$$

falls short of unity by a large proportion, while the fraction

$$\frac{I_2}{I_1} \cdot \frac{x_2a_1 + y_2b_1 + z_2c_1 + \dots}{x_2a_2 + y_2b_2 + z_2c_2 + \dots}$$

exceeds unity only by a small proportion, the economic

[1] [Cd. 4032], pp. vii and xlv.

satisfaction (as measured in money) enjoyed by our group has *probably* diminished; and that, if conditions of an opposite character are realised, it has probably increased. A like inference, it would seem, may be drawn, though with less confidence, when one fraction differs from unity in only a *slightly* greater proportion than the other. If this be so, the economic satisfaction—it will be understood that we are speaking of satisfaction as measured in money—obtained by our group *probably* decreases or increases in the second period according as either

$$\frac{I_2}{I_1} \cdot \frac{x_1 a_1 + y_1 b_1 + z_1 c_1 + \ldots}{x_1 a_2 + y_1 b_2 + z_1 c_2 + \ldots} \times \frac{I_2}{I_1} \cdot \frac{x_2 a_1 + y_2 b_1 + z_2 c_1 + \ldots}{x_2 a_2 + y_2 b_2 + z_2 c_2 + \ldots}$$

or any power of this expression, or any other formula which moves more or less as it does, is greater or less than unity. Any fraction constructed on these lines will, therefore, *probably* satisfy the conditions required of our measure.

§ 12. In former editions of this work the above commonsense view was defended by direct analysis as follows. If

$$\frac{I_2}{I_1} \cdot \frac{x_1 a_1 + y_1 b_1 + z_1 c_1 + \ldots}{x_1 a_2 + y_1 b_2 + z_1 c_2 + \ldots}$$

is less than unity by a large fraction, this means that, were our group to purchase in the second year a collection of the form C_1, its purchases of each item would be less by a large percentage than they were in the first year, and therefore—tastes and distribution being unchanged—it would probably enjoy an amount of satisfaction less than in the first year by a large amount, say by K_1. The fact that, instead of doing this, it purchases in the second year a collection of the form C_2 proves that the satisfaction yielded by its purchase of this collection in the second year does not fall short of that yielded by its purchase of the other collection in the first year by more than K_1. In like manner, if

$$\frac{I_2}{I_1} \cdot \frac{x_2 a_1 + y_2 b_1 + z_2 c_1 + \ldots}{x_2 a_2 + y_2 b_2 + z_2 c_2 + \ldots}$$

is greater than unity by only a small fraction, this means that, were our group to purchase a collection of the form C_2 in the first year, its purchases of each item would be less by only a small percentage than they are in the second year, and—tastes and distribution being unchanged—it would

F

probably enjoy an amount of satisfaction less than in the second year by only a small amount, say K_2. Hence, the satisfaction yielded by the collection actually purchased in the second year does not exceed that yielded by the collection actually purchased in the first year by more than K_2. Since, therefore, in view of the largeness of K_1 relatively to K_2, there are more ways in which the satisfaction from the second year's purchase can be less, than there are ways in which it can be more, than the satisfaction from the first year's purchase, and since, further, the probability of any one of these different ways is *prima facie* equal to that of any other, it is *probable* that the satisfaction from the second year's purchase is less than that from the first year's. This line of reasoning now seems to me to depend on *a priori* probabilities in a manner that is not correct. It is necessary to look at the matter more closely. To this end let us write

q_1 for the quantity of collection C_1 obtainable (and obtained) with the then income in period I.:

q_2 for the quantity of collection C_1 obtainable with the then income in period II.:

r_1 for the quantity of collection C_2 obtainable with the then income in period I.:

r_2 for the quantity of collection C_2 obtainable (and obtained) with the then income in period II.:

and $\phi(q_1)$, $\phi(q_2)$, $F(r_1)$ and $F(r_2)$ for the quantities of satisfaction (as measured in money) associated with these several actual and potential purchases.

We are given that

$$q_1 > q_2 \quad (1)$$
$$r_2 > r_1 \quad (2)$$
$$\frac{q_1}{q_2} > \frac{r_2}{r_1} \quad (3)$$

Then, since q_1 of C_1 is preferred in period I. to r_1 of C_2, we know that $\phi(q_1) > F(r_1)$. In like manner we know that $F(r_2) > \phi(q_2)$. Further, from (1) $\phi(q_1) > \phi(q_2)$; and from (2) $F(r_2) > F(r_1)$.

Write
$$\phi(q_1) = F(r_1) + A$$
$$F(r_2) = \phi(q_2) + B$$
$$\phi(q_1) = \phi(q_2) + H$$
$$F(r_2) = F(r_1) + K$$

Thus A, B, H and K are all positive, and, by simple transposition, $\phi(q_1) - F(r_2) = \frac{1}{2}(A - B + H - K)$. The inequality (3), at all events if the excess of $\frac{q_1}{q_2}$ over $\frac{r_2}{r_1}$ is considerable, permits us to say that *probably* H>K. But we know nothing about the values of A and B. The so-called principle of non-sufficient reason does not entitle us to educe out of this nescience the proposition that *probably* (B - A)<(H - K). It is only, however, with the help of some such proposition that we can infer that $\phi(q_1)$ is *probably* $> F(r_2)$. Hence no general proof of our common-sense view is possible. It is true that, the larger the excess of $\frac{q_1}{q_2}$ above $\frac{r_2}{r_1}$, *the more likely it is* that satisfaction in the second period will be less than satisfaction in the first; but we cannot specify any values for these quantities in respect of which satisfaction in the second period is *more likely than not* to be less than satisfaction in the first. As Mr. Keynes puts it, " We are faced with a problem in probability, for which in any particular case we may have relevant data, but which, in the absence of such data, is simply indeterminate."[1]

§ 13. If this conclusion is correct it follows that, when of the expressions

$$\frac{I_2}{I_1} \cdot \frac{x_1a_1 + y_1b_1 + z_1c_1 + \ \cdot \ \cdot \ \cdot}{x_1a_2 + y_1b_2 + z_1c_2 + \ \cdot \ \cdot \ \cdot} \qquad \text{and}$$

$$\frac{I_2}{I_1} \cdot \frac{x_2a_1 + y_2b_1 + z_2c_1 + \ \cdot \ \cdot \ \cdot}{x_2a_2 + y_2b_2 + z_2c_2 + \ \cdot \ \cdot \ \cdot} \qquad \text{one is greater and}$$

the other less than unity, there is *no* intermediate expression of which we can say in general terms that the economic satisfaction obtained by our group probably increases or decreases in the second period according as the expression is greater or less than unity. Nevertheless, when both our limiting expressions are on the same side of unity, so that there is no doubt as to whether economic satisfaction, as between the two periods, has increased or diminished, it is practically much more convenient to write down some single expression intermediate between the two limiting expressions rather than both of these. There are an infinite number of intermediate

[1] *A Treatise on Money*, vol. i. p. 112.

expressions available. In making our choice among them, since there is no deeper ground of preference, we may, as Mr. Keynes writes, "legitimately be influenced by considerations of algebraical elegance, of arithmetical simplicity, of labour-saving, and of internal consistency between different occasions of using a particular system of short-hand."[1] It is thus, I suggest, proper to make use of the two fundamental tests of technical excellence in price index numbers—for, of course, the measure we are seeking is simply the reciprocal of a price index number multiplied by the proportionate change that has taken place in money incomes —which Professor Irving Fisher has brought into prominence. First, the formula chosen should be such that " it will give the same ratio between one point of comparison and the other point, no matter which of the two is taken as base."[2] If, calculated forward, it shows that in 1910 prices were double what they were in 1900, it must not, as a so-called unweighted arithmetical index number of the Sauerbeck type would do, show, when calculated backwards, that in 1900 prices were something other than half what they were in 1910. Secondly, the formula chosen should obey what Professor Fisher calls the factor-reversal test. " Whenever there is a price of anything exchanged, there is implied a quantity of it exchanged, or produced, or consumed, or otherwise involved, so that the problem of an index number of *prices* implies the twin problem of an index number of quantities. . . . No reason can be given for employing a given formula for one of the two factors which does not apply to the other."[3] Hence, the formula chosen should be such that, assuming the aggregate money values of all the commodities we are studying to have moved between two years from E to $(E + e)$, then, if the formula, as applied to prices, gives an upward movement from P to $(P + p)$ and, as applied to quantities, an upward movement from Q to $(Q + q)$,

$$\left\{ \frac{P + p}{P} \cdot \frac{Q + q}{Q} \right\} \text{ is equal to } \frac{E + e}{E}.$$

Besides conformity with these tests we may also properly

---

[1] *A Treatise on Money*, vol. i. p. 113.
[2] *The Making of Index Numbers*, p. 64.
[3] *Loc. cit.* pp. 72 and 74.

require in our measure simplicity of structure and convenience of handling. These various considerations taken together point, on the whole, to the formula

$$\frac{I_2}{I_1} \sqrt{\frac{x_1 a_1 + y_1 b_1 + z_1 c_1 + \cdots}{x_1 a_2 + y_1 b_2 + z_1 c_2 + \cdots} \times \frac{x_2 a_1 + y_2 b_1 + z_2 c_1 + \cdots}{x_2 a_2 + y_2 b_2 + z_2 c_2 + \cdots}}$$

as the measure of change most satisfactory for our purpose. The portion of this expression to the right of $\frac{I_2}{I_1}$ is the reciprocal of that form of price index number to which Professor Fisher assigns the first prize for general merit, and which he proposes to call " the ideal index number." [1]

§ 14. The formulae discussed so far, alike the limiting formulae and the intermediate formula, have been built up on the tacit assumption that no commodities are included in either of the collections C_1 and C_2, which are not included in both. If, therefore, a commodity is available for purchase in one of any two years but not in the other, the satisfaction yielded by this commodity in the year in which it is purchased is wholly ignored by these measures. So far then as " new commodities " are introduced between two periods which are being compared, the measures are imperfect. This matter is important, because new commodities, in the sense here relevant, embrace, not merely commodities that are new physically, but also old commodities that have become obtainable at new times or places, such as strawberries in December, or the wheat which railways have introduced into parts of India where it was formerly unknown. Obviously, we must not count December strawberries along with ordinary strawberries, and so make inventions for strawberry forcing raise the price of strawberries, but must reckon December strawberries as a new and distinct commodity. Since, however, new commodities seldom play an important part in the consumption of any group till some little while after they are first introduced, the imperfection due to this is not likely to be very serious for comparisons between two years that are fairly close together. We can

---

[1] *The Making of Index Numbers*, p. 242.

ignore the existence of the new commodities and confine our calculations to the old ones without serious risk of invalidating our results. As between distant years, however, in the later of which a great number of important commodities may be available that did not exist at all in the earlier ones, a measure that ignored new commodities would be almost worthless as a gauge of changes (as defined in the preceding chapter) in the size of the national dividend.[1] Unless, therefore, some way can be found of bringing these things into account, the hope of making comparisons over other than very short intervals must, it would seem, be abandoned. A way out of this impasse is, however, available in the chain method devised by Marshall.[2] On this method, the price level of 1900 is compared with that of 1901 on the basis of the commodities available in both those years, new commodities introduced and old commodities dropped out during 1901 being ignored; the price level of 1901 is then compared with that of 1902, the new commodities of 1901 this time being counted, but those of 1902 ignored; and so on. Thus we may suppose prices in 1901 to be 95 per cent of prices of 1900; those of 1902, 87 per cent of those of 1901; those of 1903, 103 per cent of those of 1902. On this basis we construct a chain, the price level of 1900 being put at 100. With the above figures the chain will be:

$$
\begin{array}{lll}
1900 & . & . & 100 \\
1901 & . & . & 95 \\
1902 & . & . & 82 \cdot 6 \left(i.e. \dfrac{95 \times 87}{100} \right) \\
1903 & . & . & 85 \left(i.e. \dfrac{82 \cdot 6 \times 103}{100} \right).
\end{array}
$$

When the reciprocals of these price indices, which obviously

[1] Similar considerations suggest that the existence of "new commodities," or rather, in this case, different commodities, is a more serious obstacle in the way of comparing two distant than two neighbouring places, because it is much more likely that one of the two distant places (e.g. a tropical as against a polar region) than it is that one of the two neighbouring places will purchase commodities that are not known in the other. As between distant places the chain method, about to be described, could theoretically be applied via a chain of intermediate places; but practically this method of comparison would probably prove unworkable.

[2] Cf. Marshall, Contemporary Review, March 1887, p. 371, etc.

constitute indices of the purchasing power of £1, are put into our measure of the national dividend, we obtain an instrument by which years, too distant from one another to be effectively compared by any direct process, can be compared by a chain of successive stages. It is as though we were unable to construct any measuring rod capable of maintaining its shape if carried more than 100 miles. It would then be impossible to make any direct comparison between the height of the trees in places 1000 miles apart. But, by comparing the trees at the first mile with those at the 100th mile, these with those at the 199th mile, and so on continually, it would be possible to make an indirect comparison.[1] It must, indeed, be conceded that, if the successive individual comparisons embodied in the chain method, each of which admittedly suffers from a small error, are likely for the most part to suffer from errors *in the same direction*, the cumulative error as between distant years may be large. Were people equally likely to forget how to make things now in use as to

---

[1] Professor Fisher does not, as it seems to me, take sufficient account of this aspect of the chain method. If there were no new commodities to be considered, or if new commodities as between distant years were unimportant, I should not quarrel with his position. It would then be true, as he argues, that, in a comparison of 1900 and 1920, our index number should be based directly on the prices and quantities ruling in those two years, and that the prices and quantities ruling in 1910, which, if the chain method were used, would be involved, are irrelevant, and resort to them a source of error. It is easy to see, for example, that, if the position of 1900 as to quantities and prices is exactly repeated in 1920, an index made on the chain method would probably not give, as it ought to do, a number for 1920 equal to that for 1900. (Cf. *The Review of Economic Statistics*, May 1921, p. 110.) But if, say, half the expenditure in 1920 is on commodities that did not exist in 1900, a chain comparison is no longer an inferior substitute for a direct comparison : it is the only sort of comparison that it is possible to make at all. For this reason it seems to me on the whole best that, in constructing a *series* of index numbers, we should employ the chain method, and not the method of calculating a number for each year relative to one (the same) base year. In the absence of new commodities the issue would be balanced, because, whereas the chain method gives perfectly correct results only as between successive years, the other method—except with constant-weight formulae, which are inadmissible on other grounds—gives perfectly correct results only as between the base year and each other year. But the argument from new commodities tips the scale in favour of chain series. Of course, if, having constructed a chain series, we desire a more special comparison between two years (other than successive years) covered by it, and if, as between those years, the "new commodity" trouble happens to be unimportant, it will be well to calculate a new number directly for this purpose instead of using the series number. (For Fisher's view compare *The Making of Index Numbers*, p. 308, etc.)

invent new things, a large cumulative error would be unlikely. But, in fact, we know that the great march of inventive progress is not offset in this way.   Hence the errors introduced by the chain method are likely to be predominantly in one direction, in such wise that, if the method, as between two distant years, gives equal purchasing power for the £, it is *probable* that the £ really brings more satisfaction to the representative man of given tastes in the later year that in the earlier. Consequently, if our chain measure in 1900 gave 90 as the index of a £'s purchasing power, and gave 100 as the index in 1920, even though meanwhile a large number of new commodities had been introduced and old commodities abandoned, we might confidently infer that, in the conditions postulated in § 5, the amount of economic satisfaction carried to our group by a £ was larger in 1920 than it had been in 1900. But, if these indices were reversed, we could not infer with equal confidence—indeed, unless the fall of the index were very great, we could not infer with *any* confidence—that the sum of economic satisfaction carried by a £ was *smaller* in 1920 than in 1900.

§ 15. We now turn to the second main problem of this chapter.   The formula of § 13 is the one we should select if our choice was completely free.   But it cannot be employed in practice because, in order to construct it, a great deal of information would be necessary which is never in fact available.   It is, therefore, necessary to construct, from such information as we can obtain, a model, or representative, measure that shall approximate to it as closely as possible.

Our full-data measure, apart from its multiplier $\frac{I_2}{I_1}$ representing change of income, is built up of two parts: the reciprocal of the price change of the collection C_1 (containing quantities of different commodities equal to $x_1, y_1, z_1, \ldots$) and the reciprocal of the price change of the collection C_2 (containing quantities equal to $x_2, y_2, z_2, \ldots$).   Our approximate measure will, therefore, also be built up of two parts constituting approximations to the price changes of C_1 and of C_2 respectively. By what use of the method of sampling can these approximations best be made ?

§ 16. Whatever be the collection of commodities with which we are concerned, whether it be that purchased at any time by people in general, or by artisans, or by labourers, or by any other body of persons, it is likely to contain commodities drawn from several different groups, the broad characteristics of whose price movements are different. A good sample collection should contain representatives of all the groups with different characteristics that enter into the national dividend, or of that part of it which we are trying to measure.[1] Unfortunately, however, practical considerations make it impossible that this requirement should be satisfied, and even make it necessary that resort should be had to commodities that do not themselves enter into the purchases of ordinary people, but are, like wheat and barley, raw materials of commodities that do. For the range of things whose prices we are able to observe and bring into our sample collection is limited in two directions.

First, except for certain articles of large popular consumption, the retail prices charged to consumers are difficult to ascertain. Giffen once went so far as to say: " Practically it is found that only the prices of leading commodities capable of being dealt with in large wholesale markets can be made use of." This statement must now be qualified, in view of the studies of retail prices of food that have been made by the Board of Trade and the late Ministry of Food, but it still holds good over a considerable field. Even, however, when the difficulty of ascertaining retail prices can be overcome, these prices are unsuitable for comparison over a series of years, because the thing priced is apt to contain a different proportion of the services of the retailer and of the transporter, and, therefore, to be a different thing at one time from what it is at another. " When fresh sea fish could be had only at the seaside, its average price

[1] Professor Mitchell writes: " The sluggish movement of manufactured goods and of consumers' commodities in particular, the capricious jumping of farm products, the rapidly increasing dearness of lumber, etc., are all part and parcel of the fluctuations which the price level is actually undergoing. . . . Every restriction in the scope of the data implies a limitation in the significance of the results " (*Bulletin of the U.S.A. Bureau of Labour Statistics*, No. 173, pp. 66-7). This is quite correct as it stands, but it must not be interpreted to imply that both finished products and the raw materials embodied in *those same* finished products should be included.

was low. Now that railways enable it to be sold inland, its average retail price includes much higher charges for distribution than it used to do. The simplest plan for dealing with this difficulty is to take, as a rule, the wholesale price of a thing at its place of production, and to allow full weight to the cheapening of the transport of goods, of persons, and of news as separate and most weighty items." [1]

Secondly, it is very difficult to take account even of the wholesale prices of manufactured articles, because, while still called by the same name, they are continually undergoing changes in character and quality. Stilton cheese, once a double-cream, is now a single-cream cheese. Clarets of different vintages are not equivalent. A third-class seat in a railway carriage is not the same thing now as it was forty years ago. "An average ten-roomed house is, perhaps, twice as large in volume as it used to be; and a great part of its cost goes for water, gas, and other appliances which were not in the older house." [2] "During the past twelve years, owing to more scientific methods of thawing and freezing, the quality of the foreign mutton sold in this country has steadily improved; on the other hand, that of foreign beef has gone down, owing to the fact that the supply from North America has practically ceased, and its place has been taken by a poorer quality coming from the Argentine." [3] The same class of difficulty is met with in attempts to evaluate many direct services—the services of doctors, for example, which, as Pareto pointedly observes, absorb more expenditure than the cotton industry [4] —for these, while retaining their name, often vary their nature.

It would thus seem that the principal things available for observation—though it must be admitted that the official Canadian Index Number and more than one index number employed in the United States have attempted a wider survey —are raw materials in the wholesale markets, particularly in the large world markets. These things—apart, of course, from

---

[1] Cf. Marshall, *Contemporary Review*, March 1887, p. 374.

[2] *Ibid.* p. 375. Cf. also Marshall, *Money, Credit, and Commerce*, p. 33.

[3] Mrs. Wood, *Economic Journal*, 1913, pp. 622-3.

[4] *Cours d'économie politique*, p. 281.

the war—have probably of late years fallen in price relatively to minor articles, in which the cost of transport generally plays a smaller part; they have certainly fallen relatively to personal services; and they have probably risen relatively to manufactured articles, because the actual processes of manufacture have been improving. The probable tendency to mutual compensation in the movements of items omitted from our samples makes the omission a less serious evil than it would otherwise be. But, of course, the approximation to a true measure is *pro tanto* worsened; and it is almost certain, since the value of raw materials is often only a small proportion of the value of finished products, so that a 50 per cent change in the former might involve only a 5 per cent change in the latter, that it will give an exaggerated impression of the fluctuations that occur.

Nor does what has just been said exhaust the list of our disabilities. For the samples wanted to represent the several " collections " is a list, not merely of prices, but of prices multiplied by quantities purchased : and our information about quantities is even more limited than our information about prices. There are very few records of annual output— still less of annual purchases—of commodities produced at home. Quantities of imports are, indeed, recorded, but there are not very many important things that are wholly obtained by importation. The difficulty can, indeed, be turned, for some purposes, by resort to typical budgets of expenditure. These make it possible to get a rough idea of the average purchases of certain principal articles that are made by particular classes of people. But this method can scarcely as yet provide more than rough averages. It will seldom enable us to distinguish between the quantities of various things which are embodied in the collections representative of different years fairly close together.

§ 17. Let us next suppose that these difficulties have been so far overcome that a sample embracing both prices and quantities at all relevant periods is available. The next problem is to determine the way in which the prices ought to be " weighted." At first sight it seems natural that the weights should be proportioned to the quantities of the several commodities that are contained in the collection from which

the sample is drawn. But, in theory at all events, it is sometimes possible to improve upon this arrangement. For some
of the commodities about which we have information may
be connected with some excluded commodities in such a way
that their prices generally vary in the same sense. These
commodities, being representative of the others as well as of
themselves, may properly be given weights in excess of what
they are entitled to in their own right. Thus, ideally, if we
had statistics for a few commodities, each drawn from a different
broad group of commodities with similar characteristics, it
would be proper to "weight" the prices of our several
sample commodities in proportion, not to their own importance,
but to that of the groups which they represent. This, however,
is scarcely practicable. There may be certain commodities
whose representative character is so obvious that a doctored
weight may rightly be given to them, but we shall seldom have
enough knowledge to attempt this kind of discrimination.
To use our sample as it stands is, in general, the best plan
that is practically available.[1] Hence, the full-data measure
of the price change of the collection C_1 being

$$\frac{x_1a_2 + y_1b_2 + z_1c_2 + \ldots}{x_1a_1 + y_1b_1 + z_1c_1 + \ldots},$$

the best available approximation to this will be

$$\frac{x_1a_2 + y_1b_2 + \ldots}{x_1a_1 + y_1b_1 + \ldots},$$

[1] This proposition can be proved by means of the principle of inverse
probability. There are more ways in which a sample that will change in a
given degree can be drawn from a complete collection which changes in that
degree than there are ways in which such a sample could be drawn from a
collection that changed in a different degree. Therefore any given sample
that has been taken without bias from any collection is more likely to represent
that collection correctly as it stands than it would do after being subjected to
any kind of doctoring. It must be confessed, however, that the question,
whether a commodity whose price has moved very differently from the main
part of our sample ought to be included, is a delicate one. The omission of
"extreme observations" is sometimes deemed desirable in the calculation of
physical measurements. What should be done in this matter depends on
whether or not a priori expectations, coupled with the general form of our
sample, show that the original distribution, from which the sample is taken,
obeys some ascertained law of error. Whether they do this or not will often be
hard to decide. It should be added that the practical effect of omitting extreme
observations is only likely to be important when the number of commodities
included in our sample is small ; and that it is just when this number is small
that adequate grounds for exclusion are most difficult to come by.

where the number of terms is limited to the number of articles contained in the sample. It follows that the best approximation to the full-data measure of dividend change set out at the end of § 13 is

$$\frac{I_2}{I_1} \sqrt{\frac{x_1 a_1 + y_1 b_1 + \dots}{x_1 a_2 + y_1 b_2 + \dots} \times \frac{x_2 a_1 + y_2 b_1 + \dots}{x_2 a_2 + y_2 b_2 + \dots}}.$$

§ 18. In practice, as has already been hinted, we cannot usually find a reasonable sample set of articles, in regard to which the quantities of the same articles purchased in each of the two periods (or places) we are comparing are known. In these circumstances we may have to content ourselves with a sample in which quantities are given only for one of the years in our comparison. In this case we are forced to truncate our formula and adopt the form

$$\frac{I_2}{I_1} \quad \frac{x_1 a_1 + y_1 b_1 + \dots}{x_1 a_2 + y_1 b_2 + \dots}.$$

This is the type of formula (inverted) employed by the British Board of Trade in the cost of living index number. Obviously a sample of this truncated sort is inferior to a full sample. But Professor Fisher's investigations show that it does not usually yield results very widely divergent from those given by the full sample. We need not, therefore, attack the very difficult question whether there may not be some other formula founded on the same data that would give a closer approximation to the full sample.

§ 19. It is, however, desirable at this point to make plain the exact relation between the above formula and that implicit in a so-called "unweighted" index number such as Sauerbeck's. In that type of index number a certain year or average of years is taken as base, the prices of all commodities for this base-year or base-period are put at 100, and the prices for other years at the appropriate fractions of 100. If a_1, b_1, c_1, are the actual prices in the base-year, and a_2, b_2, c_2, the actual prices in the other year, the index of a £'s purchasing power for this other year will be

$$\frac{100 + 100 + 100 \dots}{100\frac{a_2}{a_1} + 100\frac{b_2}{b_1} + 100\frac{c_2}{c_1} \dots}$$

This is equivalent to the formula given in the preceding
section if and only if x_1, y_1, z_1, . . . in that formula have
values proportioned to $\dfrac{100}{a_1}$, $\dfrac{100}{b_1}$, $\dfrac{100}{c_1}$, . . . That is to say, the
Sauerbeck formula measures the changes that take place in
the aggregate price of a collection made up of such quantities
of each sort of commodity as would, in the base-year or base-
period, have sold for equal multiples of £100. It is extremely
improbable that, as a matter of fact, those quantities were the
quantities actually sold in the base-year or base-period. Therefore, it is only by an extraordinary accident that a formula
constructed on the Sauerbeck plan with any given year or
period as base will coincide with a formula modelled on the
plan of the preceding section and designed to display the
changes that occur in the aggregate price of the collection that
was actually sold in the base-year or base-period.

§ 20. To what has just been said an obvious corollary
attaches. We have seen that an index number on the
Sauerbeck plan is built up with any year or period R as
base; it measures changes in the aggregate price of a collection made up of such quantities of each commodity as in the
year R would have sold for £100. It follows that, when the
base is shifted from the year R_1 to the year R_2, the collection
whose aggregate price movements are being measured is, in
general, altered. Since, then, a different thing is being
measured, it is to be expected that a different result will be
attained; and there is no reason why the results should not
differ so far that an index number on base R_1 shows a rise in
the purchasing power of money, while a similar number (of
the Sauerbeck type) on the base R_2 shows a fall. Thus, if
we have to do with two commodities only, one of which
doubles in price while the other halves, this type of index
number will show a 25 per cent rise in the price of the two
together if the first year is taken as base and a 20 per cent
fall if the second year is taken. An excellent practical
illustration of this type of discrepancy is afforded by certain
tables in the Board of Trade publications concerning the
cost of living in English and German towns respectively.
In the Blue-book dealing with England the real wages of

London, the Midlands and Ireland are calculated by means of index numbers, in which London (corresponding in our time index, say, to the year 1890) is taken as base, and the price of consumables and the rents prevailing there are both represented by 100. On this plan, prices of consumables and rents being given weights of 4 and 1 respectively, the Board of Trade found real wages in London to be equal to those of the Midlands, and 3 per cent higher than those of Ireland. If, however, Ireland had been taken as base, the indices of real wages would have been in London 98, in the Midlands 104, in Ireland 100. A similar difficulty emerges in the Blue-book on German towns. The Board of Trade, taking Berlin as base, found real wages higher in that city than in any place save one on their list.[1] "If the North Sea ports, instead of Berlin, had been taken as base, Berlin would have appeared fourth on the list instead of second, and the order of the other districts would have been changed; and, by taking Central Germany as base, even greater changes in the order would have been effected."[2] It is true, no doubt, that *large* discrepancies of this sort are not likely to occur, except when there are large differences, or, as between different times, large fluctuations, in the prices of commodities that are heavily weighted. But that fact, though practically interesting, is not relevant to my present point.

§ 21. It may happen in some circumstances that we have no knowledge of, and no data for guessing, quantities for any of the years we wish to compare, and are, therefore, forced back, for the price index number involved in our measure, on a sample of price relatives alone without any weights at all. In these circumstances the preceding discussions make one thing quite clear. We must not construct our index by combining the price relatives in a simple arithmetical average, after the manner of Sauerbeck. The paradoxes to which that method leads are avoided if either the simple geometric mean—this will not work if the price of any of our commodities is liable to become nothing!—or the median of the price relatives is taken. Professor Fisher has an

[1] [Cd. 4032], p. xxxiv.
[2] J. M. Keynes, *Economic Journal*, 1908, p. 473.

interesting discussion of the comparative advantages of these two forms.[1] Both are plainly inferior to the weighted formula of § 18, where the data required for that formula are available.

§ 22. In conclusion we have to consider the *reliability* of the various practicable measures which are available as representatives of the full-data measure. Let us first suppose that we can obtain a sample of the same general form as the full-data measure, quantities as well as prices being available for both (or all) of the periods that we wish to compare. Five general observations may then be made. First, when the sample is drawn from most of the principal sets of commodities included in the full-data collection, which have characteristic price movements, the probable error of our measure will be less than it is when a less representative field is covered. Secondly, when the sample is large, in the sense that the expenditure upon the items included in it comprises a large part of the aggregate expenditure of our group upon the whole collection, the probable error is less than it is when the sample is small. With random sampling in the strict technical sense, the reliability increases as the square root of the number of items contained in the sample. Thirdly, when each of the items constituting the full-data collection absorbs individually a small part of the aggregate expenditure upon that collection, the probable error is less than when some of the items absorb individually a large part of the total expenditure. Fourthly, when the items included in the sample exhibit a small " scatter," the various prices changing as between the years we are comparing in very similar degrees, the probable error is less than it is when the items exhibit a wide scatter. From this consideration it follows that the magnitude of the error to which our measure is liable is greater—apart altogether from the difficulty of " new commodities " referred to in § 14—as between distant years than as between years that are close together. The reason is, as Professor Mitchell, on the basis of a wide survey of facts, has shown, that the distribution of the variations in wholesale prices as between one year and the next is highly

[1] Cf. *The Making of Index Numbers*, p. 211, etc., and p. 260, etc.

concentrated,—more concentrated than the distribution proper to the normal law of error,—but the distribution of variations as between one year and a somewhat distant year is highly scattered. " With some commodities the trend of successive price changes continues distinctly upwards for years at a time; with other commodities there is a constant downward trend; with still others no definite long-period trend appears." [1] Finally, if we are unable to obtain a sample of the same general form as our full-data measure, and have to be content with one of the truncated form described in § 18, our measure will, of course, be less reliable than one of equal range of the better type. If we have to do without quantities altogether, and must use the simple geometric mean or the median of price relatives, the measure will be less reliable still. But, it is important to notice, the damage done to reliability by the use of an inferior index formula, like the damage done by the use of a small sample, is not very great when the scatter of price movements between the years we are comparing is small or moderate, but may be very great when the scatter is large.

[1] *U.S. Bulletin of Labour*, No. 173, p. 23.

CHAPTER VII

ECONOMIC WELFARE AND CHANGES IN THE SIZE OF THE NATIONAL DIVIDEND

§ 1. It is evident that, provided the dividend accruing to the poor is not diminished, increases in the size of the aggregate national dividend, if they occur in isolation without anything else whatever happening, must involve increases in economic welfare. For, though, no doubt, economic welfare as measured in money, and, therefore, the national dividend as here defined, might be increased and economic welfare in itself—not as measured in money—at the same time diminished, if an addition to the supply of rich men's goods was accompanied by a contraction in the supply of poor men's goods, this sort of double change is ruled out by the proviso that the dividend accruing to the poor shall not be diminished. But it does not follow that every cause, which, while leaving the dividend of the poor unharmed, increases the size of the aggregate dividend, must bring about an increase in economic welfare; because it is possible that a cause which increases the size of the dividend may at the same time produce other effects adverse to economic welfare. It is desirable, therefore, to inquire how far this possibility needs to be reckoned with in practice.

§ 2. Changes in consumption that come about in consequence of an increase in facilities for obtaining some of the items contained in the dividend are liable to bring about changes in taste. But, when any particular kind of commodity becomes more readily available the resultant change of taste is *usually* an enhancement. Thus, when machines are sent out on trial, or articles presented in sample-packets, or pictures exhibited free to the public, the popular desire for these objects tends to be augmented. When public-houses, or lotteries, or libraries are easily accessible, the taste for drink, or gambling, or literature is not merely gratified, but is also stimulated. When cleanliness, or light,[1] or model dwellings, or model plots of agricultural land are set up, though it is only to be seen, and not owned, by the neighbours, the object lesson may still succeed and make plain superiorities hitherto unrecognised.[2] Thus, "free libraries are engines for creating the habitual power of enjoying high-class literature," and a savings bank, if confined to the poor, is an "engine for teaching thrift."[3] / In like manner the policy of many German cities, in subsidising theatres and opera-houses and in providing symphony concerts two or three evenings a week at a very small admission fee, is an *educational* policy that bears fruit in increased capacity for enjoyment. It is true that an increase in taste for one thing is generally associated with a decline in taste for any other things that fulfil the same or a similar purpose, *e.g.* wool as against cotton or a new "best type" of motor car as against what used to be the best type, and sometimes with a decline in taste for other quite disconnected means of enjoyment. But it is reasonable, in these circumstances, to hold that the provision made for the new taste is likely to yield *some* excess of satisfaction over that made for the old;

[1] Cf. Walpole's account of the way in which the introduction of street lamps led to an increased demand for illuminants *within* the neighbouring houses (*History of England*, i. 86). An elaborate method of advertising electric light is quoted in Whyte's *Electrical Industry* (p. 57). A company undertakes to instal six lamps in a house free of all charge for a six months' trial, the house-holder paying only for the current that he uses. After the six months, the company undertakes to remove the whole arrangement if the customer so desires.

[2] Cf. Miss Octavia Hill's practice of insisting on the cleanliness of the *stair-cases* of her houses, and Sir H. Plunkett's account of the Cork Exhibition, 1902 (*Ireland in the New Century*, pp. 285-7).

[3] Jevons, *Methods of Social Reform*, p. 32. It should be noted, however, that Dr. Marshall believes this order of consideration to have a relatively small range. He writes: "Those demands, which show high elasticity in the long run, show a high elasticity almost at once ; so that, subject to a few exceptions, we may speak of the demand for a commodity as being of high or low elasticity without specifying how far we are looking ahead" (*Principles of Economics*, p. 456).

so that the net result of an increase in facilities for obtaining some of the items contained in the dividend will be to increase economic welfare.

§ 3. The above argument does not, however, go to the root of things. It is relevant to immediate short-period effects rather than to ultimate effects. When a group of people have passed from a state of relative poverty, to which they were accustomed and adapted, to a state of relative wealth, to which they have become adapted, will they really derive more satisfaction from the last state of their environment than they did from the first? With the changed conditions the whole scheme of their desires and habits and expectations will also be changed. If a man who had all his life slept in a soft bed was suddenly compelled to sleep on the ground under the sky, he would suffer greatly; but does a man who has always slept on a soft bed enjoy his nights more than one who has always slept under the sky? Is it certain that a hundred Rolls-Royce cars in a Rolls-Royce world would yield a greater sum of satisfaction than a hundred dog-carts in a world of dog-carts? In the chapter that follows some reasons will be given for doubting whether a substantial reduction in the real consumable income of rich people, provided it were general, would, after time had been allowed for adaptation to it, appreciably diminish their economic welfare. Analogous considerations hold good of an increase in their real consumable income. The point is a very important one. If the *per capita* income of this country were, say, twenty times what it actually is, it may well be that a further increase in it would not ultimately—the population being supposed constant—add anything at all to economic welfare. As things are, however, in view of low level of average real income, we may, I think, safely conclude that an increase in the dividend—apart from the fantastic hypothesis that the whole increase goes to persons already very rich—would carry with it, ultimately and not merely immediately, an increase in economic welfare. The goal of economic betterment is not a mere illusion.[1]

[1] Cf. M. Bousquet (*Weltwirtschaftliches Archiv*, Oct. 1929, pp. 174 *et seq.*) for an opposite view. M. Bousquet argues that economic welfare depends on the

§ 4. There is, however, a further point to be considered. The economic welfare of a community consists in the balance of satisfactions derived from the use of the national dividend over the dissatisfactions involved in the making of it. Consequently, when an increase in the national dividend comes about in association with an increase in the quantity of work done to produce it, the question may be raised whether the increase in work done may not involve dissatisfaction in excess of the satisfaction which its product yields. Now, in so far as extra work is called out because, through inventions and so on, new and more advantageous means of employing it have been opened up, there is no fear of this. Nor is there any fear of it if the extra work is called out because obstacles, such as quarrels between employers and employed, which used to prevent people who wanted to work from doing so, have been removed. Nor again is there any fear of it if the extra work is called out because methods of remunerating workpeople, which reward extra work with equivalent extra pay, have been introduced. It is possible, however, that extra work may be called out in other ways than these. Suppose, for example, that the whole community was compelled by law to work for eighteen hours a day, and—which is in fact improbable—that this policy made the national dividend larger. It is practically certain that the satisfaction yielded by the extra product would be enormously less than the dissatisfaction caused by the extra labour. There is here a cause which has increased the size of the national dividend while lessening, and not increasing, the sum of economic welfare. This type of cause is not, in the modern world, practically important, because, apart from military conscription, we have to do with voluntary, not with compulsory, labour. It is, however, conceivable that, even under a voluntary system, something analogous may emerge. From a mistaken view of their own real interest, workpeople may welcome an addition to the hours of labour of a sort which augments the dividend

relation between incomes and needs, and that an increase in income involves, after time for adjustment has been allowed, such an increase of needs that the original relation between income and needs is re-established. Hence, he concludes, the economic welfare of a representative man is a constant, unaffected in the long run by changes in his income.

but damages economic welfare.   Again, under the exploitation of employers, workpeople may be forced to assent to an increase of work as a less evil than reduced earnings.   There are here a number of possible causes of additions to the dividend associated with damage to economic welfare.   Plainly, however, among the general body of causes relevant to our discussion the part they play will be small. / In general, causes which increase the size of the national dividend while involving an increase in work, as well as causes which increase it without involving this, will, the conditions of distribution being assumed, increase economic welfare.

CHAPTER VIII

ECONOMIC WELFARE AND CHANGES IN THE DISTRIBUTION
OF THE NATIONAL DIVIDEND

§ 1. IF income is transferred from rich persons to poor persons the proportion in which different sorts of goods and services are provided will be changed. Expensive luxuries will give place to more necessary articles, rare wines to meat and bread, new machines and factories to clothes and improved small dwellings; and there will be other changes of a like sort.[1]

---

[1] It should be noticed that one of the things to which people will divert consumption, if distribution is altered in favour of the poor, is the quasi-commodity, leisure. It is well established that the high-wage countries and industries are generally also both the short-hour countries and industries and the countries and industries in which the wage-earning work required from women and children in supplement of the family budget is the smallest. The former point is illustrated by some statistics of the wage rate and hours of labour of carpenters in the United States, Great Britain, France, Germany, and Belgium, published in No. 54 of the Bulletin of the U.S. Bureau of Labour (p. 1125). In illustration of the latter point, Sir Sydney Chapman notes the assertion that, whereas the German collier finds only 65·8 per cent of his family's earnings, the wealthier American collier finds 77·5 per cent (*Work and Wages*, i. p. 17). Mr. Rowntree's interesting table for York points, when properly analysed, in the same direction (*Poverty*, p. 171); and Miss Vessellitsky shows that low-paid home-work among women is found principally in those districts, *e.g.* East Anglia, "where the bad conditions of male labour make it almost indispensable for the wife to supplement the husband's earnings," whereas, in districts where men's wages are good, women only work at industry if they themselves can obtain well-paid jobs (*The Home-worker*, p. 4). Again, reference may be made to the familiar correlation found in recent English history between rising wages and falling hours. Yet again, a study of the rates of wages and hours of labour in different districts in England would, I suspect, reveal a correlation of the same type. It does so for the wages and hours statistics of bricklayers as given in the *Abstract of Labour Statistics for 1908* (pp. 42, etc.). These facts are somewhat awkward to fit in to the method of exposition followed in this book, because leisure is not included as a commodity in my definition of the national dividend : and in so far, therefore, as improved distribution causes leisure to be substituted for things, it must involve a decrease in the national dividend. Plainly, however, this sort of decrease should be ignored when we

In view of this fact, it is inexact to speak of a change
in the distribution of the dividend in favour of, or adverse to,
the poor.   There is not a single definitely constituted heap of
things coming into being each year and distributed now in one
way, now in another.   In fact, there is no such thing as *the*
dividend from the point of view of both of two years, and, therefore, there can be no such thing as a change in *its* distribution.

§ 2. This, however, is a point of words rather than of
substance.   What I *mean* when I say that the distribution of
the dividend has changed in favour of the poor is that, the
general productive power of the community being given, poor
people are getting more of the things they want at the expense
of rich people getting less of the things they want.   It might
be thought at first sight that the only way in which this
could happen would be through a transference of purchasing
power from the rich to the poor.   That, however, is not so.
It is possible for the poor to be advantaged and the rich
damaged, even though the quantity of purchasing power, *i.e.*
of command over productive resources, held by both groups
remains unaltered. // This might happen if the technical
methods of producing something predominatingly consumed
by the poor were improved and at the same time those of
producing something predominatingly consumed by the rich
were worsened, and if the net result was to leave the size of
the national dividend as defined in Chapter V. unchanged.
It might also happen if, by a system of rationing or some
other device, the rich were forced to transfer their demand
away from things which are important to the poor and which
are produced under such conditions that diminished demand
leads to lowered prices.   *Per contra*—and this point will be
seen in Part IV. to be very important practically—the share,
both proportionate and absolute of command over the country's
productive resources held by the poor may be increased, and
yet, if the process by which they acquire this greater share
involves an increase in the cost of things that play a large
part in their own consumption, they may not really gain.

---

are considering the effect of changes of distribution on economic welfare ; for
the loss of welfare associated with the constriction of production to which they
lead is necessarily less than the gain of welfare due to the leisure itself.

Thus a change in distribution favourable to the poor may be brought about otherwise than by a transference of purchasing power, or command over productive resources, to them, and it does not *mean* a transference of these things to them. None the less, this sort of transference is the most important, and may be regarded as the typical, means by which changes in distribution favourable to the poor come about.

§ 3. On this basis it is desired, if possible, to establish some connection between changes in the distribution of the national dividend and changes in economic welfare, corresponding to the connection established in the preceding chapter between changes in the size of the national dividend and changes in economic welfare. In considering this matter we must not forget that the economic welfare enjoyed by anybody in any period depends on the income that he consumes rather than on the income that he receives; and that, the richer a man is, the smaller proportion of his total income he is likely to consume, so that, if his total income is, say, twenty times as large as that of a poorer man, his consumed income may be only, say, five times as large. Nevertheless, it is evident that any transference of income from a relatively rich man to a relatively poor man of similar temperament, since it enables more intense wants to be satisfied at the expense of less intense wants, must increase the aggregate sum of satisfaction. The old "law of diminishing utility" thus leads securely to the proposition: Any cause which increases the absolute share of real income in the hands of the poor, provided that it does not lead to a contraction in the size of the national dividend from any point of view, will, in general, increase economic welfare.[1] This conclusion is further fortified by another consideration. Mill wrote: "Men do not desire to be *rich*, but to be richer than other men. The avaricious or covetous man would find little or no satisfaction in the

[1] The difficult case in which a transference leads to a contraction in the size of the dividend from the point of view of either the pre-change or the post-change period, and not from that of the other, will not be considered here. Henceforward it will be assumed that we have to do with changes in the dividend that are either positive or negative from both the relevant points of view, and, therefore, except for special reasons, we shall speak simply of increases and decreases in the dividend.

possession of any amount of wealth, if he were the poorest amongst all his neighbours or fellow-countrymen."[1]　More elaborately, Signor Rignano writes: "As for the needs which vanity creates, they can be satisfied equally well by a small as by a large expenditure of energy.　It is only the existence of great riches which makes necessary for such satisfaction a very large, instead of a very small, expenditure. In reality a man's desire to appear 'worth' double what another man is worth, that is to say, to possess goods (jewels, clothes, horses, parks, luxuries, houses, etc.) twice as valuable as those possessed by another man, is satisfied just as fully, if the first has ten things and the second five, as it would be if the first had a hundred and the second fifty."[2]　Now the part played by comparative, as distinguished from absolute, income is likely to be small for incomes that only suffice to provide the necessaries and primary comforts of life, but to be large with large incomes. ╱In other words, a larger proportion of the satisfaction yielded by the incomes of rich people comes from their *relative*, rather than from their absolute, amount.　This part of it will not be destroyed if the incomes of all rich people are diminished together.　The loss of economic welfare suffered by the rich when command over resources is transferred from them to the poor will, therefore, be substantially smaller relatively to the gain of economic welfare to the poor than a consideration of the law of diminishing utility taken by itself suggests. ╱

§ 4. It must be conceded, of course, that, if the rich and the poor were two races with different mental constitutions, such that the rich were inherently capable of securing a greater amount of economic satisfaction from any given income than the poor, the possibility of increasing welfare by this type of change would be seriously doubtful.　Furthermore, even without any assumption about inherent racial difference, it may be maintained that a rich man, from the nature of his upbringing and training, is capable of obtaining considerably more satisfaction from a given income —say a thousand pounds—than a poor man would be.

---

[1] Posthumous Essay on Social Freedom, *Oxford and Cambridge Review*, Jan. 1907.

[2] *Di un socialismo in accordo colla dottrina economica liberale*, p. 285.

For, if anybody accustomed to a given standard of living suddenly finds his income enlarged, he is apt to dissipate the extra income in forms of exciting pleasure, which, when their indirect, as well as their direct, effects are taken into account, may even lead to a positive loss of satisfaction. To this argument, however, there is a sufficient answer. It is true that at any given moment the tastes and temperament of persons who have long been poor are more or less adjusted to their environment, and that a sudden and sharp rise of income is likely to be followed by a good deal of foolish expenditure which involves little or no addition to economic welfare. If, however, the higher income is maintained for any length of time, this phase will pass; whereas, if the increase is gradual or, still better, if it comes about in such a way as not to be directly perceived—through a fall in prices, for example—the period of foolishness need not occur at all. In any case, to contend that the folly of poor persons is so great that a rise of income among them will not promote economic welfare in any degree is to press paradox beyond the point up to which discussion can reasonably be called upon to follow. The true view, as I conceive it, is admirably stated by Messrs. Pringle and Jackson in their special report to the Poor Law Commissioners: "It is in the unskilled and least educated part of the population that drink continues to hold its ground; as greater regularity of employment and higher wages are achieved by sections of the working-classes, the men rise in respectability and character. That the drink bill is diminishing, while wages are rising throughout the country, is one of the most hopeful indications of progress we possess."[1] The root of the matter is that, even when, under existing conditions, the mental constitution of poor persons is such that an enlarged income will at the moment yield them little benefit, yet, after a time—more especially if the time is long enough to allow a new generation to grow up—the possession of such an income will make possible the development in them, through education and otherwise, of capacities and faculties adapted for the enjoyment of the enlarged income. Thus in the long run differences

[1] [Cd. 4795], p. 46.

of temperament and taste between rich and poor are overcome by the very fact of a shifting of income between them.
Plainly, therefore, they cannot be used as an argument to
disprove the benefits of a transference.[1]

§ 5. After all, however, general reasoning of the above
type, though perhaps necessary to provide formal justification
for our thesis, is not necessary to convince us practically that
it is valid. For that purpose it is sufficient to reflect on the
way in which, in this country, income has in fact been
distributed in recent times. There are not sufficient data to
enable this to be calculated with any degree of accuracy.
On the basis, however, of work done by Dr. Bowley,[2] we may
hazard the following rough estimate for the period immediately
prior to the war. The 12,000 richest families in the country
received about one-fifteenth of the total national income; the
richest *fiftieth* of the population received about one-quarter,
and the richest *ninth* of the population received nearly one-
half of that total income. The remainder of it, a little more
than a half, was left to be shared among small independent
workers and salary-receivers earning less than £160 a year
and practically the whole body of wage-earners. The table
below, giving Dr. Bowley's estimate of distribution among a
portion of this last group in 1911, carries the matter a little
farther.

[1] Similarly, of course, when we are taking a long view, the argument that
a reduction in the real income of the rich inflicts a special injury, because it
forces them to abandon habits to which they have grown accustomed, loses
most of its force.

[2] *Quarterly Journal of Economics*, Feb. 1914, p. 261 ; and *The Division of
the Product of Industry before the War*, 1918, pp. 11 and 14.

[TABLE

WEEKLY MONEY WAGES OF ADULT WORKMEN IN ORDINARY
FULL WORK

(INCLUDING VALUATION FOR PAYMENT IN KIND) [1]

Wage.	Number of Men.	Per cent of whole.
Under 15/- . .	320,000 (mainly agriculture)	4
15/- to 20/- . .	640,000	8
20/- to 25/- . .	1,600,000	20
25/- to 30/- . .	1,680,000	21
30/- to 35/- . .	1,680,000	21
35/- to 40/- . .	1,040,000	13
40/- to 45/- . .	560,000	7
45/- and over .	480,000	6

In studying these figures we must, indeed, remember that in families where the man has a small income the wife and children are more likely to be earning wages than they are in families headed by richer men; so that distribution among families was probably more satisfactory than distribution among individuals. This, however, is comparatively a small matter. What the figures cited meant in the concrete is brought out very clearly in the same author's pre-war study of the conditions of life in four industrial towns. Together these towns embrace " about 2150 working - class households and 9720 persons. Of these households 293 or $13\frac{1}{2}$ per cent, of these persons 1567 or 16 per cent, are living in a condition of primary poverty," *i.e.* with incomes so low that, even if expended with perfect wisdom, they could not have provided an adequate subsistence. " Out of 3287 children who appear in our tables, 879, or 27 per cent, are living in families which fail to reach the low standard taken as necessary for healthy existence." [2] The excess incomes of the richer classes did not, of course, represent corresponding excess consumption. The dominant part

[1] From the *Contemporary Review*, Oct. 1911, p. 1.

[2] *Livelihood and Poverty*, pp. 46-7. The reason for the excess in the proportion of children in poverty is the twofold one, that poor families are apt to be larger than others, and that a large family is itself a cause of life in poverty. Cf. Bowley, *The Measurement of Social Phenomena*, p. 187.

of the annual new investments of the country—before the war perhaps 350 millions—and a large part of the expenses of central and local government—over 200 millions—had to be provided out of them; so that not more than 300 millions annually can have been spent by the rich and moderately well-off on any form of luxury. Moreover, estimates of money income tend to exaggerate the relative real income of wealthy persons, because these persons are often charged higher prices than poor persons pay for the same services. A number of London shops, for example, discriminate against " good addresses," and hotel charges are also often discriminatory. It has even been suggested that as much as 25 per cent of the money income of the rich, as spent by them, represents no equivalent in real income.[1] In like manner, estimates of money income sometimes make it appear that the real incomes of poor persons are less than they really are, by ignoring discriminations in their favour. Thus Dr. Bowley points out : " A butcher can perhaps raise his prices to his day customers without much affecting the sale, but not to those in the evening. In this case the working class would suffer a smaller rise than the richer class. This consideration applies especially to the very large volume of purchases made late on Saturday night." But, when all quali- fications have been made, the figures cited above leave no room for doubt that there was before the war, and is still, a substantial excess income in the hands of the richer classes available, in Dr. Bowley's phrase, " for attack " by way of transference.

§ 6. Some study of the post-war distribution of income in Great Britain and Northern Ireland has been made by Dr. Bowley and Sir Josiah Stamp with special reference to the year 1924. From this it appears that the proportion of the total accruing, pre-tax, to the richest classes, *i.e.* those with incomes in excess of £9400, which roughly corresponds to £5000 at the pre-war price-level, has somewhat diminished.[2] In general these writers conclude as follows. The distribution of income between wage-earners, other earners and unearned

---

[1] Urwick, *Luxury and the Waste of Life*, pp. 87 and 90.
[2] *The National Income*, 1924, p. 58.

incomes was changed slightly in favour of the earning classes. Manual workers on the average make slightly increased real earnings, and there have also been transfers for their benefit in insurance schemes and other public expenditure. In addition they have the advantage of a reduction of about one-tenth of the working week. This change can be connected with the reduction in the real income derived from house property and investments bearing fixed rates of interest. The indications are that profits as a whole, reckoned before tax is paid, form nearly the same proportion of total income at the two dates (*i.e.* 1911 and 1924). Within the wage-earning classes women and unskilled workers have received a substantial real advance in wages; the great majority of skilled workers made at least as much (after allowing for the rise of prices) in 1924 as in 1911.[1] That these changes have meant a great deal to the lives of the very poor is well brought out by Dr. Bowley's second investigation, made after the war, into the conditions of the four towns referred to in the preceding section. " Even," he writes, " on the assumption that all the families suffering from unemployment in a particular week had no adequate resources, and that their unemployment was chronic, the proportion in poverty in 1924 was little more than half that in 1913. If there had been no unemployment the proportion of families in poverty in the towns taken together would have fallen to one-third (3·6 per cent as against 11 per cent), and of persons to little over a quarter (3·5 per cent against 12·6 per cent) of the proportion in 1913."[2]   Again : " The proportion of families, in which a man is normally earning, found to be in poverty, was in 1924 only one-fifth of the proportion in 1913, if full employment is assumed; while, if the maximum effect of unemployment is reckoned, it is little over one-half."[3]   This large improvement is partly due (to the extent of about one-third of the whole) to a decrease in the average number of children per family;

[1] *The National Income*, 1924, pp. 58-9.

[2] *Has Poverty Diminished*, p. 16. The discrepancies between the percentages given in this passage for 1913 and that given in *Livelihood and Poverty* is apparently due to the fact that in the latter work 480 houses inhabited by the middle and upper classes were excluded from the calculation (cf. *Livelihood and Poverty*, p. 46, footnote).

[3] *Has Poverty Diminished*, p. 21.

but chiefly (to the extent of the remaining two-thirds) to a rise in the rate of real wages of unskilled labourers. In spite of this improvement, however, and in spite of the fact that, " when the full effects of taxation are taken into account, the real income available for saving or expenditure in the hands of the rich is definitely less than before the war,"[1] the distribution, not merely of incomes prior to taxation, but of what is left over after taxes have been taken away, is still very uneven. It was still true, for example, in 1924, that something like 100 millions a year *net*, *i.e.* about $2\frac{1}{2}$ per cent of the total income of the country, was enjoyed by 3000 families. We must not hesitate, therefore, to conclude that, so long as the dividend as a whole is not diminished, any increase, within wide limits, in the real income enjoyed by the poorer classes, at the expense of an equal decrease in that enjoyed by the richer classes, is practically certain to involve an addition to economic welfare.

§ 7. It should be noticed that the conclusion set out above is not exactly equivalent to the proposition that economic welfare will be increased by anything that, *ceteris paribus*, renders the distribution of the national dividend less unequal. If the community consisted of two members only, it would, indeed, coincide with this. But, in a community consisting of more than two members, the meaning of "rendering the distribution of the dividend less unequal" is ambiguous. Pareto measures inequality of distribution by dividing the logarithm of the number of incomes in excess of any amount x into the logarithm of x. This measure is very difficult to apply unless we accept Pareto's view that, in any given income distribution, the ratio between his two logarithms is approximately the same for all values of x; and, even so, it is a matter of dispute whether the reciprocal of his measure,—which, of course, would indicate less equality when the measure itself indicates greater equality,—is not to be preferred to that measure.[2] Among other measures of inequality the most

---

[1] *The National Income*, 1924, p. 59. It must, of course, be held in mind that a large part of the heavy taxation of rich persons goes to pay interest on war loan held by rich persons.

[2] Cf. Gini, *Variabilità e mutabilità*, p. 72.

familiar is the mean square deviation from the mean. With that criterion it can be proved that, assuming similarity of temperament among the members of the community, a diminution in the inequality of distribution *probably*, though not necessarily, increases the aggregate sum of satisfaction.[1]

[1] If A be the mean income, n the number of incomes, and a_1, a_2 . . . deviations from the mean, aggregate satisfaction, on our assumption,

$$= nf(A) + (a_1 + a_2 + \ldots)f' + \frac{1}{2!}(a_1{}^2 + a_2{}^2 + \ldots)f'' + \frac{1}{3!}(a_1{}^3 + a_2{}^3 + \ldots)f''' + \ldots$$

But we know that $\{a_1 + a_2 + \ldots\} = 0$.

We know nothing to suggest whether the sum of the terms beyond the third is positive or negative. But it is certain that $\frac{1}{2}\{a_1{}^2 + a_2{}^2 + \ldots\}f''$ is negative. If, therefore, the fourth and following terms are small relatively to the third term, it is certain, and in general it is probable, that aggregate satisfaction is larger, the smaller is $(a_1{}^2 + a_2{}^2 + \ldots)$. This latter sum, of course, varies in the same sense as the mean square deviation or standard deviation $\sqrt{\dfrac{\Sigma \overline{a^2}}{n}}$. Dr. Dalton, in the course of an interesting article on " The Measurement of the Inequality of Incomes," has shown that, in a community where many incomes diverge widely from the average, the probability which the above argument establishes is only of a low order (*Economic Journal*, Sept. 1920, p. 355).

CHAPTER IX

§ 1. IN the two preceding chapters nothing was said about the possible reactions which the changes we have been contemplating may have on the numbers of the population. This omission must now be remedied. To the broad conclusions which were reached relating respectively to the size and distribution of the national dividend, it may be objected that an increase in the income enjoyed by any group causes its numbers to increase until income per head is again reduced to its old amount, and, therefore, that it leads to no lasting benefit. In practice this argument is most often used about the effects of an increase in the income of manual workers; and it is, of course, much more plausible in this field than in any other. It will, therefore, be enough to examine this aspect of it. I shall consider it first from the point of view of the whole world, or of a single country imagined, for the purposes of the argument, to be isolated, and afterwards shall inquire how far the results achieved need to be modified for a single country constituting one among the associated family of modern nations. In the argument to be developed under these two heads it must be understood that the additions to the income of wage-earners that we have in mind do not include additions brought about by the offer, on behalf of the State, of deliberate and overt bounties upon the acquisition of large families. Under the old Poor Law in the United Kingdom bounties were, in effect, given; our present income-tax law acts in a slight degree in the same sense; and in a law passed in France [1]

---

[1] Cf. *Economic Journal*, Dec. 1913, p. 641.

shortly before the war a similar policy was adopted. This class of addition to the income of the poor has, of course, a tendency to augment population, and, in some practical problems, the point is of importance. For the present, however, we are concerned with additions that do not offer a special differential inducement to the begetting of children.

§ 2. If we provisionally ignore the deeper-seated reactions which increased income may exert upon wants and tastes, our discussion virtually resolves itself into an inquiry into the validity of the celebrated " iron law of wages." According to this " law," expanding numbers continually press the earnings of the workpeople down to " subsistence level," thus making it impossible for their real income *per head* in any circumstances to increase. It should be noted in passing that, even if there really were such a law, the proposition that better fortune for the workers increases economic welfare would not be definitely disproved. For it might still be urged that, provided the average working family attains in the whole period of life any surplus of satisfaction over dissatisfaction, an increase of numbers implies by itself an addition to economic welfare.[1] But, for my present purpose, there is no need to press this doubtful point. Population does not tend to expand in such a manner as to hold down income per head to a predetermined " subsistence level." It is true, no doubt, that the direct and immediate result of an increase in the dividend accruing to any group is likely to be *some* increase of population. It is well known that the English marriage rate was negatively correlated with wheat prices in the earlier part of the nineteenth century and was positively correlated with exports, clearing-house returns

[1] But cf. Sidgwick's observation: " It seems at least highly doubtful whether a mere increase in the number of human beings living as an average unskilled labourer lives in England can be regarded as involving a material increase in the quantum of human happiness " (*Principles of Political Economy*, p. 522, note). A population, which, in given conditions, maximises this quantum, seems to have a much better claim to be called the *optimum* population than a population which maximises *real income per head*. The practice, which has gained a certain currency, of using the term in this latter sense is, therefore, unfortunate.

and so on in the latter part:[1] and that the rate of mortality falls with growing wealth, and *vice versa*. But it is contrary to experience to assert that increased income stimulates population to so large an extent that the individual earnings of workpeople are brought down again to the level they occupied before the improvement. There are two ways in which the manual workers can use their increased claims over material things, namely, to increase their numbers and to increase their standard of comfort. The distinction between these two ways is well illustrated by the following contrasted passages from Malthus's *Principles of Political Economy*. On the one hand, he found that the greater wealth resulting from the introduction of the potato into Ireland in the eighteenth century was "spent almost exclusively in the maintenance of large and frequent families." On the other hand, when the price of corn in England fell between 1660 and 1720, a considerable portion of the workpeople's "increased real wages was expended in a marked improvement of the quality of the food consumed and a decided elevation in the standard of their comforts and conveniences."[2] It is not possible to prophesy *a priori* the proportion in which increased resources will be devoted to these two uses. The proportion will vary at different times and in different places. Leroy-Beaulieu, for example, suggests that the population use has been predominantly followed in recent times in Belgium and Germany, and the standard-of-comfort use in other European countries.[3] But—and this is the point—it is practically certain that the population use will not be allowed to absorb the *whole* fruits of increased command over nature.

§ 3. The preceding argument, as was indicated at the outset, leaves out of account the deeper-seated reactions that may be set up by expanded earnings. An important

---

[1] Cf. Pareto, *Cours d'économie politique*, pp. 88 *et seq.* Cf. also Marshall, *Principles of Economics*, pp. 189-90.

[2] *Principles of Political Economy*, pp. 252 and 254. Mr. Wright, commenting on the fall in the birth rate in the later nineteenth century, suggests that increased command over nature is more likely to be taken out in an improved standard of comfort when it manifests itself in a fall of prices than when it manifests itself in higher money wages ; for people do not readily see behind money (*Population*, p. 117).   [3] *La Répartition des richesses*, p. 439.

school of writers, headed by Professor Brentano, admits that the direct and immediate effect of enhanced material prosperity in any class will, in general, be to increase the marriage rate and, therewith, the birth rate. They maintain, however, that the enhanced prosperity will, in the long run, bring about the development of a higher spiritual and cultural level, in which more forethought is exercised about children and more satisfactions rival to that of having children come to the front. Hence, they urge, in the long run an increase in the income of any class is likely to lead to no increase at all, but actually to a decrease, in their birth rate and their numbers.[1] Thus Professor Brentano declares that a permanent improvement in wealth and culture, " as a comparison of different ranks, as well as of the same ranks and the same people at different stages of development, has shown us, results in a diminution of births. . . . As prosperity increases, so do the pleasures which compete with marriage, while the feeling towards children takes on a new character of refinement, and both these facts tend to diminish the desire to beget and to bear children." [2] Those persons, for instance, who have something to leave to their children are more affected by the fact that, if their family is large, what is left at their death must be divided into a number of small parts, than those who have nothing to leave and act apart from economic motives. Detailed confirmation of this view is afforded by Dr. Heron's statistical study of London in 1906. In certain selected districts he found the correlation co-efficients between the number of births per 100 wives and various indices of social status. The indices chosen were the proportion of occupied males engaged in professional occupations, the number of female domestic servants per 100 families, the number of general labourers per 1000 males, the proportion of the population living more than two in a room, and the number of paupers and of lunatics per 1000 of the population. A low index of prosperity and a high birth rate were found to go together.

[1] Cf. Mombert, *Archiv für Socialwissenschaft*, vol. xxxiv. p. 817. Cf. also Aftalion, *Les Crises périodiques de surproduction*, vol. i. pp. 208-9.

[2] *Economic Journal*, 1910, p. 385.

Against this result there had to be set the fact that a low index of prosperity was also accompanied by a high rate of infant mortality. Investigation, however, showed that the excess of mortality was not sufficient to balance the excess of births; and the conclusion emerged, that "the wives in the districts of least prosperity and culture (and, of course, these poor wives were married to poor husbands) have the largest families."[1] Furthermore, a comparison between the conditions of 1851 and 1901 brought out the startling fact "that the intensity of this relationship has almost doubled in the last fifty years."[2] Heron's results have been amply confirmed by later investigations over a wider field. Thus Mr. Yule writes : "At the present date (1920) there is no doubt that marriage fertility is, on the whole, broadly speaking, graduated continuously from a very low figure for the upper and professional classes to a very much higher figure for unskilled labour."[3] In like manner Dr. Stevenson, as the result of an elaborate study, concludes : "The difference in fertility between the social classes is small from marriages contracted before 1861, and rapidly increases to a maximum for those of 1891–96. The slight subsequent approximation between the classes may be apparent rather than real. The difference in fertility between the social classes is, broadly speaking, a new phenomenon."[4] Up till the middle of last century, though the upper classes, whose full earning capacity develops later than that of manual workers, tended to marry later, and so to have somewhat fewer children, this tendency was nearly balanced by the lower mortality among them.

[1] *The Relation of Fertility in Man to Social Status*, pp. 15 and 19. M. Bertillon has shown that, in general, a high birth rate and a high death rate are correlated (*La Dépopulation de la France*, pp. 66 *et seq.*). This correlation is partly due to the fact that the death of children induces parents to get more, and partly to the fact that a high birth rate often means many children born in poor circumstances and so likely to die. Thus, Dr. Newsholme suggests that the observed correlation "is probably due in great part to the fact that large families are common among the poorest classes, and these classes are specially exposed to influences producing excessive infant mortality" (Second Report on Infant Mortality [Cd. 6909], p. 57). A similar conclusion as regards the North of England is reached in Elderton's *Report on the English Birth-rate*, Part I.

[2] *The Relation of Fertility in Man to Social Status*, pp. 15 and 19.

[3] *The Fall in the Birth-rate*, p. 31.

[4] *Journal of the Royal Statistical Society*, 1920, p. 431.

Their fertility after marriage was not much less, and the survival rate among them only a little lower. Now, in consequence of the relatively large fall in their fertility, the survival rate among them is very much lower.[1] The inferences suggested by these statistical facts are, indeed, less firmly based than they appear to be at first sight. The correlation between high prosperity and low birth rate may be partly due to the fact that a man with a small family is in a better position to accumulate a fortune, and that between rich districts and low birth rate may be partly due to the accumulation of domestic servants and other dependants—a particularly infertile class—in these districts.[2] Moreover, a part of the correlation between wealth and small families is probably due to the fact that physiologically infertile stocks, having their property divided among fewer persons on inheritance, tend, on the average, to be more than ordinarily rich.[3] But these considerations, important as they are, do not, there is reason to believe, completely account for the observed facts. What has been said of the deeper-seated reactions of prosperity appreciably strengthens our conclusion that an improvement in the fortunes of the poor is not likely, in an isolated community, to cancel itself by causing a large expansion of population.

§ 4. When account is taken of the fact that, in the modern world, no country is isolated from the rest, the issue

[1] Cf. *Journal of the Royal Statistical Society*, 1920, p. 417.

[2] Cf. Leroy-Beaulieu's argument: "Il se trouve dans les quartiers riches une plus forte proportion de ménages âgés, de gens retraités, de domestiques, classe particulièrement stérile, et personnes qui ne passent qu'une partie de l'année à la ville ; la natalité enregistrée doit donc y être plus faible, sans qu'on puisse rien en inférer. On qualifie le XVIe arrondissement qui compte 135,000 habitants comme un arrondissement riche et le VIIIe également qui, de son côte, compte 104,000 habitants. Or, il est manifeste que les gens vraiment riches ne représentent pas la dixième partie, peut-être pas même la vingtième partie, de la population de ces arrondissements dits riches ; les gens opulents ne se comptent pas, même à Paris, par centaines de mille ; le gros de la population de ces arrondissements est composé de domestiques, de concierges, de petits boutiquiers et d'ouvriers d'élite. Les conclusions que l'on tire de la natalité dans les quartiers dits riches de Paris sont donc sans valeur " (*La Question de la population*, p. 399).

[3] Cf. Darwin, " Eugenics in Relation to Economics and Statistics," *Journal of the Royal Statistical Society*, 1919, p. 7.

becomes less plain. Of course, if the real income of the manual
working class anywhere is increased because the average level
of capacity among that class has been raised, no inducement
is thereby offered to immigration from elsewhere. But, if
their real income is increased through some discovery, or
invention, or stroke of policy that improves the economic
position of one country considerably more than it improves
that of others, an inducement is offered. The same thing
happens if legislative or other measures bring about a transference of income from the richer to the poorer members of
some one community—provided, of course, that poor persons
who have immigrated are not excluded from the benefits of
these measures.[1] These considerations are very important;
for they show that many causes tending to increase the real
income per head of the wage-earners in a single country will
ultimately exercise a smaller influence in that direction than
they appear likely to do at first sight. It should not be
forgotten, however, that that very immigration, which lessens
their effect at the point of primary impact, involves indirectly
an improvement in the fortunes of labour elsewhere. Hence,
in any event, the beneficial influence of the changed conditions
is not destroyed, but is merely spread over a wider area. In
the country primarily affected *some* addition to economic
welfare is necessarily secured.

§ 5. The above discussion disproves the suggestion that
the beneficial effect on economic welfare of an increase in
the real income of wage-earners will be neutralised by an
expansion of population. It does not, however, disprove
the suggestion that the beneficial effect on economic welfare
of transferences of income from the rich to the poor will
be so neutralised. For, in order to that result, it is not necessary that the gain of economic welfare to the poor should
be destroyed—only that it should be made smaller than
the loss of economic welfare to the rich. It cannot be denied
that this *might* happen. But, in a country where the distri-

---

[1] The inducement to immigration offered by old-age pensions might be kept
very small by a rule requiring previous residence of, say, 20 years as a condition
of qualification; for a far-off benefit affects action but slightly, the more so if,
as in this case, the possibility of death makes it uncertain as well as distant.

bution of wealth is as uneven as it is in the United Kingdom, and where, therefore, there are many high incomes which could be largely cut down with very little injury to economic welfare, the chance that it *will* happen may reasonably be regarded as small.

CHAPTER X

THE NATIONAL DIVIDEND AND THE QUALITY OF THE PEOPLE

§ 1. THE general conclusions of Chapters VII.-VIII. might, until quite recently, have been stated as they are there stated, without evoking quarrel or dispute. But of late years a great advance has occurred in biological knowledge. In former times economists had, indeed, to take some account of the reactions of economic causes upon the quantity of the population, and upon its quality so far as that was determined by environment : but questions about the reaction of economic causes upon the quality of the population, as determined by fundamental biological attributes, were not raised. Now, the situation is different. Biometricians and Mendelians alike have turned their attention to sociology, and are insisting upon the fundamental importance for our science of a proper understanding of the laws of heredity. Economists, it is said, in discussing, as I have done, the direct effect of the state of the national dividend upon welfare, are wasting their energies. The direct effect is of no significance; it is only the indirect effect on the size of the families of good and bad stocks respectively that really matters. For every form of welfare depends ultimately on something much more fundamental than economic arrangements, namely, the general forces governing biological selection. I have intentionally stated these claims in a somewhat indefinite form, because I am anxious to investigate the problem thus raised in a constructive rather than in a critical spirit. I shall endeavour, in the following sections, to indicate, as precisely as possible, how far the recent advance in biological knowledge really affects our science.

To this end, I shall distinguish, first, certain results of that knowledge, which, though of great value, are not strictly relevant to economics; secondly, the general claim that the method of economic study indicated in the preceding chapters is rendered by the new knowledge trivial and unimportant; and, thirdly, certain points, in respect of which the new knowledge comes directly into contact with the problems I have undertaken to investigate, and makes it necessary to qualify the conclusions that have been reached.

§ 2. By far the most important contribution of modern biological study to sociology is the assurance, which it affords, of the definite heritable character of certain inborn defects. Whatever view be taken of the physiological mechanism of inheritance, the practical result is the same. We know that persons with congenital defects are likely, if they marry, to hand down a defective organisation to some of their children. We do not possess this definite knowledge with regard to general desirable qualities, particularly on the mental side. Bateson issued a wise caution when he wrote : " Whereas our experience of what constitutes the extremes of unfitness is fairly reliable and definite, we have little to guide us in estimating the qualities for which society has or may have a use, or the numerical proportions in which they may be required. . . . There is as yet nothing in the descent of the higher mental qualities to suggest that they follow any simple system of transmission. It is likely that both they and the more marked developments of physical powers result rather from the coincidence of numerous factors than from the possession of any one genetic element." [1]   Again, Mr. and Mrs. Whetham rightly observe that desirable qualities, such as ability, moral character, good health, physical strength and grace, beauty and charm, " are, from the point of view of heredity, essentially different from some of the bad qualities hitherto considered, in that they depend on the conjunction of a great many factors. Such a conjunction must be very hard to trace in the hereditary process, where possibly each character may descend independently, or different characters

[1] *Mendel's Principles of Heredity*, p. 305.

may be linked together, or be incompatible, in far more
complicated ways than we have traced in the qualities of
plants and animals. Our present knowledge is quite insufficient to enable us to predict how a complex combination
of factors, making up the personality of an able or charming
man or woman, will reappear in their offspring." [1] We
are, in fact, in this region, surrounded by so much ignorance that the utmost caution is essential. Doncaster well
observed : " In this direction empirical rules and common
sense must still be followed, until the time shall come when
science can speak with no uncertain voice." [2] More recently,
the late Sir Francis Galton lent the weight of his authority
to this opinion : " Enough is already known to those who
have studied the question to leave no doubt in their minds
about the general results, but not enough is quantitatively
known to justify legislative or other action, except in extreme
cases." [3] It is well not to forget that Beethoven's father was
an habitual drunkard and that his mother died of consumption.[4] About definite defects our ignorance is much
less profound. These *are* the extreme cases of which Galton
was thinking. Not a few medical men have long been
urging that authoritatively to prevent propagation among
those afflicted with imbecility, idiocy, syphilis, or tuberculosis
would mean cutting off at its source a long stream of
defective humanity. This matter is especially urgent among
the mentally defective, on account of the exceptionally high
rate at which, if left to themselves, they tend to produce
children. Thus, before the Royal Commission on the Feeble-
Minded, " Dr. Tredgold, an especially experienced witness,
pointed out that the average number of children in the
families which now use the public elementary schools is about
four ; whereas, in the degenerate families, whose children are
passed over to the special schools, there is an average of
7·3 children, not including those still-born." [5] Further-

---

[1] *The Family and the Nation*, p. 74.
[2] *Independent Review*, May 1906, p. 183.
[3] *Probability the Basis of Eugenics*, p. 29.
[4] Cf. Bateson, Presidential Address to the British Association, *Nature*,
Aug. 1914, p. 677.
[5] *The Family and the Nation*, p. 71.

more, feeble-minded women often begin child-bearing at an exceptionally early age; and it must be remembered that, even if the size of families is unaffected, early marriage is not a matter of indifference; for, when the normal age of marriage in any group is reduced, "generations succeed one another with greater rapidity," so that the proportion of the whole population embraced among the descendants of the original members of that group is increased.[1] The mentally defective are not, however, the only class among which propagation might with advantage be restrained. Some writers suggest that certain forms of criminality and certain qualities conducive to pauperism might be eradicated from the race in the same way. Professor Karl Pearson makes a suggestion, which, if correct, strengthens considerably the probability that this sort of policy would reach its goal. He thinks that imperfections of quite different kinds are correlated, and that "there is something akin to germinal degeneracy, which may show itself in different defects of the same organ or in defects of different organs."[2] Bateson, to the same practical, though not to the same theoretical, effect, speaks of the existence of "indications that, in the extreme cases, unfitness is comparatively definite in its genetic causation, and can, not unfrequently, be recognised as due to the presence of a simple genetic factor."[3] In sum, as the last-quoted writer states, there is little doubt that "some serious physical and mental defects, almost certainly also some morbid diatheses, and some of the forms of vice and criminality could be eradicated if society so determined."[4] This is a conclusion of extreme importance. It is one, too,

---

[1] Haycraft, *Darwinism and Race Progress*, p. 144.

[2] *The Scope and Importance of National Eugenics*, p. 38.

[3] *Mendel's Principles of Heredity*, p. 305.

[4] *Ibid.* p. 305. It is, however, important to remember that a bad *recessive* quality cannot be eliminated merely by preventing propagation among persons who manifest it; for it will also be borne in the germ-plasm of a number of apparently normal persons. Feeble-mindedness appears to be a recessive quality (cf. Gates, *Heredity and Eugenics*, p. 159). Calculation shows that, if 3 per cent of a population now is feeble-minded, it would require 250 generations (*i.e.* about 8000 years) to reduce the proportion to 1 in 100,000 by merely segregating or sterilising those who show the characteristics. To distinguish and to prevent propagation among those apparently normal persons who bear feeble-mindedness as a recessive quality would, however, be a task far beyond our present powers (cf. *ibid.* p. 173).

that seems *prima facie* susceptible, without great difficulty, of some measure of practical application.   Occasions frequently arise when tainted persons, whether on account of crime or of dementia, are compulsorily passed into governmental institutions.   When this happens, propagation might be prevented, after careful inquiry had been made, either by permanent segregation, or possibly, as is authorised by law in certain American States, by surgical means.[1]   The knowledge we possess seems clearly sufficient to warrant us in taking some cautious steps in this direction.   There can be no doubt that such a policy would redound both to the general and to the economic welfare of the community.   For this conclusion, and for the great step forward which it is hoped may follow from it, we are indebted to modern biology. The conclusion, however, is outside the sphere of economics, and does not in any way disturb the results that were attained in the preceding chapters.

§ 3. I pass, therefore, to something of whose relevance at all events there can be no doubt, the view, namely, that biological science proves all such inquiries as we are pursuing here to be trivial and misdirected. Put broadly, the charge is this. Economic changes, such as alterations in the size, composition, or distribution of the national dividend, affect environment only; and environment is of no importance, because improvements in it cannot react on the quality of the children born to those who enjoy the improvements.   This view was crystallised by Professor Punnett, when he declared that hygiene, education and so on are but " fleeting palliatives at best, which, in postponing, but augment the difficulties they profess to solve. . . . Permanent progress is a question of breeding rather than of pedagogics ; a matter of gametes, not of training." [2]   Mr. Lock [3] is even more emphatic in the same sense.   The opinions of these writers on the practical side are substantially in agreement with those of Professor Karl Pearson.

The scientific foundation on which all such views rest is,

---

[1] The standard work on this subject is *Eugenical Sterilisation in the United States*, by Dr. H. H. Laughlin, 1922.

[2] *Mendelism* (second edition), pp. 80-81.

[3] Cf. *Recent Progress in the Study of Variation, Heredity and Evolution*, by R. H. Lock.

of course, the thesis that acquired characters, which arise
out of the influence of environment, are not inherited.   It is
held, at least as regards the more complicated multicellular
organisms, that the germ-cells, which will ultimately form the
offspring of a living being, are distinct at the outset from
those which will form the body of that being.   Thus, Mr.
Wilson writes : " It is a reversal. of the true point of view to
regard inheritance as taking place from the body of the
parent to that of the child.   The child inherits from the
parent *germ-cell*, not from the parent body, and the germ-cell
owes its characteristics, not to the body which bears it, but
to its descent from a pre-existing germ-cell of the same
kind. Thus, the body is, as it were, an offshoot from the germ-
cell. As far as inheritance is concerned, the body is merely
the carrier of the germ-cells, which are held in trust for
coming generations." [1]   Doncaster takes up substantially the
same position : " In the earlier theories of heredity it was
assumed that the germ-cells were produced by the body, and
that they must, therefore, be supposed either to contain
samples of all parts of it, or at least some kind of units
derived from those parts and able to cause their development
in the next generation.   Gradually, as the study of heredity
and of the actual origin of the germ-cells has progressed,
biologists have given up this view in favour of a belief in
germinal continuity, that is, that the germ - substance is
derived from previous germ-substance, the body being a kind
of offshoot from it.   The child is, thus, like its parent, not
because it is produced from the parent, but because both
child and parent are produced from the same stock of germ-
plasm." [2]   If this view be sound, it follows that those definite
characteristics of an organism, whose appearance is determined
by the presence of definite structures or substances in the
germ-cells, cannot be directly affected by any quality " acquired "
by an ancestor.   It is only characteristics of an indefinite
quantitative kind, such as may be supposed to arise from the
intercommunication of the germ-cells with the other cells of

[1] Wilson, *The Cell in Development and Inheritance*, p. 13 ; quoted by
R. H. Lock, *Variation, Heredity and Evolution*, p. 68.
[2] *Heredity*, p. 124.

the body and the reception of fluid or easily soluble substances from them, that can be affected in this way. The characteristics thus reserved are not, of course, wholly without significance. The question whether the submission of germ-cells to a poisonous environment reacts permanently upon the descendants of those cells does not seem to be a closed one. Professor J. A. Thomson writes: " There is a great difference between a poisoning of the germ-cells along with the body and the influencing them in a manner so specific that they can, when they develop, reproduce the particular parental modification." [1] The germ-cells do not lead " a charmed life, uninfluenced by any of the accidents or incidents of the daily life of the body which is their bearer." [2] On the contrary, there is some evidence that, not only direct poisons like alcohol, but even injuries to the parent, may, by reacting on the nutrition of the germ-cells, cause general weakness and resultant bad properties in the offspring, though how far *the offspring of their offspring* would be affected is doubtful. But the general opinion among biologists appears to be that the effect of the acquired characteristics of one generation upon the quality of the succeeding generation is, at all events, very small compared with the effect of the inborn characteristics of the one generation.[3] " Education is to man what manure is to the pea. The educated are in themselves the better for it, but their experience will alter not one jot the irrevocable nature of their offspring." [4] In like manner " neglect, poverty, and parental ignorance, serious as their results are, (do not) possess any marked hereditary effect." [5]

This biological thesis, which, since it is dominant among experts, an outsider has no title to dispute, is, as I have said, the scientific foundation of the view that economic circumstances, because they are environmental, are not, from a long-period standpoint, of any real importance. The

[1] J. A. Thomson, *Heredity*, p. 198.
[2] *Ibid.* p. 204.
[3] Lock, *Variation and Heredity*, pp. 69-71.
[4] Punnett, *Mendelism*, p. 81.
[5] Eichholz, " Evidence to the Committee on Physical Deterioration," Report, p. 14.   Dr. Eichholz's view appears to be formed *a posteriori*, and not to be an inference from general biological principles.

biological premise I accept. To the sociological conclusion,
however, I demur. Mr. Sidney Webb has uttered a genial
protest against a too exclusive attention to the biological
aspect of social problems. " After all," he writes, " it would
not be of much use to have all babies born from good stocks,
if, generation after generation, they were made to grow up
into bad men and women. A world of well‑born but
physically and morally perverted adults is not attractive." [1]
My criticism, however, goes deeper than this. Professor
Punnett and his fellow‑workers would accept Mr. Webb's
plea. They freely grant that environing circumstances can
affect the persons immediately subjected to them, but they,
nevertheless, hold that these circumstances are unimportant,
because, not being able to influence the inborn quality of
succeeding generations, they cannot produce any lasting
result. My reply is that the environment of one generation *can* produce a lasting result, because it can affect the
environment of future generations. Environments, in short,
as well as people, have children. Though education and so
forth cannot influence new births in the physical world, they
can influence them in the world of ideas; [2] and ideas, once

[1] *Eugenics Review*, November 1910, p. 236.

[2] An interesting comparison can be made between the process of evolution
in these two worlds. In both we find three elements, the *occurrence of, propagation of,* and *conflict between*, mutations.

In both worlds the *kind* of mutations that occur appear to be fortuitous,
and cannot be controlled, though in both it is sometimes suggested that the
tendency to mutate is encouraged by large changes in, and particular kinds of,
environment.   For example, Rae suggested, as conditions favourable to the
emergence of inventions, general upheavals, such as wars or migrations, and the
adoption in any art of a new material—such as steel in building—either for
lack of the old material or through the possession of a specially effective
new one, and he maintained that the stable agricultural districts rarely
yield inventions (*The Sociological Theory of Capital*, pp. 172-3). In both
worlds again, with every increase of *variability*, the chance that a "good"
mutation will occur is increased. Hence, *ceteris paribus*, environments that
make for variability are a means to good. Thus, of local governments
Marshall writes: "All power of variation that is consistent with order and
economy of administration is an almost unmixed good.   The prospects of progress are increased by the multiplicity of parallel experiments and the inter-
communion of ideas between many people, each of whom has some opportunity
of testing practically the value of his own suggestions" (*Memorandum to the
Royal Commission on Local Taxation*, p. 123 ; cf. also Booth, *Industry*, v.
p. 86 ; and Hobhouse, *Democracy and Reaction*, pp. 121-3).

The *propagation* of mutations, on the other hand, does not proceed in the
same way among ideas as among organisms. Among the latter the fertility of

produced or once accepted by a particular generation, whether
or not they can be materialised into mechanical inventions,
may not only remodel from its very base the environment
which succeeding generations enjoy,[1] but may also pave the
way for further advance. For, whereas each new man must
begin where his last ancestor began, each new invention begins
where its last ancestor left off.[2] In this way a permanent
or, rather, a progressive change of environment is brought
about, and, since environment is admittedly able to exert
an important influence on persons actually subjected to it,
such a change may produce enduring consequences. Among
animals, indeed, and among the primitive races of men this
point is not important. For there what the members of
one generation have wrought in the field of ideas is not
easily communicated to their successors. "The human race,
when widely scattered and incapable of intercommunication,
makes the same discovery a hundred times. Its efforts
and its triumphs are annihilated with the death of the
individual, or of the last member of the family in which
the invention has been passed on by oral tradition."[3] But
among civilised men the arts of writing and of printing
have rendered thought viable through time, and have thus
extended to each generation power to mould and remodel
the ideal environment of its successors. Tarde grasped

---

the mutated members that survive is not, but among the former it is, affected by
their adaptation or otherwise to successful struggle. Animals that are failures
and those that are successes are equally likely, if they survive, to have offspring.
But, among ideas, those that fail are likely to be barren and those that succeed
to be prolific.

Still more marked is the difference between the character of the *struggle*
that takes place between mutated members in the two groups. In the physical
world the process is negative—the failures are cut off. In the world of ideas it
is positive—successful ideas are adopted and imitated. One consequence of
this is that, in general, a successful experiment diffuses itself much more rapidly
than a successful "sport."

[1] This consideration affords a powerful argument for the expenditure of State
funds upon training the girls of the present generation to become competent
mothers and housewives, because, if only one generation were so taught, a family
tradition would very probably become established, and the knowledge given in
the first instance at public cost would propagate itself through successive
generations without any further cost to anybody. (Cf. Report of the Inter-
departmental Committee on Physical Deterioration, p. 42.)

[2] Cf. Fiske, *Invention*, p. 253.

[3] Majewski, *La Science de la civilisation*, p. 228.

this point when he wrote: "To facilitate further production is the principal virtue of capital, as that term ought to be understood. But in what is it inherent? In commodities or in particular kinds of commodities? Nay, rather in those fortunate experiments of which the memory has been preserved. Capital is tradition or social memory. It is to societies what heredity or vital memory,—enigmatical term, —is to living beings. As for the products that have been saved and stored up to facilitate the construction of new copies of the models conceived by inventors, they are to these models, which are the true social germs, what the cotyledon, a mere store of food, is to the embryo."[1] Bacon had already exclaimed: "The introduction of new inventions seemeth to be the very chief of all human actions. The benefits of new inventions may extend to all mankind universally, but the good of political activities can respect but some particular country of men: these latter do not perdure above a few ages, the former for ever." Marshall writes in the same spirit: "The world's material wealth would quickly be replaced if it were destroyed, but the ideas by which it was made were retained. If, however, the ideas were lost, but not the material wealth, then that would dwindle and the world would go back to poverty. And most of our knowledge of mere facts could quickly be recovered if it were lost, but the constructive ideas of thought remained; while, if the ideas perished, the world would enter again on the Dark Ages."[2] Nor is even this a full account of the matter. As Marshall observes in another place: "Any change that awards to the workers of one generation better earnings, together with better opportunities of developing their best qualities, will increase the material and moral advantages which they have the power to offer to their children; while, by increasing their own intelligence, wisdom and forethought, such a change will also, to some extent, increase their willingness to sacrifice their own pleasures for the well-being of their children."[3] Those children, in turn, being themselves rendered

[1] *La Logique sociale*, p. 352.
[2] *Principles of Economics*, p. 780.
[3] *Ibid.* p. 563.

stronger and more intelligent, will be able, when they grow up, to offer a better environment—and under the term environment I include the physical circumstances of the mother before, and immediately after, child-birth [1]—to their children, and so on. The effect goes on piling itself up. Changes in ancestral environment start forces, which modify continuously and cumulatively the conditions of succeeding environments, and, through them, the human qualities for which current environment is in part responsible. Hence, Professor Punnett's assertion is unduly sweeping.[2] Progress, not merely permanent but growing, *can* be brought about by causes with which breeding and gametes have nothing to do. Nor, indeed, must we rest content with the word *can*. There is strong reason for holding that the enormous development in the *mental* function of mankind, which has taken place during historic times, has not been associated with any significant germinal change. With growing density of population the machinery of thought has been developed through contact and co-operation among persons of not substantially greater germinal endowment than was possessed by earlier generations. " This is the paradox of the population problem. Change among species in a state of nature is based upon germinal change alone ; change among our pre-human ancestors was equally a matter of change in the quality of population ; but the explanation of the most outstanding fact in recent history broadly viewed (*i.e.* the great acceleration of progress in knowledge and power) is to be sought in a change in quantity, rather than in quality, of population." [3]   We conclude, then, that there is no fundamental difference of the kind sometimes supposed between causes operating on acquired, and causes operating on inborn, qualities. The two are of co-ordinate importance ; and the students of neither have a right to belittle the work of those who study the other.

[1] The importance of this point is illustrated by the observation of the London Education Committee of 1905, that the children born in a year when infant mortality is low have more than average physique, and *vice versa*. (Cf. Wells, *New Worlds for Old*, p. 216.)

[2] In later editions of his book Professor Punnett's argument is stated in a less sweeping form and does not conflict with what has been said above. (Cf. *Mendelism*, third edition, p. 167.)

[3] Carr-Saunders, *The Population Problem*, pp. 480-81.

§ 4. I proceed now to the third of the topics indicated for discussion in the first section of this chapter, namely, the extent to which new biological knowledge makes it necessary for us to qualify the conclusions laid down in Chapters VII. and VIII.   These conclusions, it will be remembered, were to the effect that, other things being equal, (1) an increase in the size of national dividend—provided that it is not brought about by the exercise of undue pressure upon workpeople,—and (2) a change in the distribution of the dividend favourable to the poor, would be likely to increase economic welfare and, through economic welfare, general welfare.   Against these conclusions the biologically trained critic urges an important caution.   May it not be, he asks, that advance along the first of these lines, by checking the free play of natural selection and enabling feeble children to survive, will set up a cumulative influence making for national weakness; and that advance along the second line, by differentiating in favour of inferior stocks, will have a similar evil effect?   Is there not ground for fear that the brightness of the stream of progress is deceptive, that it bears along, as it flows, seeds of disaster, and that the changes we have pronounced to be productive of welfare are, at the best, of doubtful import?   The two parts of this thesis must now be examined in turn.

§ 5. The danger to national strength that results from a growth of wealth in general has been emphasised by many writers.   In a softened environment children of feeble constitution, who, in harder circumstances, would have died, are enabled to survive and themselves to have children.[1]   It has even been suggested that in this fact may lie the secret of the eventual decay of nations and of aristocracies which have attained great wealth.   There are, indeed, mitigating circumstances, which may be urged in extenuation of this view.   First, according to the most recent biological opinion, the survival of weakly children, if their weakness is, as it were, accidental, and not due to inherited defect, is not ultimately harmful to the stock, because the children of the weakly children are quite likely to be strong.   Secondly,

[1] Cf. Haycraft, *Darwinism and Race Progress*, p. 58.

weakness in infancy is not necessarily a good index of
essential inborn weakness; and Mr. Yule, after reviewing
the available statistics by mathematical methods, is led to
suggest that, perhaps, " the mortality of infancy is selective
only as regards the special dangers of infancy, and its
influence scarcely extends beyond the second year of life,
whilst the weakening effect of a sickly infancy is of greater
duration." [1] These mitigating circumstances somewhat limit,
though they may well fail to overthrow, the thesis that
growth in wealth, unaccompanied by any safeguard, is likely
to deteriorate the inherent quality of the race. There is
also available a further mitigating circumstance, which is
less fundamental, though not less important. For, even if
the inherent quality of the race is somewhat injured, it does
not follow that the finished products, which contain, of
course, at once inherent and environmental qualities, are so
injured. If increased wealth removes influences that make
for the elimination of the unfit, it also removes influences
that make for the weakening of the fit. The total effect
of this twofold action may well be beneficial rather than
injurious. That this is in fact so is suggested by an
important report published by the Local Government Board
on the relation of infantile mortality to general mortality.
In that report Dr. Newsholme directly combats the view
that improvements making for a reduction of infant mortality,
by enabling more weaklings to survive, must be inimical
to the average health of the population. He finds, on the
contrary, " that the counties having high infant mortalities
continue, in general, to suffer somewhat excessively throughout
the first twenty years of human life, and that counties
having low infantile mortalities continue to have relatively
low death-rates in the first twenty years of life, though the
superiority is not so great at the later as at the earlier
ages. . . . It is fair to assume, in accordance with general
experience, that the amount of sickness varies approximately
with the number of deaths; and there can be no reasonable
doubt that, in the counties having a high infant death-rate,
there is—apart from migration—more sickness and a lower

[1] [Cd. 5263], p. 82 (1909–10).

standard of health in youth and in adult life than in counties in which the toll of infant mortality is less."[1] Dr. Newsholme's argument is, indeed, open to the reply that ascertained differences between the several counties in infantile death-rate and later death-rate may *both* be due to differences in the quality of the inhabitants of the several counties. The argument, therefore, fails to prove that the direct beneficial effect of better environments due to greater wealth outweighs the indirect injurious effect of the impediment they place in the way of natural selection. It may be that the injurious effect is really the stronger, but that it is masked in the statistics because it is exercised upon persons who are *ab initio* of better physique—as is, indeed, suggested by their ability to earn more and so to live in better conditions—than the average. This criticism lessens the force of Dr. Newsholme's statistical argument.[2] Still the directly observed fact that good environment removes influences tending to weaken the fit remains. In company with the considerations set out earlier in this section, that fact militates against the view that a growing dividend and the improvements that naturally accompany it carry seeds of future weakness, and so ultimately make against, rather than in favour of, economic welfare. In any event, the danger that they may have this effect can be readily and completely counteracted, if the policy of segregating the unfit, advocated in the second section, is adopted. As Professor Thomson points out, no biological evil can result from the preservation of weaklings, provided that they are not allowed to have children.[3] There is, therefore, no need to surrender our conclusion that causes, which make for an expansion of the dividend, in general make for economic and, through economic, for aggregate, welfare.

§ 6. The danger to national strength and efficiency through an improvement in the distribution of the dividend

---

[1] Report for 1909–10 [Cd. 5263], p. 17.

[2] Dr. Newsholme's argument was severely criticised—partly under a misapprehension of its purpose—by Professor Karl Pearson in his Cavendish lecture, 1912, p. 13. Dr. Newsholme replied in his second (1913) report [Cd. 6909], pp. 46-52.

[3] *Heredity*, p. 528.

might seem *a priori* to be very important. For improved distribution is likely to modify the proportion in which future generations are born from the richer and poorer classes respectively. If, therefore, the poorer classes comprise less efficient stocks than the richer classes—if, in fact, economic status is anything of an index of inborn quality—improved distribution must modify the general level of inborn quality, and so, in the long run, must react with cumulative force upon the magnitude of the national dividend. Now I do not agree with those who hold that poverty and inborn inefficiency are obviously and certainly correlated. Extreme poverty is, no doubt, often the result of feckless character, physical infirmity, and other "bad" qualities of finished persons. But these themselves are generally correlated with bad environment; and it is ridiculous to treat as unworthy of argument the suggestion that the "bad" qualities are mainly the result, not of bad original properties, but of bad original environment.[1] Nevertheless, though it is not self-evident, it is, I think, probable, that a considerable measure of correlation exists between poverty and "bad" original properties. For among the relatively rich there are always a number of persons who have risen from a poor environment, which their fellows, who have remained poor, shared with them in childhood; and this sort of movement is probably becoming more marked, as opportunities of education and so forth are being brought more within the reach of the poorer classes. In like manner, of course, among the poor are some persons who have fallen from a

---

[1] This class of difficulty is experienced in many statistical investigations of social problems. For example, an interesting inquiry into the inheritance of ability, as indicated by the Oxford class lists and the school lists of Harrow and Charterhouse, was published some years ago by Mr. Schuster. But the value of his results is in some measure—it is not possible to say in *what* measure—impaired by the fact that the possession of able parents is apt to be correlated with the reception of a good formal, and, still more, informal, education. Mr. Schuster argues (p. 23) that the error due to this circumstance is not likely to be large. (Cf. also Karl Pearson, *Biometrika*, vol. iii. p. 156.) M. Nicefero, on the other hand, in his study of *Les Classes pauvres*, lays stress on the effects of environment in promoting the physical and psychical inferiority of these classes ; but he does not seem to justify by evidence his conclusion that "tous les facteurs—en dernière analyse—plongent leur racine bien plus dans le milieu économique de la société moderne que dans la structure même de l'individu" (p. 332).

superior environment. Among the original properties of
these relatively rich there are presumably qualities making
for efficiency, which account for their rise ; while, among the
original properties of *these* relatively poor, there are, presumably, qualities of an opposite kind.[1] Hence, it is probably
true that causes affecting the comparative rate of child-
bearing among the relatively rich and the relatively poor
respectively affect the comparative rate among those with
" better " and " worse " original properties (from the point
of view of efficiency) in the same direction. If it were true
that increased prosperity in a poor class involved a higher
rate of reproduction, it would follow that an improved distribution of the dividend would increase the number and,
therewith, the proportion, of children born from parents
of stock other than the best. Since, however, as is notorious,
propagation among the lowest class of all is practically
untrammelled by economic considerations, an increase in
fortune to the poor as a whole could only increase the number
of children born to sections of the poorer classes other
than the worst. It would not, therefore, necessarily follow
that the average quality of the population as a whole would
be lowered. It is not, however, necessary to stop at this
point. Professor Brentano's investigations, which were
previously noticed, have suggested that increased prosperity
in a class tends, on the whole, to diminish rather than to
increase the reproduction rate of that class, and reason
has been shown for believing that this tendency is not
fully offset by accompanying improvements in the mortality
rate.[2] Hence, it would seem, an improvement in the distribution of the dividend may be expected actually to diminish
the proportion of children born from inferior stocks. In

[1] Pareto ignores these considerations when he argues (*Systèmes socialistes*,
p. 13 *et seq.*) that an increase in the relative number of children born to
the rich must make for national deterioration because, since the children
of the rich are subjected to a less severe struggle than those of the poor,
feeble children, who would die if born to the poor, will, if born to the rich,
survive and, in turn, have feeble children. In view of the facts noted in
the text, this circumstance should be regarded merely as a counteracting force,
mitigating, but not destroying, the beneficial consequences likely to result from
a relative increase in the fertility of the rich.

[2] Cf. *ante*, Chapter IX. § 3,

short, this biological consideration, so far from reversing the conclusion of Chapter VIII., that improved distribution makes for economic and general welfare, lends, in present conditions, some support to that conclusion. The results of that chapter, along with those of Chapter VII., therefore, remain intact.

CHAPTER XI

THE METHOD OF DISCUSSION TO BE FOLLOWED

IN the preceding chapters it has been shown that economic
welfare is liable to be affected in an important degree (1)
through the size of the national dividend and (2) through the
way in which it is distributed among the members of the
community.   If causes affecting the size of the dividend had
no influence on its distribution, and causes affecting its distribution no influence on its size, the remaining stages of our
inquiry would be simple.   Each of these groups of causes
would be examined in turn separately.   As a fact, however,
the same causes will often act along both of these channels,
with the result that an entirely satisfactory method of
exposition is difficult to devise.   After weighing up the
comparative advantages of different courses I propose to
proceed as follows.   In Parts II. and III., I shall study the
way in which economic welfare is affected by certain causes
that operate upon it through the size of the dividend.   I do
not propose to examine all the causes that might properly be
brought under review in this connection.   Inventions and
discoveries, the opening up of extensive sources of foreign
demand, improvements in the technique of marketing, and
the growth of accumulated capital will scarcely be discussed
at all.   Part II. will be concerned with the way in which
the productive resources of the community, looked at generally,
are distributed among different uses, and Part III. with the
organisation of labour in various aspects.   These discussions
having been completed, Part IV. is devoted to an inquiry as to

how far in actual fact causes that affect economic welfare in one sense through the size of the dividend are liable to affect it in a different sense through the distribution of the dividend, and to a study of the problems that arise when this sort of disharmony is manifested.

PART II

THE SIZE OF THE NATIONAL DIVIDEND AND THE DISTRIBUTION OF RESOURCES AMONG DIFFERENT USES

CHAPTER I

INTRODUCTORY

§ 1. In this Part we are concerned with causes that increase or diminish the size of the national dividend by acting on the way in which the productive resources of no matter what kind belonging to the country are distributed among different uses or occupations. Throughout this discussion, except when the contrary is expressly stated, the fact that some resources are generally unemployed against the will of the owners is ignored. This does not affect the substance of the argument, while it simplifies its exposition. The purpose of this introductory chapter is to indicate the general scope of the problem before us.

§ 2. Certain optimistic followers of the classical economists have suggested that the "free play of self-interest," if only Government refrains from interference, will automatically cause the land, capital and labour of any country to be so distributed as to yield a larger output and, therefore, more economic welfare than could be attained by any arrangement other than that which comes about "naturally." Even Adam Smith himself, while making an exception in favour of State action in "erecting and maintaining certain public works and certain public institutions, which it can never be for the interests of any individual, or small number of individuals, to erect and maintain," lays it down that "any system which endeavours, either by extraordinary encouragements to draw towards a particular species of industry a greater share of the capital of the society than what would naturally go to it; or by extraordinary restraints to force from a particular species of industry some share of the capital

which would otherwise be employed in it . . . retards, instead
of accelerating, the progress of the society towards real wealth
and greatness, and diminishes, instead of increasing, the real
value of the annual produce of its land and labour."[1]   It
would, of course, be unreasonable to interpret this passage in
any abstract or universal sense.   Adam Smith had in mind
the actual world as he knew it, with an organised system of
civilised government and contract law.   He would not have
quarrelled with the dictum of a later economist that "the
activities of man are expended along two routes, the first
being directed to the production or transformation of economic
goods, the second to the appropriation of goods produced by
others."[2]   Activities devoted to appropriation obviously do
not promote production, and production would be promoted if
they were diverted into the channels of industry.   We must,
therefore, understand him to assume the existence of laws
designed, and, in the main, competent, to prevent acts of
mere appropriation, such as those perpetrated by highwaymen
and card-sharpers.   The free play of self-interest is conceived
by him to be "confined to certain directions by our general
social institutions, especially the Family, Property, and the
territorial State."[3]   More generally, when one man obtains
goods from another man, he is conceived to obtain them by
the process, not of seizure, but of exchange in an open market,
where the bargainers on both sides are reasonably competent
and reasonably cognisant of the conditions.   There is ground,
however, for believing that even Adam Smith had not realised
fully the extent to which the System of Natural Liberty needs
to be qualified and guarded by special laws, before it will
promote the most productive employment of a country's
resources.   It has been said by a recent writer that "the
working of self-interest is generally beneficent, not because of
some natural coincidence between the self-interest of each and
the good of all, but because human institutions are arranged
so as to compel self-interest to work in directions in which it

---

[1] *Wealth of Nations*, Book iv. chapter ix., third paragraph from the end.
[2] Pareto, *Manuale di economia politica*, pp. 444-5.
[3] Cannan, *The History of Local Rates*, p. 176.   Cf. also Carver, *Essays in
Social Justice*, p. 109.

will be beneficent."[1] Thus, though it is, apart from any institutions, to the interest of each individual that all individuals, including himself, should refrain from thieving rather than that all should thieve, it would not be to the interest of any one that he personally should refrain from thieving, unless *either*, by so doing, he could induce others to follow his example—which he could not do—*or* there was a law or other sanction imposing penalties for theft. This kind of coercive legal device for directing self-interest into social channels is well illustrated by the limitations which some civilised States impose upon the absolute powers of owners of property—such limitations as the Bavarian rule forbidding owners of forests to exclude pedestrians from their land, the French and American rules restraining a man from setting fire to his own house, and the practice prevalent in all countries of expropriating private owners where their expropriation is urgently required in the general interest.[2] It is further illustrated by the attitude of the law of modern nations towards types of contract—gambling debts, contracts in restraint of trade, agreements for contracting-out of certain legal obligations—which are deemed contrary to public policy and are, therefore, treated by the courts as void.[3] This adjustment of institutions to the end of directing self-interest into beneficial channels has been carried out in considerable detail. But even in the most advanced States there are failures and imperfections. We are not here concerned with those deficiencies of organisation which sometimes cause higher non-economic interests to be sacrificed to less important economic interests. Over and above these, there are many obstacles that prevent a community's resources from being distributed among different uses or occupations in the most effective way. The study of these constitutes our present problem. That study involves some difficult analysis. But its purpose is essentially practical. It seeks to bring into clearer light some of the ways in which it now is, or eventually may become, feasible for governments to control the play of economic

---

[1] Cannan, *Economic Review*, July 1913, p. 333.
[2] Cf. Ely, *Property and Contract*, pp. 61 and 150.
[3] *Ibid.* pp. 616 and 731.

K

forces in such wise as to promote the economic welfare, and, through that, the total welfare, of their citizens as a whole.[1]

[1] Cf. Marshall's observation: "Much remains to be done, by a careful collection of the statistics of demand and supply and a scientific interpretation of their results, in order to discover what are the limits of the work that society can with advantage do towards turning the economic actions of individuals into those channels in which they will add the most to the sum total of happiness" (*Principles of Economics*, p. 475).

CHAPTER II

THE DEFINITION OF MARGINAL SOCIAL AND PRIVATE NET PRODUCTS

§ 1. CONCERNED as we are with the national dividend as a continuing flow, we naturally understand by the resources directed to making it, not a stock of resources, but a similarly continuing flow; and we conceive the distribution of these resources among different uses or places on the analogy, not of a stagnant pond divided into a number of sections, but rather of a river divided into a number of streams. This conception involves, no doubt, many difficulties in connection both with the varying durability of the equipment employed in different industries and with the dynamic, or changing, tendencies of industry as a whole. In spite of these difficulties, however, the general idea is exact enough for the present purpose. That purpose is to provide a suitable definition for the concepts which are fundamental throughout this Part, namely, *the value of marginal private* and *the value of the marginal social net product.* The essential point is that these too must be conceived as flows—as the result *per year* of the employment *per year* of the marginal increment of some given quantity of resources. On this basis we may proceed to work out our definition.

§ 2. For complete accuracy it is necessary to distinguish between two senses in which the term marginal increment of resources may be employed. It may be conceived either as being added, so to speak, from outside, thus constituting a net addition to the sum total of resources in existence, or as being transferred to the particular use or place we are studying from some other use or place. If the effect on production in a particular use or place of adding an increment of resources is independent of the quantity of resources employed elsewhere, the net products of these two sorts of marginal increment will be the same. It often happens, however, that this condition of independence is not satisfied. Thus, as will be shown more fully in a later chapter, the nth unit of resources employed in a particular firm will yield different quantities of produce according as the quantity of resources employed in other firms in the same industry is larger or smaller. The net products derived from marginal increments of resources, interpreted in the above two ways, might perhaps be distinguished as additive marginal net products and substitutive marginal net products. In general, however, the net products derived from the two sorts of marginal increment of resources in any use or place are not likely to differ sensibly from one another, and for most purposes they may be treated as equivalent.

§ 3. Waiving, then, this point, we have next to define more precisely what is meant when we speak of the marginal net product of the resources employed in any use or place as *the result of* the marginal increment of resources employed there. This is tantamount to saying that the marginal net product of a given quantity of resources is equal to the difference that would be made to the total product of these resources by adding to or subtracting from them a small increment. This, however, is not by itself sufficient. For the addition or subtraction of a small increment can be accomplished in several different ways with correspondingly different results. We are here concerned with a particular way. For us the marginal net product of any flow of resources employed in any use or place is equal to the difference between the aggregate flow of product for which that flow of resources, *when appropriately organised*, is responsible and the aggregate flow of product for which a flow of resources differing from that flow by a small (marginal) increment, *when appropriately organised*, would be responsible. In this statement the phrase *when appropriately organised* is essential. If we were thinking of marginal net product in the sense of the difference between the products of two adjacent *quantities* of resources, we should normally imagine the resources to be organised suitably to one of these quantities and, therefore, not to the other. Since, however, our interest is in the difference between the products of two adjacent *flows* of resources, it is natural to conceive each of the two flows as organised in the manner most appropriate to itself. This is the conception we need. It is excellently illustrated by Professor J. B. Clark. The marginal increment of capital invested in a railway corporation is in reality, he writes, " a difference between two kinds of plant for carrying goods and passengers. One of these is the railroad as it stands, with all its equipment brought up to the highest pitch of perfection that is possible with the present resources. The other is the road built and equipped as it would have been if the resources had been by one degree less. A difference in all-round quality between an actual and a possible railroad is in reality the final increment of capital now used by the actual corporation. The product of that last unit of capital is the difference between what the road actually produces and what it would have produced if it had been made one degree poorer." [1]

§ 4. One further point must be made clear. The marginal net product of a factor of production is the difference that would be made to the aggregate product by withdrawing *any* (small) unit of the factor. The marginal unit is thus not any particular unit. Still less is it the worst unit in existence —the most incompetent workman who is employed at all— as some writers have supposed ! It is *any* (small) unit out of the aggregate of units, *all exactly alike*, into which we imagine this aggregate to be divided. Though, however, the marginal unit is thus *any* unit, it is not any unit *however placed*. On the contrary, it is any unit *conceived as placed at the margin*. The significance of this is best understood with the help of an illustration. To withdraw a man attending a new machine or working in an easy place in any industry and to do nothing else would, of course, affect aggregate output more seriously than to withdraw a man attending an obsolete machine or

---

[1] *The Distribution of Wealth*, p. 250. I have substituted "produced" for "earned" in the sentence quoted above.

working in a difficult place would do. The marginal net product of work in that industry is then the difference that would be made to aggregate output by withdrawing for a day any (similar) man and redistributing, if necessary, the men that are left in such wise that the machine consequently left unattended or place of work left unfilled is the least productive machine or place of work of which use has hitherto been made.

§ 5. So much being understood, we have next to distinguish precisely between the two varieties of marginal net product which I have named respectively *social* and *private*. The marginal social net product is the total net product of physical things or objective services due to the marginal increment of resources in any given use or place, no matter to whom any part of this product may accrue. It might happen, for example, as will be explained more fully in a later chapter, that costs are thrown upon people not directly concerned, through, say, uncompensated damage done to surrounding woods by sparks from railway engines. All such effects must be included—some of them will be positive, others negative elements—in reckoning up the social net product of the marginal increment of any volume of resources turned into any use or place. Again an increase in the quantity of resources employed by one firm in an industry may give rise to external economies in the industry as a whole and so lessen the real costs involved in the production by other firms of a given output. Everything of this kind must be counted in. For some purposes it is desirable to count in also indirect effects induced in people's tastes and in their capacity to derive satisfaction from their purchases and possessions. Our principal objective, however, is the national dividend and changes in it as defined in Part I. Chapters III. and V. Therefore psychical consequences are excluded, and the marginal social net product of any given volume of resources is taken, except when special notice to the contrary is given, to consist of physical elements and objective services only. The marginal private net product is that part of the total net product of physical things or objective services due to the marginal increment of resources in any given use or place which accrues in the first instance—

i.e. prior to sale—to the person responsible for investing resources there.   In some conditions this is equal to, in some it is greater than, in others it is less than the marginal social net product.

§ 6. The *value* of the marginal social net product of any quantity of resources employed in any use or place is simply the sum of money which the marginal social net product is worth in the market.   In like manner the value of the marginal private net product is the sum of money which the marginal private net product is worth in the market.   Thus, when the marginal social net product and the marginal private net product are identical and the person responsible for the investment sells what accrues to him, the value of both sorts of marginal net product in respect of a given volume of resources is equal to the increment of product multiplied by the price per unit at which the product is sold when that volume of resources is being employed in producing it.[1]   For example, the two sorts of marginal net product per year of a million units of resources invested in weaving being assumed to be identical, the value of both is equal to the number of bales of cloth by which the output of a million *plus* a small increment, say a million and one, exceeds the output of a million units, multiplied by the money value of a bale of cloth when this output is being produced.[2]   This, it should be observed in passing, is different from, and must by no means be confused with, the excess—if there is an excess—of the money value of the whole product when a million and one units of resources are being employed over the money value of the whole product when a million units are being employed.

[1] This definition tacitly assumes that the realised price is equal to the (marginal) demand price.   If government limitation of price causes it to be temporarily less than this, the value of the marginal net product will need to be interpreted as the marginal (physical) net product multiplied by the marginal demand price, and the marginal demand price in these conditions will not be equal to the actual selling price.

[2] Cf. Marshall, *Principles of Economics*, p. 847.   It will be noticed by the careful reader that, even when the *additive* marginal net product and the *substitutive* marginal net product are equal, the *value* of the marginal net product will be different according as marginal net product is interpreted as additive and as substitutive marginal net product.   The difference will, however, in general, be of the second order of smalls.

CHAPTER III

§ 1. LET us suppose that a given quantity of productive resources is being employed, that there are no costs of movement between different occupations and places, and that conditions are such that only one arrangement of resources will make the values of marginal social net products everywhere equal.[1] On these suppositions it is easy to show that this arrangement of resources will make the national dividend larger than it would be under any other arrangement. This follows from the definition of changes in the size of the national dividend given in Part I. Chapter V. The value of the marginal social net product of resources in any use is the money measure of the satisfaction which the marginal increment of resources in that use is yielding. Whenever, therefore, the value of the marginal social net product of resources is less in any one use than it is in any other, the money measure of satisfaction in the aggregate can be increased by transferring resources from the use where the value of the marginal social net product is smaller to the use where it is larger. It follows that, since, *ex hypothesi*, there is only one arrangement of resources that will make the values of the marginal social net products equal in all uses, this arrangement is necessarily the one that makes the national dividend, as here defined, a maximum.[2]

---

[1] The considerations developed in Part III. Chapter IX. § 2 are here provisionally ignored.

[2] A minor point should be noticed in passing. In occupations in which *no* resources are employed, the value of the marginal net product of resources will, in general, be smaller than it is in occupations where *some* resources are employed.

§ 2. This conclusion may be extended to show that, when complete equality among the values of marginal social net products is wanting, a diminution in the degree of inequality that exists among them is likely to benefit the national dividend. This result cannot, however, be set down without explanation. If the uses in which resources are employed were only two in number, its meaning would be perfectly clear and its validity undoubted. In fact, however, these uses are very numerous. This circumstance gives rise to a difficulty, which has already been referred to in another connection.[1] The meaning of the concept of greater or less equality among a large number of values is ambiguous. Are we to measure the degree of equality by the mean deviation from the average value, or by the standard deviation, or by the "probable error," or by some other statistical measure? If we use the standard deviation as our criterion, reasoning akin to that of the footnote on p. 97 shows that a decrease in the degree of inequality subsisting among the values of marginal social net products in different uses will *probably* lead to an increase in the national dividend. But it is not certain to do this unless the decrease of inequality is brought about by a group of (one or more) changes of individual values, *each one of which taken by itself* tends to decrease inequality. Thus, if the distribution of resources is so altered that a number of values of marginal social net products which are below the average are all increased, or if a number which are above the average are all diminished, it is certain that the dividend will be increased. But, if a cause comes into play, which, while decreasing the degree of inequality among the values of marginal social net products on the whole, yet increases *some* values that are above the average and diminishes *some* that are below it, this is not certain. This type of difficulty is not, however, of great practical

---

This circumstance clearly does not imply the existence of inequality among the values of marginal net products in any sense incompatible with the maximisation of the national dividend. But, if it should anywhere happen that the value of the marginal net product of resources in an occupation where no resources are employed is larger than it is in occupations where some resources are employed, —e.g. a profitable venture which for some reason people have failed to exploit,— *that* inequality would be an effective inequality and would be incompatible with the maximisation of the dividend.

[1] Cf. *ante*, Part I. Chapter VIII. § 7.

importance, because the obstacles to equality with which
we have to deal are, for the most part, general obstacles,
and operate in the same sense at nearly all points where
they operate at all.

§ 3. Let us next take account of the fact that in real life
costs are often involved in moving resources from one place
or occupation to another, and let us inquire in what, if any,
respects this fact makes it necessary to modify the conclusions
set out above. The kernel of the matter can be displayed
as follows. Suppose that between two points A and B the
movement of a unit of resources can be effected at a capital
cost equivalent to an annual charge of n shillings for
every year during which a unit that is moved continues in
productive work in its new home. In these circumstances the
national dividend will be increased by the movement of resources
from A to B, so long as the annual value of the marginal
social net product at B exceeds that at A by more than n
shillings; and it will be injured by any movement of resources
which occurs after the excess of the value of the marginal
social net product at B has been reduced below n shillings. If
the initial distribution of resources between A and B is such
that the value of the marginal social net product at B exceeds
(or falls short of) the value of the marginal social net product
at A by any number of shillings less than n, say by $(n - h)$
shillings, the existing arrangement—that under which the
values of the marginal social net products at the two points
differ by $(n - h)$ shillings—is the best arrangement, not indeed
absolutely, since, if there were no costs, a better arrangement
would be possible,[1] but *relatively to the fact of the initial distribution and the existing costs of movement*. It is not, be it noted,
the best arrangement relatively to the existing costs of movement alone. We cannot say that, when the costs of movement
are equivalent to n shillings, the national dividend is best
served by a distribution under which the values of the marginal
social net products at A and B differ by such and such a defined
number of shillings. The only accurate statement is: when the
costs of movement between A and B are equivalent to n shillings,
the national dividend is best served by the maintenance of

---

[1] Cf. *post*, Ch. V. § 6.

the existing distribution, whatever that may be, provided that this distribution does not involve a divergence in the values of marginal social net products greater than n shillings; and, if the existing distribution does involve a divergence greater than n shillings, by a new distribution brought about by the transference of sufficient resources to bring the divergence down to n shillings.

§ 4. The results set out in the two preceding sections rest upon the assumption that there is only one arrangement of resources which makes the values of marginal social net products everywhere equal—or as nearly equal as, in view of costs of movement, it is to the interest of the national dividend that they should be made. This assumption would be justified if the value of the marginal social net product of resources employed in each several use was always smaller, the greater the volume of resources employed there. There are, however, two sets of conditions in which this is not so. First, the employment of additional resources in the production of a commodity may, after a time, enable improved methods of organisation to be developed. This means that decreasing supply price [1] prevails, in such wise that the marginal (physical) net product of a greater quantity of resources exceeds the marginal (physical) net product of a smaller quantity: and, whenever this happens, it is *possible*, though, of course, it is not *necessary*, that the value of the marginal social net product of several different quantities of resources that might be engaged in producing the commodity will be the same. Secondly, the employment of additional resources in the production of a commodity may, after a time, lead to an increase in the price per unit offered by consumers of any given quantity of it. For their taste for it may be lastingly enhanced—obvious examples are afforded by the taste for music and tobacco— through experience of it. When this happens the value per unit of a larger product will (after an appropriate interval of time) be greater than the value per unit of a smaller product. It follows that, even for commodities whose production is not subject to conditions of decreasing supply price in the sense defined above, there *may* be, though, of course,

---

[1] For a study of this concept cf. *post*, Chapter XI.

there need not be, several different quantities of invested resources, the values of whose marginal social net products are the same.[1] Hence, the conclusions set out above require to be restated in a modified form. Allowance being made for costs of movement, it is true that the dividend cannot reach the maximum attainable amount *unless* the values of the marginal social net products of resources in all uses are equal. For, if they are not equal, the dividend can always be increased by a transference of resources from the margin of some uses to the margin of others. But, when the values of the marginal social net products in all uses are equal, the dividend *need not* attain an unequivocal maximum. For, if several arrangements are possible, all of which make the values of the marginal social net products equal, each of these arrangements does, indeed, imply what may be called a *relative maximum* for the dividend; but only one of these maxima is the unequivocal, or absolute, maximum. All of the relative maxima are, as it were, the tops of hills higher than the surrounding country, but only one of them is the highest hill-top of all. Furthermore, it is not necessary that all positions of relative maximum should represent larger dividends than all positions which are not maxima. On the contrary, a scheme of distribution approximating to that which yields the absolute maximum, but not itself fulfilling the condition of equal marginal yields, would probably imply a larger dividend than most of the schemes which do fulfil this condition and so constitute relative maxima of a minor character. A point *near* the summit of the highest hill may be higher than any summit except the highest itself.

[1] If equality of the values of marginal net products is attained when 1000 units of resources are devoted to the production of a particular thing, and also, *because of decreasing supply price*, when 5000 units are so devoted, the national dividend is necessarily larger under the latter arrangement. If equality is attained with 1000 units and also, *because of reactions upon tastes*, with 5000 units, both economic welfare and the national dividend, from the point of view of the period in which the 5000 units are operating, are necessarily larger under the latter arrangement. But the national dividend, from the point of view of the other period, may be smaller under the 5000 units arrangement. In these circumstances, the definition of p. 54 compels us to conclude that, from an absolute point of view, the dividends under the two arrangements are incommensurable.

§ 5. These considerations show that, even though the values of marginal social net products were everywhere equal or differed only in ways "justified" by the costs of movement, there might still be scope for State action designed to increase the magnitude of the national dividend and augment economic welfare.   Benefit might be secured by a *temporary* bounty (or temporary protection) so arranged as to jerk the industrial system out of its present poise at a position of relative maximum, and induce it to settle down again at the position of absolute maximum—the highest hill-top of all.   This is the analytical basis of the argument for the *temporary* protection, or other encouragement, of infant industries ; and, if the right infants are selected, the right amount of protection accorded, and this protection removed again at the right time, the argument is perfectly valid.   Benefit might also be secured by a *permanent* bounty at a different rate from that contemplated above, so arranged as to force the industrial system from the summit of the hill-top on which it is found to any position, that overtops its present site, on the slope of a higher hill.   The conditions in which bounties are likely to have this effect, rather than that of shifting the economic system to a different position on the hill that it is on already, are somewhat special.   But it can be proved that, in certain states of demand and supply, *some* rates of bounty *must* have this effect.[1]

[1] The shapes of the demand and supply curves and the size of the bounty must be such that, when the demand curve is raised by the bounty, it does not cut the supply curve at any point corresponding to its former point of intersection, but does cut it at a point corresponding to a point of stable equilibrium further to the right than this.   This condition can readily be depicted in a diagram.

CHAPTER IV

RATES OF RETURN AND THE VALUES OF MARGINAL PRIVATE NET PRODUCTS

§ 1. THE rate of return per unit in money obtained from any quantity of any kind of productive resource in any use is, in general, equal to the value of the marginal private net product of that quantity of that kind of resource there. As between different occupations and places, therefore, the relation between rates of return is the same as the relation between values of marginal private net products; so that equality or inequality among rates of return is the same thing as equality or inequality among values of marginal private net products. In this and the four following chapters I shall, for convenience, sometimes use the term of rate of returns—or, more loosely, returns—in place of the longer synonym.

§ 2. Anybody who has control of any quantity of any form of productive resource will try so to distribute it among various uses that it brings him the largest possible money receipts. If he thinks that, apart from cost of carriage and so on, he can get more money by transferring a unit from any one use to any other, he will do so. It follows that the free play of self-interest, so far as it is not hampered by ignorance, tends, in the absence of costs of movement, so to distribute resources among different uses and places as to render rates of return everywhere equal. By an easy extension of the argument it can be shown that, where there *are* costs of movement, the free play of self-interest, again so far as it is not hampered by ignorance, tends, not to bring about equality in rates of return, but to prevent any divergences from equality in excess of those that, relatively to the fact that there are costs of movement, allow the sum total of returns to attain a maximum.

§ 3. It follows that, if private and social net products everywhere coincide, the free play of self-interest, so far as it is not hampered by ignorance, will tend to bring about such a distribution of resources among different uses and places as will raise the national dividend and, with it, the sum of economic welfare to a maximum.[1] The distinctions drawn in the last sections of the preceding chapter show, indeed, that several maxima are possible, so that the one which self-interest tends to bring about need not be the highest maximum attainable. This, however, is a secondary matter. The essential point for our present purpose is that, when marginal private net products and marginal social net products coincide, any obstacles that obstruct the free play of self-interest will, in general, damage the national dividend. In real life, of course, marginal private and marginal social net products frequently do not coincide. In Chapters V.-VIII. this fact will be left out of account: but in later chapters, particularly Chapters IX.-XI., the consequences that follow from it will be fully examined.

[1] The conception of the free play of self-interest must, of course, for this purpose, be taken to exclude monopoly action. Cf. *post*, Chapters XIV.-XVII.

CHAPTER V

§ 1. THE purpose of this chapter is to study the way in which the size of the national dividend will be affected by a reduction of the obstacles to the movement of productive resources that are set up by ignorance and costs of movement. It is legitimate for this purpose to ignore differences between marginal social net products and marginal private net products; for, though particular obstacles to movement may prevent equality between the values of marginal private net products in such wise as to promote equality between the values of marginal social net products, there is no reason to suppose that obstacles to movement in general act in this way. It is proper to regard divergences between social and private net products as one factor making for inequality in the values of marginal social net products, and obstacles to movement as a second factor superimposed upon this; so that to weaken the force of either factor may be expected, in general, to promote *pro tanto* the equality that is desired. Assuming this, I shall, for simplicity of diction, in this and the following chapter, speak of marginal net product without any adjective.

§ 2. If the total quantity of productive resources at work be taken as given, it would seem at first sight that a reduction effected without expense in either sort of obstacle must necessarily make the rates of return in different uses and places, that is to say, the values of marginal net products, less unequal, and, consequently, must make the dividend larger. In reality, however, things are not so simple as this. The fact that obstacles to free movement comprise both costs of movement and imperfections of knowledge complicates the situation; for

144

we have to contemplate reductions of costs while knowledge is still imperfect and improvement of knowledge while costs remain.

§ 3. It is plain that, if people think that a larger return can be obtained by sending resources away from A for employment at B, a diminution in costs will cause resources to be sent, which, as a matter of fact, would have been more productive if left where they were. It is thus certainly *possible* that a reduction of costs in actual life may render the values of marginal net products more unequal, and so lessen the national dividend. In the appended footnote, however, it is shown by a technical argument that this is, on the whole, unlikely.[1]

§ 4. There is a different kind of complication when costs of movement remain unchanged but knowledge is improved. This improvement need not lead to an increase in equality

---

[1] The proof is as follows. Let people's judgment concerning the value of the marginal net product of resources invested at B be correct, but let their estimate of the corresponding value at A differ from fact by a defined quantity k. Let the costs of movement between A and B be equated to an annual sum spread over the period during which the unit of resources that has moved may be expected to find profit in staying in its new place. This annual sum is not necessarily the same in respect of movements from A to B and movements from B to A. Transport, for example, "acts more easily down than up hill or stream [and] . . . the barrier of language acts more strongly from England to Germany than *vice versa*" (Macgregor, *Industrial Combination*, p. 24). For the present purpose, however, we may ignore this complication and represent costs in either direction by an annual sum equal to n. Construct a figure in which positive values are marked off to the right of O and negative values to the left. Mark off OM equal to k; and MQ, MP on either side of M each equal to n. It is then evident that the excess of the value of the marginal net product of resources at B over that at A—let this excess be known as h—is indeterminate and may lie anywhere between a value OQ, which may be either positive or negative, and a value OP which may also be either positive or negative. A diminution in the value of n is represented by movements on the part of the two points P and Q towards M. So long as the values

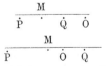

of k and n are such that P and Q lie on opposite sides of O, it is obvious that these movements make impossible the largest positive and the largest negative values of h that were possible before, and have no other effect. When, however, P and Q lie on the same side of O—in which case, of course, all possible values of h are of the same sign—they make impossible both the largest values of h that were possible before and also the smallest values. This double change seems equally likely to increase or to diminish the value of h. Hence, if it

L

among the values of marginal net products. For suppose the conditions to be such that, if perfect knowledge prevailed, the value of the marginal net product of resources at one point A would exceed the corresponding value at another point B by one shilling, and that the cost of moving a unit of resources from B to A would just balance this advantage. But, in fact, let us further suppose, knowledge is imperfect; people believe the value of the marginal net product at A to be higher than it really is; they therefore send more resources from B to A than they would do if better informed; and, therefore, the excess of the value of the marginal net product at A over that at B stands at less than n shillings. In these circumstances the growth of a more correct judgment would evidently *increase* the degree of inequality prevailing between the values of the marginal net products of resources at A and B. At the same time, however, it would evidently also increase the size of the national dividend. A reduction effected without expense in the obstacles set up by ignorance will thus always increase the national dividend; though it will not always do it by promoting equality among the values of marginal net products.

§ 5. At this point, however, we are brought up against a serious difficulty. Hitherto the total quantity of resources at work has been taken as given. In fact, however, the elimination or reduction of obstacles to the movement of productive resources may modify the quantity of these resources that come into action. We have, therefore, to ask whether the quantity of resources at work will ever be reduced, as a consequence of obstacles being removed, in such a way that the national dividend is made smaller and not larger than

---

were the fact that the points P and Q always lay on the same side of O, we could not infer that diminutions of the value of n would be likely to affect the value of h either way. In fact, however, it must often happen that P and Q lie on opposite sides of O. When account is taken of these cases as well as of the others, we can infer that, over the mass of many cases, diminutions in the value of n are likely to reduce the value of h. In other words, diminutions in the costs of movement are likely, in general, to make the values of the marginal net products of resources at A and B less unequal. Furthermore, it is evident that, when the distances MP and MQ are given, the probability that P and Q will both lie on the same side of O and, therefore, the probability that a diminution in the distances MP and MQ will be associated with an increase in the value of h, is smaller the smaller is the value of k.

before. That this result may be possible is suggested by an argument of Cournot's, in which he shows that, when "communication is opened between two markets, previously separated by a barrier, the total quantity produced of any commodity, which now begins to be exported from one market and imported to the other, will not necessarily be increased."[1] The increase in the output of the (hitherto) cheaper market will not, in some conditions, be as large as the decrease in that of the (hitherto) dearer market. By analogy it would seem that the opening up of communication between occupations and places hitherto separate might cause the aggregate quantity of labour at work, or of capital created, to be reduced; and the reduction might, in some circumstances, suffice to cause a reduction in the size of the national dividend in spite of the fact that part of the labour or capital still left would be operating under more favourable conditions than before. We must, I think, admit that, as a result of the opening up of communication, the amount of labour at work or of capital created may be reduced. I have difficulty, however, in imagining conditions in which the national dividend, as I have conceived it, could be diminished. For why should anybody choose more leisure than before unless the new conditions had given him a bigger aggregate income from work than before; and why should any one choose to save less than before unless the new conditions had given him a bigger aggregate income from savings than before? It may be that a full analysis would reveal possibilities in this matter that I have failed to see; but the possibilities are certainly remote. There can be no doubt that, in a broad general way, the conclusions reached in the preceding sections on the assumption that the quantity of resources at work is given are also valid when that assumption is removed.

§ 6. It remains to clear up an important issue. This has to do with the effect of State bounties designed to lessen ignorance or to reduce the costs of movement.[2] A cheapening of knowledge and movement to individuals, brought about

---

[1] Cf. Cournot, *Mathematical Theory of Wealth*, ch. xi., and Edgeworth, "Theory of International Values," *Economic Journal*, 1894, p. 625.

[2] Cf. *post*, Part III. Ch. IX. §§ 11-14.

by the transference of a part of the cost of these things to the State, is quite a different thing and works quite differently from a cheapening brought about by a real fall in cost. The two sorts of cheapening have the same tendency to promote — apart from the exceptional cases noticed above — increased equality among the values of marginal net products at different points.   But, when the cheapening is due to transference, the resultant increase of equality is an increase beyond what, *relatively to existing conditions*, is most advantageous. *Prima facie* this sort of cheapening, though it will generally make the values of marginal net products more equal, is likely to injure the national dividend.[1]

[1] To obviate misunderstanding two modifying considerations should be added.   First, the presumption just established against the grant of a bounty to the industry of promoting mobility is merely a special case of the general presumption against the grant of a bounty to any industry.   It may, therefore, be overthrown if there is special reason to believe that, in the absence of a bounty, investment in the industry in question would not be carried so far as is desirable.   Secondly, when the State takes over the work of providing either information or the means of movement, and elects for any reason to sell the result of its efforts either for nothing or below cost price, we have, in general, to do, not merely with the grant of a bounty on these things, but at the same time with a real cheapening due to the introduction of large-scale methods.   Even, therefore, though the bounty element in the new arrangement were proved to be injurious, it might still happen that that arrangement as a whole was beneficial.

CHAPTER VI

HINDRANCES TO EQUALITY OF RETURNS DUE TO IMPERFECT KNOWLEDGE

§ 1. In the present chapter I shall study in some detail the obstructive influence of ignorance. A flowing stream of resources is continually coming into being and struggling, so far as unavoidable costs of movement allow of this, to distribute itself away from points of relatively low returns towards points of relatively high returns. Success in this struggle is interfered with by imperfect knowledge on the part of those in whose hands the power to direct the various branches of the stream resides. To obtain an idea of the scale of the damage which results from this cause, it is desirable to study briefly certain aspects of modern business finance.

§ 2. First, it must be observed that the returns, which are important as a guide to the right distribution of resources, are those that are accruing in different uses from resources turned into them at each successive moment. The quotient obtained by dividing the net income of a business by the sum of all the money investment made in it in the past would, in a stationary state, afford a true measure of the returns to current investment there. But in actual conditions the measure thus obtained will often be hopelessly misleading. For example, a man may have put £100,000 into a factory for making some particular thing, and the factory may have been destroyed by fire or may have become worthless through obsolescence. An investment of £10,000 now might have just yielded him a return of £2000, or 20 per cent on the new investment, but the return on the total investment will appear as £2000 on £110,000, or less than 2 per cent. This

sort of difficulty could hardly fail to obscure relevant facts
however excellently business accounts were drawn up and
however fully they were published.

§ 3. The next thing that calls for comment is the
general character of the accounts as they actually are. In
businesses conducted by private firms no statement of
profits is made public. In businesses conducted by joint
stock companies a certain amount of publicity is enforced
by law. But stock-watering and other devices are often
used to conceal from outsiders the rate of return that is
obtained on the capital actually invested, so that, even when
this would afford a reasonable guide to the return on current
investment, and, therefore, to future prospects, the way is
blocked to anybody other than a specialist. The difficulty is
still further enhanced by the fact that the prospects which it
is necessary to forecast refer, not to immediate returns only,
but to returns spread over a considerable period. It is
evident that, as regards these returns, even correct knowledge
of the immediate past gives but imperfect guidance. In view
of these facts, it might seem that, in existing conditions, ignorance
will almost entirely inhibit the tendency towards equality
among the returns to resources flowing at any time into different
uses. Such a view, however, would be unduly pessimistic.
"Though it may be difficult," Marshall writes, "to read the
lessons of an individual trader's experience, those of a whole
trade can never be completely hidden, and cannot be hidden at
all for long. Although one cannot tell whether the tide is rising
or falling by merely watching half-a-dozen waves breaking on
the seashore, yet a very little patience settles the question ;
and there is a general agreement among business men that
the average rate of profits in a trade cannot rise or fall much
without general attention being attracted to the change before
long. And though it may sometimes be a more difficult task
for a business man than for a skilled labourer to find out
whether he could improve his prospects by changing his trade,
yet the business man has great opportunities for discovering
whatever can be found out about the present and future of
other trades ; and, if he should wish to change his trade,
he will generally be able to do so more easily than the

skilled workman could."[1]   In short, though individual firms
may successfully conceal their position, industries as wholes
can hardly do so.   Ignorance as to the comparative returns to
be got by using resources to start new businesses in different
occupations may be very great among the general public, but
it is probably much less important than it appears to be
at first sight among those persons by whose agency the flow
of resources is, in the main, directed.   Nevertheless, there
is clearly room for improvement in the matter of business
publicity,[2] and, if such improvement were made, ignorance
would be lessened, equality in the values of marginal net
products promoted, and the size of the national dividend
consequently increased.

§ 4. I turn next to the relation between ignorance and
the quality of the persons by whom the employment of resources is controlled.   In a primitive community investment
is carried on almost exclusively by entrepreneurs actually
engaged in the various industries and devoting to the conduct
of them resources belonging to themselves.   Their quality
alone is relevant to our problem ; and it is obvious that the
range of error in the forecasts that are made is likely to be
larger or smaller according as able men are or are not content
to adopt business as a career.   In the modern world a very
large part of the investment made in industry still comes
from the people actually engaged in particular businesses,
who reinvest their profits in them or obtain funds from
partners or friends of their own who are fully conversant
with all relevant circumstances.   It has been suggested
that methods of this sort, lying outside the organisation of the money market proper, are employed to direct
more than half the total stream of new home investment.[3]
In addition, however, to these methods, the modern world
also has resort to others.   A very important part of
industry is financed from resources belonging to a great
number of other people besides those who actually
manage businesses.   These other people include, on the one

---

[1] *Principles of Economics*, p. 608.

[2] Cf. Layton, *Capital and Labour*, ch. iv.

[3] Lavington, *The English Capital Market*, p. 281.

hand, professional financiers, company promoters or promoting syndicates, and, on the other hand, moneyed people among the general public, whom these promoters induce to invest in their ventures. "The promoter's special province," writes Professor Mitchell, "is to find and bring to the attention of investors new opportunities for making money, new natural resources to be exploited, new processes to be developed, new products to be manufactured, new organisations of existing business enterprises to be arranged, etc. But the promoter is seldom more than an explorer who points out the way for fresh advances of the army of industry. . . . There are always being launched more schemes than can be financed with the available funds. In rejecting some and accepting others of these schemes, the men of money are taking a very influential, though not a very conspicuous, part in determining how labour shall be employed, what products shall be used, and what localities built up." [1] In modern industry, then, the direction of a large part of the community's investment is in the joint control of professional financiers interested in company promotion and of the moneyed part of the general public. What is to be said about the capacity and business judgment of this complex directing agency?

§ 5. The comparative capacity for detecting good new openings for enterprise of the professional financier and of the ordinary business man—the entrepreneur investor of former days—is not difficult to determine. First, the professional financier is a specialist in this particular work, whereas to the ordinary business man an opportunity for undertaking it would come, if at all, only at rare intervals. Clearly the specialist is likely to make better forecasts than the general practitioner. Secondly, the international character which the development of the means of communication has in recent times given to many industries has made the advantage enjoyed by the specialist much greater than it used to be when a knowledge of *local* conditions, such as an intelligent business man would naturally possess, afforded a sufficient basis for a good forecast. Lastly, the fact of specialisation gives freer play to the selective agency of bankruptcy, in eliminating persons who undertake

[1] Mitchell, *Business Cycles*, pp. 34-5.

to choose openings for new enterprises and cannot choose well. When the functions of financier and manufacturer are rolled together in one man, the man may flourish through his manufacturing skill—good business tactics—despite of incompetent business strategy. When the two functions are separated, anybody who undertakes the one in which he is incompetent relatively to other people is apt to lose his money and be driven from the field. Furthermore, the efficiency of this natural selection is augmented by the fact that a professional financier undertakes a great number of transactions, and that, therefore, the element of chance plays a small part, and the element of efficiency a large part, in the result. Hence there can be no doubt that the advent into any industry of professional financiers means the advent of persons better able than those immediately concerned in the industry to forecast future conditions. Against this has to be set the fact that the great bulk of those members of the general public, who ultimately supply the funds for the enterprises that professional financiers have organised, are much less capable than ordinary business men of forecasting future conditions. If promoters always looked for the openings most profitable on the whole, as distinguished from those that can be so manipulated as to become most profitable to themselves, this ignorance on the part of people who follow their lead would not, perhaps, greatly matter. Unfortunately, however, it is often to the interest, and it is usually in the power, of the professionals, by spreading false information and in other ways, deliberately to pervert the forecasts of their untutored colleagues. It is this fact that makes the net effect of the modern system upon the distribution of the community's investments among openings of varying merit somewhat doubtful. The prospect of advantage is probably increased when, as in Germany before the war, the flotation of new companies on the basis of shares of extremely low nominal value is forbidden by law; for then a certain number of the poorer and, perhaps, more ignorant persons, who might be easily tricked, are driven away.[1] Again, any legislative enactment,

[1] In Germany shares were, in no case, permitted of a lower denomination than £10, and they were not usually permitted of a lower denomination than

capable of being enforced, that checks the fraudulent exploitation of incompetent investors by dishonest professionals tends
pro tanto to diminish the range of error to which the general
mass of operative forecasts made in the community is liable.
" The public regulation of the prospectuses of new companies,
legislation supported by efficient administration against fraudulent promotion, more rigid requirements on the part of the
stock exchanges regarding the securities admitted to official
lists, and more efficient agencies for giving information to
investors fall under this head."[1]

§ 6. A more fundamental remedy is introduced when the
work of promotion itself is kept in the hands of bankers—
whose reputation, of course, depends upon the *permanent*
success of the business undertakings that they have founded.
This is done in Germany.   Big German banks retain a staff
of technical experts to investigate and report upon any
industrial ventures that may be proposed, decide, after elaborate
inquiries, which ventures to promote and, in short, constitute
themselves a financial general staff to industry.   The contrast with the English system is well pointed out in the following passage : " The English joint stock companies (*i.e.* the
banks), conforming to the theory, have abstained in a *direct*
way from flotations and the underwriting business, as well
as from bourse speculation.   But this very fact causes
another great evil, namely, that the banks have never shown
any interest in the newly founded companies or in the
securities issued by these companies, while it is a distinct
advantage of the German system that the German banks,
even if only in the interest of their own issue credit, have
been keeping a continuous watch over the development of
the companies which they founded."[2]   No doubt, this
practice of banks acting as promoters involves great risks
and absolutely requires that their capital resources shall be,
as they are in Germany,[3] very much larger relatively to

£50. (Cf. Schuster, *The Principles of German Civil Law*, p. 44.) In 1924
the minimum denomination was reduced to £1 (20 marks), and the usual
denomination to £5 (100 marks).
  [1] Cf. Mitchell, *Business Cycles*, p. 585.
  [2] Riesser, *The German Great Banks*, p. 555.
  [3] The general practice of the English banks is to supply " banking
facilities," that is to say advances, whether by discount of bills or otherwise,

their liabilities than is usual among English banks; for otherwise losses sustained in the promotion business, or even the temporary "solidification" of funds locked up in this business, might render the banks unable to meet their obligations to their depositors. Moreover, it must be remembered that the position of this country as the banking centre of the world, and, until recently, the principal free market for gold, would make the locking up of bank resources in long ventures more dangerous than in other countries. I make no suggestion, therefore, that the general policy hitherto pursued by British banks has been other than well advised. Nevertheless, there can be no doubt that, when conditions are such as to allow banks safely to undertake the work of promotion, a real advantage results. They are more likely than are certain types of private financiers to look out for openings which really are sound, as distinguished from openings which can be made for a short time to appear sound. It is, indeed, possible that, in some circumstances, where the rival interests of different nationalities are affected, powerful banking institutions operating along these lines may be made the instruments of a *political* movement, and may allow their conduct to be swayed by other than economic considerations. But this aspect of the matter is unsuited for discussion here.

§ 7. It is not, however, only by acting as promoting agents that bankers can help to direct resources into

---

that have a short currency only, and not "financial facilities," *i.e.* advances with a long currency. It is sometimes claimed that this practice handicaps those British industries in which opportunities may arise for the profitable expansion of plant at short notice,—to make possible, for example, their acceptance of some large order which might throw open for them the entry into some new market; for the raising of fresh capital by an issue of shares or debentures necessarily takes time. It is also sometimes claimed that our banking practice makes it difficult for British traders to make their way in those foreign markets where purchasers are accustomed to expect very long credits. It was with a view to meeting these complaints that Lord Farringdon's Committee on Financial Facilities (1916) recommended that an institution should be established with a large capital, not undertaking ordinary deposit banking, but prepared to provide financial facilities both for the development of industries at home and, where necessary, for the conduct of foreign trade. This recommendation was acted upon, and an institution of the kind contemplated—the British Trade Corporation—was granted a Charter in April 1917.

productive channels. It is true that ordinary bankers in their loans to traders, whether made directly or through bill-brokers, are concerned only with the safety of the debt. The judgment that they make about the capacity of would-be borrowers to meet their obligations involves, when acceptable security is offered, no judgment as to the comparative profitableness of the undertakings into which different would-be borrowers will put the money they succeed in raising. But, when bankers are required to make loans to persons who are not in a position to offer full banking security, they are compelled to assume a more important rôle. They cannot lend on a mere promise to pay, but are bound, in their own interest, to make elaborate inquiry both as to the trustworthiness of the borrower and also as to the purpose to which he proposes to devote the proceeds of the loan. Speaking of the peasant borrowers of India, Sir Theodore Morison writes: " It is useless, however amiable, to believe that the ryot is only thirsting for capital in order to invest it at once in the improvement and development of his estate." [1]   Again, in the Report on the working of the Co-operative Credit Societies Act in Burma, issued in 1907, it is urged that "in Burma borrowing is mostly due to habit and want of forethought, and not to necessity ; that the capital really required to finance cultivation (apart from luxury) is very much less than what is generally supposed, and that mere provision of cheap money, through co-operative societies or otherwise, tends, owing to the existing state of public feeling, to induce waste of income rather than thrift ; and, lastly, that in Burma very special care will be necessary to see that the societies are managed in such a way that the prevention of waste and inculcation of thrift are effectively impressed on the members' minds." [2]   The recognised machinery for exercising this type of control and supervision is provided by People's Banks, such as the Raiffeisen Banks in Germany and their Italian counterparts. These banks evoke the necessary knowledge by a double process. First, the persons brought together as members

---

[1] *The Industrial Organisation of an Indian Province*, p. 110.
[2] Report, p. 15.

of the Bank, and, therefore, as potential borrowers, are gathered from a small area only, in such wise that the controlling committee can easily obtain intimate personal information concerning all of them. Only those persons are allowed to become members, of whose probity and general good character the committee have satisfied themselves. In some banks—in the Italian Banchi Popolari, for instance— the committee draw up, *ab initio* and independently of any particular application, a list of the sums which, in their opinion, may safely be lent to the various members.[1] This list is afterwards used as a basis for loans, just as the lists of the communal *bureaux de bienfaisance* in France are used as a basis for the grant of Poor Relief. Secondly, the grant of a loan is often made conditional on its being employed for a specified purpose, and subject to certain rights of supervision reserved for the lender. Thus, whereas in most land-banks (where material security is taken) " the proceeds of mortgages may be used as the borrower pleases, *e.g.* in paying off loans, in portioning younger sons, etc.," in the Raiffeisen Banks careful inquiry is undertaken into the purpose for which the loan is required, and provision is made for its recall should the borrower divert it from that purpose.[2] The general tendency of this arrangement is to lessen the number of investments made under the impulse of ignorance in undertakings that yield an abnormally low return, and so indirectly to augment the national dividend.

[1] Cf. Wolff, *People's Banks*, p. 154.

[2] For an account of Raiffeisen and kindred Banks, cf. Fay, *Co-operation at Home and Abroad*, Part I.

CHAPTER VII

HINDRANCES TO EQUALITY OF RETURNS DUE TO IMPERFECT
DIVISIBILITY OF THE UNITS IN TERMS OF WHICH
TRANSACTIONS ARE CONDUCTED

§ 1. ALONGSIDE of imperfect knowledge, as discussed in the preceding chapter, stands the cost of movement. Some part of this cost is, of course, represented by the payments that have to be made to various agents in the capital market, promoters, financing syndicates, investment trusts, solicitors, bankers, and others, who, in varying degrees according to the nature of the investment concerned, help in the work of transporting capital from its places of origin to its places of employment.[1] But there is also a less obvious and more peculiar part of the cost of movement, of which some more detailed study is desirable. A pure mathematical treatment of economic problems always assumes that, when there is opportunity anywhere for the profitable employment of given quantities of the several factors of production, each factor can be received there in units that are indefinitely small and are capable of being separated completely from units of any other factor. In so far as this assumption is not warranted, it is readily seen that the tendency to equality of returns will be imperfectly realised. For, on the one hand, if an enterprise is only financed, in respect of any one factor, by means of units, each of which has the value of £1000, it may well be that, though the transference of £1000 worth of the factor to or from elsewhere could not, when equilibrium is established, bring about an increased aggregate return, the transference

[1] For an excellent account of these agencies cf. Lavington, *The English Capital Market*, ch. xviii.

158

of a sum less than £1000 could, if it were permitted, do this. In short, when the units, in terms of which transactions are made, are not indefinitely small, the tendency to equality of returns in all uses degrades into a tendency to limitation of inequality—a limitation the extent of which is diminished with every increase in the size of the units. On the other hand, if an enterprise is only financed, in respect of any two factors, by means of units which combine factor A and factor B in a definite proportion, it may well be that, though the transference of one of these complex combined units to or from elsewhere could not, when equilibrium is established, bring about an increased aggregate return, the transference in isolation of some quantity of either of the two factors might have this effect. Hence, when the units, in terms of which transactions are made, are compounded of fixed proportions of two or more factors, the tendency to equality of returns in all uses again degrades into a tendency to limitation of inequality. It follows that largeness and complexity in the units in terms of which transactions are made act in the same way as costs of movement. In general they obstruct the tendency of self-interest to make the returns obtainable by each several factor of production equal in all uses.

§ 2. At one time it may have been true that the units in which capital transactions were made were noticeably large. Of recent years, however, the size of those units has been greatly reduced in two ways. Of these one is obvious, the other relatively obscure. The obvious way is the diminution in the value of individual deposits which banks will accept—the Savings Bank, for example, allows pennies to be deposited separately—and a similar, though less extensive, diminution in the value of the individual shares issued by companies.[1] The more obscure way depends upon the fact that a unit of capital is a two-dimensional entity. A man can reduce the quantity of capital which he provides, not only by altering the number of pounds that he lends over a defined time, but also by altering the

---

[1] It must be remembered, as was indicated in § 5 of the preceding chapter, that this tendency is not without incidental disadvantages.

time over which he lends a defined number of pounds. Reduction in the time-extension of the units in which capital is borrowed is of great importance in practice, because, whereas most enterprises require funds for a long period, many lenders are only willing to cut themselves off inexorably from their resources for a short period. There have been evolved in the modern world two devices through which the required reduction in time-extension has been effected. The first of these is the actual acceptance of loans for short terms by entrepreneurs, in dependence partly on the elasticity of the wants of their enterprise, and partly on the chance of opportunities for reborrowing elsewhere. The second is the organisation of the Stock Exchange, by resort to which the funded debts of enterprises can be transferred, —a device which is, from the lender's point of view, the next stage to permission to recall his loan from the enterprise itself. These two devices have fairly distinct spheres. To rely too largely on short loans is felt to be dangerous. "In proportion as enterprises depend upon short-time credits rather than upon paid-up capital or permanent loans are they in danger of failure in times of stress" [1]—through inability to renew the credits. There has, therefore, grown up a rough general understanding that short-time paper is an unsuitable means of raising money for things like new equipment, from which the turn-over is necessarily slow ; it should be used only to finance expenditure on materials and labour employed in making commodities that are likely to be sold before the maturity of the paper.[2] This distinction between the two devices is not, however, important for the present purpose. Both of the devices are essentially similar, for both depend on the general probability that the willingness of the aggregate community to lend will be less variable than that of a representative individual. In consequence of this, on the one hand, a company, by discounting bills through banks, borrows part of its capital for a series of short terms from different people, thus enabling any one of them to lend for a few months only. On the other hand, a man, who makes

---

[1] Burton, *Financial Crisis*, p. 263.
[2] Cf. Meade, *Corporation Finance*, p. 231.

savings for a "treat" or to meet an accident, instead of
storing what he expects to want, invests it in long-time
securities, in reliance on the organisation of the Stock
Exchange to enable him to realise his capital at need. These
devices are not perfect. In times of stress the discounting
of new bills may prove very difficult and costly, and the
realisation of capital by the sale of shares may not be
possible except at heavy loss. They have availed, however,
to bring about a large and important reduction in the time-
extension of the units in terms of which capital transactions
are conducted. As regards labour transactions, it is plain
enough that the units are fairly small. Hence, in the modern
world, apart from certain special problems of land transfer that
cannot conveniently be discussed here, the only department
in which largeness in the units of transactions obstructs the
tendency of self-interest to bring about equality of returns
in different occupations would seem to be that of employing
power. The average wielder of employing power cannot
be regarded as indefinitely small, as compared with the
aggregate quantity of employing power that is in action
in any use. This fact brings it about that the returns to
employing power in different uses are checked from approaching very closely towards equality ; and, hence, that the national
dividend is rendered smaller than it would be if employing
power were more fully divisible.

§ 3. Let us next consider complexity, or compound character, in the units in terms of which transactions are made.
Here, as before, it is capital which calls for the greatest
amount of discussion. For capital, as ordinarily conceived
in business, is not a pure elementary factor of production.
In the concrete, of course, it appears in the form either of
plant and equipment or of a system of connections called
goodwill. But this concrete capital is always made up
of a combination, in varying proportions, of two factors,
namely, waiting and uncertainty-bearing.[1] Under primitive

---

[1] The nature of the service of "waiting" has been much misunderstood.
Sometimes it has been supposed to consist in the provision of money, sometimes
in the provision of time, and, on both suppositions, it has been argued that no
contribution whatever is made by it to the dividend. Neither supposition is
correct. "Waiting" simply means postponing consumption which a person

conditions, if an enterprise was undertaken by more than one person, it was practically necessary for *each* of the several contributors to furnish waiting and uncertainty-bearing in the proportions in which these factors were required in the aggregate. They would, in effect, pool their capital, taking upon each £ lent an equal measure of uncertainty-bearing. They would be partners, or, if we wish to suppose them in the enjoyment of limited liability, joint shareholders in a company whose capital consisted entirely of ordinary shares. In modern times, however, this is no longer necessary. An enterprise that requires, say, x units of waiting *plus* y units of uncertainty-bearing, need no longer obtain from each subscriber of one unit of waiting $\frac{y}{x}$ units of uncertainty-bearing also. By the device of guarantees its demand can be separated into two streams, in such wise that waiting alone is drawn from one set of people and uncertainty-bearing alone from another set. Guarantees may assume a great variety of forms. They are given to industrialists by insurance companies, which undertake, for a consideration, that the industrialists' earnings shall be unaffected by fire or accident. They are given by Exchange Banks, such as those which, in India before 1893, bought importers' and exporters' bills at the time of their bargain, and so, for a

---

has power to enjoy immediately, thus allowing resources, which might have been destroyed, to assume the form of productive instruments and to act as "harness, by which natural powers are guided so as to assist mankind in his efforts" (Flux, *Principles of Economics*, p. 89). The unit of "waiting" is, therefore, the use of a given quantity of resources—for example, labour or machinery—for a given time. Thus, to take Professor Carver's example, if a manufacturer buys one ton of coal a day on each day of the year and buys each day's supply one day ahead, the waiting he supplies during that year is one ton of coal for one year—a year-ton of coal (*Distribution of Wealth*, p. 253). In more general terms, we may say that the unit of waiting is a year-value-unit, or, in the simpler, if less accurate, language of Dr. Cassel, a year-pound. The graver difficulties involved in the conception of uncertainty-bearing are discussed in Appendix I. A caution may be added against the common view that the amount of capital accumulated in any year is necessarily equal to the amount of "savings" made in it. This is not so even when savings are interpreted to mean net savings, thus eliminating the savings of one man that are lent to increase the consumption of another, and when temporary accumulations of *unused* claims upon services in the form of bank-money are ignored; for many savings which are meant to become capital in fact fail of their purpose through misdirection into wasteful uses.

price, insured them against loss (or gain) from any fluctuations in the exchange which might occur in the interval between the bargain and the realisation of the bills. Where industrialists have to do with staple goods, for which grading permits the establishment of future markets, they are given, for the more general risks of business, by speculators. For a miller or cotton merchant, undertaking an order to supply flour or cotton goods, can buy the speculator's promise to provide him with his raw material in the future for a stipulated sum, irrespective of the price which may then prevail in the market. Like guarantees are given to a banker preparing to discount a bill for an industrial enterprise, when a second banker, or a bill-broker, or some independent person, consents to accept, or endorse, the bill, or, as is usual with "cash credits" in Scotland, to stand surety for the original borrower.[1] They are given to a Central Bank, when a People's Bank, working, either on unlimited liability or with a subscribed capital of guarantee, in effect borrows money on behalf of its local clients.[2] They are given finally to a banker or other lender when a borrower obtains a loan from him by a deposit of "collateral" security. By far the most effective form of security consists in government scrip and the share certificates of industrial enterprises. For the deposit of these, unlike the deposit of chattel security, involves no present loss to the depositor, while their ultimate assumption, unlike the foreclosure of a mortgage, threatens no difficulty to the person in whose favour the deposit has

[1] The essence of the guarantee given by the acceptor's signature is the same whether the bill be drawn in respect of goods received, or is an accommodation bill endorsed by an accepting-house, which lends its name for a consideration. The variety of accommodation bills known as "pig-on-bacon," where the acceptor is a branch of the drawing house under an *alias*, is, of course, different, because these bills, in effect, bear only one name ; and the same thing is substantially true when the fortunes of the endorsing house and the original borrower are so closely interwoven that the failure of the one would almost certainly involve the failure of the other.

[2] The controversy between the advocates of limited and unlimited liability has sometimes been keen. In the ordinary banks and in the Schulze-Delitzsch People's Banks limited liability is the universal rule. On the other hand, in the People's Banks of Italy and originally, before their absorption by the Imperial Federation, in the Raiffeisen Banks of Germany (except that the law insists on some *small* shares) the method of unlimited liability was adopted, for the reason that the poor people, for whom the banks were designed, would find difficulty in becoming shareholders to any substantial extent.

been made.   Furthermore, the "continuous market" provided
for securities by the Stock Exchanges of the world safeguards the holders of them against the danger of slumps in
value so sudden and large as those to which persons holding,
as collateral, the title-deeds of parcels of real estate are liable.[1]
In recent times, partly in consequence of the supersession
of partnerships by joint stock companies,[2] the proportion of
national wealth represented by stocks and shares, and, therefore, available as collateral security, has enormously increased.
According to Schmoller's estimate of a few years before
the war, whereas 100 years ago only a very small proportion
of any country's wealth was in this form, to-day in Germany
17 per cent—Riesser says 33 per cent—and in England
40 per cent, of it is covered by paper counterparts.[3]   According to Mr. Watkins's investigations, 77 per cent of the capital
value owned by residents in the United Kingdom, on which
estate duty was levied in 1902–3, was "personalty," and,
out of personalty, 70 per cent was paper property.[4]   As
a natural consequence the area over which the device
of guarantees can be employed, and, therefore, the segregation
of waiting from uncertainty-bearing brought about, has been
greatly extended.

§ 4. This device is not, however, the only method by
which modern ingenuity has broken up the complex unit
of capital into its component parts.   It enables waiting to
be separated from uncertainty-bearing.   But uncertainty-
bearing is itself not a single simple thing.   To expose a
£ to an even chance of becoming 21s. or 19s. is a different
thing from exposing it to an even chance of becoming
39s. 10d. or 2d.   There are, in short, a great number of
different schemes of uncertainty, which different people are
ready to shoulder.   Over against these there are a great number
of different schemes of uncertainty which the undertaking
of various business enterprises involves.   It is evident that
what is offered can be adjusted to what is wanted more
satisfactorily when any given demand of industry can be

[1] Cf. Brace, *The Value of Organized Speculation*, p. 142.
[2] Cf. Fisher, *The Rate of Interest*, p. 208.
[3] Quoted by Watkins, *The Growth of Large Fortunes*, p. 42.
[4] *Ibid.* pp. 48-9.

met by combining together a number of different schemes that
individually do not fit with it. This can now be done.
When enterprises, for which capital had to be provided by
several people, were worked on the partnership plan, all
those concerned submitted the resources invested by them
to the same scheme of uncertainty.   Consequently, unless
a sufficient number of people could be found ready to undertake that particular scheme of uncertainty, profitable enterprises
were liable to be hung up.   In the modern world this difficulty
has been, in great part, overcome by the device, which joint
stock companies now invariably adopt, of raising capital by
means of different grades of security.   Instead of an arrangement, under which every pound invested in an enterprise
is submitted to the same scheme of uncertainty, we have
systems of capitalisation combining debentures, cumulative
preference shares, non-cumulative preference shares, ordinary
shares and, sometimes, further special sub-varieties.   Each
of these classes of security represents a different scheme,
or sort, of uncertainty-bearing. This specialisation of shares
into a number of different classes has the same kind of effect
in facilitating the distribution of resources in the way most
advantageous to the national dividend as the simpler specialisation into two grades, one involving some uncertainty and the
other involving none.

§ 5. There is yet one more form of specialisation.
Hitherto we have tacitly assumed that a given type of holding
in a company will always remain what it was when it was
first taken up.   In fact, however, this is not so : for, as a
company becomes established, holdings, that at first involved
much uncertainty-bearing, often cease to do so.   The modern
system of industrial finance enables adjustment to be made to
this fact, so that shares of companies are, in general, held by one
set of people while the companies are new, and by a different
set of people when they become established.   Thus, when an
important " proposition " is floated, the funds are provided
in the first instance by a contributing syndicate—or are
guaranteed by an underwriting syndicate—consisting of
persons who are willing to risk large losses in the hope of
large gains, but are not prepared to lock up their capital for

long. The syndicate in its early stages may succeed in disposing of many shares to speculators on margins and others, who are similarly willing to provide uncertainty-bearing but not waiting;[1] and these, in turn, after a short "flutter," may sell again to others like unto themselves. At a later stage, when trial has shown what the concern is really like, and so has greatly reduced the element of uncertainty-bearing involved in taking up its shares, the "investing public," those who are anxious to furnish waiting without much alloy, come into the field and purchase the shares. In this way providers of uncertainty-bearing and providers of waiting are both afforded an opportunity of playing the parts for which they are respectively fitted.

§ 6. The broad result of these modern developments has been to break up into simple and convenient parts the compound units in terms of which it was formerly necessary for capital transactions to be conducted. In transactions affecting labour and land—apart from the fact, to be examined in Part III., that the family must sometimes be taken as the unit of migration—there has never been any great complexity in the units. In the field of "enterprise" complexity still rules, in so far as employing power can only find an engagement if it brings with it a certain amount of capital. But the advent of salaried managers, working on behalf of joint stock companies, has done much to break down the complex unit here also. In general, therefore, we may conclude that, in the modern world, complexity in the structure of the units in which transactions are conducted is not an important hindrance to adjustments making for equality of returns in different occupations.

[1] For details cf. Meade, *Corporation Finance*, pp. 153-7.

CHAPTER VIII

HINDRANCES TO EQUALITY OF RETURNS DUE TO RELATIVE VARIATIONS OF DEMAND IN DIFFERENT OCCUPATIONS AND PLACES

§ 1. WE have now to introduce a new conception, that of the relative variations of demand in different parts of the industrial field. If the amount of any sort of productive resource demanded at a given price at all points collectively is constant, and the amounts demanded at the several points individually are variable, the relative variation of demand between two periods, say, between two successive years, may be measured by the sum of the excesses of the amounts demanded in the second year, at those points where there are excesses, over the amounts demanded in the previous year at the same points. If the demand for the productive resource at all points collectively is not constant, this variation may be measured, either by the sum of the excesses of the amounts demanded in the second year over the amounts demanded in the previous year at the same points, or by the sum of the deficiencies of the amounts so demanded over the corresponding amounts of the previous year, *according as the one or the other of these sums is the smaller.*

§ 2. On the basis of this description, it can readily be shown that the influence of impediments to movement, in causing departures from equality of returns, is, in general, greater, the greater are the relative variations of demand in the sense just explained. For let attention be concentrated upon those impediments, which are not adequate to prevent returns from being equalised in " the long run," but suffice to prevent the movements required to equalise them immediately.

If the various parts of the industrial field are fluctuating relatively to one another, impediments of this order will keep returns *always* unequal. Mill's illustration from wave movements on the ocean is wholly apposite. Under the influence of gravity, there is a constant tendency to equality of level in all parts ; but, since, after any disturbance, this tendency takes time to assert itself, and since, before the necessary time has elapsed, some fresh disturbance is always introduced, equality of level does not in fact ever occur. It is evident that the average amount of inequality of level depends in part on the magnitude of these disturbances. It is, similarly, evident that the average degree of inequality of returns depends in part, in respect of any system of impediments to movement, upon the size of the relative variations which the demands for productive resources at different points in the industrial field undergo. It is the task of the present chapter to distinguish the principal influences upon which the magnitude of these relative variations in different circumstances depends.

§ 3. First, it is plain, in so far as the demands for the services of productive resources in different occupations and places are affected by independent causes, anything that promotes variations in any particular occupation or place is likely to enhance the relative variations of demand as a whole. Thus all the factors affecting particular industries, which we shall be studying for a different purpose in Chapter XX. of Part III., are also relevant here.

§ 4. Secondly, when the demands for a commodity that is being produced in several centres fluctuate as between the centres, anything that prevents variations of demand for the commodity from being reflected in variations of demand for productive resources lessens the relative variations of demand for these resources. The practice followed by some firms of giving out work on commission in times of over-pressure to other firms in the same industry that are temporarily slack has this effect. When the firms engaged in an industry combine into a single concern, this device can, of course, be carried further. Orders, at whatever point they originate, can be spread among the members of the combination in such wise that there are no relative variations in the several demands for resources to meet these orders.

§ 5. Thirdly, there are sometimes at work causes which bring about definite transfers of demand from one group of occupations to another. The most obvious of these are seasonal changes in climatic conditions; in the summer, for example, people want less gas for lighting but more petrol for motoring than they do in the winter. Shiftings of taste, under the influence of fashion, from one class of luxury article to another are on the same plane. Yet again, even when every individual's tastes remain unaltered, the transfer of income from people with one set of tastes to people with another set involves a transfer of demand from the products favoured by the first class to those favoured by the second. Thus an improvement in the incomes of the poor at the expense of the rich would cause the demand for poor men's goods to grow, and that for rich men's to contract: and this change would be reflected in the demands for productive resources to make the two sorts of goods.

§ 6. Fourthly, there are at work certain general causes, which affect the demand for productive resources in a large number of occupations in the same sense, but in different degrees. Thus the psychical, monetary and other factors that underlie what are commonly called cyclical fluctuations in industry involve, for reasons which I have endeavoured to explain elsewhere,[1] much more violent swings in the demand for instrumental goods than in that for the general run of consumption goods. This, of course, means that demands for productive resources to produce these two sorts of goods fluctuate relatively to one another. Any policy, therefore, that succeeded in mitigating the swing of cyclical industrial fluctuations, would, incidentally, also lessen the *relative* variations in the demands of different industries.

§ 7. If we suppose ourselves starting from a position of equilibrium and imagine *any* relative variation of demand to occur as between two occupations, until the appropriate transfer of productive resources has taken place the national dividend must fall below its maximum. But, nevertheless, it

---

[1] Cf. my *Industrial Fluctuations*, Part I. chapter ix.

is for some purposes important to distinguish between relative variations in which the demands in both occupations have moved in the same direction and relative variations in which one demand has risen and the other fallen. *Where wage earners maintain rigid rates of wages in the face of falling demand*, it will be possible for those displaced from a depressed industry to find employment in an expanded one, but not possible for them to find employment in one which, though less depressed, is itself depressed in some degree. To eliminate obstacles to movement—provided that the expense of doing this were not too great—would, therefore, help the national dividend in the first case, but would have no effect upon it in the second.

§ 8. In conclusion it should be noted that relative variations in the demand for productive resources, whether between places or between occupations, may be expected to have different effects according as they take place rapidly or slowly. If one occupation or place declines slowly while another expands slowly, adjustment may be made to the new conditions without it being necessary for any actual transfer of resources to take place between them. All that need happen is that in the declining occupation or place, capital, as it wears out, and workpeople, as they retire or die, are not fully replaced; while newly created capital and young men and women coming to industrial age are turned into the expanding place or occupation to the extent required to fit the enlarged demand. In these conditions, no actual transfer of capital or labour being required, obstacles in the way of transfer do no harm to the national dividend. When, however, relative variations of demand take place rapidly, adjustment cannot be fully made in the way described, and, if it is to be made, actual transfers must take place. Here, therefore, obstacles to movement necessarily injure the dividend, and the elimination of them (if this could be accomplished without too great cost) would benefit it. Where exactly the line between "gradual" and "rapid" relative variations lies from the standpoint of this discussion, depends on the rates at which, in the occupations and places concerned, capital equipment normally decays and the labour force normally requires replacement. As will be observed presently in another connection, the proportion of the annual flow to total stock is, in general, much larger among women workers than among men workers.[1]

[1] Cf. *post*, Part III. Chapter IX. § 6.

CHAPTER IX

§ 1. In general industrialists are interested, not in the social,
but only in the private, net product of their operations.
Subject to what was said in Chapter V. about costs of movement, self-interest will tend to bring about equality in the values
of the marginal private net products of resources invested in
different ways. But it will not tend to bring about equality in
the values of the marginal social net products except when
marginal private net product and marginal social net product
are identical. When there is a divergence between these two
sorts of marginal net products, self-interest will not, therefore,
tend to make the national dividend a maximum; and, consequently, certain specific acts of interference with normal
economic processes may be expected, not to diminish, but to
increase the dividend. It thus becomes important to inquire
in what conditions the values of the social net product and
the private net product of any given (r^{th}) increment of
investment in an industry are liable to diverge from one
another in either direction. There are certain general sorts
of divergence that are found even under conditions of simple
competition, certain additional sorts that may be introduced
under conditions of monopolistic competition, and yet others
that may be introduced under conditions of bilateral monopoly.

§ 2. If there existed only one type of productive resource,
say, labour of a given quality, this statement of the issues
would be complete. It would also be complete if several types
of productive resources existed, but they were everywhere and
in all circumstances combined together in exactly the same

proportions. In real life there are a number of different types of resource and they are combined in various proportions, not only in different industries, but in the same industry in respect of different quantities of output. Hence the expression "the rth increment of investment in an industry," which was employed in the preceding section, calls for further elucidation. In a given industry y units of output are produced as a result of the joint operations of a, b and c (physical) units of three types of productive resource, or factors of production. When the output of the industry is increased to $(y + \Delta y)$, the quantities of the several factors become a', b' and c'. There being no reason to suppose that $\dfrac{a' - a}{a}$, $\dfrac{b' - b}{b}$ and $\dfrac{c' - c}{c}$ will be equal, it is impossible to describe unambiguously the change in the quantities of productive resources taken collectively that has led to a given change in the output of the commodity. If, therefore, the rth increment of investment is to have a precise meaning, it must be interpreted as the rth (physical) increment of some one sort of productive resource (*e.g.* labour of a given quality) *plus* whatever additions to the quantities of the other sorts *properly go with* that increment. These quantities are perfectly definite, being determined by the condition that, in respect of any given quantity of output, the various factors of production must be combined in such wise as to make their aggregate money cost a minimum.[1] The above definition appears at first sight objectionable, because under it the rth "unit" of investment is, in general, of different physical constitution from the $(r + h)^{\text{th}}$ "unit." This objection would, of course, be fatal if we were concerned to compare the net products of different increments or units of investment. But in fact we are concerned to compare two sorts of net product —social and private as yielded by *given increments of investment*. For this purpose the relation in which different incre-

---

[1] Thus, let y be the output of the commodity in question, and a, b, c the (physical) quantities of the several factors of production combined in making it. Then $y = \mathrm{F}(a,b,c)$. Let $f_1(a)$, $f_2(b)$ and $f_3(c)$ be the prices of these factors. Then, in respect of any quantity of output, the quantities of the several factors are determined by the equations

$$\frac{1}{f_1(a)} \cdot \frac{\partial \mathrm{F}(a,b,c)}{\partial a} = \frac{1}{f_2(b)} \cdot \frac{\partial \mathrm{F}(a,b,c)}{\partial b} = \frac{1}{f_3(c)} \cdot \frac{\partial \mathrm{F}(a,b,c)}{\partial c}.$$

ments, or different "units," stand to one another is irrelevant.
Our definition simply removes an ambiguity, and enables us
to proceed unhampered with the line of analysis outlined in
the preceding section.

§ 3. The source of the general divergences between the
values of marginal social and marginal private net product that
occur under simple competition is the fact that, in some occupations, a part of the product of a unit of resources consists of
something, which, instead of coming in the first instance to
the person who invests the unit, comes instead, in the first
instance (*i.e.* prior to sale if sale takes place), as a positive or
negative item, to other people. These other people may fall
into any one of three principal groups : (1) the owners of
durable instruments of production, of which the investor is a
tenant ; (2) persons who are not producers of the commodity
in which the investor is investing ; (3) persons who are
producers of this commodity. The divergences between the
values of social and private net product that are liable to arise
in respect of this last class of persons will be discussed
separately in Chapter XI. In the present chapter attention
is confined to the other two classes of divergence.

§ 4. Let us consider first the class connected with the
separation between tenancy and ownership of certain durable
instruments of production. The extent to which the actual
owners of durable instruments leave the work of maintaining
and improving them to temporary occupiers varies, of course,
in different industries, and is largely determined by considerations of technical convenience. It also depends in
part upon tradition and custom, and is further liable to vary
in different places with the comparative wealth of the owners
and the occupiers. It appears, for example, that in Ireland,
owing to the poverty of many landlords, the kinds of expenditure on land which they leave wholly to their tenants are
more numerous than in England.[1] Details thus vary, but
there can be no doubt that over a wide field some part of
the investment designed to improve durable instruments
of production is often made by persons other than their
owners. Whenever this happens, some divergence between

[1] Cf. Bonn, *Modern Ireland*, p. 63.

the private and the social net product of this investment is liable to occur, and is larger or smaller in extent according to the terms of the contract between lessor and lessee. These terms we have now to consider.

§ 5. The social net product of an assigned dose of investment being given, the private net product will fall short of it by an especially large amount under a system which merely provides for the return of the instrument to the owner at the end of the lease in the condition in which the instrument then happens to be. Under this arrangement the private net product of any r^{th} increment of investment falls short of the social net product by nearly the whole of the deferred benefit which would be conferred upon the instrument. It need not fall short of it by quite the whole of this deferred benefit, because a tenant, who is known to leave hired instruments in good condition, is likely to obtain them more easily and on better terms than one who is known not to do this. So far, careful tenancy yields an element of private, as well as of social, net product. Since, however, separate contracts are often made at considerable intervals of time, this qualification is not especially important. Passing it over, therefore, we notice that, since the effects of investment in improving and maintaining instruments generally exhaust themselves after a while, the contraction of private net product below social net product, which the form of tenancy just described brings about, is not likely to be considerable in the earlier years of a long lease. In the later years of such a lease, however, and during the whole period of a short lease, it may be very considerable. Indeed, it is often found that, towards the close of his tenancy, a farmer, in the natural and undisguised endeavour to get back as much of his capital as possible, takes so much out of the land that, for some years afterwards, the yield is markedly reduced.[1]

§ 6. The form of tenancy just described is illustrated by that primitive type of contract between landlord and tenant, in which nothing is said about the condition of the land at the end of the lease. But it is by no means

[1] Cf. Nicholson, *Principles of Economics*, vol. i. p. 418.

confined to this type of contract. Another very important field in which it is present is that of "concessions" to gas companies, electric lighting companies and so forth. An arrangement, under which the plant of a concessionaire company passes ultimately, without compensation, into the hands of the town chartering it, corresponds exactly to the system of land leases without provision for compensation for tenants' improvements. Such an arrangement at one time governed the Berlin Tramways. The Company's charter provided that, "at the end of the contract, all property of the road located in the city streets, including poles, wires, any waiting-rooms built on city property, and patents, come into the possession of the city without charge." [1] From the present point of view, this system is similar to that of the British Tramways Act of 1870 and Electric Lighting Act of 1881, which provided for the taking over of the company's plant "upon terms of paying the then value (exclusive of any allowance for past or future profits of the undertaking, or any compensation for compulsory sale or other consideration whatever)." For the "reproduction cost," which value in .this sense seems to represent, of a concern established many years back might be expected to fall far short of its value as a going concern. It follows that, under the German and English plans alike, the terminating franchise system must, unless some plan is adopted to obviate that result,[2] reduce the private net product of investments, alike in the original plant and in later extensions, below their social net product, thus causing them to be carried less far than the best interests of the national dividend require. Furthermore, it is obvious that the restrictive

---

[1] Beamish, *Municipal Problems*, p. 565.

[2] Of course, the English plan is not so severe as the German in respect of investments in plant made near the end of the lease ; for, presumably, for a short time the cost of manufacturing such plant will remain fairly constant. But for investments designed to create goodwill, and, through this, future business, it is exactly similar. Thus, after the agreement of 1905, by which the Post Office undertook to buy up in 1911 such part of the National Telephone Company's plant as proved suitable, at the cost of replacement, the Chairman of the Company stated that "the Company would not attempt to build up business that would require nursing as well as time to develop; it would confine itself to operations that from the start would pay interest and all other proper charges " (H. Meyer, *Public Ownership and the Telephones*, p. 309). A device for getting over the difficulty considered in the text was embodied in

influence will be most marked towards the close of the concession period. In view of this fact, M. Colson recommends a policy, under which negotiations for the renewal of concession charters would be taken up some 15 or 20 years before these charters are due to expire.[1]

§ 7. The deficiency of the private, as compared with the social, net product of any r^{th} increment of investment, which arises in connection with what I have called the primitive type of tenancy contracts, can be mitigated in various degrees by compensation schemes. These may conveniently be illustrated from the recent history of land tenure. Arrangements can be made for compensating tenants, when they leave their holdings, for whatever injury or benefit they may have caused to the land. Negative compensation for injury is practically everywhere provided for in the terms of the leases. In its simplest form it consists in monetary penalties for failure on the part of tenants to return their land to the owner in "tenantable repair." These penalties may be made operative directly, through an explicit legal contract; or they may be made operative indirectly, by a rule forbidding the tenant to depart from the local customs of husbandry; or, again, they may be made operative through a modification in this rule concerning local customs, so arranged as to free enterprising tenants from the burden which the rule in its simple form imposes, without sacrificing the purpose of the rule. Thus, under the Agricultural

the contract extending the franchise of the Berlin Tramway Company to 1919. This contract provided, *inter alia* : "If, during the life of the contract, the city authorities require extensions within the city limits, which are not specified in the contract, the company must build as much as 93 miles, double track being counted as single. But the company should receive from the city one-third of the cost of construction of all lines ordered between Jan. 1, 1902, and Jan. 1, 1907 ; and one-half of the cost on all lines ordered between Jan. 1, 1908, and Jan. 1, 1914. For all lines ordered after that the city must pay the full costs of construction, or a full allowance towards the cost of operation, as determined by later agreement. The overhead trolley was to be employed at first, except where the city demanded storage batteries ; but, if any other motor system should later prove practicable and in the judgment of the city authorities should appear more suitable, the company may introduce it ; and, if the city authorities request, the company must introduce it. If increased cost accrue to the company thereby, due allowance being made for benefits obtained from the new system, the city must indemnify the company " (Beamish, *Municipal Problems,* p. 563).

[1] Cf. Colson, *Cours d'économie politique,* vol. vi. p. 419.

Holdings Act, 1906, a tenant may depart from local custom, or even from a contract, as to cropping arable land, provided that he shall make " suitable and adequate provision to protect the holding from injury or deterioration "—except in the year before the expiration of the contract of tenancy. If the tenant's action under this section does injure the holding, the landlord is entitled to recover damages and to obtain, if necessary, an injunction against the continuance of the tenant's conduct. Positive compensation was of some-what later growth. Rules about it were at first a matter of voluntary arrangement in the yearly leases made by landlords. Mr. Taylor quotes a Yorkshire lease, in which the landlord covenants to allow the tenant " what two different persons shall deem reasonable," in payment for the capital put into the land in the course of ordinary farming operations during the last two years of the lease.[1] Gradually compensation schemes have been given a legal status. Something in this direction was done in Ireland under the Act of 1870—the need for it being specially great in a country where the English custom, under which the landlord provides the buildings and permanent improvements, seldom applied.[2] In 1875 an Act laying down conditions for compensating the outgoing tenant in England and Wales was passed, but contracting-out was permitted. In 1883 a new Act, the Agricultural Holdings Act, was passed, in which contracting-out was forbidden. This Act distinguished between improvements for which the landlord's consent was necessary and those for which it was not necessary.[3] Scotland is now under a similar Act. It has largely superseded the old long leases, and these are now practically being modified out of existence.[4] In the detailed drafting of all Acts of this class difficulty is caused by the fact that some " improvements " do not add to the enduring value of the estate the equivalent of their cost of production. If the compensation for these improve-ments is based upon their cost, the private net product is raised above the social net product. In practice this danger

---

[1] Cf. Taylor, *Agricultural Economics*, p. 305.

[2] Cf. Smith-Gordon and Staples, *Rural Reconstruction in Ireland*, p. 20.

[3] Cf. Taylor, *Agricultural Economics*, pp. 313 *et seq.*

[4] Cf. Taylor, *ibid.* p. 320.

is largely overcome by the rejection of initial cost as a basis of compensation value, coupled with the requirement of the landlord's consent to some kinds of improvement. Under the Town Tenants (Ireland) Act, 1906, for example, when a tenant proposes to make an improvement he must give notice to the landlord, and, if the latter objects, the question, whether the improvement is reasonable and will add to the letting value of the holding, is determined by the County Court. The British Landlord and Tenant Act (1927) contains a similar provision for compensation for improvements and goodwill on the termination of tenancies of business premises. But even on this plan the private net product may be slightly in excess. In order that private and social net product may coalesce, the value of an improvement, for compensation purposes, should in strictness be estimated subject to the fact that, at interchanges of tenants, the land may stand for a time unlet, and that during this time the improvement is not likely to yield its full annual value. If this is not done, it will pay a tenant to press investment slightly—very slightly—further than it will pay either the landlord or society to have it pressed; and hence, where, as in market-gardening, improvements can be made without the landlord's consent, it will check landlords from letting land. It is, thus, theoretically an error in the Agricultural Holdings Act of 1906, that it defines the compensation, which an outgoing tenant may claim for improvements, as " such sum as fairly represents the value of the improvements to an incoming tenant." The standard ought to be " the value to the landlord." But, when, as is usual, improvements exhaust themselves in a few years, the practical effect of this slight error is negligible, and does not cause the private and social net products of any r^{th} increment of investment to diverge appreciably.

§ 8. These compensation arrangements, as so far considered, possess one obvious weakness, which generally impedes the adjustment they are designed to effect between private and social net product. It is true that a tenant can claim compensation for improvements on quitting. But he knows that the rent may be raised against him on the strength of his improvements, and his compensation claim does not come into force unless he takes the extreme step of giving up his farm.   Hence the private net product of investment is still contracted below the social net product.   This result is partially mitigated under the Agricultural Holdings Act of 1906— somewhat strengthened in 1920—where it is provided that: "When the landlord, without good and sufficient cause, and for reasons inconsistent with good estate management, terminates a tenancy by notice to quit," or when the tenant leaves in consequence of a proved demand for increased rent consequent upon tenants' improvements, the tenant may claim, not merely compensation for the improvements, but also "compensation for the loss or expense directly attributable to his quitting the holding," in connection with the sale or removal of household goods, implements of husbandry, and so forth.   The above remedy is, however, defective in several respects.   In the first place, since a tenant quitting his holding under the conditions contemplated obtains no compensation for the loss of "good-will" or the non-monetary inconveniences of a change of home, he will still be very unwilling to leave, and the landlord will still possess a powerful weapon with which to force him to consent to an increase of rent.   In the second place, notice to quit on account of sale is not held to be "incompatible with good estate management."   Consequently, when the land farmed by a sitting tenant is sold by one landlord to another, the tenant, if he leaves, obtains no secondary compensation of the kind just described.   He will, therefore, be even more unwilling to leave.   Should he elect, however, to rent the farm under the new landlord, he "is liable to the rent on any improvement which he has executed, without receiving any compensation."[1]   It is probably a recognition of this danger that has given rise to the growing demand among farmers for legislation permitting them, when the landlord wishes to sell,

[1] *Report of the Committee on Tenant Farmers* [Cd. 6030], p. 6.   Notice given to a sitting tenant on the ground that his land is wanted for building is also "not incompatible with good husbandry" and carries no secondary compensation. There would plainly be danger in the grant of such compensation here, since it would encourage the investment of resources in agricultural improvements at the cost of a *more than equivalent* social injury in postponing the use for building of land that has become ripe for it.

to purchase their holdings on the basis of the old rent. A provision for secondary compensation on disturbance similar to that of the Agricultural Holdings Act is contained in the Town Tenants (Ireland) Act, 1906. Here, under the circumstances specified, compensation may also be claimed for "goodwill." But even with this provision it is apparent that the adjustment secured cannot be more than partial.[1]

§ 9. In view of these imperfections in compensation arrangements, it is often contended, in effect, that for a really adequate adjustment, not merely compensation for tenants vacating their holdings, but legal security of tenure, coupled with the legal prohibition of renting tenants' improvements, is required. Of course, in some circumstances the state of things which this policy is designed to bring about is attained without any legislative intervention. In Belgium, for example, it is substantially established everywhere by the force of custom :[2] and, no doubt, many English landlords conduct the management of their estates in a like spirit. It is plain, however, that the willingness of landlords to refrain from using economic power for their own advantage, when the use of this power is permitted by law, cannot always be assumed; indeed, if it could be assumed, the whole elaborate development of compensation laws, which we have been discussing, would have been unnecessary. We are thus led forward to a consideration of the policy of legally enforced security of tenure *plus* "fair rents." In the way of this policy there are two principal difficulties. In the first place, the security of tenure that is granted cannot be absolute; for, if it were, considerable economic waste might sometimes result. It would appear, therefore, that security must be conditional upon reasonably good farming. Furthermore, it must be "conditional upon the land not being required in the public

---

[1] The argument for compensation, it should be noted, is not that it would benefit the tenant. Professor Nicholson is right when he observes "that compensation for improvements will not benefit the tenant so much as is generally supposed, because the privilege itself will have a pecuniary value ; that is to say, a landlord will demand, and the tenant can afford to give, a higher rent in proportion. Under the old improving leases, as they were called, the rent was low because ultimately the permanent improvements were to go to the landlord " (*Principles of Economics*, vol. i. p. 322). Cf. Morison's account of Indian arrangements (*The Industrial Organisation of an Indian Province*, pp. 154-5). [2] Cf. Rowntree, *Land and Labour*, p. 129.

interest, whether for small holdings, allotments, labourers'
cottages, urban development, the working of minerals, or the
making of water-courses, roads and sanitary works.   When it
is required for any of these purposes the Land Court should
have the power to terminate the tenancy, while ensuring
adequate compensation to the tenant." [1]   The precise drafting
of appropriate conditions is not likely to prove altogether easy.
In the second place, security of tenure being plainly illusory
if the landlord can force the tenant to give notice by arbitrary
increases of rent, it is necessary that fair rents be somehow
enforced.   This cannot be done by a mere prohibition of *any*
increases of rent, for in some circumstances an increase would
be fair.   There would be no justice, for example, in taking from
the landlord and giving to the tenant the benefit of an addition
to the value of the land brought about by some general change
in agricultural prices wholly independent of the tenant's action.
Hence this policy seems to involve the setting up of a tribunal
to fix rents, or, at all events, to settle disputes about rents,
when invoked for that purpose.   Were the Land Court, or
whatever the body set up may be, omniscient and all-wise,
there would, indeed, be no objection to this.   But, in view of
the necessary imperfection of all human institutions, there is
some danger that a tenant may be tempted deliberately to let
down the value of his holding in the hope of obtaining a
reduced rent.   Under the Irish system of judicial rents, a
defence against this abuse was nominally provided in the form
of permission to the Courts to refuse revision.   But this
remedy was not utilised in practice.   Very often "not productivity, but production, and more especially the evidences of
production in the fifteenth year, were the determining factors"
in rent revision. [2]   Professor Bonn illustrates the result thus :
"Two brothers divided a farm into two shares of equal values
—the good husbandman got a rent reduction from the Courts
of $7\frac{1}{2}$ per cent, the bad got one of $17\frac{1}{2}$ per cent." [3]   It is not,
therefore, by any means obvious that the policy of fixity of
tenure and judicial rents will really bring marginal private net

[1] *Land Enquiry Report*, p. 378.
[2] Smith-Gordon and Staples, *Rural Reconstruction in Ireland*, p. 24.
[3] Bonn, *Modern Ireland*, p. 113.

product and marginal social net product more closely together than they are brought by simple compensation laws. The gap between the two marginal net products can only be completely closed if the person who owns the land and the person who makes investments in it are the same. But this arrangement is frequently uneconomic in other ways. For, especially if the farmers are small men, they are likely, as owners, to find much difficulty in raising the capital required for those larger improvements, which, under the English land-system, it is now usual for the landlord to undertake. It is beyond the scope of this volume to attempt a detailed discussion of the controversial topics thus opened up. What has been said, however, will suffice to illustrate one type of discrepancy between marginal private net product and marginal social net product, that is liable to arise in occupations where resources have to be invested in durable instruments by persons who do not own the instruments.

§ 10. I now turn to the second class of divergence between social and private net product which was distinguished in § 3. Here the essence of the matter is that one person A, in the course of rendering some service, for which payment is made, to a second person B, incidentally also renders services or disservices to other persons (not producers of like services), of such a sort that payment cannot be exacted from the benefited parties or compensation enforced on behalf of the injured parties. If we were to be pedantically loyal to the definition of the national dividend given in Chapter III. of Part I., it would be necessary to distinguish further between industries in which the uncompensated benefit or burden respectively is and is not one that can be readily brought into relation with the measuring rod of money. This distinction, however, would be of formal rather than of real importance, and would obscure rather than illuminate the main issues. I shall, therefore, in the examples I am about to give, deliberately pass it over.

Among these examples we may set out first a number of instances in which marginal private net product falls short of marginal social net product, because incidental services are performed to third parties from whom it is technically

difficult to exact payment. Thus, as Sidgwick observes,
" it may easily happen that the benefits of a well-placed light-
house must be largely enjoyed by ships on which no toll
could be conveniently levied." [1]   Again, uncompensated
services are rendered when resources are invested in private
parks in cities; for these, even though the public is not
admitted to them, improve the air of the neighbourhood.
The same thing is true—though here allowance should be
made for a detriment elsewhere—of resources invested
in roads and tramways that increase the value of the
adjoining land—except, indeed, where a special betterment
rate, corresponding to the improvements they enjoy, is levied
on the owners of this land.   It is true, in like manner, of
resources devoted to afforestation, since the beneficial effect
on climate often extends beyond the borders of the estates
owned by the person responsible for the forest.   It is true
also of resources invested in lamps erected at the doors of
private houses, for these necessarily throw light also on the
streets.[2]   It is true of resources devoted to the prevention
of smoke from factory chimneys: [3] for this smoke in large
towns inflicts a heavy uncharged loss on the community, in
injury to buildings and vegetables, expenses for washing
clothes and cleaning rooms, expenses for the provision of
extra artificial light, and in many other ways.[4]   Lastly and

[1] *Principles of Political Economy*, p. 406.

[2] Cf. Smart, *Studies in Economics*, p. 314.

[3] It has been said that in London, owing to the smoke, there is only 12
per cent as much sunlight as is astronomically possible, and that one fog in five
is directly caused by smoke alone, while all the fogs are befouled and prolonged
by it (J. W. Graham, *The Destruction of Daylight*, pp. 6 and 24).   It would
seem that mere ignorance and inertia prevent the adoption of smoke-preventing
appliances in many instances where, through the addition they would make
to the efficiency of fuel, they would be directly profitable to the users.   The
general interest, however, requires that these devices should be employed beyond
the point at which they "pay."   There seems no doubt that, by means of
mechanical stokers, hot-air blasts and other arrangements, factory chimneys can
be made practically smokeless.   Noxious fumes from alkali works are suppressed
by the law more vigorously than smoke (*ibid.* p. 126).

[4] Thus the Interim Report of the Departmental Committee on smoke and
Noxious Vapours Abatement 1920 contains the following passages :

" 17. *Actual economic loss Due to Coal Smoke.*—It is impossible to arrive at
any complete and exact statistical statement of the amount of damage
occasioned to the whole community by smoke.   We may, however, quote the
following investigations.

" A report on an exhaustive investigation conducted by an expert Committee

most important of all, it is true of resources devoted alike to the fundamental problems of scientific research, out of which, in unexpected ways, discoveries of high practical utility often grow, and also to the perfecting of inventions and improvements in industrial processes. These latter are often of such a nature that they can neither be patented nor kept secret, and, therefore, the whole of the extra reward, which they at first bring to their inventor, is very quickly transferred from him to the general public in the form of reduced prices. The patent laws aim, in effect, at bringing marginal private net product and marginal social net product more closely together. By offering the prospect of reward for certain types of invention they do not, indeed, appreciably stimulate inventive activity, which is, for the most part, spontaneous, but they do direct it into channels of general usefulness.[1]

Corresponding to the above investments in which marginal private net product falls short of marginal social net product, there are a number of others, in which, owing to the technical difficulty of enforcing compensation for incidental disservices, marginal private net product is greater than marginal social net product. Thus, incidental uncharged disservices are rendered to third parties when the game-preserving activities of one occupier involve the overrunning of a neighbouring occupier's land by rabbits—unless, indeed, the two occupiers stand in the relation of landlord and tenant, so that compensation is given in an adjustment of the rent. They are rendered, again, when the owner of a site in a residential quarter of a city builds a factory there and so destroys a great

---

of engineers, architects, and scientists in 1912 in Pittsburgh, U.S.A., estimated the cost of the smoke nuisance to Pittsburgh at approximately £4 per head of the population per annum.

"18. A valuable investigation was made in 1918 by the Manchester Air Pollution Advisory Board into the comparative cost of household washing in Manchester—a smoky town—as compared with Harrogate—a clean town. The investigator obtained 100 properly comparable statements for Manchester and Harrogate respectively as to the cost of the weekly washing in working-class houses. These showed an extra cost in Manchester of 7½d. a week per household for fuel and washing material. The total loss for the whole city, taking the extra cost of fuel and washing materials alone, disregarding the extra labour involved, and assuming no greater loss for middle-class than for working-class households (a considerable under-statement), works out at over £290,000 a year for a population of three quarters of a million."

[1] Cf. Taussig, *Inventors and Money Makers*, p. 51.

part of the amenities of the neighbouring sites; or, in a less
degree, when he uses his site in such a way as to spoil
the lighting of the houses opposite:[1] or when he invests
resources in erecting buildings in a crowded centre, which,
by contracting the air space and the playing-room of the
neighbourhood, tend to injure the health and efficiency of the
families living there. Yet again, third parties—this time
the public in general—suffer incidental uncharged disservices
from resources invested in the running of motor cars that wear
out the surface of the roads. The case is similar—the
conditions of public taste being assumed—with resources
devoted to the production and sale of intoxicants. To enable
the social net product to be inferred from the private net
product of the marginal pound invested in this form of
production, the investment should, as Mr. Bernard Shaw
observes, be debited with the extra costs in policemen and
prisons which it indirectly makes necessary.[2] Exactly similar
considerations hold good in some measure of foreign investment in general. For, if foreigners can obtain some of the
exports they need from us by selling promises, they will not
have to send so many goods; which implies that the ratio of
interchange between our exports and our imports will become
slightly less favourable to us. For certain sorts of foreign
investments more serious reactions come into account. Thus,
when the indirect effect of an increment of investment made
abroad, or of the diplomatic manœuvres employed in securing
the concession for it, is an actual war or preparations to
guard against war, the cost of these things ought to be
deducted from any interest that the increment yields before
its net contribution to the national dividend is calculated.
When this is done, the marginal social net product even of
investments, which, as may often happen in countries where
highly profitable openings are still unworked and hard bargains
can be driven with corrupt officials, yield a very high return
to the investors, may easily turn out to be negative. Yet

[1] In Germany the town-planning schemes of most cities render anti-social
action of this kind impossible; but in America individual site-owners appear to
be entirely free, and in England to be largely free, to do what they will with
their land. (Cf. Howe, *European Cities at Work*, pp. 46, 95 and 346.)

[2] *The Common Sense of Municipal Trading*, pp. 19-20.

again, when the investment consists in a loan to a foreign government and makes it possible for that government to engage in a war which otherwise would not have taken place, the indirect loss which Englishmen in general suffer, in consequence of the world impoverishment caused by the war, should be debited against the interest which English financiers receive.   Here, too, the marginal social net product may well be negative.   Perhaps, however, the crowning illustration of this order of excess of private over social net product is afforded by the work done by women in factories, particularly during the periods immediately preceding and succeeding confinement ; for there can be no doubt that this work often carries with it, besides the earnings of the women themselves, grave injury to the health of their children.[1]   The reality of this evil is not disproved by the low, even negative, correlation which sometimes is found to exist between the factory work of mothers and the rate of infantile mortality.   For in districts where women's work of this kind prevails there is presumably—and this is the cause of the women's work—great poverty.   This poverty, which is obviously injurious to children's health, is likely, other things being equal, to be greater than elsewhere in families where the mother declines factory work, and it may be that the evil of the extra poverty is greater than that of the factory work.[2]   This consideration explains the statistical facts that are known.   They, therefore, militate in no way against the view that, *other things equal*, the factory work of mothers is injurious.   All that they tend to show is that prohibition of such work should be accompanied

[1] Cf. Hutchins, *Economic Journal*, 1908, p. 227.

[2] Cf. Newsholme, *Second Report on Infant and Child Mortality* [Cd. 6909], p. 56.   Similar considerations to the above hold good of night work by boys. The *Departmental Committee on Night Employment* did not, indeed, obtain any strong evidence that this work injures the boys' health.   But they found that it reacts injuriously on their efficiency in another way, *i.e.* by practically precluding them from going on with their education in continuation classes and so forth.   The *theory* of our factory laws appears to be that boys between 14 and 18 should only be permitted to work at night upon continuous processes of such a kind that great loss would result if they did not do so.   The *practice* of these laws, however, permits them to be employed at night on unnecessary non-continuous processes which are carried out in the same factory as continuous processes. Consequently, the Committee recommend that in future "such permits should be granted in terms of processes, and not of premises, factories, or parts of factories without reference to processes" ([Cd. 6503], p. 17).

by relief to those families whom the prohibition renders necessitous.[1]

§ 11. At this point it is desirable to call attention to a somewhat specious fallacy. Some writers unaccustomed to mathematical analysis have imagined that, when improved methods of producing some commodities are introduced, the value of the marginal social net product of the resources invested in developing these methods is less than the value of the marginal private net product, because there is not included in the latter any allowance for the depreciation which the improvement causes in the value of existing plant; and, as they hold, in order to arrive at the value of the marginal social net product, such allowance ought to be included.[2] If this view were correct, reason would be shown for attempts to make the authorisation of railways dependent on the railway companies compensating existing canals, for refusals to license motor omnibuses in the interests of municipal tramways, and for the placing of hindrances in the way of electric lighting enterprises in order to conserve the contribution made to the rates by municipal gas companies. But in fact the view is not correct. The marginal social net product of resources devoted to *improved methods of producing a given commodity* is not, in general, different from the marginal private net product; for whatever loss the old producers suffer through a reduction in the price of their products is balanced by the gain which the reduction confers upon the purchasers of these products. This is obvious if, after the new investment has been made, the old

---

[1] Cf. *Annual Report of the Local Government Board*, 1909-10, p. 57. The suggestion that the injurious consequences of the factory work of mothers can be done away with, if the factory worker gets some unmarried woman to look after her home in factory hours, is mistaken, because it ignores the fact that a woman's work has a special personal value in respect of her own children. In Birmingham this fact seems to be recognised, for, after a little experience of the bad results of putting their children out to "mind," married women are apt, it was said before the war, to leave the factory and take to home work. (Cf. Cadbury, *Women's Work*, p. 175.)

[2] For example, J. A. Hobson, *Sociological Review*, July 1911, p. 197, and *Gold, Prices and Wages*, pp. 107-8. Even Sidgwick might be suspected of countenancing the argument set out in the text (cf. *Principles of Political Economy*, p. 408). It does not seem to have been noticed that this argument, if valid, would justify the State in prohibiting the use of new machinery that dispenses with the services of skilled mechanics until the generation of mechanics possessing that skill has been depleted by death.

machines continue to produce the same output as before at reduced prices. If the production of the old machines is diminished on account of the change, it seems at first sight doubtful. Reflection, however, makes it plain that no unit formerly produced by the old machinery will be supplanted by one produced by the new machinery, except when the new machinery can produce it at a *total cost* smaller than the *prime cost* that would have been involved in its production with the old machinery : except, that is to say, when it can produce it at a price so low that the old machinery would have earned nothing by producing it at that price. This implies that every unit taken over by the new machinery from the old is sold to the public at a price *reduced* by as much as the whole of the net receipts, after discharging prime costs, which the old machinery would have obtained from it if it had produced that unit. It is thus proved that there is no loss to the owners of the old machines, in respect of any unit of their former output, that is not offset by an equivalent gain to consumers. It follows that to count the loss to these owners, in respect of any unit taken over from them by the new machinery, as a part of the social cost of producing that unit would be incorrect.

An attempt to avoid this conclusion may, indeed, still be made. It may be granted that, so far as direct effects are concerned, ordinary commercial policy, under which investment in improved processes is not restrained by consideration for the earnings of other people's established plant, stands vindicated. There remain, however, indirect effects. If expensive plant is liable to have its earnings reduced at short notice by new inventions, will not the building of such plant be hindered ? Would not the introduction of improved processes on the whole be stimulated, if they were in some way guaranteed against too rapid obsolescence through the competition of processes yet further improved ? The direct answer to this question is, undoubtedly, yes. On the other side, however, has to be set the fact that the policy proposed would retain inferior methods in use when superior methods were available. Whether gain or loss on the whole would result from these two influences in combination, is a question to which it seems difficult to give any confident answer. But this impotent conclusion is not the last word. The argument so far has assumed that the rapidity with which improvements are invented is independent of the rapidity of their practical adoption ; and it is on the basis of that assumption that our comparison of rival policies fails to attain a definite result. As a matter of fact, however, improvements are much more likely to be made at any time, if the best methods previously discovered are being employed and, therefore, watched in actual operation, than if they are being held up in the interest of established plant. Hence the holding-up policy indirectly delays, not merely the adoption of improvements that have been invented, but also the invention of new improvements. This circumstance almost certainly turns the balance. The policy proper to ordinary competitive industry is, therefore, in general and on the whole, of greater social advantage than the rival policy. It is not to the interest of the community that business men, contemplating the introduction of improved methods, should take account of the loss which forward action on their part threatens to other business men. The example of some municipalities in postponing the erection of electric-lighting plant till their gas plant is worn out is not one that should be imitated, nor one that can be successfully defended by reference to the distinction between social and private net products. The danger that beneficial advances may be checked by unwise resistance on the part of interested municipal councils is recognised in this country in the rules empowering the central authority to override attempts at local vetoes against private electrical enterprise. The policy followed by the Board of Trade is illustrated by the following extract from their report on the Ardrossan, Saltcoats and District Electric Lighting Order of 1910 : " As the policy of the Board has been to hold that objection on the grounds of competition with a gas undertaking, even when belonging to a local authority, is not sufficient reason to justify them in refusing to grant an Electric Lighting Order, the Board decided to dispense with the consent of the Corporation of Ardrossan." [1]

§ 12. So far we have considered only those divergences

---

[1] Cf. Knoop, *Principles and Methods of Municipal Trading*, p. 35.

between private and social net products that come about through
the existence of uncompensated services and uncharged disservices, the general conditions of popular taste being tacitly
assumed to remain unchanged.   This is in accordance with
the definition of social net product given in Chapter II. § 5.
As was there indicated, however, it is, for some purposes,
desirable to adopt a wider definition.   When this is done, we
observe that a further element of divergence between social
and private net products, important to economic welfare
though not to the actual substance of the national dividend,
may emerge in the form of uncompensated or uncharged
effects upon the *satisfaction that consumers derive from the
consumption of things other than the one directly affected.*
For the fact that some people are now able to consume
the new commodity may set up a psychological reaction
in other people, directly changing the amount of satisfaction
that they get from their consumption of the old commodity.
It is conceivable that the reaction may lead to an *increase*
in the satisfaction they obtain from this commodity, since
it may please them to make use of a thing just because it
is superseded and more or less archaic.   But, in general, the
reaction will be in the other direction.   For, in some measure,
people's affection for the best quality of anything is due simply
to the fact that it is the best quality ; and, when a new best,
superior to the old best, is created, that element of value in
the old best is destroyed.   Thus, if an improved form of motor
car is invented, an enthusiast who desires above all " the very
latest thing " will, for the future, derive scarcely any satisfaction from a car, the possession of which, before this new invention, afforded him intense pleasure.   In these circumstances
the marginal social net product of resources invested in producing the improved type is somewhat smaller than the
marginal private net product.[1]   It is *possible* that the introduction of electric lighting into a town may, in some very slight
degree, bring about this sort of psychological reaction in regard

[1] It should be noticed that the argument of the text may be applicable even
where the product formerly consumed is wholly superseded by the new rival,
and where, therefore, nobody is actually deriving diminished satisfaction from
the old product : for it may be that complete supersession would not have come
about unless people's desire for the old product had been reduced by the psycho-

to gas : and this possibility may provide a real defence, supplementary to the fallacious defence described in the preceding section, for the policy of municipalities in delaying the introduction of electricity. This valid defence, however, is almost certainly inadequate. The arguments actually employed in support of the view that municipalities should not permit competition with their gas plant are those described in the preceding section. They are, in general, independent of any reference to psychological reactions, and are, therefore, like the arguments which persons interested in canals brought against the authorisation of the early railways, wholly fallacious.

§ 13. It is plain that divergences between private and social net product of the kinds we have so far been considering cannot, like divergences due to tenancy laws, be mitigated by a modification of the contractual relation between any two contracting parties, because the divergence arises out of a service or disservice rendered to persons other than the contracting parties. It is, however, possible for the State, if it so chooses, to remove the divergence in any field by " extraordinary encouragements " or " extraordinary restraints " upon investments in that field. The most obvious forms which these encouragements and restraints may assume are, of course, those of bounties and taxes. Broad illustrations of the policy of intervention in both its negative and positive aspects are easily provided.

The private net product of any unit of investment is unduly large relatively to the social net product in the businesses of producing and distributing alcoholic drinks. Consequently, in nearly all countries, special taxes are placed upon these businesses. Marshall was in favour of treating in the same way resources devoted to the erection of buildings in crowded areas. He suggested, to a witness before the Royal Com-

logical reaction we have been contemplating. Furthermore, the preceding argument shows that inventions *may* actually diminish aggregate economic welfare ; for they may cause labour to be withdrawn from other forms of productive service to make a new variety of some article to supersede an old one, whereas, if there had been no invention, the old one would have continued in use and would have yielded as much economic satisfaction as the new one yields now. This is true, broadly speaking, of inventions of new weapons of war, so far as these are known to all nations, because it is of no advantage to one country to have improved armaments if its rivals have them also.

mission on Labour, "that every person putting up a house in a district that has got as closely populated as is good should be compelled to contribute towards providing free playgrounds."[1]   The principle is susceptible of general application.   It is employed, though in a very incomplete and partial manner, in the British levy of a petrol duty and a motor - car licence tax upon the users of motor cars, the proceeds of which are devoted to the service of the roads.[2]   It is employed again in an ingenious way in the National Insurance Act.   When the sickness rate in any district is exceptionally high, provision is made for throwing the consequent abnormal expenses upon employers, local authorities or water companies, if the high rate can be shown to be due to neglect or carelessness on the part of any of these bodies.   Some writers have thought that it might be employed in the form of a discriminating tax upon income derived from foreign investments.   But, since the element of disadvantage described in § 10 only belongs to some of these investments and not to others, this arrangement would not be a satisfactory one.   Moreover, foreign investment is already penalised to a considerable extent both by general ignorance of foreign conditions and by the fact that income earned abroad is frequently subjected to foreign income tax as well as to British income tax.

The private net product of any unit of investment is unduly small in industries, such as agriculture, which are supposed to yield the indirect service of developing citizens suitable for military training.   Partly for this reason agriculture in Germany was accorded the indirect bounty of protection.   A more extreme form of bounty, in which a governmental authority provides *all* the funds required, is given upon such services as the planning of towns, police administration, and, sometimes, the clearing of slum areas.   This type of bounty is also not

---

[1] *Royal Commission on Labour*, Q. 8665.

[2] The application of the principle is incomplete, because the revenue from these taxes, administered through the Road Board, must be devoted, "not to the ordinary road maintenance at all, however onerous it might be, but exclusively to the execution of new and specific road improvements" (Webb, *The King's Highway*, p. 250).   Thus, in the main, the motorist does not pay for the damage he does to the ordinary roads, but obtains in return for his payment an additional service useful to him rather than to the general public.

O

infrequently given upon the work of spreading information about improved processes of production in occupations where, owing to lack of appreciation on the part of potential beneficiaries, it would be difficult to collect a fee for undertaking that task.   Thus the Canadian Government has established a system, "by means of which any farmer can make inquiry, without even the cost of postage, about any matter relating to his business"; [1] and the Department of the Interior also sometimes provides, for a time, actual instruction in farming.[2]   Many Governments adopt the same principle in respect of information about Labour, by providing the services of Exchanges free of charge.   In the United Kingdom the various Agricultural Organisation Societies are voluntary organisations, providing a kindred type of bounty at their subscribers' expense.   An important part of their purpose is, in Sir Horace Plunkett's words, to bring freely "to the help of those whose life is passed in the quiet of the field the experience, which belongs to wider opportunities of observation and a larger acquaintance with commercial and industrial affairs." [3]   The Development Act of 1909, with its provision for grants towards scientific research, instruction, and experiment in agricultural science, follows the same lines.

It should be added that sometimes, when the inter-relations of the various private persons affected are highly complex, the Government may find it necessary to exercise some means of authoritative control in addition to providing a bounty.   Thus it is coming to be recognised as an axiom of government that, in every town, power must be held by some authority to limit the quantity of building permitted to a given area, to restrict the height to which houses may be carried, — for the erection of barrack dwellings may cause great overcrowding of area even though there is no overcrowding of rooms,[4]—and generally to control the building

[1] Mavor, *Report on the Canadian North-West*, p. 36.

[2] *Ibid.* p. 78.

[3] C. Webb, *Industrial Co-operation*, p. 149.

[4] Mr. Dawson believes that this type of overcrowding prevails to a considerable extent in German towns.   He writes : "The excessive width of the streets, insisted on by cast-iron regulations, adds greatly to the cost of house-building, and in order to recoup himself, and make the most of his profits, the builder begins to extend his house vertically instead of horizontally" (*Municipal Life*

activities of individuals. It is as idle to expect a well-planned town to result from the independent activities of isolated speculators as it would be to expect a satisfactory picture to result if each separate square inch were painted by an independent artist. No " invisible hand " can be relied on to produce a good arrangement of the whole from a combination of separate treatments of the parts. It is, therefore, necessary that an authority of wider reach should intervene and should tackle the collective problems of beauty, of air and of light, as those other collective problems of gas and water have been tackled. Hence, shortly before the war, there came into being, on the pattern of long previous German practice, Mr. Burns's extremely important town-planning Act. In this Act, for the first time, control over individual buildings, from the standpoint, not of individual structure, but of the structure of the town as a whole, was definitely conferred upon those town councils that are willing to accept the powers offered to them. Part II. of the Act begins : " A town-planning scheme may be made in accordance with the provisions of this Part of the Act as respects any land which is in course of development, or appears likely to be used for building purposes, with the general object of securing proper sanitary conditions, amenity, and convenience in connection with the laying out and use of the land, and of any neighbouring lands." The scheme may be worked out, as is the custom in Germany, many years in advance of actual building, thus laying down beforehand the lines of future development. Furthermore, it may, if desired, be extended to include land on which buildings have already been put up, and may provide "for the demolition or alteration of any buildings thereon, so far as may be necessary for carrying the scheme into effect." Finally, where local authorities are remiss in preparing a plan on their own initiative, power is given to the appropriate department of the central Government to order them to take action. There is ground for hope, however, that, so soon as people

and Government in Germany, pp. 163-4). Hence German municipalities now often control the height of buildings, providing a scale of permitted heights which decreases on passing from the centre to the outlying parts of a town.

become thoroughly familiarised with town-planning, local patriotism and inter-local emulation will make resort to pressure from above less and less necessary.

§ 14. So far we have been concerned with forms of divergence between social and private net products that are liable to occur even under conditions of simple competition. Where conditions of monopolistic competition [1]—competition, that is to say, between several sellers each producing a considerable proportion of the aggregate output—are present, the way is opened up for a new kind of investment. This consists in competitive advertisement directed to the sole purpose of transferring the demand for a given commodity from one source of supply to another.[2] There is, indeed, little opportunity for this as regards goods of a kind whose quality is uniform and, as with salt, lumber or grain, can be easily tested ; but, where quality cannot be easily tested, and especially where goods are sold in small quantities, which can readily be put into distinctive packages for the use of retail customers, there is plenty of opportunity.[3] Not all advertisement is, of course, strictly competitive. Some advertisement, on the contrary, fulfils a social purpose, in informing people of the existence of articles adapted to their tastes. Indeed, it has been said " that advertising is a necessary consequence of sale by description," and represents merely a segregated part of the complex work formerly done by those middlemen who exhibited, as well as sold, their goods.[4] Without it many useful articles, such as new machines, or useful services, such as that of life insurance, might not be brought at all to the notice of potential purchasers who have a real need for them. Furthermore, some advertisement serves to develop an entirely new set of wants on the part of consumers, the satisfaction of which involves a real addition to social well-being; and the development of which on a large scale at the same time enables the commodity that satisfies them to be produced on

[1] Cf. *post*, Part II. Ch. XV.

[2] Under simple competition, there is no purpose in this advertisement, because, *ex hypothesi*, the market will take, at the market price, as much as any one small seller wants to sell. Practically monopolistic competition comprises all forms of imperfect competition.

[3] Cf. Jenks and Clark, *The Trust Problem*, pp. 26-7.

[4] Cf. Shaw, *Quarterly Journal of Economics*, 1912, p. 743.

a large scale and, therefore, cheaply.[1]   Under this head it is possible to make out a case in favour of the peculiar system of advertisement arranged on behalf of the general body of its currant growers (without the mention of individual names) by the Greek Government:[2] though, of course, the development of a taste for currants is probably in part at the expense of the taste for something else.   It is not, however, necessary to my purpose to attempt an estimate of the proportion which strictly competitive advertisement bears to advertisement in the aggregate—an aggregate the cost of which has been put, for the United Kingdom, at eighty million pounds, and, for the world, at six hundred million pounds per annum.[3]   That a considerable part of the advertisement of the modern world is strictly competitive is plain.[4]   This is true alike of the more obvious forms, such as pictorial displays, newspaper paragraphs,[5] travellers, salesmen, and so on; and of the more subtle forms, such as a large exhibit of jewellery in the shop window, the according of credit, with the consequential expenditure on book-keeping and on the collection of recalcitrant debts, expenditure in keeping shops open at hours inconvenient and costly to the sellers, and other such forms.   It is plain that, up to a point, investment of this type, in so far as it retains, or gains, for the investor "a place in the sun," yields, like expenditure upon national armaments, a considerable private net product.   A curve, representing the private net products yielded by successive increments of it, would indicate positive values for a long distance.   What relation does this curve bear to the corresponding curve representing the social net products of successive increments?

[1] Cf. the discussion of "constructive" and "combative" advertisements in Marshall's *Industry and Trade*, pp. 304-7.

[2] Cf. Goodall, *Advertizing*, p. 49.   [3] *Ibid.* p. 2.

[4] It should be observed that this type of advertisement, which aims in effect at diverting custom from a rival to oneself, may be pressed to lengths that the laws of modern States will not tolerate.   Thus in some European States certain definite false statements about awards alleged to have been won at exhibitions or about an exceptional offer of bankrupt stock, direct disparagement of a rival's character or produce, and attempts to pass off one's own goods as the goods of a well-known house are punishable offences.   (Cf. Davies, *Trust Laws and Unfair Competition*, ch. x.)

[5] Of course the "resources" invested in these things are measured by the actual capital and labour involved in the production of the paragraphs, not by a monopoly charge—if such is made—exacted for them by the newspaper concerned.

First, it may happen that the net result of the expenditures made by the various rivals in conflict with each other is to bring about an alliance between them. If this happens, the expenditures induced by a state of monopolistic competition are responsible for the evolution of simple monopoly. It does not seem possible to determine in a general way the comparative effects on output that will be produced by simple monopoly and by monopolistic competition. Consequently no general statement can be made as to whether the curve representing the social net products of successive increments of investment will indicate positive values over any part of its course.

Secondly, it may happen that the expenditures on advertisement made by competing monopolists will simply neutralise one another, and leave the industrial position exactly as it would have been if neither had expended anything. For, clearly, if each of two rivals makes equal efforts to attract the favour of the public away from the other, the total result is the same as it would have been if neither had made any effort at all. This point was set in a very clear light in Mr. Butterworth's Memorandum to the Board of Trade Railway Conference in 1908. He pointed out that, under competitive arrangements, the officers of rival companies spend a great part of their time and energy in " scheming how to secure traffic for their own line, instead of in devising how best to combine economy with efficiency of working. At present much of the time and energy of the more highly-paid officials of a railway company is taken up with work in which the trading community has no interest, and which is only rendered necessary in the interest of the shareholders whom they serve by the keen competition which exists between companies." [1] In these circumstances the curve representing the social net products of successive increments of investment will indicate negative values throughout.

Thirdly, it may happen that the expenditures lead simply to the substitution in a market of goods made by one firm for the same quantity of equivalent goods made by another firm. If we suppose production, both under A's auspices and under B's,

[1] [Cd. 4677], p. 27.

to obey the law of constant supply price, and to involve equal cost per unit, it is clearly a matter of indifference to the community as a whole from which of these two producers the public buys. In other words, all units of resources expended by either producer in building up goodwill as against the other have a social net product equal to zero. If conditions are such that a diminution in the aggregate cost of production of the commodity would be brought about by the transference of some of the orders from B to A, some units of resources employed by A to abstract orders from B would yield a positive social net product, while all units of resources employed by B to abstract orders from A would yield a negative social net product. If we suppose the more efficient and the less efficient firms to expend resources in these hostilities in about equal measure, in such wise that their efforts cancel one another and leave things much as they would have been had the efforts of both been removed, it is obvious that the social net product of any compound unit of these efforts taken as a whole is, again, zero. There is, however, some slight ground for believing that firms of low productive efficiency tend to indulge in advertisement to a greater extent than their productively more efficient rivals. For, clearly, they have greater inducements to expenditure on devices, such as special packages, designed to obviate comparison of the bulk of commodity offered by them and by other producers at a given price. This consideration suggests that the curve representing the social net products of successive increments of investment is likely to indicate negative values throughout.

The discussion of the preceding paragraphs makes it plain that, speaking generally, the social net product of any r^{th} increment of resources invested in competitive advertisement is exceedingly unlikely to be as large as the private net product. The consequent waste might be diminished by special undertakings among competitors not to advertise, such as hold good among barristers, doctors and members of the London Stock Exchange. Failing this, the evil might be attacked by the State through the taxation, or prohibition, of competitive advertisements — if these could be distinguished from advertisements which are not strictly competitive. It could be removed altogether if conditions of monopolistic competition were destroyed.

§ 15. We now turn to conditions of bilateral monopoly, that is to say, conditions under which the relations between individual buyers and sellers are not rigidly fixed by a surrounding market. The presence of bilateral monopoly in this sense implies an element of theoretical indeterminateness, and, therefore, opens up the way for the employment of activities and resources in efforts to modify the ratio of exchange in favour of one or other of the " monopolists." The nature of the indeterminateness present is different according as the monopolists are, as it were, solidified units, such as single individuals and joint-stock companies, or representative units, such as Trade Unions or Employers' Federations, whose officials negotiate to establish a rate of pay, but whose individual members, when this rate is established, are still free at will to continue or to abandon business. This distinction is, for some purposes, important and ought not to be ignored.[1] It does not, however, bear directly upon our present inquiry. For, whatever the nature of the indeterminateness, it is plain that activities and resources devoted to manipulating the ratio of exchange may yield a positive private net product ; but they cannot—even the earliest dose of them cannot—yield a positive social net product, and they may in some conditions yield a negative social net product.[2] The activities here contemplated consist chiefly— for physical force exercised in direct plunder does not operate through exchange—in the brain work of " bargaining " proper and in the practice of one or other of two sorts of deception. These latter are, first, deception as to the physical nature of a thing offered for sale, and, secondly, deception as to the

[1] With solidified units the *settlement locus*—i.e. the range of possible bargains—lies along the contract curve, and with representative units along portions of the two reciprocal demand (or supply) curves. For a technical discussion of this and connected points cf. my paper "Equilibrium under Bilateral Monopoly" (*Economic Journal*, Jan. 1908, pp. 205 *et seq.*) ; also my *Principles and Methods of Industrial Peace*, Appendix A.

[2] It will be understood that net product here means net product of dividend. It is not, of course, denied that, if a poor man outbargains a rich one, there is a positive net product of economic satisfaction, and, if a rich man outbargains a poor one, a corresponding negative net product of satisfaction.

future yield that it is reasonable to expect from a thing
offered for sale, when the physical nature of that thing has
been correctly described.

§ 16. Of bargaining proper there is little that need be
said. It is obvious that intelligence and resources devoted to
this purpose, whether on one side or on the other, and whether
successful or unsuccessful, yield no net product to the community as a whole. According to Professor Carver, a considerable part of the energies of business men is devoted
to, and a considerable part of their earnings arise out of,
activities of this kind.[1] These activities are wasted. They
contribute to private, but not to social, net product. But
this conclusion does not exhaust the subject. It is often
pointed out that, where their clients, be they customers or
workpeople, can be squeezed, employers tend to expend their
energy in accomplishing this, rather than in improving the
organisation of their factories. When they act thus, the social
net product even of the earliest dose of resources devoted
to bargaining may be, not merely zero, but negative. Whenever that happens, no tax that yields a revenue, though it
may effect an improvement, can provide a complete remedy.
For that absolute prohibition is required. But absolute
prohibition of bargaining is hardly feasible except where
prices and conditions of sale are imposed upon private
industry by some organ of State authority.[2]

§ 17. Deception as to the physical nature of a thing
offered for sale is practised through false weights and measures,
adulteration and misnaming of goods, and dishonest advertisement. Before the days of co-operation "the back streets
of the manufacturing towns swarmed with small shops, in
which the worst of everything was sold, with unchecked
measures and unproved weights."[3] To a less degree similar
practices still prevail. There is little temptation to adopt
them in marketing "production goods," where the buyers
are large industrial concerns, like railway companies, which

[1] Cf. *American Economic Association*, 1909, p. 51.

[2] The legislation of many States concerning private labour exchanges is
relevant here. For an account of this legislation, cf. Becker and Bernhardt,
Gesetzliche Regelung der Arbeitsvermittelung.

[3] Aves, *Co-operative Industry*, p. 16.

possess elaborately organised testing departments. But, in selling "consumption goods"—particularly semi-mysterious consumption goods like patent medicines—to poor and ignorant buyers, and even in selling production goods to less skilled buyers, such as farmers, there is still some temptation. It is always profitable for sellers to "offer commodities which seem, rather than are, useful, if the difference between seeming and reality is likely to escape notice."[1] Deception as to the future yield, which it is reasonable to expect from a thing offered for sale, is practised, in the main, by unscrupulous financiers selling stocks and shares. Among the methods employed are the manipulation of dividend payments, "matched orders," the deliberate publication of false information,[2] and — a practice less clearly over the border line of fairness—the deliberate withholding of relevant information.[3] It is evident that, up to a point, activities devoted to either of these forms of deception bring about a positive private net product, but not a positive social net product. Furthermore, they often lead to enhanced purchases and, therefore, enhanced production of the thing about which deception has been practised. Hence they divert to the

[1] Sidgwick, *Principles of Political Economy*, p. 416.

[2] For a lurid account of some of these methods *vide* Lawson, *Frenzied Finance*, *passim*, and for an analysis of the protective devices embodied in the celebrated German law of 1884, *vide* Schuster, "The Promotion of Companies and the Valuation of their Assets according to German Law," *Economic Journal*, 1900, p. 1 *et seq.* It should be observed that the device of "matched orders" may be made difficult by a rule forbidding offers and bids for large amounts of stock on the terms "all or none." For, when such a rule exists, there is more chance that a seller or buyer operating a matched order may be forced unwillingly to make a deal with some one other than his confidant. (Cf. Brace, *The Value of Organised Speculation*, p. 241.)

[3] It is interesting to observe that, whereas the law often, and public opinion generally, condemns a seller who withholds relevant information, a buyer who acts in this way is generally commended for his "good bargain." Thus to pick up a piece of valuable oak furniture in an out-of-the-way cottage for much less than it is worth is thought by some to be creditable; and nobody maintains that the Rothschild, who founded the fortunes of his house by buying government stock on the strength of his early knowledge of the battle of Waterloo, was bound in honour to make that information public before acting on it. The reason for this distinction probably is that the possessor of an article is presumed to have full opportunity of knowing its real value, and, if he fails to do this, becomes, for his carelessness, legitimate prey. A director of a company who bought up shares in that company on the strength of knowledge gained in the Board room, and so not available to the shareholders generally, would be universally condemned.

production of this thing resources that would otherwise have been devoted to investments yielding the normal marginal return.   Therefore, when this indirect consequence is taken into account, the social net product even of the earliest dose of resources devoted to deception, is, in general, not zero but negative.   If the thing in question is something the production of which involves no expenditure of resources, like the fictitious situations created by fraudulent registry offices, the social net product does not, indeed, sink below zero, for extra production of these imaginary entities involves no withdrawal of resources from elsewhere.   As a rule, however, the social net product of any dose of resources invested in a deceptive activity is negative.   Consequently, as with bargaining, no tax that yields a revenue, though it may effect an improvement, can provide a complete remedy, and absolute prohibition of the activity is required. Attempts to establish such prohibition have been made, on the one side, in various laws concerning false weights and measures and the adulteration of foods, and, on the other side, in various laws—laws, which to be effective, must be enforceable at the instance, not of the damaged party, but of public inspectors or commissioners [1]—designed to control and regulate the practice of company promotion.   In other fields the evil can be met in a more direct way by the establishment of Purchasers' Associations, in which the interests of the sellers and the buyers are unified.[2]

[1] Cf. Van Hise, *Concentration and Control*, pp. 76-8.
[2] Cf. *post*, Part II. Ch. XIX.

CHAPTER X

MARGINAL PRIVATE AND SOCIAL NET PRODUCTS IN RELATION TO INDUSTRIAL FORMS

§ 1. In the preceding chapter we were engaged in a study of the differences between the marginal social net product and the marginal private net product of resources devoted to various occupations or industries. It is now necessary to conduct an analogous inquiry about resources devoted to various forms of economic organisation within the several occupations or industries. Marshall long ago observed: " As a general rule the law of substitution—which is nothing more than a special and limited application of the law of the survival of the fittest— tends to make one method of industrial organisation supplant another when it offers a direct and immediate service at a lower price. The indirect and ultimate services, which either will render, have, as a general rule, little or no weight in the balance." [1] These indirect services constitute the difference between the social net product and the private net product of a unit of resources invested in any form of economic organisation. Our present task is to distinguish the principal fields in which they play an important part.

§ 2. One very important indirect service is rendered by the general economic organisation of a country in so far as, in addition to fulfilling its function as an instrument of production, it also acts, in greater or less degree, as a training ground of business capacities. In order that it may do this effectively, the size of business units must be so graded that persons possessed of good native endowments can learn the principles of enterprise in some small and simple concern, and thereafter

[1] *Principles of Economics*, p. 597.

can gradually move upwards, as their capacity improves with practice, to larger and more difficult posts. The point may be put in this way. When the separate steps in the agricultural or industrial ladder are large, it is difficult for a man adapted, if adequate practice is obtained, for life at one stage, but standing by some accident at another stage, to move to his proper place. Thus—to take a hypothetical example—if agriculture or industry were worked exclusively in large units consisting of one or two large entrepreneurs assisted by a number of mere labourers, any capacity for management and direction that might be born among people in the labouring class would have no opportunity for use or development. Many persons endowed with native capacity would thus be compelled to be watchers only and not doers. But, as Jevons has well taught, it is doing, and not watching, that trains. "A few specimens probed thoroughly," he wrote, "teach more than thousands glanced at through a glass case. The whole British Museum accordingly will not teach a youth as much as he will learn by collecting a few fossils or a few minerals, *in situ* if possible, and taking them home to examine and read and think about."[1] The point was put even more forcibly by Marshall in his address to the Co-operative Society in 1885: "It is a better training in seamanship to sail a fishing-boat than to watch a three-masted ship, the tops of whose masts alone appear above the horizon."[2] Thus it would seem that, in the absence of a proper ladder, a great deal of the business capacity born among the working classes must run to waste. If, however, industry or agriculture is organised by way of units of many different sizes, a workman possessing mental power beyond what is normal to his class can, without great difficulty, himself become the entrepreneur of a small establishment, and gradually advance, educating his powers the while, higher up the ladder that is provided for him.

§ 3. This train of thought suggests that, in a community organised on the general lines of a modern industrial State, associations of workers combined together in small co-partner-

---

[1] *Methods of Social Reform*, p. 61.
[2] *Loc. cit.* p. 17.

ship workshops constitute an industrial form, investment in which is likely to yield a marginal social net product considerably in excess of the marginal private net product. For such workshops provide the first stage of the ladder that is needed to lift upwards the great fund of capacity for management that is almost certainly lying latent among the manual labouring classes. They furnish, as it were, a first school in which this capacity can be developed, and, in so doing, contribute for the service of the community, not merely boots and shoes, but well-trained, competent men, by whose work the national dividend will afterwards be augmented. Much the same thing holds good of the analogous workers' businesses in agriculture. Gardens and small allotments near their cottages for workmen in regular employment elsewhere, large allotments for workmen occasionally taking odd jobs elsewhere, and small holdings for those who devote themselves entirely to work on these holdings, provide in combination a complete ladder from the status of labourer to that of independent farmer. This ladder yields a product of human capacity over and above its immediate product of crops. That element of social net product, however, does not accrue to those persons by whom the size of agricultural holdings is regulated, and is not included in the marginal private net product of the resources invested in them. This is enough to establish a *prima facie* case for the "artificial encouragement," by State action or by private philanthropy, of Workers' Associations and of various grades of allotments and small holdings. Such encouragement is given to Workers' Associations, in England by the support of Retail Co-operative Societies, and in France and Italy by the grant of special facilities for tendering on Government work. The movement for developing allotments and small holdings has also, in this country, received governmental help.

§ 4. The same line of thought, looked at from the other side, suggests that the marginal social net product of activities devoted to bringing about any widespread "trustification" of industry is likely to be smaller than the marginal private net product. For large combinations—this does not apply to

those Kartels whose members remain separate and independent on the productive side—by lessening the opportunities for training in the entrepreneur function, tend to
prevent the level of business ability from rising as high as it
might otherwise do. "The development of a high order of
undertaking genius in the few seems to depend upon a wide
range of undertaking experience in the many." With the
main part of industry organised into million dollar combines,
the ladder connecting different stages of managing ability
would be gravely damaged. Nor would the opportunity for
obtaining positions as managers of departments in a giant concern
go far to make up for this ; for, apart from the limited degree
of independent initiative which the management of a department,
as compared with the control of a business, necessarily involves,
departments will not vary in size so widely, or reach so low
down in the scale, as private businesses may do. In his address
to the Royal Economic Society in 1908, Marshall called
attention to the educative possibilities of small businesses, illus-
trating his thesis from the present organisation of the milk trade.
He pointed out that, so far as the working of industries by the
State—and the same thing, of course, applies to the working
of them by large commercial combinations—does away with
this sort of educative ladder, the mere proof that it was *immediately* more economical than private management would
not suffice to show that it was more economical on the whole.[1]
This is the same thing as saying that the marginal social net
product is less than the marginal private net product. The
practical inference, so far as the present argument goes, is
plain. Though in the special emergency of the Great War,
when immediate output was absolutely essential and had to
be won even though the future suffered, the State might
rightly intervene to *enforce* various forms of combination that
would not have come about without it, yet in normal times of
peace it should always hesitate before encouraging, and should

[1] We may notice that, when, as in such a country as India, the narrowness
of the markets and other causes prevent the development of any large-scale
industries, the top end of the industrial ladder is cut off, and there is a difficulty,
analogous to the difficulty discussed in the text, about the provision of an
adequate training-ground for the higher forms of business ability. (Cf. Morison,
The Industrial Organisation of an Indian Province, p. 186.)

perhaps in some instances impede, any threatened excess in
the growth of giant businesses, whether these are publicly
or privately owned. What has been said above, however,
obviously does not exhaust the considerations relevant to this
problem. Further discussion of it will be found in Chapters
XIV. and XXI.

§ 5. Considerations of the same general character as the
above are relevant to certain developments in the method
and practice of standardised production.[1] It has long been
known that, by specialisation to a limited number of standard
forms, great economy of cost and increase of output can be
achieved. This economy, furthermore, is not confined to the
point at which standardisation is first applied; for, if one
industry agrees to standardise its product, the industries which
make machines and tools for making that product are in turn
enabled to standardise theirs. The Standards Committee of
the Engineering Trade of this country has done much work in
drawing up, for screws, nuts, certain motor parts and various
other things, standard specifications which have been adopted
throughout the engineering industry of the country generally.
The experience of the Great War, in which military equipment
and munitions had necessarily to be of uniform patterns,
brought out more clearly than before the enormous scope for
direct economies which, partly by making possible the employment of relatively unskilled labour, standardisation of
product is able, in favourable circumstances, to create. The
urgent need for immediate large output at a minimum of
cost even led to standardisation, under Government authority,
of such things as ships and boots. The essence of the matter
is that the standardisation of certain products over the whole of
an industry, by enabling the firms that make them, and the
other firms that make tools for making them, to specialise more
closely than would otherwise be possible, leads immediately to
an enormously increased output of these products. This increased output we may call, if we will, the private net product of
the method of standardisation. If, however, attention is concen-

[1] In *Industry and Trade*, Bk. ii., chapters ii. and iii., Marshall, after
distinguishing between standards *particular* to an individual producer and
standards that are *general* to the greater part of an industry, has much interesting discussion of modern developments in standardisation.

trated exclusively upon this, the net advantages of the method will sometimes be greatly exaggerated. For standardisation almost inevitably checks the development of new patterns, new processes and new ideas. It is all very well to make rules for revising periodically the standard specifications. This is not an adequate remedy, because the real danger of standardisation is, not so much that it will prevent the adoption of new things when their superiority has been recognised, but that it will greatly lessen the inducement to manufacturers to devise and try new things. For in normal industry the profit which a man gets out of an improvement is chiefly won in the period when he is ahead of his competitors, before the improvement is adopted generally. With a rigid system of standardisation nobody would be able to be ahead of anybody else or to introduce a new pattern till the whole trade did so. The whole line, in short, must advance together; and this means that no part of it has any great inducement to advance at all. Other things being equal, the marginal social net product of effort devoted towards standardising processes falls short of the marginal private net product, in so far as it indirectly checks inventions and improvements and so lessens productive powers in the future. Obviously the gap thus indicated is not equally wide for all commodities. It is difficult to believe, for example, that the establishment of standard sizes and standard forms for such things as screws and nuts is likely to prevent the development of any important improvement. In these simple things there is little or no room for improvement. But with complex manufactures the position is altogether different. Even in the course of the Great War, when large output was of overwhelming importance, it would have been madness to standardise the production of aeroplanes ; the opening for discovery and for the development of better types was so wide. In many other finished manufactures it is impossible to feel any confidence that the final form has already been evolved. There is, therefore, always the danger that, by standardisation, we shall augment enormously the production of the good at the cost of never attaining to the better. In any action that the State may take to foster standardisation for the sake of the immediate and direct stimulus which it gives to output this danger must be carefully borne in mind.

§ 6. Yet again, the analysis here developed is applicable to certain aspects of that method of business organisation that has come to be known as "scientific management." The general characteristics of that system are well known. Elaborate study of the various operations to be performed is undertaken by trained experts, who analyse these operations into their separate elements, and, on the basis of this analysis, coupled with careful observation of the methods actually followed by a number of good workmen, construct, by combination, an ideal method superior to any yet in vogue. The kind of improvement to which this process leads is illustrated by the results of Mr. Gilbraith's investigation of the problem of laying bricks. He " studied the best height for the mortar box and brick pile, and then designed a scaffold, with a table on it, upon which all of the materials are placed, so as to keep the bricks, the mortar, the man, and the wall in their proper relative positions. These scaffolds are adjusted, as the wall grows in height, for all of the bricklayers, by a labourer especially detailed for this purpose, and by this means the bricklayer is saved the exertion of stooping down to the level of his feet for each brick and each trowelful of mortar and then straightening up again. Think of the waste of effort that has gone on through all these years, with each bricklayer lowering his body, weighing, say, 150 pounds, down two feet and raising it up again every time a brick (weighing about 5 pounds) is laid in the wall ! And this each bricklayer did about one thousand times a day." [1] This device is, however, merely one example of what scientific management endeavours to achieve in general. The central conception involved in it is that of handing over the task of planning methods to trained experts, and then explaining to the workmen in elaborate detail what it is they have to do, including even the pauses and rest periods that they should take between successive operations and movements. "The work of every workman is fully planned out by the management at least one day in advance, and each man receives in most cases complete written instructions, describing in detail

[1] Taylor, *The Principles of Scientific Management*, p. 78.

the task which he is to accomplish, as well as the means to be used in doing the work. And the work planned in advance in this way constitutes a task which is to be solved, as explained above, not by the workman alone, but in almost all cases by the joint effort of the workman and the management. This task specifies, not only what is to be done, but how it is to be done and the exact time allowed for doing it." [1] The work of teaching the workmen how to do it, and of seeing that they properly understand and carry out their instructions, is entrusted to a new class of officials known as " functional foremen." These officials, working in conjunction with the accounting officer, can ascertain at once how far the costs of any particular workman's output exceed the proper costs laid down beforehand, and can then concentrate attention and instruction at any point where there is *prima facie* reason to hope for improvement. [2] Now it is perfectly plain that this type of industrial organisation is likely to yield large immediate economies, and that the careful teaching involved in it must *up to a point* yield much permanent good. It is a paradox that, " though in the athletic world instructors exist to teach boxers how to balance themselves and use their arms, and cricket professionals are constantly at work improving the efficiency of batsmen and bowlers, and coaches are a necessity to teach a boat's crew collectively and individually how and when to move their bodies and hands, yet in the industrial world the value of teaching operatives how to earn their livelihood is hardly yet recognised." [3] Nevertheless, there is real danger lest this new-found science should be pushed too far. Carried to excessive lengths it *may*, from a long period point of view, defeat its own ends. First, it is not proper to assume that there is only one best method of doing a thing independent of the psychological and physical qualities of the individual doing it. There may be several first-class methods, some more fitted to bring out the best in one man, another more

[1] Taylor, *The Principles of Scientific Management*, p. 39.

[2] Cf. Emerson, *Efficiency*, ch. vii. Mr. Dicksee draws some instructive comparisons between these methods and the various forms of drill practised among soldiers. (*Business Methods and the War*, Lecture 2.)

[3] Health of Munition Workers Committee, *Interim Report*, p. 77.

suited to another man.[1]   Secondly, so far as the operations
of the individual workman are reduced to a mechanical
plan, the original source from which the directing authority
derived its standard methods—namely, a combination of
the best points in the *varied* individual methods of different
workmen—would be dried up.   Overt suggestions from
workpeople for improvements in method would also, perhaps,
be rendered less probable.   No doubt, this loss could be
partly atoned for by the employment of scientific experts
specially charged with the task of experimenting in new
methods.   But, after all, these are available under ordinary
systems of works' management and cannot, therefore, be
regarded as a peculiar asset of the Taylor system, to be set
against its peculiar failings.   Nor is it only in respect of
specific suggestions and devices that injury may be indirectly
wrought by this system.   There is grave reason to fear lest
the *general* initiative and independent activity of workpeople
may be injured by their complete subordination to the detailed
control of functional foremen, much as the *general* initiative
of soldiers is injured by the grinding of an over-rigid and
mechanical military system.   By the removal of opportunities
for the exercise of initiative, capacity for initiative may be
destroyed, and the quality of the labouring force may in this
way be subtly lowered.   In so far as this happens, the
marginal social net product of resources invested in the
development and application of scientific management falls
short of the marginal private net product.   Unless the State or
philanthropy intervenes, there is a danger that this method
of industrial organisation may be carried further and applied
more widely than the interest of the national dividend—not
to speak of the more general interest of society—when viewed
as a whole, demands.

[1] Cf. Miers, *Mind and Work*, p. 192.

CHAPTER XI

§ 1. IN Chapter IX. § 3 attention was drawn to a type of divergence between private and social net product additional to the two types that were studied in that chapter. This type of divergence arises when a part of the effect of employing a unit of resources in any occupation consists of something, which, instead of coming in the first instance to the person who invests the unit, comes instead, in the first instance, to other persons engaged in the occupation. To simplify the study of these divergences I shall imagine that there exists an archetypal industry, in which the values of the marginal private net product and of the marginal social net product of investment are *both* equal to one another and *also* stand at a sort of central level representative of industries in general.[1] In any actual industry conducted under conditions of simple competition—that is to say, conditions such that each seller produces as much as he can at the ruling market price, and does not restrict his output in the hope of causing that price to rise—investment and output must be carried to a point at which the value of the marginal private net product of investment there conforms to the central value. It follows that the value of the marginal social net product of investment in the industry can only diverge from this central value if and in so far as it diverges from the value of the marginal private net product. The present

---

[1] It is not necessary to suppose that this central value is actually attained in any industry ; it is rather to be conceived as the level which would be attained under conditions of simple competition in an industry of constant supply price.

chapter is concerned exclusively with conditions of simple competition.

§ 2. Let us place ourselves in imagination in a country where the flow of resources coming annually into being has to be distributed regularly among a variety of occupations. It is assumed that, when any given quantity of resources is devoted to a given occupation, the concrete form assumed by these resources—their distribution, for example, into many or few individual firms and so forth—is the most economical form available (from the standpoint of the period of time relevant to our problem) for that quantity of new resources; and that, when a slightly greater quantity is devoted to the occupation, the concrete form assumed is the most economical form available (from the same standpoint) for that quantity. When this assumption is made, it is plain that, if one unit is added to the resources *of any given sort*[1] that normally flow into any one occupation, that unit will yield the same net product as each of the other units in the flow. All the units are interchangeable in this sense. But, none the less, the presence of an extra unit may alter the output of the other units, in such wise that the addition made to aggregate output is either more or less than proportionate to the difference made to the quantity of resources invested. In so far as the other units belong to the investor of the given unit and the difference made to the output of the other units comes in the first instance to him, it enters into the private net product as well as into the social net product of the extra unit. But, in so far as the other units belong to people other than the investor of the given unit, the difference made to the output of these units enters into the social net product, but not into the private net product of the given unit. The two sorts of marginal net product in the particular industry, and hence their values, therefore, differ. Since then investment under competitive conditions is carried to the point at which the value of the marginal private net product of the resources placed there is equal to the central value, the value of the

---

[1] In view of the definition of an increment of investment given in Chapter IX. § 2, we must not speak of units being added to *the* resources without qualification that flow into an occupation.

social net product in that industry must diverge from the central value; and the national dividend is not maximised.[1]

§ 3. This statement has now to be brought into connection with the familiar economic concept of increasing, constant and diminishing returns, or, as some prefer to say, decreasing, constant and increasing costs. As a preliminary it will be convenient to provide ourselves with an appropriate terminology. The expressions cited above, used in the present connection,[2] are designed to describe certain relations between the output of a commodity and the expenses, measured in money, that are incurred in producing it. Diminishing and increasing returns mean diminishing and increasing yields of commodity per unit of money expenses as the output of the commodity increases; increasing and decreasing costs mean increasing and decreasing money expenses per unit of the commodity as the output increases. The two sets of terms are thus,

---

[1] In an industry, for whose product the demand has an elasticity equal to unity, the amount of resources devoted to production will obviously be the same whether, the social net product of any r^{th} increment of investment being given, this social net product of that increment is equal to or greater than the private net product. Therefore, when there is an excess of social over private net product in respect of the marginal unit of resources invested, the effect of the existence of this excess, in conditions of competition, is that consumers obtain for nothing exactly this excess: and the effect of there being an excess of (the given) social above private net product in respect of the other units of invested resources is that they obtain for nothing the aggregate of all these excesses. In industries, however, in which the elasticity of demand is not equal to unity, the existence of an excess of (the given) social above private net product of various quantities of investment causes the quantity of investment made to be different from what it would otherwise have been. This implies that the effect on the consumers' material estate, due to the existence of an excess of social over private net product in respect of the unit of investment which is marginal when there is such an excess, is not simply the amount of that excess. In like manner the effect on their material estate of the sum of all the excesses of the units of resources that are in fact employed is not simply the sum of those excesses. It follows, of course, that the effect on their satisfaction (as expressed in money) is not measured, as it is in the case of unitary demand elasticity, by the excess of their aggregate demand price for the quantity of product they do secure over their aggregate demand price for the quantity that they would have secured had (the given) social net product throughout been equal to private net product. These considerations render it inappropriate, except when the elasticity of demand is unitary, to speak of the excess of marginal social net product over marginal private net product as equivalent, in conditions of competition, to what "accrues" to the consumer in consequence of there being such an excess. For this reason I have in the present text modified the phraseology employed in the corresponding passages of the third edition.

[2] For another use cf. *post*, Part IV. Ch. III.

so to speak, reciprocals of one another.   Both alike, however, are open to an objection.   It is not clear, on the face of things, whether the returns per unit of money expenses, or expenses per unit of returns, to which they refer, are average or marginal returns or expenses; and, when diminishing returns (or increasing costs) hold for some amounts of output and increasing returns (or decreasing costs) for other amounts, there must, it would seem, be certain amounts in respect of which marginal returns are increasing (or marginal expenses decreasing) while average returns are decreasing (or average expenses increasing), and *vice versa*.   It is, therefore, best, as I think, to surrender both the above forms of expression, and to distinguish industries according as they conform to conditions of *increasing, constant or decreasing supply price.* It will be shown in Appendix III. that, in competitive industries, the supply price of any quantity of output is equal both to the marginal expenses and to the average expenses of what I call the equilibrium firm engaged in the industry; and that it is a concept free from ambiguity. That discussion need not be repeated here.   For the reader not interested in refinements of analysis it is sufficient to say that my laws of increasing, constant and decreasing supply price correspond, for practical purposes, to what are ordinarily known as the laws of diminishing, constant and increasing returns, or increasing, constant and decreasing costs.[1] It is, of course, with long-period or " normal," not with any form of short-period supply price, that we here have to do.

§ 4. The relations which these laws express between variations in supply price and variations in output are not necessarily the relations which do subsist between these things in history, but the relations which would subsist subject to the condition *other things being equal.*   In real life, with the general advance of knowledge, new methods of

---

[1] Professor Cannan has objected to the use of the term " law " in connection with diminishing and increasing returns as defined above, on the ground that, whereas in some industries diminishing, and in others increasing, returns prevail, a scientific law is a statement that holds true in all, and not only in some, circumstances (*Wealth*, p. 70).   It might be answered that in fact this is only true of the most general laws of physics.   Biologists, for example, regularly speak of Mendel's law of inheritance, without any implication that all inheritance obeys this law.   But in any event the point is a verbal one.

production are being continually introduced and new technical appliances invented. Some of these changes are due to factors which would operate *even though the scale of output of the industry remained constant*. Others are the result of the changes in the scale of output, being called out in response to changes in demand. Of course, in practice, it may often be impossible to say whether a particular invention in, say, the process of steel manufacture is or is not due to changes in the scale of output. Logically, however, the distinction is quite clear. For the present purpose changes not due to changes in the scale of output are definitely ruled out of consideration. Therefore an industry may display continually falling supply price through a long series of years, and yet may not be operating under conditions of decreasing supply price [1] as understood here. In like manner, when, for example, the coal seams of a country are being gradually worked out, an industry may display continually rising supply and yet may not be operating under conditions of increasing supply price.[2] An industry is said to conform to increasing, constant or decreasing supply price, when, apart from changes in technique or other inventions not due to changes in the scale of output, increase of output would be associated, as the case may be, with increasing, constant or decreasing supply prices.

§ 5. Attention must next be called to a distinction, which, for the present purpose, is fundamental. When we speak without qualification of laws of increasing, constant or decreasing supply price, we have in view the relation between variations in the output of a commodity and variations in the supply price per unit *from the standpoint of the industry producing the commodity*. These variations are not always or necessarily the same as the variations in the supply price per unit of the commodity *from the standpoint of the community*. Consider an industry which purchases from others factors of production only. When, with a given measure of increase

---

[1] Geometrically the continuous fall in costs would be represented by a lowering of the whole supply curve.

[2] In this case the extent to which the seams are worked out at any time is, of course, a result of the scale of output that ruled in the past ; but this leaves my distinction intact.

in the output of anything, the money expenses per unit of
output incurred by the equilibrium firm increase, because
for each unit of output it has to buy, at the same price as
before, greater quantities of one or another factor, the two sorts
of variation are identical.   But, when the expenses per unit
increase because it has to pay for the factors of production
which it employs a higher money price, the extra payment
that it makes is offset by an equal and opposite extra payment
which the owners of the several factors of production receive.
From the point of view of the community as a whole no extra
expense per unit of output is incurred.   In like manner, when
the expenses per unit to the equilibrium firm in an industry
decrease because it pays for the factors it employs a lower
money price, from the point of view of the community as a
whole there is no saving of expenses per unit of output.
This matter is examined in more detail in Appendix III.
We say, then, that an industry conforms to the law of
increasing, constant or decreasing supply price *simpliciter*,
when it so conforms from the standpoint of the industry
under review, *i.e.* when the variations in supply price, calculated without any allowance for the transfer elements
distinguished above, that are associated with increases of output, are positive, nil or negative respectively.   We say that
it conforms to the law of increasing, constant or decreasing
supply price from the standpoint of the community, when
these variations, corrected so as to eliminate transfer elements,
are positive, nil or negative.[1]

---

[1] This conception, though mathematically simple, needs to be handled
carefully when translated into ordinary language.   An industry conforms to
conditions of decreasing, constant or increasing supply price *simpliciter* according as the rate of increase, from the standpoint of the industry, of the supply
price (associated with increasing output) is negative, nil or positive : it
conforms to conditions of decreasing, constant or increasing supply price from
the standpoint of the community according as the rate of increase from the
standpoint of the community is negative, nil or positive.   The rate of increase
from the standpoint of the industry of the supply price is a differential, the
integral of which is the supply price.   The rate of increase from the standpoint
of the community of the supply price is also a differential, but the integral
which corresponds to it has no real significance.   *The rate of change from the
standpoint of the community in the supply price* does *not* mean *the rate of
change in the supply price from the standpoint of the community*.   There is
no separate supply price from the standpoint of the community : there is only
one supply price from all standpoints.

§ 6. Conditions of decreasing supply price *from the stand-point of the community* are clearly possible in a material as well as in a formal sense. For, when the scale of an industry increases, this change often leads to changes in the internal structure and methods of working of the firms engaged in it, or in the proportions in which the several factors of production are employed, of a kind which would lower the cost of production per unit, even though the prices per unit of all the factors of production employed were unaltered. Thus many writers have called attention to the fact that, when an industry is on a small scale, the firms belonging to it all engage in producing a number of different types or varieties of their commodity. They are, more or less, firms of all work. There is not a sufficiently wide or assured market to allow of close specialisation. As, however, the general demand grows, it becomes more and more worth while for firms to specialise on particular types. Thus Sir Sydney Chapman has observed that the relatively large scale of the cotton industry in England is associated, not only with specialisation between the processes of spinning and weaving, but with further specialisation between firms spinning fine counts and those spinning coarse counts. In contrast to this : " The range of work undertaken by the typical factory in Germany is far greater than that undertaken by the typical factory in England. Hence naturally the skill of the operatives is less in Germany ; more time is wasted and factory organisation is less perfect." [1] The increased specialisation of its component firms made possible by an enlargement in an industry as a whole often involves a large reduction in costs. This reduction might, so far as pure theory goes, be accompanied by no change, or even by a decrease, in the size of the typical firm. In practice it is likely to be accompanied by some increase in this size. Thus Marshall writes : " An increase in the aggregate volume of the production of anything will generally increase the size, and, therefore, the internal economies possessed by (such) a representative firm." [2] This, however, is a secondary consideration. The essential point is that an increase in the scale to

---

[1] *Work and Wages*, vol. i. p. 166.
[2] *Principles of Economics*, p. 318.

which an industry is producing frequently alters—in general diminishes—the average (and marginal) costs of the equilibrium firm contained in it, whether or not it also alters its size. There is, then, no difficulty in seeing that the law of decreasing supply price from the standpoint of the community is not merely formally possible, but is likely to be followed in practice by many manufacturing industries.

§ 7. Conditions of increasing supply price *from the standpoint of the community* are, however, in different case. We consider, as before, an industry which purchases for its own use factors of production, but no other ingredients. At the worst the equilibrium firm is in a position to maintain its original scale of output: and it will, in fact, do this unless some other scale now makes possible a lower cost per unit of output. Hence, in order that the law of increasing supply price from the standpoint of the community may prevail, conditions must be such that a mere increase in the output of the industry as a whole would cause the average expenses of the equilibrium firm —which are equal, as is shown in Appendix III., to the supply price of the industry—to increase, even though that firm continued to produce exactly the same output as before and paid exactly the same prices for the factors of production employed by it. It is *possible*, no doubt, that diseconomies of this character— injuries to the efficiency of old firms brought about by the mere existence of new ones—may occur. But their occurrence is, on the face of things, highly improbable; and that they should occur in sufficient measure to outweigh the factors, described in the preceding section, that make for decreasing supply price is more improbable still. In general, therefore, we may conclude that an industry, whose purchases embrace only factors of production, cannot conform to the law of increasing supply price from the standpoint of the community, *i.e.* when variations in supply price are expressed in such a way that transfer elements are eliminated.

§ 8. When an industry, besides purchasing ultimate factors of production, purchases also materials, machinery and so on, the matter is less simple. The price variations in these things, if such occur, do not now necessarily represent only transfer expenditure. They do not do so, for example, when an increase in the size of the cotton industry enables textile machinery to be produced with more help from specialisation and standardisation, and, therefore, more cheaply. The fall in price of textile machinery brought about in this way when the cotton industry expands is relevant to the law of supply price in that industry, not merely from the standpoint of the industry, but also from that of the community. Since, however, what is sold to one industry, other than factors of production, must be the product of another industry, it follows from the discussion of the preceding section that an increase in the output (and, therefore, in the demand for materials and machinery) in a given industry cannot involve an increase in the price of the things it buys, except by causing an increase in the price of the factors of production that make them. Therefore, in this complex case, no less than in the simpler one, conditions of increasing supply price from the standpoint of the community are excluded. From the cosmopolitan point of view they are excluded absolutely. From the point of view of a particular country purchasing materials from abroad they may, however, be present. For, though, if the price of imported materials rises as a consequence of an increase in the scale of the given industry, this can only be because a transfer is made to the owners of the factors that help to make them, these owners belong to other countries, and, therefore, so far as the one country is concerned, the transfer does not cancel itself.

§ 9. We may now return to the argument of § 2. In that argument, it will have been noticed, no reference was made to the prices of the several factors of production that are at work. Quantities of resources in a physical sense were related directly to quantities of output, so what was said was complete. Now, provided that (small) variations in output in a given industry do not involve variations in the prices of any factor of production, variations in the quantities of the several factors employed may, with propriety, be measured by the variations in the amount of money which is expended by the industry in purchasing them for its use. In these conditions the argument of § 2 can be translated into an inverse form thus. The marginal private net product of the equilibrium firm is equal to the average net product of the equilibrium firm per unit cost; and is thus the reciprocal of the supply price of the product. The marginal social net product, on the other hand, is the reciprocal of the marginal supply price of the product to the industry, *i.e.* of the difference made to the total money expenses of the industry by adding a small increment of output. Hence to say that the marginal private net product of investment in any industry is greater (or less) than the marginal social net product is the same thing as to say that the supply price is less (or greater) than the marginal supply price to the industry. This fact, taken in conjunction with the argument of Appendix III. §§ 16-17, implies that in a many-firm industry the value of the marginal private net product of any quantity of investment is greater than, equal to or less than the value of the marginal social net product, according as the industry conforms to conditions of increasing, constant or decreasing supply price from the standpoint of the industry—which in the conditions supposed is the same as the standpoint of the community. When, in a competitive industry, variations in output involve variations in the price of some of the factors of production employed, so that the rates of change in supply price, regarded from the two standpoints, differ, an extension of the above argument shows that the value of the marginal private net product of investment is greater than, equal to or less than the value of the marginal social net product according as the industry conforms to conditions of increasing, constant or decreasing supply price from the standpoint, not of the industry, but of the community.[1]

§ 10. It remains to inquire in this last case what, if any, light can be thrown on the relation between the values of the marginal social and marginal private net products, if we know of an industry merely that it conforms to one or other of the laws of increasing, constant or decreasing supply price *simpliciter* (*i.e.* from the standpoint of the industry). The conclusions that flow from the preceding analysis are then as follows: First, it is on the face of things very improbable that an increase in the output of any commodity will cause a *fall* in

[1] Cf. Appendix III. § 17.

the aggregate money price that would have to be expended to secure the same quantities of all the factors collectively as were employed before the increase.[1]   Therefore, when conditions of decreasing supply price *simpliciter* rule, conditions of decreasing supply price from the standpoint of the community must, *in general*, also rule, and, therefore, under competitive conditions, the marginal private net product of investment in the industry will, in general, fall short of the marginal social net product. When, however, conditions of increasing supply price *simpliciter* rule, it need not happen that conditions of increasing supply price from the standpoint of the community also rule : indeed, except in the special circumstances described in § 8, this cannot happen.   Therefore the law of increasing supply price *simpliciter* does not imply that, under competitive conditions, the marginal private net product of investment in the industry exceeds the marginal social net product ; on the contrary it may fall short of it.   Hence, while, with rare exceptions, simple competition always causes too little investment to be made in industries of decreasing supply price (*simpliciter*), it does not always, or even generally, cause too much to be made in industries of increasing supply price (*simpliciter*).   On the contrary, in a number of those industries it may cause too little investment to be made.   British agriculture, for example, though obviously conforming to conditions of increasing supply price (*simpliciter*), may well be an industry of decreasing supply price from the standpoint of the community, and as such, in danger of suffering from a shortage of investment.

§ 11. If the amount of investment in any industry was carried exactly to the point at which the value of the marginal social net product there is equal to the central value of

---

[1] It is not, it should be understood, impossible that this should happen. For example, if an industry employed only a small proportion of the total supplies of two factors of production and nearly the whole supply of a third, and if an increase in the scale of output caused new methods to be introduced which led to an absolute decrease in the amount of this third factor that was wanted, the prices of the first two factors would be practically unchanged, while that of the third would fall substantially.   As a result a units of the first plus b units of the second plus c units of the third might cost less money than before.   Plainly, however, such a combination of circumstances is not likely to occur.

marginal social net products, the national dividend, so far as that industry is concerned, would be maximised. Disregarding the possibility of multiple maximum positions, I propose, for convenience, to call the investment that would then be made in the industry the ideal investment and the output that would be obtained the ideal output. Under conditions of simple competition, if in any industry the value of the marginal social net product of investment is greater than the value of the marginal private net product, this implies that the output obtained is less than the ideal output: if the value of the marginal social net product is less than the value of the marginal private net product, this implies that the output obtained is greater than the ideal output. It follows that, under conditions of simple competition, for every industry in which the value of the marginal social net product is greater than that of the marginal private net product, there will be certain rates of bounty, the granting of which by the State would modify output in such a way as to make the value of the marginal social net product there more nearly equal to the value of the marginal social net product of resources in general, thus— provided that the funds for the bounty can be raised by a mere transfer that does not inflict any indirect injury on production— increasing the size of the national dividend and the sum of economic welfare; and there will be one rate of bounty, the granting of which would have the *optimum* effect in this respect. In like manner, for every industry in which the value of the marginal social net product is less than that of the marginal private net product, there will be certain rates of tax, the imposition of which by the State would increase the size of the national dividend and increase economic welfare; and one rate of tax, which would have the *optimum* effect in this respect. These conclusions, taken in conjunction with what has been said in the preceding paragraphs, create a presumption in favour of State bounties to industries in which conditions of decreasing supply price *simpliciter* are operating, and of State taxes upon industries in which conditions of increasing supply price from the standpoint of the community are operating. They do *not*, of course, create a presumption in favour of fiscal interference with industries selected at haphazard or operated through rates of bounty or tax so selected. It is true that particular drugs consumed in particular quantities at particular times may cure diseases; but it is no less true that the consumption of drugs in general in a miscellaneous manner is highly injurious to health.

§ 12. Moreover, it may be well to make explicit a further consideration. When it was urged above that in certain industries a wrong amount of resources is being invested because the value of the marginal social net product there differs from the value of the marginal private net product, it was tacitly assumed that in the main body of industries these two values are equal, and, therefore, that there is scope for increasing the national dividend by shifting resources between the particular industry under review and this body of industries. If in all industries the values of marginal social and marginal private net product differed to exactly the same extent, the *optimum* distribution of resources would always be attained, and there would be, on these lines, no case for fiscal interference. It would still be possible, however, to defend a system of bounties to industries in general, the funds for which should be collected by some kind of lump-sum taxation, by arguing that the sum total of effort and waiting devoted to industry could be increased with advantage to economic welfare. Moreover, even when attention is confined to the distribution of resources among the several industries, what has been said does not imply that the mere prevalence in all industries of some degree of decreasing supply price from the standpoint of the community would rule out fiscal interference. It would still be possible—at all events in theory—to increase the national dividend by shifting resources from industries in which the law of decreasing supply price acted only weakly to industries in which it acted strongly.

§ 13. For completeness — though strictly this matter lies outside our formal limits—attention may be called, in parenthesis, to a type of reaction analogous to that discussed in § 12 of Chapter IX. The investment of an increment of resources in an industry, besides yielding a product to the purchasers, not reflected in the investor's profit, by altering costs of production, may yield a further

Q

product of a like kind by altering the amount of satisfaction which the purchasers derive from a given quantity of their purchases. This form of indirect product may be either positive or negative. Among commodities, the desire for which is partly a desire to possess what other people possess, the creation of the 1000th unit adds to aggregate satisfaction more satisfaction than it carries itself, because it makes every unit of the commodity more common. Top-hats are examples. Among commodities, the desire for which is partly a desire to possess what other people do not possess, the creation of the 1000th unit adds to aggregate satisfaction less satisfaction than it carries itself, because it makes every unit of the commodity more common. Diamonds are examples.[1] Among industries whose products are desired for their own sake, and not as means to any form of distinction, the creation of the 1000th unit adds to aggregate satisfaction exactly as much satisfaction as it carries itself. On the basis of this analysis, inferences analogous to those set out in § 11 are easily obtained. For every industry, the desire for whose products is enhanced if they become less common, there must be certain rates of tax, the levy of which on the industry would increase economic welfare; and for every industry, the desire for whose products is enhanced if they become more common, there must be certain rates of bounty, the imposition of which would produce a like effect. But there is reason to believe that the great bulk of ordinary commodities consumed by the mass of the population are desired almost entirely for their own sake, and not as a means to any form of distinction. The sphere of usefulness that could belong, even under a perfectly wise and perfectly virtuous Government, to these fiscal devices is, therefore, probably smaller than it might appear to be at first sight.

§ 14. These results, like the companion results which

[1] It should be added that, when commonness or rareness is an element in the esteem in which a person holds a thing, it is often not general commonness or general rareness alone, but, in many instances, both commonness among one set of people and also rareness among another set. As Mr. McDougall writes of the followers of fashion : " Each victim is moved not only by the prestige of those whom he imitates but also by the desire to be different from the mass who have not yet adopted the fashion " (*Social Psychology*, p. 336). This aspect of the matter cannot, however, be pursued here.

will be established presently in connection with monopoly, are results in pure theory. Attempts to develop and expand them are sometimes frowned upon on the ground that they cannot be applied to practice. For, it is argued, though we may be able to say that the size of the national dividend and the sum of economic welfare would be increased by granting bounties to industries falling into one category and by imposing taxes upon those falling into another category, we are not able to say to which of our categories the various actual industries of real life belong. In other words, it is maintained that the economic boxes and sub-boxes, labelled increasing, constant and decreasing supply price (whether *simpliciter* or from the standpoint of the community) and so on, are *empty* boxes and, therefore, useless except as toys. This conclusion does not, however, appear to be well grounded. Even though we should be for ever unable to fill these boxes and sub-boxes, the labour involved in studying them would not be thrown away. By means of it we are enabled to see, for example, what conditions are implicitly assumed when it is stated that the imposition of a tax or the introduction of monopolistic policy will have such and such consequences. We are thus put in a position to detect and expose sophistical dogmatism. It is better to know exactly what facts are required to make the answering of a question possible, even though those facts are unattainable, than to rest in a fog of vague and credulous opinion. But this is not all. Difficult as it must necessarily be to classify industries into the categories which analysis has distinguished, we need not yet conclude that it is impossible. Statistical technique, by itself, in spite of the growing volume and improving quality of the material available, will not enable us to accomplish this; for statistics refer only to the past. But able business men with a detailed realistic knowledge of the conditions of their several industries should be able to provide economists with the raw material for rough probable judgments. Economists unaided cannot fill their empty boxes because they lack the necessary realistic knowledge; and business men unaided cannot fill them because they do not know where or what the boxes are. With collaboration, however, it is not unreasonable to hope that some measure of success may eventually be achieved. At least the effort is worth making. It is premature, in impatience at the present shortage of straw, to scrap our brickmaking machinery. It is the better part to advertise abroad the urgent need for straw, and to call for students to produce it.[1]

[1] Cf. a paper by Dr. Clapham on " Empty Economic Boxes " in the *Economic Journal* for September 1922, and a reply by the present writer in the December issue of the same journal.

CHAPTER XII

STATE REGULATION OF COMPETITIVE PRICES

§ 1. THE preceding discussion seems at first sight to prove that, apart from divergences between private and social net product, State interference, designed to modify in any way the working of free competition, is bound to injure the national dividend; for this competition left to itself will continually push resources from points of lower productivity (in terms of economic satisfaction as measured in money) to points of higher productivity, thus tending always away from less favourable, and towards more favourable, arrangements of the community's resources. We have now to confront this general presumption with the extensive policy of price regulation which was followed by the British, as by most other Governments, during the course of the great European War. I propose first to give a general account of that policy and then to inquire how far, if at all, the experience gained should modify the conclusions reached in preceding chapters.

§ 2. Broadly put, the position was as follows. The war caused in two ways a great shortage in certain things. On the one hand, for munition articles, army clothes and so forth, there was an enormous new Government demand much in excess of normal supplies. On the other hand, for various articles of ordinary civilian use, the contraction of available tonnage and the withdrawal of labour for the army and munition work caused supplies to fall much below the normal. The shortage brought about in one or other of these ways put it in the power of persons who happened to hold stocks of short commodities, or to be able to produce them quickly, to charge for them prices very much higher than usual. When the shortage was due to increased Government demand, the scale of business done by these persons being as large as, or larger than, before, the high prices that they were enabled to charge necessarily yielded them abnormally large profits. When it was due to contraction of supply (*e.g.* through the withdrawal of labour or other obstacles to output), the gain from high prices *might* be cancelled by loss due to lessened sales; so that abnormally large profits were not obtained. For a great number of things, however, the conditions of demand are such that a shortage of, say, 10 per cent in the supply causes the price offered by purchasers to rise by much more than 10 per cent. For the sellers of articles of this class the shortage, even when it was due to a supply contraction, often meant abnormal profits. Of course, some of these abnormal profits were more apparent than real, for, if prices all round are doubled, a doubling of money profits will only enable a man to get the same amount of things as before. Very often, however, the money profits were enhanced very much more than in proportion to the rise in general prices. Wherever this happened, certain specially favoured persons were benefiting greatly as a direct consequence of the war. This state of things naturally caused resentment, and suggested State interference.

§ 3. This interference might follow either of two principal lines. On the one hand, fortunately situated sellers might be allowed to charge such prices as the market would bear, thus collecting abnormal profits in the first instance; but, thereafter, be deprived of the bulk of these for the benefit of the Exchequer by a high excess profits tax. On the other hand, the prices they were allowed to charge might be limited by authority to rates at which it was estimated that abnormal profits would not accrue to them. Apart from points of technique and administration, the choice between these two plans makes no difference to the fortunately situated seller. But it does make a difference to the people who happen to need the particular goods or services that he sells. For, whereas under the maximum price plan they are left untouched, under the excess profits plan a special levy is, in effect, placed upon them for the benefit of the general taxpayers.

It follows that, where the taxpayers themselves, through the Government, are the principal buyers, or where the public are buyers more or less in the proportion in which they are tax-payers, it does not greatly matter which of the two plans is chosen. But where, as with all the staple articles of food, poor people play a much larger part, compared with rich people, as buyers of an article which is short than they play as tax-payers, it does greatly matter. For, if the State were to adopt the excess profits plan in preference to the maximum prices plan, it would be relieving the well-to-do of a large block of taxation, and throwing it, by a roundabout and semi-secret process, upon the shoulders of the poor. Whatever might be thought of the desirability of exacting a larger contribution to the expenses of the war from relatively poor persons, it was obvious that a device of that kind would never be tolerated. Consequently, over a large part of the field, the excess profits plan could not practically be made the *main* engine for preventing fortunately situated sellers from making fortunes out of the war. Resort had of necessity to be had to the plan of maximum prices.

§ 4. In the actual working out of that plan, a great number of difficulties emerged, which it will be well to set out in order. The first of these was the difficulty of definition. The same name often covers a great variety of different qualities of article, which it may be extremely hard to disentangle in any formal schedule. When this condition prevails it is impossible to exercise control over prices by general rules, and it becomes necessary to fall back upon the cumbrous device of individual appraisement. Thus, under the Raw Cocoa Order of March 1918, it was laid down that no raw cocoa might be sold except at "a fair value," this fair value being determined by a person authorised by the Food Controller to determine the grade of the various lots of cocoa. A similar plan was adopted at the end of 1917 for controlling the prices of cattle and sheep sold by live weight at market. Obviously, however, this plan could not be employed on a large scale, owing to the vast amount of labour that it involves. Conse-quently, in general, some modification of it was essential, and some general classification of grades had, in spite of the openings for evasion that this permits, to be, in one way or another, relied upon.

A second difficulty, when the problem of *defining* grades of quality was overcome, resulted from the mere fact that grades were often very numerous. The task of fixing prices directly for a great variety of these might well be more than any authority, at all events in the earlier stages of its operation, was prepared to enter upon. When there were only a few grades, it was comparatively easy, with the help of advice from experts, to do this; but, when there were a great many, it was thought better to rely, not on a schedule of maximum prices, but on a general Order determining the relations between the prices that might be charged in the future and those that had been charged in the past. An example of this plan was the Order of the Ministry of Munitions, issued in August 1916, by which sellers of 'machine tools were forbidden, except with the sanction of the Minister, henceforward to charge prices higher than they were charging in July 1915.

An analogous difficulty had to be faced when a commodity, about the grading of which, perhaps, there was no need to trouble, was produced under different conditions in a number of different localities, in such wise that a single maximum price would not treat different producers fairly. Here, too, inability to construct a schedule as varied as the circumstances required forced the controlling authority to fall back on the plan of fixing, not future prices themselves, but the relation between future prices and past prices. Thus, in May 1917, an Order was issued that no imported soft wood should be sold at prices above those that ruled *in each several locality* in the week ending 31st January 1917. This Order was subsequently modified as regards imports from Scandinavia; but with that we are not concerned.

So far it has been tacitly assumed that the maximum price aimed at for any one commodity of a given grade is a single price. For some commodities, however, no one uniform price ruling throughout the year is adapted to the conditions of their production and sale, and a series of maxima is needed. Plainly, a series is more difficult to determine correctly than a single price. Consequently, here again the controlling authority was driven to the method of regulating the *relation* between future and past prices. Thus, in July 1917, it was ordered that the wholesale price of milk per imperial gallon should not henceforward anywhere exceed by more than 6½d. the price charged in the corresponding month a year before, and that the retail price per imperial quart should not exceed this corresponding price by more than 2d. The same plan was followed in the Price of Coal (Limitation) Act of 1915, which decreed that no colliery company should charge a price exceeding by more than 4s. (afterwards raised to 6s. 6d.) the price charged on a similar sale at a similar date in 1913–14.

Plainly, all these indirect and roundabout methods of control left the way open for evasion and were likely to prove difficult to enforce. Consequently, controlling authorities, as they got a better grip and better knowledge of the conditions of various industries, tried to step forward to the more precise method of maximum price schedules. More and more this became the predominant plan. The producers' and wholesalers' prices of most of the more important articles of food came to be fixed directly by schedule, as were also the prices of most of the commodities controlled by the Ministry of Munitions. For most things it was found sufficient to set up a single schedule. But sometimes different producers' prices were fixed for different parts of the country. For hay, for example, Scotland was given one price, England another. Sometimes, too, a series of schedules were set up to apply to different parts of the year. For potatoes the Order of February 1917 fixed one price up till March 31st, and another higher price after that date; and for peas and beans an Order of May 1917 fixed three prices, diminishing in amount, for sales in June, July and later months. Similarly for wheat, oats and barley, to be harvested in the United Kingdom, the Food Controller, in August 1917, fixed a series of prices rising gradually in each successive two months from November 1917 on to June 1918. A later Order fixing maximum milk prices made a similar differentiation between different parts of the year. It is plain that the direct establishment of maximum prices is, if the appropriate prices can once be worked out satisfactorily, likely to prove much more effective than any roundabout plan.

So far we have only taken account of industries so simply organised that the producers sell a finished product direct, without any intermediary, to ultimate consumers. In most industries, however, there are several stages between the original material or service and the finished product in consumers' hands. This fact gives rise to further problems. The conditions of demand for any finished product being given, when an artificial price is fixed for any material or service used in the course of making and selling it, the price of the finished product need not be lowered correspondingly, but it is in the power of other persons in a line between the provider of this material or service and the finished product to add on to their charges the equivalent of whatever has been knocked off the charges of the regulated sellers. Thus, if the price of coal at the pit-mouth were reduced by State action, and nothing else were done, the only effect might be that dealers in coal could buy more cheaply while retaining the old price of sale. Again, if the price of cattle were forced down, and nothing else done, retail prices might remain unaltered, while butchers and meat dealers gained enormously. Yet again, if freight-rates on imported materials were kept artificially low by Government action, the various people who use these materials in their industries might get the whole benefit. Nor is it merely *possible* that this *might* happen. In general it *would* happen, except in so far as the people, on whom a power of exaction was thus conferred, deliberately from patriotic motives, or from fear of popular resentment, decided to forgo their advantage. In order to prevent this, the fixing of maximum prices at the earlier stages of production had to be coupled with control over the profits which manufacturers or dealers at a later stage may make by adding further charges on to these prices. One way in which this control was exercised was by limiting the *percentage* addition that might be made by any seller in the line. In May 1917, for example, it was decreed that no timber from Russia should be sold at an advance of more than 10 per cent on the purchase price; and in September 1917 a schedule of prices for fish was fixed as between fish-curers and wholesale dealers, and other sellers (with the exception of retailers) were prohibited from adding more than 10 per cent on to the scheduled prices. More usually it was not the *percentage*, but the *amount*, of addition that was limited. Thus, under the Cheese Order of August 1917, first-hand prices of various sorts of British-made cheese were fixed as from the maker, and it was provided that no dealer other than the maker should add on to them more than the actual charge for transport *plus*, in general, 6s. per cwt. In October it was provided further that retailers should not add on to the prices actually paid by them more than $2\frac{1}{2}$d. per lb. In the same month the prices of the various sorts of leather were regulated on the same general plan. In like manner the price of horse and poultry mixture was controlled, in November 1917, by an Order forbidding the maker to charge a price exceeding the cost to him of his ingredients by more than £1 : 10s. per ton ; and the amount that other sellers might add on was limited to 1s. per cwt. on sales of 6 cwt. and more, 3s. per cwt. on sales of from 3 to 6 cwt., and so on. In meat a variant on this plan was adopted, in the first instance, on account of difficulties due to the custom among retailers of obtaining different proportions of their profit from the sale of different joints. In an Order of September 1917 it was laid down that no person shall in any fortnight sell meat by retail at such prices as cause the aggregate price received by him to exceed actual costs to him by more than a prescribed percentage (20 per cent or $2\frac{1}{2}$d. per lb., whichever shall be less). In August 1917 a rule on similar lines was laid down for retailers of bacon and hams.

It is evident that plans of this kind for controlling the charges to be made at the later stages of a commodity's progress to the consumer suffer from the same sort of disadvantage that roundabout attempts to control producers' charges suffer from. They are liable to evasion. Consequently, the controlling authorities sought, as they became more masters of their work, to evolve some more satisfactory arrangement. One stage in this evolution is illustrated by the Butter Prices Order of August 1917. In that Order it was laid down that retailers should not add to the price of butter sold by them more than 2½d. per lb. above the actual cost of it to them; but it was provided further that local Food Control Committees *might* prescribe a scale of maximum retail prices in accordance with the general directions of the Order (which includes rules about maker's, importer's and wholesaler's prices), although conformity with that scale should not relieve any retailer from the obligation not to add on more than 2½d. per lb. A slightly more advanced stage is illustrated by the plan adopted for regulating the retail prices of coal. The general principle was laid down that retailers should not add on to their own purchase price more than 1s. per ton over and above the costs of actual handling and dealing with the coal (including office expenses apart from the trader's own salary). But this principle was not left, as it were, in the air. It was provided that local authorities, after consultation and inquiry, should work it out and apply it in the form of a definite list of retail prices applicable to their district. Yet a further stage is reached when the controlling authority itself fixes lists of maximum prices at more than one point on the way from production to consumption. The Potato Order of September 1917 was of this type. Maximum prices were fixed for growers; wholesale dealers were forbidden to sell in any week at prices that yielded them more than 7s. 6d. a ton beyond their total costs on all purchases of potatoes—costs which varied with the transport conditions of different districts; and an elaborate scale of retail prices was fixed, which related the permitted price per lb. to the price per cwt., including price of transport, that the retailer had actually paid for different classes of potatoes. The final stage is reached when definite schedules are fixed throughout—for producer, wholesaler and retailer equally—by the controlling authority itself. This was the arrangement to which the Ministry of Food steadily progressed. It was definitely attained in regard to British onions, most sorts of fish, beef and mutton, fruit for jam and jam, peas and beans, and hay, oats and wheat straw. Lest, through imperfect knowledge, the special circumstances of particular districts should have been neglected in the construction of these scales, a safeguard was sometimes provided in the form of a rule empowering local Food Committees, with the sanction of the Food Controller, to vary the maxima in their district. This provision was introduced into the Order of January 1918 fixing maximum prices for rabbits. In like manner it was provided in an Order of September 1917, that, where the Food Controller or a local Food Committee was satisfied that, by reason of some exceptional circumstance, flour or bread could not be sold by *retail* at the official maximum price "so as to yield a reasonable profit," a licence might be issued, either for the whole or for a part of any Committee's area, permitting higher prices to be charged. The Order of January 1918, fixing a schedule of maximum prices for most kinds of fish, was made subject, as regards *retail* prices, to similar local revision, as was also the Milk Prices Order of March 1918. A like power of varying local retail prices, with the sanction of the Food Controller, was accorded to the local Food Committees under the Potato Prices Order of September 1917.

Hitherto attention has been confined to commodities that come into the consumer's hands in much the same form as that in which they leave the hands of producers. Further complications are introduced when we have to do with raw materials that are worked up into elaborately finished articles. Here, owing to the various parts which the raw material plays in different types and grades of finished goods, it is not generally possible to fix schedules of prices beyond the raw material. Consequently, for two important articles, boots and clothes, an ingenious roundabout plan was adopted. An attempt was made to induce or compel manufacturers to devote a considerable part of their plant to making "standard articles" to be sold at prices calculated on a basis of conversion costs, in the hope that the competition of these articles in the market would indirectly keep down the price that it was profitable to charge for similar articles that were not standardised. In boots, manufacturers were ordered to devote one-third of that part of their plant which was engaged on civilian work to making

" standard boots." In clothes, no fixed proportion of plant was forced into making standard goods, but manufacturers were tempted to take up this kind of work by relatively favourable treatment in the matter of the quota of raw wool allowed to them. In cotton goods, though the price of raw cotton was artificially controlled, no corresponding control of the finished commodity was attempted, the argument being that cotton manufacturers were sufficiently burdened by having to provide a special levy to pay benefit to workpeople thrown out of work by the reduction in the number of spindles and looms that might be operated.

§ 5. The foregoing account of the difficulties encountered and the expedients employed in the exercise of price control suggests a question of some theoretical interest. It is plain enough that, in the earlier stages of control, practical considerations make it necessary to begin at the producer's, rather than the retailer's, end ; for the local differentiations needed in a retail schedule are generally much more serious and require much more knowledge to allow of their being fairly made. As has been shown, however, as the controlling authority became more expert and got a better grip on its industries, it tended to make price schedules all along the line from the producer to the final seller. Thus, in the end, retail maximum prices often were fixed. The point in doubt is whether, when this has all been arranged, there is any real need to continue the earlier stages of control. Will not maximum retail prices be reflected back all along the line, and so automatically stop " profiteering " at earlier stages ? The view that this will be so seems to have guided the work of some of the Ministry of Food's controls. For example, the prices of turnips and swedes were regulated by a rule that *nobody* might sell them for more than 1½d. per lb., and the price of chocolates and sweets by a rule that *nobody* might sell them for more than 3d. per oz. and 2d. per oz. respectively. In general, however, it was thought better to maintain price schedules at the earlier stages, separate from, and adjusted to, the retail maxima. In a world of pure competition it does not appear that this would really have been necessary. If the retail maxima were rightly arranged, everybody in line would automatically be forced to charge prices that yielded them about the ordinary rate of profits. The artificial restriction upon retail price would act in exactly the same way as a fall in the public demand for the commodity sufficient to counteract the shortage of supply. It is probable, however, that this adjustment would not, in real life, be made without a certain amount of friction, and that some of the traders affected might be in a position to exercise quasi-monopolistic pressure against particular shopkeepers or others who happened to be mainly dependent on them. Consequently, when schedules of maximum prices for the earlier stages had already been worked out, to drop them, in the hope that the retailers' schedules subsequently superimposed would by themselves achieve the whole of the ends desired, would probably have been unwise.

§ 6. We have now to consider the broad analytical problem which these expedients of war time suggest. What *exactly* is to be said of the relation between the kind of price regulation that was then attempted and the size of the national dividend? The great upheaval of the war had caused the existing distribution of resources to be uneconomic, in the sense that the value of the marginal net product (social and private alike) of those employed in making certain specially scarce articles was abnormally high. Apart from outside interference abnormal values of marginal net products mean abnormal returns to the investor; and these abnormal returns tend to draw resources from occupations of relatively low productivity to those occupations of greater productivity in which they rule. When prices are cut down by law, the value of the marginal net product of any given quantity of resources in any occupation is, indeed, necessarily cut down also, because we have defined this value as the marginal physical net product multiplied by the realised price. Plainly, however, this definition tacitly assumes the realised price to be identical with the demand price. When these two are artificially divorced, our definition must be changed. The values of the marginal net products of resources, which it is to the interest of the national dividend to make equal everywhere, consist in the marginal physical net products multiplied by the demand prices. When this is understood, it is evident that an artificial reduction of price, while lowering returns in the industry affected by it, leaves the true value of the marginal net product of any quantity of resources invested there unchanged. The desirability, from the standpoint of the national dividend, of a transference of resources is thus unaltered, while the principal influence tending to bring it about is weakened. To put the same point in more general terms, any external limitation imposed on the price of an article produced under competitive conditions (*i.e.* otherwise than by a monopolist) must lessen the inducement that people have to make that article. Normally it is just through high prices and high profits that a shortage of anything corrects itself. The prospect of exceptional gain directs free resources into the industry which makes the thing that is short. Cut off this prospect, and that increase of supply, which the interest of the national dividend demands, will be checked, and checked more severely the greater is the cut made from the "natural" price.

§ 7. In the special circumstances of the Great War this injurious tendency of price limitation was largely counteracted by other influences. For the State itself, in many departments of industry, took over the task of allocating resources among different occupations. It built up munition works, controlled shipbuilding, and urged on agricultural production by the promise of land, tractors, and labour drawn from the Army. Thus, though price regulation might weaken the directive force normally exercised by economic motives, the task of direction was taken over by another and more powerful agency. No doubt, had prices in any occupation been artificially pushed down so low that profits to the "representative" firm fell actually below the ordinary money level, capital and labour would have gone elsewhere in spite of government pressure. But, of course, prices were not artificially pushed down to this extent in any occupation. On the contrary, complaint was often made that they were left high enough to yield abnormally large profits, not merely to firms that could fairly be regarded as "representative," but even to those very weak and inefficient firms which, in the ordinary course, would have been making losses and decaying out of business.[1] On the

---

[1] It might have proved practicable to fix prices at a considerably lower level if the good and bad firms had been formed into a kind of pool, and the objective

whole, therefore, we may conclude that, as things were, in view of the abnormal activity of the State, and, it should be added, of the effectiveness of appeals to patriotism, price control in the peculiar circumstances of the war probably caused very little damage to the volume of the national dividend.

§ 8. It would, however, be a great error to infer from this that a general permanent policy of control, designed to prevent groups of producers from reaping abnormal profit on occasions when the conditions of the market give them power to do so, would be equally innocuous. People, in choosing their investments, take account of these ups and downs, and, so far as their judgment is correct, place their resources in such a way that, on the average and on the whole, the marginal yield works out about equally in different occupations. In these circumstances it is obvious that any general State policy of cutting down prices in any industry below the competitive level, on occasions when the conditions of demand and supply would enable that industry to obtain exceptional profits, must, in effect, penalise it as compared with stable industries. For, if, in a hilly district where the average level of peaks and valleys is the same as it is on a plateau, the tops of the peaks are removed, the average level there will, of course, be reduced below that of the plateau. The discouraging effect of this differential action cannot be made good by any direct manipulation of production by the State. For here we have to do, not merely with a tendency for free resources to go elsewhere *at the time* when the régime of price control is at work, but with a tendency that operates continually and checks the general flow of resources that would otherwise seek investment in building up the permanent equipment of the threatened industry. If, for example, this country adopted a general policy of forbidding farmers to charge high prices when they have power to do

sought been normal profits for the pool as a whole. Professor Taussig has pointed out that, before an arrangement of this kind could be worked, very serious administrative difficulties would have to be overcome and an elaborate system of detailed costings set up (*Quarterly Journal of Economics*, Feb. 1919). Besides this technical objection, there is the further more general objection that efficient management in individual firms would be very greatly discouraged, since it would reap very little reward.

so on account of a bad world harvest, this would check investment in British agriculture; because people expect bad world
harvests from time to time and look to high prices then to set
against low prices in bumper years.   While, therefore, on the
one hand, our analysis does not imply that the policy of price
limitation adopted in the abnormal circumstances of the war
worked injury to the national dividend, on the other hand,
the experience of the war gives no ground for doubting that
a general permanent policy of price limitation, in non-
monopolised industries, would produce this effect.   This conclusion is, of course, subject to the considerations set out in
the preceding chapter.   It is subject, too, to the qualification
that, if maximum prices are fixed so high as to leave all
ordinary sales unaffected and merely to protect an occasional
weak purchaser from exploitation by unscrupulous dealers,
they will not interfere with the way in which resources
are distributed between different uses, and will not, therefore,
injure the national dividend.   Moreover, if State interference
to prevent any group of producers from making excessive
earnings in good times were balanced by interference to
prevent them from making abnormally low earnings in bad
times, the net result, though it would necessarily involve a
redistribution of their production between good times and bad,
would not necessarily involve a contraction in the aggregate
amount of their production.

CHAPTER XIII

§ 1. IT is not only in the matter of prices that the war afforded examples of Government interference with competitive industry. Extensive interference also took place with the free distribution of commodities among different industries, different firms within the same industry, and different ultimate consumers. This interference had to be undertaken in order to get over difficulties to which the price regulations described in the preceding chapter gave rise. For, when prices in competitive industries are artificially reduced below the level that they tend naturally to assume, the ordinary market influences regulating the distribution of commodities between different purchasers are thrown out of gear. When there are no price restrictions, at any price everybody buys for every purpose as much of a thing as, at that price, he wants, and this process exhausts the whole supply. But, when, *in competitive industries*, prices are artificially kept down, the sum of the demands of all purchasers for all purposes is greater, and may be much greater, than the supply. In the United States, where the wheat for the whole year comes from the national harvest, the result of price limitation unaccompanied by rationing was that everybody got all he wanted in the earlier part of the harvest year and had to fall back on substitutes in the later part.[1] There was, in short, a bad distribution through time. For most commodities, however, production as well as consumption is continuous. Thus, at no time can everybody get all he wants, but there is a

[1] Cf. Supplement to *American Economic Review*, March 1919, p. 244.

continuous shortage. Distribution becomes, if nothing is done, the sport of accident, influence, and ability to stand for a long time without fainting in a queue. There is no reason to expect that the distribution reached through these agencies will be, in any sense, a good distribution. Consequently, when, during the course of the war, the policy of controlling prices was adopted, it was, in general, found necessary to control distribution also, and, with that object, to establish some criterion for fixing the shares available for different purchasers. It was not, indeed, only where prices were regulated that supplies to individuals were controlled. In some instances, where there was no price regulation, they were controlled in order to prevent private persons from absorbing for their own use an undue quantity of things and services urgently needed by the Government for war. Here the control limited aggregate private consumption and did not merely regulate the distribution of an aggregate already limited. The technical problems involved are, however, the same whether control of supplies is or is not associated with the fixing of maximum prices.

§ 2. When the commodity dealt with was a material that could be employed for several alternative purposes, the obvious criterion was relative urgency, from the point of view of national war service, of these several purposes. The simplest method of applying this criterion was to make rules cutting off the supply of material from the least urgent uses either in part or altogether, thus leaving more available for more urgent uses. Examples of this method were:

(1) The imposition of Treasury restrictions upon the investment of new capital abroad and, in a less degree, in civilian home industries.

(2) The enunciation of a rule that no building costing more than £500, and no building whatever containing structural steel, should be put up without a licence.

(3) The reduction of railway service for all forms of civilian, as distinguished from military, use.

(4) The prohibition of the use of petrol for pleasure.

(5) The withdrawal of materials, etc., from the less important tramways and light railways to others of greater national importance.

(6) The regulation of the use of horses in towns and on farms and the control of road transport generally.

(7) The prohibition of the use of paper for newspaper contents bills, and, under certain conditions, for traders' circulars, and the abolition of " Returns."

(8) The prohibition by the Timber Supplies Department against packing various articles in wooden cases and crates.

(9) The prohibition of the use of electricity for lighting shop fronts, and the order restricting the hours during which hotel and restaurant dining-rooms might use artificial light or theatres might remain open.

This method is entirely negative: the least urgent uses are ruled out, either by a general order, or by making a licence —refused to the least urgent uses—a condition of action.

§ 3. Obviously, devices of this character are of limited application. They take no account of the fact that uses other than the least urgent are not all of equal urgency. Consequently, if the material or labour available is insufficient for all the uses that are left when the least urgent uses have been cut off, it becomes necessary to arrange for some system of priority among those that are left. The simplest way in which this was attempted was as follows. The material was left in private hands, but a system of Priority Certificates was instituted, which only permitted sales to would-be buyers with certificates of lower urgency after those with certificates of higher urgency had been satisfied. Government work had the first grade of certificate, work of special national importance (e.g. export work deemed valuable for protecting the foreign exchanges) the next, and so on in successive stages. Iron and steel products were dealt with on this plan, and quarry stone and other road material on less elaborate, but substantially equivalent, lines. When the proportion of the available commodity that is needed for Government war work or other especially urgent need is very large, the plan of priority certificates by itself is not always safe. The Government may get less than it needs. To meet this risk it is tempted itself, either by purchase or requisition, to become an owner (or hirer) of so much of the commodity as is of specially urgent need. It may then hand over to firms engaged on Government work, or other specially urgent work, the supplies that are required for that work; but, even so, it will need to distribute the surplus on some system of priority to other firms. This plan was followed in a rough general way with imported leather and flax and with a number of metals.

§ 4. The application in these different forms of the criterion of comparative urgency among competing uses presented very considerable difficulties during the war. These difficulties, however, were necessarily much less than those which would have to be overcome if a similar criterion had to be applied to normal conditions of peace. For the comparative urgency of different uses in war time depends on the contribution which they severally make to national war efficiency. This provides a definite standard to which to work. It is obvious that food and munitions and the support of the armed forces must take precedence over everything else; and, though, as the rivalry between the demands of munitions and of ships for steel made plain, it is difficult, still it is not impossible, by conferences between representatives of the various Ministries, to work out a fairly satisfactory scheme of priorities. The reason for this is that everything is subordinated to a single relatively simple end. Under a régime of established peace—apart, of course, from possible " key " industries, for which the natural method of assistance is bounties or a tariff, and not the allocation of material—there is no single end of this kind. We have no longer to deal with the Government's wants for war service, but with the wants of an immense and varied population for necessaries, comforts and luxuries. In war time it is clearly more important to bring steel into the country than it is to bring paper, and to manufacture army baking ovens than private kitchen ranges. But in peace time simple propositions of this kind cannot be laid down. Those things ought to be made which are most wanted and will yield the greatest sum of satisfaction. But the Government cannot possibly decide what these things are; and, even if it could decide what they are at one moment, before its decision had been put into effect conditions would very probably be changed, and they would have become something entirely different. It is not easy to see how this obstacle to a permanent policy of rationing materials among the several industries of the country could be satisfactorily overcome.

§ 5. To allocate materials to different uses according to the comparative national urgency of these uses was not a complete solution of the war problem. Within each grade of use purchases are sought by a number of rival firms anxious to work up the material into the finished product. Normally price would have established itself at such a level that each firm obtained the quantity of material which, at that price, it desired. With restricted prices it is necessary to provide an alternative basis for distribution among these firms, as well as among the different categories of urgency. The basis adopted by the British Government was that of comparative pre-war purchases. It is illustrated by—

(*a*) The regulation of the Cotton Control Board (1918), limiting the proportion of machinery that any firm might keep at work on American cotton ;

(*b*) The condition imposed on importers by the Paper Control, that they should supply their customers (*i.e.* manufacturers) in the same proportions as in 1916–17.

In highly organised trades, like the cotton industry, there was no technical difficulty in applying regulations on these lines. But in many of the metal trades a special organisation had to be created for the purpose. It is clear that this basis of allocation could not be employed in connection with any policy designed to last for more than a short period. For an arrangement, which tended to maintain the various firms engaged in an industry always in the same relative position as they occupied in an arbitrarily chosen year, would constitute a quite intolerable obstacle to efficiency and progress.

§ 6. When the prices of finished products as well as of their raw materials were limited by regulation, a problem exactly analogous to the above had to be faced as regards distribution among ultimate consumers. To organise a plausible basis for this is only practicable in connection with commodities in wide, regular and continuous consumption. The basis aimed at here was, not comparative pre-war purchases, but an estimate of comparative current need. For coal, gas and electricity an objective measure of this was sought in the number and size of rooms and the number of inhabitants in different people's houses. For food products, while some differentiation was attempted by means of supplementary rations to soldiers, sailors, heavy workers, invalids and children, in the main the knot was cut by assuming the needs of the general body of all the civil population to be equal, and rationing all alike. This sort of distributional arrangement is fundamentally different from the other two kinds. The passage from war to peace does not destroy or render violently unsuitable the criterion adopted for it. Plainly, however, in peace, as indeed in war also, its necessarily rough and arbitrary character constitutes a very serious objection to it. "The proportion in which families of equal means use the different 'necessaries of life' are very different. In ordinary times they distribute their expenditure among the different necessaries in the manner which seems best, some getting more bread, some more meat and milk, and so on. By equal rationing all this variety is done away with; each household is given the same amount per head of each commodity; allowance for age, sex, occupation and other things can only be introduced with difficulty."[1] There can be little doubt that British Food Rationing during the war, in spite of this disability, led to a much more satisfactory result than would have been attained from the scramble—a scramble in which rich people would have been able to exercise various sorts of pull upon tradesmen—that must have resulted had food prices been limited but distribution left to take care of itself. In peace time, however, when presumably the alternative to rationing would be less intolerable, the inconvenience and inequalities attaching to it have correspondingly greater weight.

§ 7. If we are content to regard the various arrangements which I have been describing as merely supplementary to price restrictions already decided upon, it is plain that, though

[1] Cannan, *Economic Journal* Dec. 1917, p. 468.

they may affect the size of the national dividend, as it were, at the second remove—if, for example, they grant priority to steel for making machinery rather than motor-cars—they cannot affect it directly or fundamentally. They modify the way in which certain elements in the dividend are shared out, but not the quantities of the elements contained in it. These are modified by the price regulations in the way that was explained in the preceding chapter. They are not modified further by any distributional supplements to those regulations. Consequently, from the standpoint of the present Part, no further analysis is required; though in Part IV., where the distributional relations of rich and poor are examined, something more will have to be said about the rationing of food.

CHAPTER XIV

THE CONDITIONS OF MONOPOLISATION

§ 1. WE may now return to the main argument. In
Chapter XI. we supposed self-interest to act along the
route of simple competition. We showed that in these
circumstances, apart from divergences of the types discussed
in Chapter IX., the value of the marginal private net
product of resources in any industry tends to equality with
the central value of marginal net products in general, and
inquired in what circumstances the value of the marginal social
net product of resources in the given industry would diverge
from the value of the marginal private net product there.
We have now to consider other routes along which self-
interest may act. As has already been observed, an essential
note of "simple competition" is that the supply of each
seller constitutes so small a part of the aggregate supply
of the market that he is content to "accept market prices
without trying, of set purpose, to modify them."[1] When
any seller's output constitutes a substantial part of the
whole, there is scope for various sorts of monopolistic action ;
and, when any sort of monopolistic action is present, self-
interest does not tend to evolve an output such that the
value of the marginal private net product of resources devoted
to its production is equal to that yielded by resources employed
elsewhere. In future chapters I shall examine monopolistic
action in detail. Before that is done, however, convenience
suggests that some study should be made of the conditions
which determine the appearance of monopolistic power.

§ 2. First, other things being equal, circumstances, which,

[1] Pareto, *Cours d'économie politique*, i. p. 20.

when the aggregate scale of an industry is given, make it structurally economical for the typical individual establishment to be large, *pro tanto* increase the likelihood that a single *seller* will market a considerable part of the aggregate output of his industry; for such circumstances necessarily increase the probability that a single *establishment* will market a considerable part of that output. Whether any single establishment will, in fact, become big enough, relatively to the whole of an industry, to procure an element of monopolistic power, depends on the general characteristics of the various industries concerned. Such an event is more than usually likely in industries that produce fancy goods liable to become "specialities." For in these industries there often exist, within the broad general market, minor markets, to a certain extent non-competitive among themselves; and, when this is so, a single establishment may supply a considerable proportion of its own minor market without itself being of very great size absolutely. In a few peculiar industries, among those concerned with staple goods and services, it may also well be that the prospect of internal economies will lead to the evolution of single establishments large enough to control a predominant part of the whole output of the industry. One of the most notable instances of this is afforded by the industry of railway transportation along any assigned route. In view of the great engineering cost of preparing a suitable way, it will, obviously, be much less expensive to have one or, at most, a few railways providing the whole of the transport service between any two assigned points than to have this service undertaken by a great number of railways, each performing an insignificant proportion of the whole service. Similar remarks hold good of the industries of furnishing water, gas, electricity, or tramway service to a town. The existence of many separate establishments involves a large number of main pipes, wires and rails. But the whole business of any ordinary district can be worked with a very small number of these mains. Therefore the existence of many separate establishments implies the investment of a great quantity of capital in mains that are only employed up to a very small proportion of their capacity. There is an obvious economy in avoiding such investment. This economy is the *ultimate* reason for the tendency, which appears strongly in the class of industry just discussed, for individual establishments to furnish a large proportion of the total supply. The truth is partly veiled by the fact that the *immediate* reason is, in general, unwillingness, on the part of national and local government authorities, to allow the right of eminent domain to be invoked, or the streets to be disturbed, on more occasions, or by more people, than is absolutely necessary. It is, however, the extra expense of such procedure that lies behind this unwillingness on the part of the authorities. In the general body of industries concerned with staple goods and services the conditions peculiar to railways and their allied industries are not reproduced. Internal economies reach their limit at different points in different kinds of industry, at one point in the cotton industry, at another in the iron and steel industry; generally at a less advanced stage where the part played by labour relatively to capital is large and at a more advanced stage where it is small; but always long before the individual establishment has grown to any appreciable fraction of the whole industry of which it is a part.[1] When this happens, internal economies evidently cannot be responsible for monopolistic power.

§ 3. Secondly, other things being equal, circumstances, which, when the aggregate scale of an industry and the size of the typical individual establishment are given, make it structurally economical for the typical individual unit of business management—a number of establishments, for example, controlled by one authority—to be large, *pro tanto* increase the likelihood that a single seller will market a considerable part of the aggregate output of his industry. This proposition has, in recent times, become of predominant importance, and it is, therefore, necessary to examine carefully the various structural

[1] Cf. Van Hise's account of the development of various important industries in the United States (*Concentration and Control*, pp. 42 *et seq.*) and Sir Sydney Chapman's discussion of the normal size of individual factories in the cotton industry (*Journal of the Royal Statistical Society*, April 1914, p. 513).

economies, for which large scale control may, in different situations, be responsible.

Much has been made by some writers of the fact that, when a number of parallel establishments are grouped under a single head, the different plants can be thoroughly specialised to particular grades of work; and of the other kindred fact that the orders in any place can be met from the plant nearest to that place, and that, thus, cross freights are saved. That the economies resulting from close specialisation upon particular articles or even particular processes may, in some circumstances, be very great has been abundantly proved in the British engineering industry during the war. But it does not appear that a single control over many separate establishments is essential in order to secure these economies. Even though the different establishments were to remain separate, it might be expected, when once their great importance is realised, that the industrial organism would tend, under the sway of ordinary economic motives, to evolve them. In the paper industry of the United States, for example, each mill confines itself as a rule to the manufacture of some one quality of paper;[1] and in the Lancashire cotton industry, not only are fine spinning, coarse spinning, and weaving localised separately, but individual firms frequently specialise on a narrow range of counts for spinning.[2] The same thing is true of the economies obtainable from the utilisation of by-products. Nor does it appear that those economies in respect of marketing, which some writers ascribe to large-scale control, are a dominating factor making for combination. For, "if a manufacturer is purchasing raw material, there is generally a market price for it which all must pay, and which any one can obtain it for, so long as he buys the customary minimum quantity; while, if what he requires is a partly manufactured article, purchases amounting in value to hundreds of pounds per annum, accompanied by prompt payment, can generally be made at the cheapest possible rate. The sole advantage enjoyed by the largest concerns in the purchase of raw materials seems to me to lie in the possibility of occasionally

---

[1] Cf. Chapman, *Work and Wages*, vol. i. p. 237.
[2] Cf. Marshall, *Industry and Trade*, p. 601.

clearing the market of raw materials or of a surplus output of partly manufactured stuff, by some purchase quite out of the power of a smaller concern to compass. Such an operation, however, partakes of the nature of a speculation, and the profit, when gained, is hardly to be called a cheapening of the cost of production, if only for the reason that the opportunity for such a special purchase cannot be relied upon to occur very often, and, when it does occur, is perhaps as likely to result in a loss as in a gain."[1] Nor, again, should much importance be attached to those advantages of large-scale management which have been summarised as "concentration of office work, provision of central warehouse for goods, centralisation of insurance and banking, establishment of a uniform system of accounts, enabling easy comparison to be made of the working of branches, institution of a uniform system of costing and of a central sales agency,"[2] and so forth. For these economies are scarcely practicable under the lower types of price-fixing Kartel, which are common in Germany, and, even in fusions and holding companies,[3] they are very soon outweighed by the immense difficulty of finding people competent properly to manage very large businesses.

There are, however, certain structural economies of large-scale management which are of a different order and have a wider reach. First, greater size, implying, as it does, greater wealth, makes it possible and profitable to spend more money on experiment. The Committee on Scientific and Industrial Research report: "Our experience up to the present leads us, indeed, to think that the small scale on which most British industrial firms have been planned is one of the principal

---

[1] Hobson, *The Industrial System*, p. 187, quoted from W. R. Hamilton, *The Cost of Production in Relation to Increasing Output*.

[2] McCrosty, *Economic Journal*, Sept. 1902, p. 359.

[3] Dr. Liefmann writes: "Einige Trusts, so der Zucker- und Spiritustrust, bildeten sich zu *einer einzigen Gesellschaft* um, also im Wege der vollständigen Verschmelzung, der Fusion, d.h. die betreffenden Unternehmungen gehen alle in einer einzigen derart auf, dass sie als besondere wirtschaftliche Organisation aufhören zu existieren. Die meisten aber nahmen in neuester Zeit nach verschiedenen Versuchen die Form der sogenannten *Holding Company*, einer *Kontrollgesellschaft*, wie wir es nennen können, an, d.h. die Gesellschaft erwarb alle oder doch die Mehrheit der Aktien sämtlicher zum Trust gehörender Einzelgesellschaften" (*Kartelle und Trusts*, p. 114).

impediments in the way of the organisation of research with a view to the conduct of those long and complicated investigations which are necessary for the solution of the fundamental problems lying at the basis of our staple industries." [1]   This is obviously a very important matter ; though it is not clear why a number of small firms should not, while retaining full independence in other respects, agree to collaborate in promoting research.   Secondly, the union into one of what would have been many firms means that, instead of each wielding only the secret processes discovered by itself, each can wield the secrets of all ; and in some circumstances this may involve large savings.   Thirdly, a business combining many establishments is, in general, in contact with a number of different markets, in which the fluctuations of demand are, in some measure, independent.   It is, therefore, in a position so to adjust things that the output of each of its component establishments shall vary through a narrower range than it would do if the several components were under separate control.   But, if an establishment produces an average output A made up of $(A + a)$ units one year and $(A - a)$ the next, its costs are bound to be less than if it produces the same average output made up of $(A + 2a)$ units one year and $(A - 2a)$ units the next; for in the latter case it must have a capital equipment adequate to a "peak load" of $(A + 2a)$ units instead of the one of $(A + a)$ units.   That this is an important matter is illustrated by the eagerness of co-operative societies—creameries and so on—to assure themselves of the "loyalty" of their members, and of Shipping Companies to "tie" their customers to them by deferred rebates or in other ways.[2]   Furthermore, even though, apart from combination, the sum of the ranges of variation in the output of the component establishments were already reduced to a minimum, *i.e.* to equality with the range of variation in aggregate output, combination might still lead to economies, by enabling the bulk of the plant to be run steadily, and reserving, after the pattern of the Sugar Trust, one specially adapted plant to adjust its output to the fluctuations in aggregate

[1] *Report*, p. 25.   Cf. Marshall, *Industry and Trade*, p. 24, footnote.
[2] Cf. *post*, Part II. Chap. XIX. § 4.

demand.[1] Fourthly, since it is much easier to forecast the incidence of various sorts of good and ill fortunes upon the aggregate of a number of separate concerns than it is to forecast the incidence upon each one individually, the operation of a business combining many establishments involves in the aggregate less uncertainty-bearing than the operation of its parts would involve if they were separated. The general economy resulting from this fact may manifest itself in the greater facility with which loans can be obtained, or in the lower price that has to be paid for them, or in the smaller proportionate reserve fund that the concern needs to keep for equalising dividends, or in other ways. The essential point is that the general economy, however it manifests itself, is necessarily there. The larger the unit of individual control, the larger is this economy. After a point, indeed, its growth, as the unit grows, becomes exceedingly slow. But, until the unit has reached a very large size, it grows rapidly, and constitutes a powerful force making for larger units— though, no doubt, among commodities suitable for grading, a speculative market may be developed, and may enable small concerns, through the practice of hedging, to put themselves, for *some* sorts of uncertainty, on a level with large concerns.[2] One further point may be mentioned. In certain special industries large-scale control not only achieves a direct economy by lessening the uncertainty-bearing that is involved in given fluctuations in the individual fortunes of different firms; it also achieves an indirect economy by reducing the probability that fluctuations will occur. It does this in occupations where public confidence is important, and where largeness of capital resource is calculated to · create confidence. This condition is fulfilled in banking—the more so since publicity of bankers' accounts has become common. The reason that banks differ in this respect from other concerns is, of course, that their customers are their creditors, and not, as in most trades, their debtors.[3]

---

[1] Cf. Jenks and Clark, *The Trust Problem*, p. 43.

[2] Cf. Brace, *The Value of Organised Speculation*, p. 210.

[3] For a very full study of the subject-matter of §§ 2-3, cf. Marshall, *Industry and Trade*, Bk. ii. chaps. iii.-iv.

§ 4. So far we have considered exclusively what I have called *structural* economies. There is also another sort of economy that, in certain circumstances, favours the growth of large-scale management. So long as an industry is occupied by a number of establishments separately controlled, expenditure is likely to be incurred by all in defending their market against the others. A large part of the expenditure upon advertisements and travellers is, as was indicated in Chapter IX., of this character. But when, instead of a number of competing firms, there appear, in any section of an industry, a number of firms under a single authority, a great part of this expenditure can, as was also indicated in that chapter, be dispensed with. A and B being united, it is no longer to the interest of either to spend money in persuading people, whether through travelling salesmen or in other ways, to prefer the one to the other. It was stated, in regard to railways, before the Board of Trade Conference of 1908 : " It is well known that railway companies find it necessary to spend large sums of money in canvassing against one another, and, if competition were removed by judicious amalgamation, the greater part of this money could be saved." [1] This economy is, of course, liable to be largest where, apart from unification, " competitive " advertisement would be largest, namely, not in staple industries providing easily recognised standard articles, but in various sorts of " fancy " trades.[2]

§ 5. Let us next suppose that the size of the individual firm and the size of the individual unit of control in an industry have been adjusted to the structural and other economies obtainable, and that the · units evolved in this way are not large enough to exercise any element of monopolistic power. It is then clear that monopolistic power will

[1] *Railway Conference*, p. 26.

[2] The suggestion, that combination enables savings to be made in respect of the number or quality of travelling salesmen and so on, is not upset by the fact that, in some instances, after the formation of a combination, the aggregate annual wages paid to salesmen have increased. For the increase was probably due to attempts on the part of the combination to extend its market into fields which were not formerly occupied by any of its constituent members, or in which the business accessible to *single* firms was not enough to make it worth while for any of them to have salesmen there. .

S

not be called into being incidentally, as a by-product of developments that take place without reference to it. But there still remains, as an influence tending to produce it, the direct expectation of the gains to which it may lead. When promoters have reason to believe that amateur speculators will expect a particular monopoly to prove more profitable than it really will do, this fact promises extra gains to those who form amalgamated companies, because it enables them to unload their shares at inflated values.[1] Apart from this special consideration, however, we may lay it down that the magnitude of the gains obtainable from monopolisation depends, the conditions of supply being given, on the elasticity of the demand — *i.e.* the fraction obtained by dividing a (*small*) percentage change in price into the associated percentage change in quantity purchased—for relevant quantities of the commodity concerned.[2] The less elastic the demand, the greater, *ceteris paribus*, are the probable gains. Incidentally, it may be observed, this circumstance, coupled with that noted in the next paragraph, makes it profitable for a monopolist to extend his control over products that compete

---

[1] The following passage from Mr. J. M. Clark's *The Economics of Overhead Costs* is interesting in this connection. "How great are the economies of combination ? So far as horizontal combination goes, the most definite quantitative evidence is afforded by Dewing's study of thirty-five combinations, all of which merged at least five concerns which had formerly competed and all of which had had a ten-year history before 1914, when the disturbances due to the world-war made further comparisons irrelevant. He finds that the promoters of these combinations prophesied sufficient savings to increase their net earnings, on the average, about 43 per cent above their previous level. This average included only serious estimates, taking no account of what were obviously sheer exhibitions of rosy imagination. The outcome told another story, however, for the net earnings of the first year after consolidation averaged about 15 per cent less than the previous earnings of the constituent parts, while the result for the ten years following combination was still worse ; about 18 per cent less than the previous earnings of the constituent parts, without allowing for the fact that considerable amounts of new capital were invested during the ten-year period " (*loc. cit.* pp. 146-7).

[2] If x is the quantity purchased and $\phi(x)$ the demand price per unit, the elasticity of demand is represented by $\dfrac{\phi(x)}{x\,\phi'(x)}$. If this is equal to unity for all values of x, the demand curve is a rectangular hyperbola. The verbal definition of the text is an approximate translation of the above technical definition, so long as the term *small* contained in it is emphasised. But, of course, a 50 per cent fall in price must be accompanied, if the elasticity of demand is to be equal to unity, by a 100 per cent rise in consumption. It will be understood, of course, that, when we speak of the gains from

with his own; for example, for the "Big Five" meat-packers of the United States to absorb both (a) non-American meat and (b) non-meat foods.[1] The principal conditions of highly inelastic demand have now to be set out.

The first condition is that the commodity shall be of a kind for which it is not easy to find convenient substitutes. The demand for mutton is made comparatively elastic by the existence of beef, the demand for oil by the existence of gas, and the demand for the service of trams by the existence of omnibuses. In like manner, the demand for the service of transport by rail is probably more elastic in England than in continental America, because "the long broken coast-line of England and the great number of ports" render the competition of water carriage exceedingly powerful;[2] and the demand for the services of any particular line of railway is, in general, fairly elastic, even where no water competition exists, in consequence of the indirect competition of lines running to other markets.[3] From another field a good example of the point I am now considering is furnished by Jevons, in his book on the Coal Question: "When the Government of the Two Sicilies placed an exorbitant tax on sulphur, Italy having, as it was thought, a monopoly of native sulphur, our manufacturers soon had resort to the distillation of iron pyrites or sulphide of iron."[4] As regards the kinds of commodity for which it is likely that substitutes can be employed little of general interest can be said. It should be observed, however, that the products of a district, or a country, whose efforts are directed

---

monopolisation depending on the elasticity of demand, there is a tacit implication that the elasticities as defined above, at the several points on the relevant range of the demand curve, do not greatly differ from one another. Mr. Dalton has suggested (The Inequality of Incomes p. 192 et seq.) that, when the price of anything increases by any finite percentage, the term "arc elasticity" should be used to represent this percentage change divided into the corresponding percentage change of quantity. But, since there would generally be a different arc elasticity for every different amount of price change from a given starting point, this new term might, in unpractised hands, easily lead to confusion.

[1] Cf. Report of the Federal Trade Commission, 1919, on the Meat-packing Industry, pp. 86 and 89.

[2] Cf. Macpherson, Transportation in Europe, p. 231.

[3] Cf. Johnson, American Railway Transportation, pp. 267-8.

[4] The Coal Question, p. 135.

to leadership in quality as distinguished from quantity, are less exposed to the competition of substitutes than other products. For example, the prime qualities of beef and mutton in Great Britain have not been affected by the development of the American and Australian trade to nearly the same extent as the inferior qualities.[1] It is, therefore, a commercially important fact that English manufacturers enjoy a very marked leadership of quality in wall-papers, fine textiles and cables, whereas in the electrical and chemical industries they are in a decidedly inferior position.[2] Obviously, from the present point of view, we must include among the substitutes for any commodity produced by a seller exercising monopolistic power the same commodity produced by other sellers. The larger, therefore, is the proportion of the total output of product that a seller exercising monopolistic power provides in any market, the less elastic the demand for his services will be. Inelasticity of demand for monopoly goods is, therefore, promoted in industries where importation from rival sources is hindered by high transport charges, high tariffs, or international agreements providing for the division of the field between the combined producers of different countries. Furthermore, in order that the elasticity of demand may be affected by substitutes, it is not necessary that the rival source of supply should be actually existing. In some industries manufacture by people who are normally purchasers is itself a possible rival source of supply. Thus the Committee on Home Work observe: "Unless the price at which these articles (baby linen and ladies' blouses and underclothing) are sold to the wives and daughters of the better-paid working men and small middle-class people is low, those who would otherwise be purchasers will buy the materials and make the articles at home." The same remark seems to apply to laundry-work and charing. The poor housewife has the power, if reason offers, to do these things for herself. Consequently, the demand for the services of specialists at such tasks is exceptionally elastic.[3] For example, it has been

---

[1] Cf. Besse, *L'Agriculture en Angleterre*, pp. 45 and 85.
[2] Cf. Levy, *Monopole, Kartelle und Trusts*, pp. 227, 229, 237.
[3] Cf. Chapman, *Unemployment in Lancashire*, p. 87.

remarked of Birmingham : " The washerwomen are among the first to suffer in any period of trade depression, for, as the first economy in bad times is to do your own washing, the tiny laundry with a very local connection is soon emptied." [1]

The second condition, making for inelasticity of demand, is that a commodity shall give rise to only a small proportion of the total cost of any further commodities in the production of which it may be employed. The reason, of course, is that, when this proportion is small, a large percentage rise in the price of the commodity, with which we are concerned, involves only a small percentage rise in the price of these further commodities, and, therefore, only a small percentage contraction of consumption. Dr. Levy suggests that this condition makes the demand for the ordinary raw materials of industry highly inelastic.[2] A similar line of thought brings out the fact that the elasticity of the demand for commodities at wholesale will be smaller, the larger is the proportionate part played by retailing and transport expenses in the cost of the commodities to consumers.

The third condition is that the further commodities, if any, in whose production our commodity is employed, shall be such that substitutes cannot easily be found for them. Thus the raw materials of the building trade should be subject, other things being equal, to a less elastic demand than those of the engineering trade, because foreign machines can compete with English machines much more easily than foreign houses can compete with English houses.[3]

The fourth condition is that the other commodities or services which co-operate with our commodity in the making of a finished product shall be easily " squeezable," or, in technical language, shall have an inelastic supply schedule.

[1] Cadbury, *Women's Work*, p. 172. It may be added that, from a short-period point of view, the elasticity of the demand for new production of certain durable goods is made greater than it would otherwise be by the fact that half-worn-out garments and other such things are possible substitutes for new ones. (Cf. Chapman, *The Lancashire Cotton Industry*, p. 120.)

[2] *Monopole, Kartelle und Trusts*, p. 280.

[3] It should be noticed, however, that, though houses as wholes cannot be imported, it is becoming always easier to import *parts* of them. The imports of wrought stone, marble and joinery doubled between 1890 and 1902 ; whereas from the provinces to London the "imports" of these things have increased still more largely (Dearle, *The London Building Trades*, p. 52).

All these four conditions, which Marshall has distinguished, refer directly to the nature of people's *desire* for different commodities. There is yet another condition, dependent on the fact that the demand schedule derived from a given desire schedule for any commodity is only identical in form with the desire schedule, provided that the proportion of people's incomes spent on the commodity is so small that variations in the quantity of their purchase make no appreciable difference to the "marginal utility" of money to them. When this condition is not realised, the following considerations become relevant. Suppose that there is only one sort of commodity in the world, and that it is impossible to store money. Then, whatever the form of people's desire schedule for this commodity, their demand schedule is necessarily such that the same sum will be spent on it whatever the amount of it available; in other words, the elasticity of demand, in respect of all possible amounts of consumption, is necessarily equal to unity. From this we may generalise as follows : Given the elasticity of the desire for any commodity, the elasticity of the demand for it will diverge from this elasticity to a greater extent, and will approach more closely towards unity, the larger is the proportionate part of people's income that is normally spent on this commodity. Thus, the demand for commodities which absorb a large part of people's incomes cannot be either so inelastic or so elastic as it is possible for the demand for commodities which only absorb a small part of their incomes to be.[1]

§ 6. The preceding considerations suggest that units of control adequate to exercise monopolistic power will often be found, even though neither structural economies nor advertisement economies dictate their formation. The tendency towards this result is opposed by the difficulty and cost involved in bringing about agreements among competing sellers. This difficulty and cost depend upon the following general circumstances. First, combination is easier when the number of sellers is small than when it is large ; for small numbers both facilitate the actual process of negotiation and diminish the chance that some party to an agreement will subsequently violate it. An attempt to form a Kartel in the German

[1] Cf. Birck, *Theory of Marginal Values*, pp. 133-4.

match trade in 1883 is reported by Liefmann to have failed because no less than 245 separate producers had to be consulted.[1] Secondly, combination is easier when the various producers live fairly close to one another, and so can come together easily, than when they are widely scattered. The reason why combination prevails in the German coal industry, and not in the English, is partly that, in Germany, the production of coal is localised, and not spread over a number of different districts, as it is in this country.[2] A similar reason probably accounts, in great measure, for the excess of combination that appears among sellers in general, as compared with buyers in general; for, it may be observed, at auctions, where buyers also are closely assembled, combination among them is not infrequent. Thirdly, combination is easier when the products of the various firms are simple, of constant quality, not adjusted to individual tastes, and, therefore, capable of being intelligently and more or less precisely defined. Marshall wrote: " It is almost impossible to arrange a uniform price list for carpets or curtain stuffs into which wool of different qualities, cotton, jute and other materials are worked in varying proportions and with incessant changes in fabric as well as in pattern. There is no room for cartellisation of such things as biscuits, or ladies' hats, in which versatility is demanded as well as high quality." [3] One writer suggests that a reason why English firms are combined to a less extent than foreign firms is that they concern themselves, as a rule, with the higher qualities, and the more specialised kinds, of commodities, rather than with " mass goods "; [4] and another, in like manner, attributes the greater ease with which Coke Kartels are formed in Germany, as against Coal Kartels, to the greater uniformity of quality generally found in coke.[5] Fourthly, combination is easier when the tradition and habit of the country is favourable, than when it is unfavourable, to joint action in general. When employers have been accustomed to act together in Chambers

1 *Unternehmeverbände*, p. 57.
2 Cf. Levy, *Monopole, Kartelle und Trusts*, p. 172.
3 *Industry and Trade*, p. 549.
4 Levy, *Monopole, Kartelle und Trusts*, p. 187.
5 Walker, *Combinations in the German Coal Industry*, p. 43.

of Commerce, in agreements as to discounts and rebates, or in negotiations with unions of workpeople, the friction to be overcome in making a price agreement is evidently less than it would be if they came together for the first time for that purpose. Thus : " The Association—such as the Merchants' Association of New York—has, indeed, no monopoly power, but it is, nevertheless, of very great importance, owing to its socialising effects and its tendency to prepare the way for a stronger organisation, the combination or pool." [1]   In like manner, the New Zealand arbitration law " forces employers into unions, for only thus can they defend themselves under the Act, and these naturally evolve into organisations for restricting competition." [2]   Yet again, there can be no doubt that the various forms of joint action which British engineering firms, for example, were compelled to take during the Great War must have done much to smooth the way for future combination.   Perhaps the opposing friction is also somewhat smaller when the producers concerned are companies than it is when they are private firms, in whose operations the sense of personal importance plays a larger part.

§ 7. The preceding section has tacitly implied that, where the gain from unification exceeds the cost and trouble involved, unification will, in fact, occur.   This implication, however, is not warranted.   It does not necessarily follow that, because an opportunity for agreement advantageous to all parties exists, an agreement will in fact be made.   The reason is that mutual jealousy may cause A and B to leave the melon of common gain uncut, rather than that either should allow the other to obtain what he considers a share unduly large relatively to his own.   Shall " participation " be proportional to the capacity of the several combining firms, or to their average product during recent years, or to the amount of the investment that has been made in plant and goodwill, or to some other quantity ?   " One manufacturer has patents and special machinery, which have cost him a great deal of money, and by which he sets much store.   He will not enter the proposed combination unless these costs are made up to

---

[1] Robinson, *American Economic Association*, 1904, p. 126.
[2] V. S. Clark, *United States Bulletin of Labour*, No. 43, p. 1251.

him.   Another manufacturer may have a large productive capacity, fifty nail machines, for example.   He may have been unable to find a market for the output of more than half his machines, but in the combination, he contends, all his capacity will become available.   He, therefore, insists that productive capacity should be the basis on which the allotment of shares in the trust should be made.   A third man, by the excellence of his equipment and the energy of his methods, has been able to run his plant at its full capacity, while his competitor, with a larger productive capacity but a less favourable location or a less capable body of subordinates, has operated only half time.   The successful manufacturer contends that average sales should be the basis of allotment." [1]   Disputes on these lines may easily prevent agreement if direct negotiation between the different firms is attempted.   It should, however, be noticed that they can, in great part, be obviated, and that the difficulty of combination can be correspondingly reduced, when an amalgamation is effected gradually by the process of absorption (exemplified among English banks), or when a company promoter, undertaking to buy up and consolidate a number of competing concerns, negotiates terms separately with each of them, without stating into what arrangements he has entered with the others.

[1] Meade, *Corporation Finance*, p. 36.

CHAPTER XV

MONOPOLISTIC COMPETITION

§ 1. A _CONDITION_ of monopolistic competition exists when each of two or more sellers supplies a considerable part of the market with which they are connected. In these circumstances it can be shown that there is no tendency for them to devote to the industry in which they are employed that amount of resources which I have called the ideal investment, namely, that amount which will make the value of the marginal social net product there equal to the central value of marginal social net products in general.[1] A demonstration of this proposition, possible differences between social and private net product of the type examined in Chapter IX. being ignored, can be given in ordinary language as follows.

§ 2. Let us first ignore all forms of action which aim, by sacrifice in the present, at obtaining an advantage against rivals in the future. We have, then, to do with the pure problem of " multiple monopoly." This problem assumes its simplest form when two monopolists only are supposed to be present; and, in this form, it has been much discussed among mathematical economists. Cournot decided, as is well known, that the resources devoted to production under duopoly are a determinate quantity, lying somewhere between the quantities that would have been so devoted under simple competition and under simple monopoly respectively. Edgeworth, on the other hand, in an elaborate critique, maintained that the quantity is indeterminate. In more recent discussions there is apparent some measure of return towards Cournot. If, it is held, each of two monopolists, in regulating his action,

[1] Cf. *ante*, pp. 223-4.

assumes that the other will not alter his *output* in consequence
of what he does, the quantity of resources devoted to production
by the two together is determinate at the amount calculated
by Cournot.   If each monopolist assumes that the other will
not alter his *price* in consequence of what he does, then, in a
perfect market, the quantity of resources devoted to production
by the two together is determinate at the amount proper to
simple competition ; in an imperfect market—that is to say,
a market in which some of the buyers have a *preference* for
one monopolist over the other—this quantity is determinate
at an amount less than that proper to simple competition, and
falling short of it more largely the more imperfect the market
is.[1]   More generally, if each seller makes and holds to *any*
definite assumption about the conduct of the other, it would
seem that the quantity of resources devoted to production by
both together is determinate at some amount not greater than
that proper to simple competition, and not less, in a perfect
market than the Cournot amount, in an imperfect market
than the amount proper to simple monopoly.   In real life,
however, it is, I suggest, very unlikely that either seller will
hold any consistent view about his rival's state of mind.   His
judgment will be variable and uncertain.   As in a game of
chess each player will act on some forecast of the other's
reply ; but the forecast he acts on may, according to his mood
and his reading of that opponent's psychology, be one thing or
another thing.   Hence, as it seems to me, we may properly
say that the aggregate amount of resources to be devoted to
production is indeterminate in the sense that from a mere
knowledge of the demand conditions and of the cost conditions
affecting the two monopolists—whether the cost conditions
are independent or inter-linked—we cannot foretell what it
will be.   The range of indeterminateness extends over a
distance which is larger in a perfect than it is in an imperfect
market, and in either sort of market is diminished as the
number of monopolists is increased above two.   In no case
can the aggregate investment be greater than the quantity
proper to simple competition.   We have learned, however, from
Chapter XI. that, except in industries in which imported

[1] G. Hotelling, "Stability in Competition," *Economic Journal*, March 1929.

materials subject to increasing supply price are employed, this last quantity cannot be greater than the ideal investment.   It follows that, except in these industries, the investment which is forthcoming under multiple monopoly cannot be greater than the ideal investment.   It may, however, easily be, and, in view of what has been said, in general seems likely to be, substantially less than this.

§ 3. Hitherto we have specifically excluded the effects of price warfare designed to secure future gains by driving a rival from the field or exacting favourable terms of agreement from him.   The indeterminateness just described exists under monopolistic competition, even though neither of the monopolists "hopes to ruin the other by cut-throat prices." [1]   In many instances of monopolistic competition, however, price warfare —or cut-throat competition—does, in fact, take place.   It consists in the practice of selling at a loss in order to inflict injury on a rival.   It must be distinguished carefully from the practice of reducing prices down to, or towards, prime cost, which frequently occurs in periods of depression.   This latter practice may involve large reductions of price below the "normal," and it is certain to do this when demand is variable and prime cost is small relatively to supplementary cost ; but it does not involve "selling at a loss" in the strict sense. Cut-throat competition proper occurs only when the sale price of any quantity of commodity stands below the short-period supply price of that quantity.   When it occurs, the range of possible aggregate investment no longer has, as an upper limit, the quantity proper to simple competition, but is liable to exceed this quantity to an extent determined by the opinion entertained by each of the combatants about the staying power of his opponent and by other strategical considerations.   There is, obviously, no tendency for it to approximate to the ideal investment ; but we can no longer say, as we could when cut-throat competition was ignored, that it is likely to be less than the ideal investment.

[1] Edgeworth, *Giornale degli economisti*, November 1897, p. 405.

CHAPTER XVI

SIMPLE MONOPOLY

§ 1. A CONDITION of simple monopoly exists when a single seller only is exercising monopolistic power—whether or not there are other sellers in the market who accept the price fixed by this seller—and when, allowance being made for cost of carriage and so forth, the same price rules throughout the whole of his market. In order that the effects of simple monopoly, as distinguished from simple competition, may be made clear, we must, of course, presume that the economies and technique of production are the same under both.[1] The fact that in real life they are often not the same gives rise to further problems, which will be discussed in Chapter XXI. Simple monopoly works out in two different ways, according as, on the one hand, the entry to the industry is so far restricted that no resources are drawn into it other than those actually finding employment in it, or, on the other hand, entry to the industry is free. I shall study first industries of restricted entry.

§ 2. In Chapter XI. it was shown that, in the absence of divergences between social and private net product of the

---

[1] Thus, if y be the aggregate output of an industry and x the output of a firm of typical size, then, writing $F(x, y)$ for the total cost of its output to this firm, we have x determined by the equation $\frac{\partial}{\partial x}\left\{\frac{F(x, y)}{x}\right\} = 0$. We must *not* suppose monopoly to come about because the introduction of a new technique has changed F into ψ, in such wise that, for a given value of y, $\frac{\partial}{\partial x}\left\{\frac{\psi(x, y)}{x}\right\} = 0$ gives a larger value of x than $\frac{\partial}{\partial x}\left\{\frac{F(x, y)}{x}\right\} = 0$ does, thus reducing the number of firms in that industry, and so making the formation of a price agreement easier. We must suppose F to be the same under both systems.

types discussed in Chapter IX., simple competition makes actual output less than ideal output in industries subject to decreasing supply price from the standpoint of the community; equal to ideal output in industries of constant supply price in this sense; and greater than ideal output in industries of increasing supply price in this sense. When simple monopoly prevails, it is to the interest of the monopolist so to regulate his output as to make the excess of his aggregate receipts over his aggregate costs (including earnings of management and so forth) as large as possible. It follows that under simple monopoly output will always, other things being equal, be less than it would have been under simple competition. Hence in industries of decreasing supply price from the standpoint of the community the substitution of simple monopoly for simple competition will cause actual output, which is now below ideal output, to fall further below it: in industries of constant supply price in this sense, it will cause actual output, which is now equal to ideal output, to fall below ideal output; in industries of increasing supply price in this sense, it will cause actual output, which is now above ideal output, to contract, and it *may* cause it to contract in a measure that brings it closer to ideal output than it has been hitherto. The conditions in which it will do this can be determined mathematically, but, unless unusual assumptions are introduced, they cannot be stated in simple terms. This, however, does not greatly matter. For in practice simple monopoly is much more likely to be introduced into industries of decreasing supply price from the standpoint of the industry, which, as was shown in Chapter XI., *in general* implies decreasing supply price from the standpoint of the community, than into other industries; and hence there is no uncertainty about the result.

§ 3. When monopolistic power is exercised by a combination of sellers through the agency of a price-agreement, the restrictive influence upon investment may be enhanced in an indirect way by a further circumstance. It is not practicable to make an agreement touching more than one or two roughly defined grades of service. Consequently, since an adapted charge cannot be made for them, the intermediate grades tend to disappear, even though numerous purchasers—some of whom, as things are, buy nothing— would have bought these grades, if they had been obtainable at a proportionate charge. Therefore resources, which, under a perfectly constructed monopoly agreement, would have been devoted to the production of these grades, are excluded by the imperfect character of actual agreements. This effect is chiefly found among railway and shipping companies, which are bound by freight-rate conventions but compete in the frequency, speed and comfort of their trains or ships.[1] Thus first-class rapid vessels may be employed to carry things for which they are quite unnecessary, because agreements preclude the offer of lower rates if slower and cheaper vessels are used;[2] and so forth. The misdirection of resources that arises in this way is additional to the misdirection due to a simple exercise of monopolistic power.

§ 4. Some qualification of the above results is necessary in industries where temporary low prices may lead to the development of new demands. For, when a prospect of this kind exists, particularly if conditions of decreasing supply price rule and if the current rate of interest on investments is low, it may pay a monopolist to accept low prices for a time, even though to do so involves production at a loss, for the sake of the future gain ; whereas it would not pay any one among a large number of competing sellers to do this, since only a very small proportion of the future gain resulting from his action would accrue to himself. It is important, however, to observe that the creation of a new demand, which may thus sometimes be credited to monopoly, is only a social gain when the demand is really new, and not when it is merely a substitute for some other demand which is at the same time destroyed. It is not, for example, a social gain if a railway company, by temporary low prices, "develops the traffic" 'from one district at the expense of destroying the traffic from another equally well-situated district; and it is not a social gain if, by a like

---

[1] The agreements, short of pooling, between railways sometimes embrace agreements as to speed ; those between the members of some, but not all, shipping conferences, agreements as to the relative number of sailings permitted to the various members (*Royal Commission on Shipping Rings, Report*, p. 23).

[2] *Royal Commission on Shipping Rings, Report*, p. 108.

policy, some ring of traders causes people, who used to obtain
a given measure of satisfaction from crinolines and no satisfaction from hobble-skirts, to obtain the like given measure
of satisfaction from hobble-skirts and no satisfaction from
crinolines. This consideration suggests that the transitional
advantage of simple monopoly, that has just been set out,
is not generally very important in comparison with the
long-period disadvantages previously explained.

§ 5. There should be added a further consideration of some
importance. It was shown in Part II. Ch. III. § 11 that to hold
back new inventions and so on in order to keep up the value
of existing forms of equipment *in general* inflicts more damage
on the public than the benefits it confers on the owners of
the equipment, and it was shown further that under simple
competition there is no tendency for this kind of hold-up to
occur. Under monopoly, on the other hand, there always is
such a tendency; for the private monopolist is interested in the
gain to him that monopoly implies, but not in the associated
loss of consumers' satisfaction. It was recognised in the chapter
cited that, when the introduction of new models of finished
goods lessens the satisfaction which owners get from existing
models, there is a substantial set-off to the gains of " progress,"
so that this tendency of private monopoly need not always
be anti-social. But, when it is a question of new instruments
and processes for making finished goods, there can be no such
set-off, and hold-up policies must be socially injurious. The
point is of great practical interest in view of the rapidity with
which new inventions and minor improvements of method are
normally made. This is illustrated by the fact that in the
United States, over industry in general, twice as much is, it
is estimated, normally written down against obsolescence as
against depreciation;[1] and by the further fact that, out of
200 representative firms questioned for the President's Survey,
43·6 require new equipment to return its cost in two years:
64·1 per cent in three years or less.[2]

§ 6. In the discussion so far we have assumed the entry
to industries, in which simple monopoly prevails, to be so

---

[1] *Changes in the Structure of World Economics since the War*, p. 158.
[2] *Recent Economic Changes*, p. 139.

far obstructed or restricted that no resources are drawn into
them other than those actually finding employment there.
As a rule this condition is fulfilled, because, when it is not
fulfilled, the trouble of forming monopolistic agreements will
seldom be worth undertaking.   Still, monopolistic agreements without restriction of entry are sometimes made.   It
is easy to show that, under these agreements, the national
dividend suffers more than it would do if the same monopolistic price policy prevailed in conjunction with restriction
of entry to the industry.   For, broadly speaking, what
happens is this.   The marginal social net product of resources
actually finding employment in the monopolised industry is
the same as it would be under a system of restricted entry.
But, besides these resources, other resources have been drawn
away from employment elsewhere and have become attached
to the industry.   These extra resources will either be all
idle themselves, or will make a corresponding quantity of
resources already in the industry idle.   The dividend, therefore, will be reduced below what it would have been under
a system of restricted entry, by the difference between the
productivity of that quantity of resources which it pays to
set to work in the monopolised industry and the productivity of that quantity for which the receipts of the
industry would suffice to provide normal earnings.   This consideration does not, of course, prove that restriction of entry
to an industry, in which monopoly prevails, is socially
desirable ; for it may well happen that free entry would compel
the monopolist to change his policy, and to adopt one
approximately equivalent to that dictated by competition.
It only proves that restriction is advantageous in those—
probably exceptional — monopolies where the removal of
restriction cannot affect price policy.[1]

[1] Attention may be called here to a peculiar case.   Suppose the same
process to yield two joint products, one of which is controlled monopolistically
but the other is not.   Then, as shown above, if entry to the industry can be
restricted, simple monopoly will make the outputs of both products less than
they would be under simple competition.   The whole of the non-monopolised
joint product that is produced will be sold, but, provided that the demand for
the monopolised product has an elasticity less than unity, and that, in respect
of the most profitable scale of output, the demand price for the non-monopolised
product exceeds the supply price of the process that produces both products, a

T

part of the monopolised product will be thrown away. If entry to the industry is not restricted, more resources will flow into it than would so flow under simple competition. On the assumption that these are actually set to work and not left standing idle, this will mean that, in the above conditions, the output and sale of the non-monopolised joint product is larger than it would have been under simple competition. It is *possible*, though improbable, that, as a net result, there may be evolved a larger sum of consumers' surplus than simple competition would allow.

CHAPTER XVII

DISCRIMINATING MONOPOLY

§ 1. Up to this point we have supposed that monopolisation, when it occurs, will be of the simple form which does not involve discrimination of prices as between different customers. We have now to observe that this variety of monopolisation is not the only possible sort. Discriminating power will sometimes exist alongside of monopolistic power, and, when it does, the results are affected. It is, therefore, important to determine the circumstances in which, and the degree to which, monopolists are able to exercise, and find advantage in exercising, this power.

§ 2. The conditions are most favourable to discrimination, that is to say, discrimination will yield most advantage to the monopolist, when the demand price for any unit of a commodity is independent of the price of sale of every other unit. This implies that it is impossible for any one unit to take the place of any other unit, and this, in turn, implies two things. The first of these is that no unit of the commodity sold in one market can be transferred to another market. The second is that no unit of demand, proper to one market, can be transferred to another market. The former sort of transference needs no description, but the latter is somewhat subtle. It would occur if the promulgation of different rates for transporting coal originating in A and coal originating in B enabled the more favoured district to increase its production of coal, and, therefore, its demand for carriage, at the expense of the less favoured district. In order that the conditions most favourable to discrimination may prevail, this sort of transferability, as well as the other, must be excluded. Under the monopolistic arrangements practicable in real life the above kinds of transferability are absent or present in varying degrees. I propose to set out a series of examples under each of the heads just distinguished.

§ 3. Units of commodity are entirely non - transferable when the commodity in question consists of services applied directly by the sellers to the persons of their customers, such as the services of medical men, barristers, teachers, dentists, hotelkeepers and so forth. A medical man's offer to charge any one set of persons less than any other set cannot lead to the one set becoming middlemen for the services which the other set desire. Services applied directly by the seller to commodities handed to them for treatment, such as the service of transporting different articles, are also entirely non-transferable. A railway's offer to charge one price for a ton-mile of transport service to copper merchants and a lower price to coal merchants cannot lead to any middleman device, because it is physically impossible to convert copper into coal for the purpose of transport and afterwards to reconvert it. A slightly, but only slightly, lower degree of non-transferability exists among services that are normally rendered in physical connection with the private dwellings of purchasers. Gas and water supplied to private houses are instances in point. Here transference is not entirely excluded, because it is *possible*, at sufficient cost of money and trouble, to detach the commodities from the distributing plant along which they are brought and to carry them elsewhere. Lesser degrees of non-transferability exist among commodities whose transference is obstructed merely by high costs of transportation or by tariff charges. The degree of non - transferability in these circumstances may, evidently, be large or small, according as the distance, or the rate of customs duty, that separates two markets between which discrimination is attempted is large or small. In like manner, various degrees of non-transferability can be brought about artificially by enforcing upon purchasers contracts that penalise re-sales. For example, in the Ruhr coal district, the (pre-war) agreement made by the syndicate with industrial purchasers provided " that re-sale to railways, gas works, brick works or lime-kilns, or any reshipment from the original point of destination, shall be penalised by an addition of 3 marks per ton to the selling price." [1]   If no agreement of this kind, no cost of carriage, and no tariff exist, complete transferability will prevail.

§ 4. Units of demand are almost completely non-transferable from one market to another, when the commodity concerned is something ready for final consumption, and when the markets, between which discrimination is to be made, are distinguished according to the wealth of the purchasers. It is clear, for instance, that the willingness of doctors to charge less to poor people than to rich people does not lead to any rich people, for the sake of cheap doctoring, becoming poor.   In like manner, the provision of the service of transport at different rates to coal merchants and to copper merchants does not lead to any copper merchants, for the sake of the cheap transportation, becoming coal merchants. No doubt, in both these examples some slight transference *may* be achieved through successful fraud, such as a pretence on the part of rich people that they belong to the poorer group, and the smuggling of copper in the guise of coal; but this kind of thing is of no practical importance.   It is interesting to note that sellers often attempt artificially to create the above type of non-transferability by attaching to different grades of their product trade marks, special brands, special types of packing and so on—all incidents designed to prevent possible purchasers of the grades that are highly priced relatively to the cost of production from becoming, instead, purchasers of the grades that are sold at a lower rate of profit.[2] A smaller degree of non-transferability exists between the markets for hotel accommodation in the season and out of the season; for heavy discrimination might cause a considerable number of people to change the time of their

---

[1] Walker, *Combination in the German Coal Industry*, p. 274.

[2] It must be added, however, that, though trade marks are sometimes mere devices for creating monopoly power, there is, nevertheless, a valid reason for protecting them against infringement by legal enactments, because "an inducement is thereby given to make satisfactory articles and to continue making them." (Cf. Taussig, *American Economic Review Supplement*, vol. vi., 1916, p. 177.)

holiday. A still smaller degree of non-transferability exists between the markets for railway transport from A to B, which are provided respectively by traders in A wishing to send a given commodity direct to B, and by traders in C wishing to send this commodity to B through A. For a large difference in the rates charged would cause production, that would normally occur at the less favoured, to take place instead at the more favoured, point. Perfect transferability exists when the markets are distinguished by some badge, the attachment of which involves no cost, as, for example, if railways charged one fare to passengers carrying pencils and another fare to passengers without pencils. The immediate effect of this discrimination would be to transfer *all* demands from the less to the more favoured market, and discrimination would yield *no* advantage to the monopolist.

§ 5. When a degree of non-transferability, of commodity units on the one hand or of demand units on the other hand, sufficient to make discrimination profitable, is present, the relation between the monopolistic seller and each buyer is, strictly, one of bilateral monopoly. The terms of the contract that will emerge between them is, therefore, theoretically indeterminate and subject to the play of that " bargaining " whose social effects were analysed at the end of Chapter IX. When a railway company is arranging terms with a few large shippers, the indeterminate element may have considerable importance. Usually, however, where discrimination is of practical interest, the opposed parties are, not a single large seller and a few large buyers, but a single large seller and a great number of relatively small buyers. The loss of an individual customer's purchase means so much less to the monopolistic seller than to any one of the many monopolistic purchasers that, apart from combination among purchasers, all of them will almost certainly accept the monopolistic seller's price. They will recognise that it is useless to stand out in the hope of bluffing a concession, and will buy what is offered, so long as the terms demanded from them leave to them *any* consumers' surplus. In what follows I assume that the customers act in this way. So assuming, we may distinguish three degrees of discriminating

power, which a monopolist may conceivably wield. A
first degree would involve the charge of a different price
against all the different units of commodity, in such wise
that the price exacted for each was equal to the demand
price for it, and no consumers' surplus was left to the buyers.
A second degree would obtain if a monopolist were able to
make n separate prices, in such wise that all units with
a demand price greater than x were sold at a price x, all with
a demand price less than x and greater than y at a price
y, and so on.   A third degree would obtain if the monopolist
were able to distinguish among his customers n different
groups, separated from one another more or less by some
practicable mark, and could charge a separate monopoly price
to the members of each group.   This degree, it will be
noticed, differs fundamentally from either of the preceding
degrees, in that it may involve the refusal to satisfy, in one
market, demands represented by demand prices in excess of
some of those which, in another market, are satisfied.

§ 6. These three degrees of discriminating power, though
all theoretically possible, are not, from a practical point of
view, of equal importance.   On the contrary, in real life the
third degree only is found.   No doubt, we can imagine
conditions in which discrimination even of the first degree
could be achieved.   If all consumers had exactly similar
demand schedules,[1] it could be achieved by the simple device
of refusing to sell in packets of less than the quantity which
each consumer required per unit of time, and fixing the
price per packet at such a rate as to make it worth the
consumer's while, but only just worth his while, to purchase
the packet.   Thus, if every demander would give for a
hundredth physical unit of commodity, when he already has
ninety-nine units, the sum of one shilling, but would prefer
to give 300 shillings for a hundred units rather than have
no units at all, the monopolist may make his unit of sale
one hundred physical units and charge for this unit of
sale a price of 300 shillings.   If there is no combination

[1] A person's demand schedule for any commodity is the list of different
quantities of that commodity that he would purchase at different price levels.
Cf. Marshall, *Principles of Economics*, p. 96.

among the buyers, the number of units sold will then
be the same as would have been sold at a price of
one shilling per physical unit, and, in effect, the physical
units satisfying demands of different keenness will have
been sold at different prices.   But this method of discrimination, whether in a complete or a partial form, is
scarcely ever practicable, because the individual demand
schedules, of which the market demand schedule is made
up, are, as a rule, very far indeed from being similar.   For
this reason an analysis of the method is of academic interest
only.[1]   Apart from this method, discrimination of the first
degree might still conceivably be established by detailed
separate bargaining with every separate customer.   But that
method would involve enormous cost and trouble.   Furthermore, since it implies separate bargains with individuals,
it opens the way, not only to error, but also to the perversion
of agents through bribery.   These considerations are, in
general, sufficient to make monopolists themselves unwilling
to adopt the method; and, even if they were not thus
unwilling, it would be hardly possible for the State, in view
of the large opportunities for "unfair" competition which
the method affords, to leave their hands free.   "Whatever
financial advantage there may be in charging against each
act of transport a rate adapted to its individual circumstances,
the arbitrary nature of a system of rates arranged on this
plan implies so much uncertainty and lends itself to such
serious abuses, that we are compelled to condemn it."[2]   Thus
a powerful influence is always at work persuading or com-
pelling monopolists to act on general rules, with published

[1] For such an analysis, cf. my paper "Monopoly and Consumers' Surplus,"
Economic Journal, September 1904.
[2] Colson, *Cours d'économie politique*, vol. vi. p. 211.   Special opportunities
for injurious discrimination of this sort exist when a railway company is
itself a large producer of some commodity, say coal, which it also transports
for rival producers.   To prevent the obvious abuses to which this state of things
may lead, the "commodity clause" of the Hepburn Act passed in 1906 in the
United States made it unlawful for any railway to engage in interstate
transport of any commodity which had been mined or manufactured by itself.
The law does not, however, prevent a railway from transporting a commodity
produced by a company in which it holds a majority of the shares, and it can,
therefore, be evaded without great difficulty.   (Cf. Jones, *The Anthracite Coal
Combination*, pp. 190 *et seq*.)

tariffs, guarded, as effectively as may be, against the under-
mining influence of unpublished rebates. This means that
they cannot, except in extraordinary circumstances, introduce
either the first or the second degree of discrimination, and
that the third degree is of chief practical importance.

§ 7. Monopoly *plus* discrimination of the third degree is
not a determinate conception. It is theoretically possible
to divide any market in an indefinitely large number of
different ways, of which some would be more, and others less,
advantageous to the monopolist. If the monopolist had an
absolutely free hand in the matter, the division he would
choose would be such that the lowest demand price in sub-
market A exceeded the highest demand price in sub-market
B, and so on throughout. If the aggregate demand of the
markets collectively had an elasticity greater than unity
throughout, the resulting system would be identical with
that proper to the second degree of discrimination, for the
lowest demand price in each group would also be the price
calculated to yield maximum monopoly revenue from that
group. If the aggregate demand had not an elasticity greater
than unity throughout, the maximising price in some groups
would be greater than the lowest demand price in those groups,
and the system would, therefore, be different from the above.
In any event the separation of markets, in such wise that the
lowest demand price in the first exceeds the highest demand
price in the second, and so on, would obviously be better,
from the monopolist's point of view, than any other kind of
separation. But in practice the monopolist's freedom of action
is limited by the need, already referred to, of acting on general
rules. This consideration makes it necessary that he shall
choose, for his sub-markets, groups that are distinguishable
from one another by some readily recognisable mark. Moreover, since a hostile public opinion might lead to legislative
intervention, his choice must not be such as to outrage the
popular sense of justice. Thus, he will not distinguish and
bring together entirely new groups, but will make use of
distinctions already given in nature. Nor is this all. For in
some circumstances the condition of non-transferability holds
good, not generally, but only as between certain markets, which

are constituted independently of the monopolist's volition. Thus, the existence of an import tariff or of high transport charges on imports to all parts of his country's frontier—a condition easiest to realise when that country is an island—may make it possible for a seller to charge a lower price for his goods abroad than at home without the risk of inviting the return and resale of his exports. Clearly, therefore, a monopolist cannot hope to find a series of sub-markets that conforms to his ideal altogether, but he may find one in which only a comparatively small number of the demand prices embraced in the first sub-market are lower than the highest demand price of the second sub-market, and so on throughout all the sub-markets.

§ 8. I now pass to an analysis of consequences, and, as in the preceding chapter, I shall begin with monopolised industries to which entry can be restricted. The analysis, to be complete, would need to take account of the fact that, in real life, the demand of one purchaser for any r^{th} unit of a commodity is sometimes, in part, dependent upon the price at which this commodity is being sold to other purchasers.[1] When markets are interdependent in this way, the issue is complicated, but the broad results, though rendered less certain, are not, it would appear, substantially altered. Consequently in the following pages I shall assume that the quantity demanded in each sub-market depends only on the price ruling in that sub-market. This procedure enables resort to be had to the same general method that has been pursued hitherto.

§ 9. As already explained, practical interest centres upon monopoly *plus* discrimination of the third degree. But, before studying this, we may, with advantage, glance at the simpler problem presented by the two higher forms of discrimination. It is easily seen that, *in industries in which the rates of change in supply price from the standpoint of the industry are identical with the rates of change from the standpoint of the community*, under monopoly *plus* discrimination of the first degree, it will always pay the monopolist to make the ideal amount of investment and to produce the ideal output. This implies that, under conditions of constant supply price, monopoly *plus* discrimination of the first degree will make

---

[1] Cf. *ante*, Part II. Ch. XI. § 13.

the national dividend the same as simple competition would have made it. Under conditions of decreasing and of increasing supply price it will always improve on the result of simple competition. The extent to which it improves on it will be measured by the extent to which the output proper to simple competition differs from the ideal output. This is evidently greater, the more elastic is the demand for the commodity produced by the industry and the more markedly the conditions of the industry depart in either direction from those of constant supply price. Finally, it should be observed that, when conditions of decreasing supply price prevail, monopoly *plus* discrimination of the first degree *may* increase the size of the national dividend in a more special way. It *may* bring about a considerable amount of socially desirable investment in an industry, in which, under a régime of simple competition, it would not have been to anybody's interest to make any investment at all. It is shown in Appendix III. that this result is most likely to be realised (1) if, other things being equal, supply price decreases sharply, in such wise that a small increase of output involves a large fall in supply price per unit, and (2) if, other things being equal, the demand for the commodity or service is elastic till fairly low price levels have been reached.[1]

§ 10. In industries where the rates of change of supply price from the standpoint of the industry and of the community are not identical, matters are slightly more complicated. As was shown in Chapter XI. §§ 6-8, we are entitled to presume that the rate of change from the standpoint of the community will, in general, be a smaller negative or a larger positive quantity than the rate from the other standpoint. It can be inferred that the output proper to discriminating monopoly of the first degree will be less than the ideal output. In industries of decreasing supply price from the standpoint of the industry, it will be greater than the output proper to simple competition, and, therefore, nearer than that output to the ideal output. In industries of increasing supply price from the standpoint of the industry, it will be less than the output proper to simple competition. But the output proper to simple competition *may* in this case be greater than the ideal output. It is,

---

[1] Cf. Appendix III. § 26.

therefore, possible that the output proper to discriminating monopoly of the first degree may be further than the output proper to simple competition from the ideal output. Since, however, as was observed in Chapter XVI. § 2, monopolistic action is chiefly to be expected in industries of decreasing supply price, this possibility is of small importance.

§ 11. It is readily seen that the effects of monopoly *plus* discrimination of the second degree approximate towards those of monopoly *plus* discrimination of the first degree, as the number of different prices, which it is possible for the monopolist to charge, increases; just as the area of a polygon inscribed in a circle approximates to the area of the circle as the number of its sides increases. Let us call the output proper to discrimination of the first degree, that is to say, the ideal output, a. Then monopoly of the second degree would lead to an output less than a, but approaching more nearly towards it the larger is the number of the different price groups which the monopolist is able to distinguish; and the value of the marginal social net product of resources invested in our industry would, in like manner, approach more nearly towards equality with the value of the marginal social net products in general, the larger is this number.

§ 12. The study of monopoly *plus* discrimination of the third degree is more complicated than that of either of the two higher forms. In the discussion of these we have been able to make use of a simple relation between the aggregate output which comes about in various circumstances and the output which I have called the ideal output. According as actual output exceeds, falls short of, or is equal to the ideal output, we could conclude that the value of the marginal social net product of resources invested in our industry falls short of, exceeds, or is equal to the value of the marginal social net product of resources in general. But, under monopoly *plus* discrimination of the third degree, the relation between actual output and ideal output no longer suffices for a criterion. The reason is that, when a demand represented by a demand price p is satisfied, it is not necessary, as it has been necessary so far, that all the demands represented by demand prices greater than p shall have been satisfied.

On the contrary, the monopolist may, in one market, be satisfying all demands represented by demand prices higher than p, while, in another market, he is refusing to satisfy any demands whose demand prices fall short of $(p + h)$. It follows that the resources invested in the industry fall into a number of different parts, in each of which the value of the marginal social net product is different. Consequently, we have no longer to ask how the value of the marginal social net product of resources invested *in the industry* is related to the value of the marginal social net product of resources in general, but how the various values of marginal social net products of resources invested to cater for *each of the several markets of the industry* are related to that standard. Our ideal output ceases to be a single output of the whole industry, and becomes a number of separate outputs sold in separate markets. A given output of the whole industry may be broken up in different ways among these markets, and the system of values of marginal social net products will be different according to the way in which it is, in fact, broken up. Hence a study of the effect which monopoly *plus* discrimination of the third degree produces upon output is only a first step to a study of the effect which it produces, as compared with that which simple monopoly and simple competition respectively produce, upon the relation between the values of marginal social net products in different parts of the industrial field. Nevertheless, it is well that such a study should be made. To facilitate it, let us suppose that the demands for the product of an industry can be broken up into two markets A and B, between which price discrimination is feasible; and let us ask, first, whether output under discriminating monopoly of the third degree will be absolutely greater or smaller than output under simple monopoly and simple competition respectively.

§ 13. To compare the output proper to discriminating monopoly of the third degree with that proper to simple monopoly, we may conveniently distinguish three principal cases. First, let the conditions be such that, under simple monopoly, some of the commodity, in which we are interested, would be consumed in both A and B. In these conditions there is no adequate ground for expecting either that output under discriminating monopoly of the third degree will exceed, or that it will fall short of, output under simple monopoly ; if the curves of demand and supply are straight lines, the two outputs will be equal.[1] Secondly, let the conditions be such that, under simple monopoly, some of the commodity would have been consumed in A, but none in B. In these conditions it is impossible that the introduction of discriminating power should lead to diminished output. On the contrary, if there is any substantial demand in B, it must lead to increased output. The amount of the increase will be specially great if the demand in B is elastic, and if the commodity obeys the law of decreasing supply price (*simpliciter*). These conditions are often fulfilled among Kartels selling regularly at specially low rates in markets, foreign and other, where they are exposed to competition. An interesting practical inference is that, if a commodity, whose production obeys the law of decreasing supply price, is monopolised, it is to the interest of the consumers in the producing country that the Government should allow the monopolist to make sales abroad at lower prices than at home, rather than that, while still permitting monopoly, it should forbid this discrimination. This inference cannot be upset by reference to the more advanced industries that use the commodity as a raw material, because the sales abroad, being at market prices there, —prices which the monopolistic exports cannot in ordinary circumstances sensibly affect—do not enable foreign users to get it appreciably more cheaply than they could before. Finally, let the conditions be such that, under simple monopoly, none of the commodity would have been consumed in either A or B. In these conditions it is obviously impossible that the introduction of discriminating power should lead to diminished output. It is possible that it may lead to increased output. The condition for this is the same as the condition, mentioned in the next paragraph, that enables discriminating monopoly of the third degree to yield some output, though simple competition would yield none.

§ 14. We have now to compare the output proper to

[1] Cf. Appendix III. § 28.

discriminating monopoly of the third degree with that proper to simple competition. Under conditions of constant and of increasing supply price it is obviously impossible for discriminating monopoly of any degree to make output greater than it would be under simple competition. Discriminating monopoly of the third degree must make it smaller than it would be under that system. When, however, conditions of decreasing supply price prevail, the question is more complex. It has been proved in an earlier section that, in that event, monopoly *plus* discrimination of the first degree must raise output above the quantity proper to simple competition. Furthermore, it is evident that discrimination of the third degree approximates towards discrimination of the first degree as the number of markets into which demands can be divided approximate towards the number of units for which any demand exists. Hence it follows that, under decreasing supply price, monopoly *plus* discrimination of the third degree *may* raise output above the competitive amount, and is more likely to do this the more numerous are the markets between which discrimination can be made. Sometimes, but not, of course, so frequently as with discrimination of the first degree, discriminating monopoly of the third degree will evolve some output where simple competition would have evolved none. In view, however, of the limitation, which practical considerations impose, alike upon the number of markets that can be formed, and upon the monopolist's freedom to make up the several markets in the way most advantageous to him, it appears, on the whole, exceedingly improbable that, in an industry selected at random, monopoly *plus* discrimination of the third degree will yield an output as large as would be yielded by simple competition.

§ 15. In the preceding paragraphs we have compared *the absolute amount* of output under discriminating monopoly of the third degree with the absolute amount under simple monopoly and simple competition respectively. The next step is to compare the measure of approximation towards the ideal output that is attained under these different systems. What has been said enables us to conclude broadly that, whatever law of supply price prevails, discriminating monopoly

of the third degree is likely to yield an output nearer to the
ideal output than simple monopoly yields; but that it is not
likely to yield an output nearer to it than simple competition yields. When, however, the conditions are such
that (1) there is an ideal output (other than a zero output),
(2) simple competition yields no output, and (3) discriminating
monopoly of the third degree yields some output, this output
must be nearer to the ideal output than the zero output of
simple competition.

§ 16. I now return to the considerations suggested in
§ 12. It was there pointed out that the measure of corre-
spondence between the actual aggregate output of an industry
and the ideal output is not, when discriminating monopoly
of the third degree is in question, the decisive index that it
is in other circumstances. Suppose, for example, that discriminating monopoly of this degree brings about an output
closer to the ideal output than either simple monopoly or
simple competition would bring about. We cannot infer from
this that the value of the marginal social net product of
resources employed in the industry is brought nearer to the
value of marginal social net products in general. For there
is no longer any such thing as the value of the marginal social
net product of resources employed in the industry. There
are different values of marginal social net product in different
portions of the industry. The value of the marginal social
net product of resources that serve the needs of low-priced
markets is smaller than the value of the marginal social net
product of those that serve high-priced markets. Hence,
even when, in any industry, discriminating monopoly makes
aggregate output more nearly conformable to ideal output
than simple monopoly or simple competition would do, it does
not follow that it will involve greater equality between the
values of marginal social net products over industry as a
whole. Nor need we stop at this negative result. It can
be shown, further, that the establishment in any industry of a
given output associated with discriminating prices is likely to
conduce less towards equality among the values of marginal
social net products as a whole than the establishment of the
same output associated with uniform prices. For let the

value of the marginal social net product of resources in general be P; and let the quantity of resources invested in our industry be such that, if the product is sold at the same price in all markets, the value of the marginal social net product of the resources employed to supply each of them will be equal to p. Then, if this same quantity of resources is invested in the industry, but the product is sold at a higher price in some markets than in others, the value of the marginal social net product of the resources utilised for the higher-priced markets will be greater than p, and that of the resources utilised for the lower-priced markets will be less than p. This implies that the mean square deviation (our measure of inequality) of these various values from P is likely to be greater than it would have been if all of them had stood at p. Hence the probability that discriminating monopoly of the third degree will be more favourable to equality among the values of marginal social net products than simple monopoly or simple competition is less than the probability that it will be more favourable than they are to the production of the ideal output. The probability that it will be more favourable than they are to the national dividend is, therefore, also less than that probability.

§ 17. So far we have supposed that discriminating monopoly is coupled with power to restrict the entry to the monopolised industry. When this condition is not satisfied, reasoning analogous to that employed at the close of the preceding chapter is applicable. Resources tend to be attracted into the industry till the point is reached at which the expectation of earnings there is equal to that ruling elsewhere. So long as monopoly prices are maintained, this means that a considerable part of the resources so attracted is standing idle and is yielding no net product whatever. It is evident, therefore, that the national dividend suffers more from discriminating monopoly without restriction of entry than it does from discriminating monopoly *plus* restriction of entry. But, as with simple monopoly, so also here, it may, nevertheless, be desirable that restriction should be forbidden, because, when it is absent, there is a better chance that the entrenchments of monopolistic power will ultimately be broken down.

U

CHAPTER XVIII

THE SPECIAL PROBLEM OF RAILWAY RATES

§ 1. THE discussion of the preceding chapter has necessarily been somewhat abstract. It has, however, practical applications of very great importance in connection with the problem of arranging the charges to be made for such things as water, gas, and electricity, when these commodities are supplied to different groups of consumers or for different purposes. Still greater interest attaches to it in connection with the rates chargeable by railway companies. Considerable controversy has taken place between those who hold that these rates should be based on " the cost of service principle " and those who would base them on the " value of service principle." [1] The " cost of service principle " is, in effect, the simple competition discussed in Chapter XI. : " the value of service principle " is discriminating monopoly of the third degree. In the light of what has been said, the issue between them can be clearly set out ; and it will, in the present chapter, be examined. We have no concern with the circumstance, explained in Chapter XVI., that, in certain conditions, a railway with power to discriminate may find it profitable, *as a temporary measure*, to charge exceptionally low rates for transport between certain places or for certain selected commodities, with a view to building up a new demand ; nor yet with the related circumstance that this policy, if the demand is really a new one, and not merely a substitute for another that has been supplanted, may be

---

[1] It is interesting to note that the problem of how retail shops should distribute their charges for the act of retailing over the various commodities that they sell is very closely analogous to the problem of railway charges. Among retail shops, however, there is the additional complication that a retailer is sometimes able to obtain a general advertisement for his shop by selling particular well-known goods practically free of retailer's profit.

more advantageous to economic welfare, if not to the national dividend,[1] than anything which simple competition—unless it were modified by a system of State bounties—could evolve. These matters call for no further investigation here. Leaving them aside, I propose to exhibit the meaning, in concrete form, of the cost of service principle—or simple competition —and of the value of service principle—or discriminating monopoly of the third degree,—and to compare their respective consequences.

§ 2. It is generally agreed that, except in so far as the transport services sold to one set of purchasers are " supplied jointly " with those sold to another set, simple competition would tend to bring about a system of uniform rates per ton-mile for similar services.[2] For these services the level of the uniform rate would be such that the demand price and the supply price would coincide; and, when the service of railway transport was sold in conjunction with some other service, such as cartage or packing, an appropriate addition would be made to the charge. This general analysis can be briefly developed as follows.

First, the actual level of the uniform mileage rate, to which simple competition would lead on any particular railway, will depend on the circumstances and position of the railway. *Ceteris paribus,* a specially high rate would be appropriate if the route lay through districts where, as with mountain railways, the engineering costs of making a line are specially great, or where the traffic is very irregular from

---

[1] Cf. *ante,* Part II. Chapter III. § 4, footnote.

[2] It is, indeed, sometimes maintained that this will only happen if " simple competition " is defined to include complete transferability of the things that are sold among customers, and it is pointed out that competition, apart from this condition, has proved compatible with discriminating charges for services sold to different sets of persons by shipping companies and by retailers ; different sorts of cargoes are carried at different rates, and the absolute charge for retailing work is different in regard to different articles. (Cf. G. P. Watkins, "The Theory of Differential Rates," *Quarterly Journal of Economics,* 1916, pp. 693-5.) Reflection, however, shows that, when competition really prevails, seller A must always endeavour to undersell seller B by offering to serve B's better-paying customers at a rate slightly less than B is charging, and that this process must eventually level all rates. The explanation of the discriminations cited above is, not the absence of complete transferability, but the fact that custom and tacit understandings introduce an element of monopolistic action.

one time to another;[1] because, in these conditions, the supply prices of all quantities of transportation along the route are specially high. In like manner, *ceteris paribus*, a specially high rate would be appropriate if the route lay through sparsely populated regions where little traffic can be obtained, or through regions where the configuration of the country renders water transport a readily available substitute for land transport for certain classes of commodities between the terminals; because, in these conditions, the demand schedule is specially low, and the supply conforms to conditions of decreasing supply price; the expenses involved in building and working a railway adapted for a small amount of traffic being proportionately greater than those involved in the production of transport service on a large scale. It is, no doubt, in recognition of these considerations that the *maxima*, imposed in the British parliamentary freight classification, are made different for different lines, though the classification itself is, of course, the same for all of them.

Secondly, departures from the uniform mileage rate would occur under simple competition, in so far as buyers of a ton-mile of transportation require, along with this, other incidental services involving expense. The adjustments needed are exactly analogous to the adjustments made in the price of plain cotton cloth delivered c.i.f. to buyers who live at different distances from the seat of manufacture. Thus rates should be comparatively low for the transport of any class of goods, when the method of packing adopted is convenient to the railway. It is more costly, other things being equal, to carry small consignments than large. "Small consignments mean to a railway three distinct sources of serious additional expense: separate collection and delivery; separate handling, invoicing, accounting, etc., at the terminal stations; and bad loading in the railway waggons."[2] It is, therefore, proper that, in the British parliamentary classification, goods, which are placed in class A——the cheapest class——when loaded in lots of 4 tons, are raised to class B when despatched in loads of between 2 and 4

[1] Cf. Williams, *Economics of Railway Transport*, p. 212.
[2] Acworth, *Elements of Railway Economics*, p. 120.

tons, and to class C when despatched in loads of less than 2 tons. On a like principle, it is proper that English railway companies should voluntarily make arrangements, under which certain goods are put into a class lower than the parliamentary classification requires, on condition that they are loaded in certain quantities or packed in certain ways. Further, when the method of packing is given, it is proper that rates per ton should vary with conditions that affect the cost of handling, such as bulk, fragility, liquidity, explosiveness, structure and so on; and also with the speed and regularity of the service required.[1] This point is clearly brought out in one of the decisions of the United States Railway Commissioners. They declared: "Relatively higher rates on strawberries appear to be justified by the exceptional character of the service connected with their transportation. This exceptional service is necessitated by the highly perishable character of the traffic, requiring refrigeration *en route*, rapid transit, specially provided trains, and prompt delivery at destination. There is also involved in this service extra trouble in handling at receiving and delivering points, the 'drilling' of cars in a train, reduction of length of trains to secure celerity of movement, partially loaded cars, the return of cars empty, and, perhaps, other similar incidentals."[2] Finally, it is proper that the rate for carrying from A to B goods that are to go forward to C on the same line should, in general, be less than the rate for so carrying goods destined for consumption at B. In so far as terminal charges are paid for in the rate, this is obvious, because, on the former class of goods, terminal charges at B are saved altogether. Even apart from terminals, however, the journey from A to B, as a part of a longer journey, is less costly than the same journey undertaken as an isolated whole. The reason is that, roughly speaking, the interval of idleness for engines and plant, following upon any journey, involves a cost properly attributable to that journey, and the length of the interval does not vary with the length of the journey which it follows. Thus, "long hauls get more mileage out of

---

[1] Cf. Haines, *Restrictive Railway Legislation*, p. 148.
[2] *Quarterly Journal of Economics*, November 1910, p. 47.

engines, waggons, train-staff, etc., than a number of short
hauls, necessarily with waits between; engines and waggons
are better loaded, and the line is more continuously utilised." [1]
This consideration points to some form of tapering rate for
the service of carriage, apart from terminal charges. The
English (pre-war) classification of merchandise rates accepts
this. It provides for one maximum ton-mile rate for the first
20 miles, a lower maximum for the next 30 miles, a still
lower one for the next 50 miles, and the lowest of all for
further distances. This scale does not include terminal
charges, which are fixed independently of distance. [2]

Thirdly, attention must be called to the fact that services,
though physically similar, are not necessarily similar in
respect of cost when they are rendered at different times
or seasons of the year. This consideration is in practice
chiefly important as regards the supply of electricity. In
order that it may be possible to provide the current required
at "the peak of the load," a large quantity of equipment
must be erected additional to what would be required if
there were no hours or seasons of exceptional demand. Let
us suppose that during one-fifth of the time 2 million units
per hour are wanted and during the rest of the time
$1\frac{1}{2}$ million units, and that, in consequence, the equipment
costs $\frac{4}{3}$ times what it would have done had $1\frac{1}{2}$ million units
been required always. Then the real cost of the peak-load
current, so far as it depends on cost of equipment, can be
calculated as follows: the equipment cost of producing
the units needed in the aggregate of off-peak times is $\frac{4}{5}$ times
$\frac{3}{4}$ths (i.e. $\frac{3}{5}$ths) of the total equipment cost, and the equipment
cost of producing the units needed in peak times is $\frac{1}{5}$ times
$\frac{3}{4}$ths of the total equipment cost, plus the whole of $\frac{1}{4}$ of that cost,
i.e. $\frac{2}{5}$ths of the whole. That is, the cost of providing 2 million
units at the peak is equal to $\frac{2}{3}$rds that of providing 6 million
units off the peak: or, in other words, the equipment cost (apart
from prime cost) of peak-load service is twice as much per
unit as the equipment cost of normal service. This shows that
simple competition, or the cost of service principle, involves

---

[1] Acworth, *Elements of Railway Economics*, footnote, pp. 122-3.
[2] Cf. Marriott, *The Fixing of Rates and Fares*, p. 21.

different charges for electricity supplied at different times. The same thing obviously holds good of telephone service and cable service—not to speak of hotel and lodging-house service in places that cater specially for seasonal visitors. In industries, the product of which can be stored in slack times, and where, therefore, the equipment can be adjusted to produce continuously the average output demanded, these differences should not exceed the cost and the loss of interest involved in storage. Railways, however, at least in the matter of passenger transport, are directly akin to electricity concerns, in that they provide a service which must be produced at the time that it is supplied. Consequently, the cost of service principle would seem to warrant higher fares for travel at busy seasons and at busy hours of the day than are charged at other times. Differential charges of this character are not, of course, exactly adjusted. Indeed, as a matter of fact, it so happens that, for other reasons, it is just for the most crowded parts of the day and week that the cheapest tickets (workmen's tickets and week-end tickets) are issued. In a concealed form, however, differential charges of this type do exist: for, when a man travelling as a straphanger in the London Tube at 5 o'clock in the evening pays the same absolute price as he does when travelling in comfort at 3 o'clock, he is paying that price for a different and much inferior service. There is just as real a differentiation as there would be if he travelled in equal comfort on both journeys and paid a considerably higher fare at the crowded time.

Lastly, the cost of service principle in some conditions leads logically to lower charges to people whose purchases are continuous than to those who buy intermittently. One reason for this is that a man taking continuous service cannot contribute to the peakiness of a peak load, whereas one taking intermittent service is likely, in some degree, to do this. Hence, if it is impracticable to charge differential rates directly as between peak and off-peak service, this may sometimes be attempted indirectly by differentiation between continuous and intermittent services. The device is an imperfect one, because a consumer, whose demand is intermittent but wholly off-peak, involves less cost than one whose demand is continuous. In practice this type of differentiation is found only in industries where special equipment has to be laid down to enable the service to be supplied to the various customers severally. Obviously, if this equipment is used rarely, a greater sum will have to be charged for each act of service than if it is used frequently. If desired, adjustment can be made by exacting a lump charge, or an annual rent, for the installation of the equipment and, thereafter, charging the same rate to everybody per unit of service obtained through it. This is, broadly, the plan in vogue with telephones. When, however, for any reason this plan is not followed, and the whole charge is levied through the price of the service, the cost of service principle necessarily leads to overt differentiation against customers whose individual load factor is small. But this consideration has no direct application to railway rates, since, apart from special sidings for which direct charges are made, railways do not provide equipment specialised to the service of particular customers.

§ 3. The results so far obtained are only valid in so far as transport services sold to different groups of purchasers are not jointly supplied. If they are jointly supplied, simple competition, or the cost of service principle, would no longer imply that, subject to the reservations of the preceding section, all ton-miles of transportation must be sold at the same price. It would not imply this any more than it implies that a pound of beef and a pound of hides must be sold at the same price. For, when two or more commodities or services are the joint result of a single process, in such wise that one of them cannot be provided without facilitating the provision of the other, simple competition evolves, not identical prices per pound (or other unit) of the various products, but prices so adjusted to demand that the whole output of all of them is carried off. Thus, if the transport of two commodities A and B, or the transport of commodity A for two purposes X and Y, were joint products, simple competition might well evolve for them different rates per ton-mile. It is, therefore, of great importance to determine how far the various services provided by railway companies are in fact joint products in the sense defined above.

§ 4. Many writers of authority maintain that joint costs play a dominant part in the industry of railway transportation. They believe that the transport of coal and the transport of copper along a railway from any point A to any point B are essentially and fundamentally joint products ; and that the same thing is true of the transport from A to B of commodities to be consumed at B and the transport from A to B of commodities to be carried forward to C. This argument is developed by Professor Taussig as follows. First, he observes : " Whenever a very large fixed plant is used, not for a single purpose, but for varied purposes, the influence of joint cost asserts itself." [1] Further : " The labour which built the railway—or, to put the same thing in other words, the capital which is sunk in it—seems equally to aid in carrying on every item of traffic. . . . Not only the fixed capital of a railway, but a very large part, in fact much the largest part, of the operating expenses, represents outlay, not separate for each item of traffic, but common to the whole of it or to great groups of it." [2] The existence of a large mass of common supplementary costs is not, in Professor Taussig's view, by itself sufficient to bring joint supply into action. For that it is essential that the plant be used for *varied purposes*. Thus he writes : " Where a large plant is used for producing one homogeneous commodity —say steel rails or plain cotton cloth—the peculiar effects of joint cost cannot, of course, appear." [3] Further, he is willing to admit that the transport of tons of different things and the transport of the same thing for different purposes from A to B do constitute, *in one sense*, a single homogeneous commodity, on precisely the same footing as plain cotton cloth. The fact that some " carrying of tons " is sold to copper merchants and some to coal merchants does not imply that two different services are being provided, any more than the fact that some plain cotton cloth is sold to one purchaser

[1] *Principles of Economics*, vol. i. p. 221. Cf. also vol. ii. p. 369.
[2] Taussig, "Theory of Railway Rates," in Ripley's *Railway Problems*, pp. 128-9.
[3] *Principles of Economics*, vol. i. p. 221.

and some is sold to another implies that two different commodities are being provided. He holds, however, that these
different transports, though homogeneous in one sense, are
not homogeneous " in the sense important for the purpose
in hand—namely as regards *the conditions of demand*." [1]
Thus his essential contention is that, when a commodity, in
the production of which supplementary general costs play
a large part, is supplied, not to different people in a single
unified market, but in a number of separated markets, the
provision to one market is supplied jointly with the provision
to the other markets, in such wise that simple competition
might be expected to evolve a system of divergent prices.

Now, whether or not the term joint products should be
used of services related in the way that Professor Taussig is
contemplating is, of course, a verbal question : but whether
these services are joint products *in such wise that simple competition might be expected to evolve a system of divergent prices*
is a real question. In my view, the conjunction of large common
supplementary costs · with separation between the markets
to which their yield is supplied does not make railway services
joint products in this—the only significant—sense. In order
that they may be joint products, it is further necessary, not
merely that additional investment in plant and so on may
be used alternatively to facilitate the supply to either market,
but that such additional investment cannot be used to
facilitate the supply to one market without facilitating the
supply to the other. The point may be illustrated as follows.
When cotton goods are provided for two distinct and isolated
markets, the costs of furnishing these different markets are,
in great part, *common* : for they consist, to a large extent,
of the supplementary expenses of the cotton industry, which
cannot be allocated specifically to the goods destined for the
different markets. A given addition to investment does not,
however, necessarily add anything to the output available
for *each* of the two markets. If, before it occurred, the first
market received x units of cotton and the second y units, after
it has occurred the extra cotton may be divided between
them, or it may go wholly to the first, or wholly to the

second. When, however, cotton fibre and cotton seed are provided for two distinct and isolated markets by one and the same process, a given addition to investment does necessarily add something to the output available for each of the two markets. In the latter case it is easily seen that simple competition will, in general, lead to divergent prices. In the former case, however, it will not do this. For, if there are a number of competing sellers supplying transportation, or anything else, to several markets with separate demand schedules, and if the price in one of these markets is higher than in another, it is necessarily to the interest of each individual seller to transfer his offer of service from the lower-priced market to the higher-priced market; and this process must tend ultimately to bring the prices in the different markets to a uniform level. This result, *when conditions of simple competition prevail*, obviously holds good independently of the question whether or not the commodity or service under discussion is one in the production of which supplementary costs are large relatively to prime costs. Hence Professor Taussig's argument cannot be accepted. Joint supply, in the sense in which we are here using the term, does not prevail in the industry of railway transport in that fundamental and general way that he supposes it to do.[1]

---

[1] On the general subject of the relation of the concept of joint costs to railway service, cf. a discussion between Professor Taussig and the present writer in the *Quarterly Journal of Economics* for May and August 1913. Two further points should be added.

First, it is sometimes maintained that the concept of joint costs, in the sense assigned to it in the text, is applicable where only one sort of commodity is produced, provided that the units of process, by which the commodity is made, are large relatively to the units of commodity. When, for instance, the marginal unit of process produces 100 units of product, it may be argued that 100 units must yield a price sufficient to remunerate one unit of process, but that it is immaterial to the suppliers by what combination of individual prices the aggregate price of 100 units is made up. This suggestion, however, *when stated in the above general form*, ignores the fact that 100 units of product can be removed, not only by abstracting one unit from the fruit of each of a hundred units of process, but also by abolishing one unit of process, and that, under free competition, if any units of product were refused a price as high as $\frac{1}{100}$th part of the supply price of a unit of process, this latter method of abstraction would naturally be employed. This shows that physically identical products, yielded by the same process at the same time, are not, *in general*, joint products in any sense, even though the marginal unit of the process of production is large. But this reply is not relevant, and the concept of joint supply cannot be ruled out, when the number of units of process that are actually being provided

§ 5. At the same time it should be clearly recognised that, in the services rendered by railway companies, joint supply does play *some* part. This is conspicuously true as between transportation from A to B and transportation in the reverse direction from B to A. The organisation of a railway, like that of a steamship company, requires that vehicles running from A to B shall subsequently return from B to A. The addition of a million pounds to the expenditure on moving vehicles necessarily increases both the number of movements of vehicles from A to B and the number of movements from B to A. This implies true jointness. It follows that a competitive system of railway or shipping rates would not, in general, make the vehicle charges the same for journeys from A to B and from B to A, but the direction, for which the demand was higher, would be charged a higher rate. This is, of course, the reason why outward

---

is the minimum number that it is practicable to provide so long as any are provided. In these circumstances there is nothing incompatible with the analysis of the text in regarding the resultant units of product as jointly supplied. The costs of constructing through any region the least expensive railway that it is possible to construct at all are joint costs of all the various items of service rendered by the railway. It is possible by following this line of analysis to reach the results obtained by the different line of analysis to be followed in § 8. In the special problem of the least expensive railway that it is possible to construct at all, the two lines are equally admissible. (Cf. *Quarterly Journal of Economics*, August 1913, p. 688.) Since, however, analysis by way of joint supply is only applicable in a single and peculiar type of problem, whereas analysis by way of discriminating monopoly, to be adopted in the text, is applicable to all problems, the latter method should be given preference.

Secondly, the concept of joint supply can, if desired, be applied to the same services rendered at different times by the same fixed plant. Thus the services of railways for night travelling and day travelling may be called joint, and different rates advocated on that ground. This consideration is especially important with electricity rates. It justifies differentiation of a form designed to carry off nearly equal supplies throughout the day or year. The same result can be obtained on a different route if we regard the services supplied at the two times as being the same service but subject to varying demands. The point of distinction, as against a railway carrying different things *at the same time*, is that the railway can be adjusted to carry any quantity of things, so that to carry A does not involve power to carry B ; but a railway fitted to carry A in the day cannot be provided except in a form that gives power to carry A also at night. The distinction would, of course, lose most of its significance if the capital equipment were expected to maintain its full value over a *defined period of use* and not over a defined period of time ; for then less night use now would make possible more day use later on. But in fact plant largely wears out *through time* independently of use ; *e.g.* rails and ties deteriorate with weather (cf. Watkins, *Electrical Rates*, p. 203), and also tend to become obsolete.

freights from England are generally low, relatively to inward freights, for commodities of similar value. Our imports being largely food and raw materials, and our exports, apart from coal, mainly finished manufactures, the former naturally make a greater demand for shipping accommodation. If it were not for our coal exports, the disparity would be much greater than it is. There is a similar relation in the transport of goods—though not of passengers—between eastward and westward travel in the United States; because "those who supply the world with food and raw materials dispose of much more tonnage than they purchase."[1] This element of jointness is, however, of comparatively small importance. Contrary to the general opinion of writers on railway economics, the services provided by railway companies are, in the main, not jointly supplied. Hence, the conclusion emerges that, subject to the reservations set out in § 2, simple competition would, in general, evolve a system of equal ton-mileage rates for all commodities, whatever their character, and whether they are to be consumed at B or be sent on from B for some further part of a "long haul."

§ 6. The meaning in concrete form of "the value of service principle," or monopoly *plus* discrimination of the third degree, is more complicated. It was shown in the last chapter that a monopolist adopting this principle will divide the total market served by him into a number of minor markets, by discriminating between which he may make his aggregate advantage as large as possible. It was shown, further, that the kind of division best calculated to promote this end is one under which the separate markets are arranged, so far as practical considerations allow, in such a way that each higher-priced market contains as few demands as possible with a demand price lower than the highest demand price contained in the next market. When once the minor markets have been separated, the determination of the rates to be charged

---

[1] Cf. Johnson, *American Railway Transportation*, p. 138. It should be noticed that, whereas there is little jointness as between first and third class passenger service on railways, there is probably a considerable element of such jointness as between first and third class service on ships ; because the structure of a ship necessarily involves the provision at the same time of more and of less comfortable parts of the vessel.

in them presents no analytical difficulty, and can be expressed in a simple mathematical formula.[1] It is not, indeed, true, as is sometimes supposed, that the relative rates charged to different markets will depend, if this plan is adopted, simply upon the comparative elasticities (in respect of some unspecified amount of output) of the demands of these markets, nor yet that they will depend simply upon the comparative demand prices (also in respect of some unspecified amount of output) ruling in these markets. The true determinant is the whole body of conditions represented in the complete demand schedules of the different markets.[2] Still, though the determinant is, in general, complex, when once the constitution of the different markets has been settled, it is precise. The real difficulty lies in the choice, limited, as it is, by practical conditions, which a railway company has to make between various possible systems of minor markets. The search for the most advantageous system—from the company's point of view—has evolved, in practice, elaborate schemes of classification both for passenger traffic and for goods traffic. To show the application of the value of service principle in practice, some description of these schemes is required.

In passenger traffic railway companies find the value of service principle most nearly satisfied by a classification based, in the main, on the relative wealth of different groups of persons, the presumption being that most of the demands for the transport of richer people yield demand prices higher than most of the demands for the transport of poorer people.

---

[1] Thus, let $\phi_1(x_1)$, $(\phi_2)x_2$ . . . represent the demand prices in n separate markets, and $f(x)$ the supply price.

The prices proper to the separate markets under monopoly *plus* discrimination of the third degree are given by the values of $\phi_1(x_1)$, $\phi_2(x_2)$ . . . that satisfy n equations of the form :

$$\frac{\partial}{\partial x_r}[x_r\{\phi_r(x_r) - \Sigma x_r f(x_1 + x_2 + \ . \ . \ .)\}] = 0.$$

These n equations are sufficient to determine the n unknowns.

[2] Where the curves representing the demand schedules are straight lines, this complex determinant dissolves into a simple one, namely, the comparative demand prices of those units which are most keenly demanded in each of the several markets. Under these conditions, if conditions of constant supply price prevail, the monopoly price proper to each market can be shown to be equal to one half of the difference between the supply price and the demand price of the unit that is most keenly demanded there.

Since it is impracticable to make a classification founded directly on differences of wealth, various indices or badges, generally associated with varying degrees of wealth, are employed. Thus, in the United States, certain railways make specially low rates for immigrants—lower than those required from native Americans,—even though the latter are willing to travel in immigrant cars.[1] In certain colonies there is a discriminating rate according to the *colour* of the traveller; black men, who are supposed, in general, to be less well-to-do, being charged lower fares than white men.[2] Again, in England, and still more markedly in Belgium,[3] railway companies charge specially low rates for workmen's tickets. This procedure is exactly analogous to that of those London shopkeepers who charge to customers with "good addresses" prices different from those charged to others, and of the Cambridge boatmen who used to charge a collective customer of five persons 5s. for the hire of a boat for an afternoon, while to a single person they would let the same boat for one shilling. A classification based on indices of wealth alone is, however, somewhat crude, since people of the same wealth will desire a given journey with very different intensities on different occasions. In recognition of this fact railway companies have constructed a variety of cross-groupings, based on such incidents as the degree of comfort or of speed with which, or the hour at which, journeys are undertaken, or the presumed purpose which these journeys serve. Thus the fares for first-class accommodation, or for conveyance by certain express trains, are made to exceed those for inferior accommodation or lower speed by more than the difference in the cost of providing these different sorts of service;[4] and specially low fares are sometimes charged for journeys made in the early morning.[5] In like manner, attempts are made to separate holiday journeys, of pre-

---

[1] *Quarterly Journal of Economics*, November 1910, p. 38.

[2] Cf. Colson, *Cours d'économie politique*, vol. vi. p. 230.

[3] Cf. Rowntree, *Land and Labour*, p. 289.

[4] M. Colson suggests that a plan, under which all trains should take third class passengers, the fast trains charging a supplement, would be superior to the present Continental plan, under which a passenger, who wishes to travel fast, has to pay the whole difference between third and second class fare.

[5] Cf. Mahaim, *Les Abonnements d'ouvriers*, p. 12.

sumed low demand, from necessary business journeys, by the supply, on special terms, of tourist, week-end and excursion tickets.

In goods traffic railway companies find the value of service principle most nearly satisfied by a classification based, in the main, upon the relative value of the different commodities claiming transport, the presumption being that most of the demands for the transport of a more valuable group of goods yield demand prices higher than most of the demands for the transport of a less valuable group. The reason for this presumption is as follows. The demand price for the transport of any n^{th} unit of any commodity from A to B is measured by the excess of the price of that commodity in B over its price in A, which would prevail if the said n^{th} unit were not transported. But, on any law of distribution, the probable difference between the prices of any article in A and B respectively, which would arise if these two places were not connected by the assigned act of transport, is greater, the greater is the absolute price that would prevail in either of them ; just as the probable difference in the heights of poplars in A and B is greater than the probable difference in the heights of cabbages. There is no reason to expect that the percentage difference will be greater for valuable than for cheap commodities, but there is reason to expect that the absolute difference will be greater. A study of the details of the classification adopted for British railways under the Railway Rates and Charges Act shows that, in the main, the value of the commodities concerned was taken as a basis. Broadly speaking, the lower the position of any class in the list, the cheaper are the goods that it contains.[1] In like manner, several of the decisions of the United States Railway Commissioners have been founded on the proposition that less expensive articles ought not to be put in a higher class than more expensive articles—chair materials than finished chairs, raisins than dried fruits, and so on.[2]

Sometimes it is practically inconvenient for a company

[1] Cf. Marriott, *The Fixing of Rates and Fares*, p. 27 *et seq.*, for these lists.
[2] Cf. *Quarterly Journal of Economics*, November 1910, pp. 13, 15 and 29.

or a regulating authority to group goods directly in accordance with their value. When this is so, a like result can be obtained indirectly by grouping them according to indices whose differences are likely to correspond to differences of value. Thus, since the valuable qualities of any commodity are generally packed better than the cheap qualities, rates are sometimes made to vary with the elaboration of the packing employed. For example, in France, where good wines are generally packed "en barriques de 220 à 230 litres" and common wines "en demi-muids de 650 à 700 litres ou en wagons-réservoirs," [1] wines in "barriques" are charged on a higher scale.

It must be added that, as with passenger service, so also with goods service, a classification based exclusively on the value of the commodities transported is necessarily somewhat crude. In consequence of this, cross-groupings based upon other incidents have also been employed. Thus, within each group of commodities of given value transported from A to B, a subdivision may be made between those which B can easily make for itself, or obtain elsewhere than from A, and those which it cannot so make or obtain; and a higher rate may be charged to the latter group. Again, within a homogeneous group made up of units of the same commodity, sub-groups are constructed. For example, vegetables imported from Germany to England during the weeks before the English crop is ready used to be charged more than vegetables imported from Germany to England after this crop had appeared; and the same thing is true of vegetables sent from the south to the north of France.[2] Sometimes, again, an attempt is made to charge different rates for the transport of the same thing according to the use to which it is to be put—bricks for building, paving bricks and fire bricks being put in different classes. It should be observed, however, that the United States Interstate Commerce Commission has declined to recognise the validity of a classification on this basis.[3] More important is the subdivision according

---

[1] Colson, *Cours d'économie politique*, vol. vi. p. 227.

[2] Cf. *ibid.* p. 227.

[3] Ripley, *Railroads, Rates and Regulation*, p. 318.

to ultimate place of destination. Thus commodities sent
from A to B, to be consumed at B, are placed in a different
group, and charged, for that act of transport, a different rate,
from commodities sent from A to B to be forwarded from
B to C. The reason is that different parts of the world
do not differ in nature in proportion as they differ in distance.
There is not much ground for expecting *a priori* that the
cost of producing a given commodity in B will differ from
the cost in A to a greater extent if A is 500, than if it is
100, miles away. Consequently the demand for any r^{th}
mile's worth of carriage is probably less in long transports
of goods than in short transports. This consideration applies
with especial force to articles of food and raw material, which
are physically adapted to growth over a wide range of
temperature and climate. But it has some relation to all
sorts of goods and is, no doubt, partly responsible for the
systems of tapering rates for goods,—but not for passengers,—
that prevail in England, France and Germany.[1] The case
for discriminating rates is, however, much stronger, when
A is connected with C by direct water transport, as well as
by a railway from A to B *plus* either more railway or water
from B to C. In these circumstances the demand price
of *many* units of transportation from A to B, of any commodity to be consumed at B, is likely to be much higher than
the demand price of *any* unit of transportation from A to B,
of the same commodity to be carried on from B to C.
Grouping in accordance with this fact is responsible for the
occurrence of rates from Cheshire to London, for goods
imported through Liverpool, much below the rates for corresponding goods originating in Cheshire. On the same principle,
"special rates have been granted by the Prussian State
Railways for the conveyance of grain traffic from Russia
to oversea countries (Sweden, Norway, England, etc.), and
the rate per ton per kilometre from the frontier to the
German harbours, Königsberg, Danzig, etc., is lower than
the charge for German grain between the same points.
. . . It was pointed out that this specially low rate was
granted with the object of securing the traffic to the Prussian

[1] Cf. Marriott, *The Fixing of Rates and Fares*, p. 43.

railways, as it need not necessarily pass over the Prussian lines, but could go via Riga, Reval and Libau, and would have done so without this reduction in the rates."[1]

§ 7. We are now in a position to compare the principle of cost of service and the principle of value of service from the point of view of the national dividend. It is well known that, in common opinion, the determination of railway rates by the value of service principle, or, in the alternative phrase, by what the traffic will bear, is unquestionably superior to its rival. The popular view, however, as I understand it, rests, in the main, upon two confusions. The first of these starts from the assumption that the transport of copper and the transport of coal, and the transport from A to B when further transport respectively is, and is not, required, are joint products. This assumption was shown to be unwarranted in § 4. It proceeds by means of the further assumption that to charge for joint products rates adapted to comparative marginal demands is to charge in accordance with the value of service principle. This assumption is no less unwarranted than the other. A moment's reflection shows that to charge for joint products in this way would be to follow the guidance of the cost of service principle, or— what is another name for the same thing—of simple competition. The second confusion is an *ignoratio elenchi*. Arguments are advanced to prove that the value of service principle, in the proper sense of discriminating monopoly, is superior to simple monopoly. Thus it is pointed out that, when the conditions are such that the rate most advantageous to himself which the monopolist can make, subject to the condition that equal rates shall be charged for the transport of copper and of coal, will cause him to stop transporting coal altogether while continuing to transport copper at a high rate, the national dividend could be increased by permission to discriminate between the two rates.[2] Such an argument, it is obvious, though valid in its own field, is wholly irrelevant to the question whether discriminating monopoly of the third degree is superior, not to simple . monopoly, but to simple

---

[1] *Report of the Railway Conference*, 1909, p. 99.
[2] Cf. *ante*, Part II. Chapter XVII. § 13.

competition. When these confusions are swept away, the issue between the value of service principle and the cost of service principle in railway rates is seen to constitute a special case of the general issue, set out in the preceding chapter, between the said discriminating monopoly of the third degree and the said simple competition.

§ 8. The result of the discussion on that issue was that simple competition is, in general, the more advantageous. There emerged, however, one set of conditions, in which the advantage lies with its rival. These conditions are that, while no uniform price can be found which will cover the expenses of producing *any* quantity of output, a system of discriminating prices is practicable, which will make *some* output profitable. They have been illustrated by Principal Hadley, with special reference to discriminations between the charges for carriage from A to B that are made for goods going to B for consumption at B and for goods going to B for further transport to C. "Suppose," he writes, "it is a question whether a road can be built through a country district, lying between two large cities, which have the benefit of water communication, while the intervening district has not." To meet water competition, the charge for carriage from one extreme A to an intermediate point B must be low for goods to be carried forward to the other extreme C; so low that, if it were applied to all carriage from A to B, it would make the working of this part of the road unprofitable. But the demand for carriage from A to B, in respect of goods to be retained at B, is so small that this alone cannot support the road, no matter how low or how high the rates are made. "In other words, in order to live at all, the road must secure two different things—the high rates for its local traffic, and the large traffic of the through points, which can only be attracted by low rates. If they are to have the road, they must have discrimination."[1] An exactly analogous argument can be constructed in favour of discriminations in the ton-

[1] *Railroad Transportation*, p. 115. It may conceivably be objected to the construction of a railway in these circumstances that it will injure the rival industry of water carriage to an extent that will offset the advantages to which it leads. This objection can, however, be shown to be inapplicable, so long as the railway as a whole pays its way. Cf. *ante*, Part II. Chapter IX. § 11.

mile rates that are charged on different commodities, when the conditions are such that, apart from discrimination, there would be no quantity of transportation units, the proceeds of whose sale would cover their expenses of production. On the same principle, it may be argued that in some circumstances a roundabout line should be permitted to charge abnormally low rates between its terminal points, with the effect of preventing the development of a direct line between these points; for conditions may be such that, apart from this arrangement, no roundabout line could be profitably built, and so centres which it might serve would suffer. I have no quarrel with the proposition that these conditions *may* occur in practice. Principal Hadley and his followers, however, not content with demonstrating that they are possible, implicitly add, without argument, that they are typical of the whole railway world, and suppose themselves, therefore, to have proved that the value of service principle ought to be followed in the determination of all railway rates. Such an unargued inference is, plainly, illegitimate. A careful inquiry is necessary concerning the range over which conditions of a sort to justify the value of service principle are likely to extend in practice.

§ 9. From an analytical point of view, the situation is simple. As explained in the preceding chapter, in order that monopoly *plus* discrimination of the first degree may create an output where simple competition fails to do so—I take the simplest case, in which the demand in one market is independent of the price in the other—certain relations, which were there described, between the general conditions of demand and of supply must exist. The conditions enabling monopoly *plus* discrimination of the third degree to lead to this result are less precise. Circumstances, in which discrimination of the first degree would only just succeed, will not, in general, enable discrimination of the third degree to succeed. We may conclude, roughly, however, that discrimination of the third degree will have a good chance of succeeding—a chance that is better, the more numerous are the markets between which discrimination is made, and the more satisfactory, from the monopolist's standpoint, is their constitution—when the conditions are such that discrimination of the first degree would succeed with a wide margin. Our problem is to determine how far this state of things is likely to occur in practice.

First : it has been shown that the likelihood of this is greatest in forms of investment in which the law of decreasing supply price acts strongly.[1] Among railways there is ground for believing that, at all events until considerable development has been reached, this condition is generally satisfied. The reason is that the fixed plant of a railway cannot, in practice, be so made as to be capable of effecting less than a certain considerable minimum of transportation. The aggregate costs of arranging for rail transport for one ounce per week are very nearly as great as those of arranging for the transport of many thousand tons. For the same heavy expenditure must be undertaken for surveying and legal charges, bridging valleys and torrents, tunnelling through rock, erecting stations and platforms, and so on. This implies that the law decreasing supply price acts strongly till a large investment has been made, and afterwards less strongly. So far, therefore, conditions in which discriminating monopoly would prove superior to simple competition are more likely to occur in railway service than in some other industries.

Secondly, it has been shown that the likelihood of discriminating monopoly yielding some output when simple competition yields none is greatest in forms of investment where the demand for the product is elastic.[2] In railway service, when once rates have been brought down to a moderate level, there is reason to believe that a small reduction of rates would call out a large increase of demand, not only from commodities that might otherwise have been transported by some other agency, but also from commodities that otherwise would not have been transported at all. In other words, there is reason to believe that the demand is, in general, elastic. Here, too, then, it may be said that railway service is more apt to yield conditions suitable for discriminating monopoly than some other industries.

Granted, however, both that the law of decreasing supply price acts strongly until considerable density of traffic has been

---

[1] Cf. *ante*, Part II. Chapter XVII. § 9, and Appendix III. § 26.
[2] *Ibid.*

attained, and that the demand for the service of railway transport is elastic, these conditions alone are by no means sufficient to ensure that discriminating monopoly would evolve some output, while simple competition would fail to do this. It is necessary, further, that the actual levels of demand price and supply price for a small quantity of service—more generally, the demand schedule and the supply schedule as a whole—shall be related in a particular way. Clearly, if the demand price for a small quantity is greater than the supply price, some output will be evolved under simple competition, and, therefore, the conditions we have in view do not arise. Clearly, again, if the demand price for a small quantity is very much less than the supply price, it is unlikely that any output will be evolved either under simple competition or under discriminating monopoly, and, therefore, again these conditions do not arise. In order that they may arise, a sort of intermediate position must, it would seem, be established. Thus, on the one hand, the district affected must not be too busy and thickly populated; on the other hand, it must not be too little busy and sparsely populated. There is a certain intermediate range of activity and population that is needed. This range, compared with the total range of possibility, is naturally not extensive. Hence the probability that the conditions necessary to make discriminating monopoly more advantageous to the national dividend than simple competition will be present in any railway selected at random at any time seems *a priori* to be very small. There are, indeed, many *dicta* of practical experts which suggest that they have in fact a wide range. But, as Edgeworth, who lays stress upon this point, recognises, "the testimony of high authorities would, no doubt, carry even greater weight if it should be repeated with a full recognition of the *a priori* improbability" to which it is opposed.[1]

§ 10. It must be observed, however, that, as population and aggregate wealth in any country expand, the demand schedule for railway service, along any assigned route, gradually rises. Hence, though, at any moment selected

[1] *Economic Journal*, 1913, p. 223.

at random, it is improbable that the conditions affecting
any route, selected at random, are such that a railway rate
system based on the value of service principle would be
more advantageous to the dividend than one based on the
"cost of service principle," it is not improbable that any
route, selected at random, will *pass through a period* during
which the conditions are of this kind. Such conditions tend
to emerge when one point in the growth of wealth and
population has been reached, and to disappear when another
somewhat later point has been reached. If the cost of
service principle ruled universally, and if no State bounties
were given, certain lines would not be built till the arrival
of the latter point—when there is hope of " building up "
a demand by experience of supply, this point need not, of
course, be such that the railway pays at the moment—
despite the fact that they could have been built, with
advantage to the community, on the arrival of the earlier
point. The inference is that discrimination, or the value
of service principle, should be adopted when any route is
in the intermediate stage between these two stages, and that
this principle should give place to simple competition, or the
cost of service principle, as soon as population has grown
and demand has risen sufficiently to lift it out of that
stage.[1] The period proper to the value of service principle
would seem, in most ordinary lines, to be a comparatively
brief one.[2]

[1] Mr. Bickerdike (*Economic Journal*, March 1911, p. 148) and Mr. Clark
(*Bulletin of American Economic Association*, September 1911, p. 479) argue, in
effect, that the transition from the one system to the other should occur, not
when rising demand lifts the railway in question out of the stage just described,
but when, if ever, it rises so high as to impinge on that point of the supply
curve at which a negative slope passes into a positive one. There is not, in
my opinion, any adequate ground for this view.

[2] It is possible to maintain, on lines similar to the above, that, after a
railway has been built, and has reached the stage of profitable working on the
cost of service principle, another stage will presently arrive, at which a return
to the value of service principle would enable a second track to be laid down
with advantage to the community, though, under a rate system based on the
cost of service principle, such an extension would not as yet be profitable to
the company. This argument justifies the establishment of a system of
discriminating rates, *to be applied to traffic carried on the new track only* ; and
a modification of it justifies the establishment of such a system, to be applied
exclusively to traffic carried in any *additional* train or truck which, apart from
discrimination, it is just not worth while to run. In practice, however, it is

§ 11. Even this limited application of the principle is only warranted on the assumption that there is no third way between the pure value of service principle and the pure cost of service principle. In fact, however, there is a third way. The cost of service principle may be maintained and the State may give a bounty. Plainly, with the help of a bounty exactly the same effect in speeding up the building of a railroad could be accomplished under the cost of service principle as would be accomplished under the value of service principle without a bounty. The community as a whole would be providing out of taxes the necessary profit for the railway, which, on the other plan, would come from the charges made to the people who buy the most highly charged freight service. Since the building of the railway is in the general interest, it would seem, on the whole, to be fairer that the taxpayers, and not a special class of traders—or rather, in the end, the consumers of these traders' products—should provide these funds. In view of the practical awkwardness of changing from a discriminating to a non-discriminating system of rates when the intermediate stage described in the preceding paragraph is passed, the plan of giving a bounty for a time and withdrawing it when it is no longer needed is also superior from the side of administrative convenience. If, on account of the indirect advantages of cheap railway transport in facilitating the division of labour between different parts of the country, making possible the development of large - scale localised industries, and, through the improved communication of markets, lessening local price fluctuations—all changes which, in one way or another, benefit production—it is held that the railway industry is one to which a general bounty should be accorded permanently, it is obvious that a second instrument for doing what bounties can do by themselves is not required and that no place is left for the value of service principle.

§ 12. Of the relative advantages of the cost of service principle, or prices proper to simple competition, and the

---

impossible to apply the value of service principle in this limited way. If it is introduced for the traffic proper to the second track or the extra truck, it must, in real life, be introduced for all the traffic carried on the line. The argument set out above does not justify this.

value of service principle, or prices proper to discriminating monopoly, this is all that need be said. There is, however, yet another possible arrangement. Control might be exercised in such a way that a railway company should only secure competitive or normal profits on the whole, but these profits might be obtained by a combination of some charges below cost with others above cost, just as a doctor's profits are obtained by a combination of low prices to poor patients and high prices to rich patients. In one field of railway service there is a plain *prima facie* case for an arrangement of this kind. Great social advantage can be derived from the provision of cheap workmen's tickets: for in favourable circumstances this makes it possible for workpeople to live in the country, though working in towns, and thus to bring up their children in healthy surroundings.[1] Such provision can be ensured if railway companies (whose earnings are supposed to be kept down by regulation to a normal competitive level) are compelled to make it, and are allowed to recoup themselves by " monopolistic " charges upon other traffic. Plainly, however, exactly the same result can be achieved if the reimbursement required for the railway companies is provided out of the national revenue. There seems to be no good reason for throwing this burden upon persons who make use of the service of railways rather than upon the general body of taxpayers. For, though it may well be that railway service is a suitable object through which to impose a tax on these persons, we can hardly suppose that the extent to which they ought to be taxed through this object exactly corresponds to the amount of funds required for the bounty to poor purchasers of railway service. There is still less reason for allowing discriminated rates, determined, not in the purchasers' interest,

---

[1] In Belgium the system of cheap workmen's tickets, which has been carried to great perfection, seems to act in this way. (Cf. Rowntree, *Land and Labour*, p. 108.) Dr. Mahaim offers some confirmation of the view that it acts so in the fact that Belgium is a land of "large towns" rather than of "great cities," a much larger proportion of the population living in communes of from 5000 to 20,000 inhabitants in that country than in France or Germany (*Les Abonnements d'ouvriers*, p. 149). At the same time, Dr. Mahaim admits that the cheap tickets have also an adverse effect. "On commence par aller à la ville ou à l'usine en revenant tous les soirs ou tous les samedis chez soi ; puis on s'habitue peu à peu au nouveau milieu, et l'on finit par s'y implanter" (*ibid.* p. 143). In fact the cheap tickets "apprennent le chemin de l'émigration."

but at the choice of the railway companies themselves. Hence this system of discriminated charges coupled with regulated profits cannot, on the whole, be justified. We are thus left with the cost of service principle, modified at need, sometimes by general bounties, sometimes by bounties on particular services deliberately sold for less than cost price.

§ 13. One last point remains. To apply this cost of service principle accurately involves, as was shown in § 2, a number of delicate adjustments. For the principle leads, not to a single price for everybody, but to prices that vary with the incidental costs attaching to each service and with the time at which it is furnished in relation to the peak of the load. To provide for these adjustments in practice is often a very difficult matter involving costly technique and account-keeping. It is, therefore, always a question how near to the ideal it is desirable to approach ; at what point the advantage of getting closer is outweighed by the complications, inconveniences and expense involved in doing so. In the early days of the telephone service the desire for simplicity and ease in rate making led to a system in which flat rates were charged for the use of instruments, without any reference whatever to the number of calls made; and water rates are even yet often based, not on any measurement of the supply that is actually taken, but on an estimate of what is likely to be taken, derived from the rental of the houses served. For electricity, while ingenious meters have been devised, which not only record the supply taken, but also weight more heavily the part of it which is taken in the peak hours, nevertheless the high cost of any sort of meter still causes the service of small houses to be charged in many districts on a flat unmetered rate. In like manner, though for the transport of parcels it has been thought worth while to take account, in the charges made, of those differences in the cost of service which arise out of differences of weight, for the transport of letters this is not done : and for neither parcels nor letters are charges adjusted to the distance (within the British Empire) over which they have to be conveyed. On similar grounds of simplicity and cheapness, a railway administration, which had decided to base its rating system upon the cost of service principle, must, nevertheless, ignore,

within considerable limits, differences in the weight of luggage
which different passengers carry. This class of consideration
shows that there is not necessarily any departure from the
spirit of the cost of service principle when a railway administration elects to utilise a system of zone tariffs. A street
railway system obviously must do this; for the mere fact that
there is no coin smaller than a farthing makes it physically
impossible to fix different fares for every different distance of
journey. So long as the zones are narrow, zone tariffs on
ordinary railways have an equally good defence. If, however,
the zones are made broad, the cost of service principle is
deliberately violated. A system under which the rates are
the same for all places in broad zones involves substantial
differentiation in favour of firms situated far from their
markets, as against firms situated nearer to them. In effect,
it confers upon them a kind of bounty at the expense of
their rivals. It can, indeed, be shown that differentiation
in favour of one source of supply as against another
source may, in certain circumstances and if introduced in a
certain manner, be advantageous to the national dividend.
The sort of differentiation that results from the zone system is,
however, random differentiation, not specially designed to
favour a carefully chosen list of selected firms. It is, thus, on
the average, like differentiation in favour of one set against
another set of *similar* firms. This sort of differentiation causes
the production (including transport) of some part of the
commodity concerned to be carried out at greater real cost
than is necessary; for the marginal real costs of producing
anything in the distant source and bringing it to the market
must necessarily be greater than the marginal real costs of
producing it in the nearer source and bringing it to the market.[1]
It is possible to maintain that the direct loss resulting from
this may be balanced by the effect of the zone system in
scattering the producing firms belonging to an industry, and
so making combination, with the opportunity which this gives
for anti-social monopolistic action, more difficult.[2] But this

[1] Cf. *Quarterly Journal of Economics*, February 1911, pp. 292-3, 297-8 and
300: also *Departmental Committee on Railway Rates*, p. 10.
[2] Cf. *Quarterly Journal of Economics*, May 1911, pp. 493-5.

argument does not appear to have great force. It is not, in itself, desirable to check the formation of large productive units, since such units introduce economies. As will be argued presently, it would seem a better policy to attack the evil consequences of monopolistic action, which combination threatens, directly, rather than indirectly by attempts to discourage unification.[1]

[1] Cf. *post*, Part II. Chapter XXI. § 2.

CHAPTER XIX

PURCHASERS' ASSOCIATIONS

§ 1. THE results of the preceding chapters make it plain that, in many industries, neither simple competition, nor monopolistic competition, nor simple monopoly, nor discriminating monopoly will make the value of the marginal social net product there equal to the value of marginal social net products generally, and, therefore, that they will not maximise either the national dividend or economic welfare. It will have been noticed, however, that the systems so far investigated have all been systems under which goods are produced by one set of people and sold to another set. The failures of adjustment, to which they lead, have, therefore, all been dependent on this fact. Hence the question naturally arises: Could not these failures be eliminated by the device of voluntary groups of purchasers undertaking for themselves the supply of the goods and services they need?

§ 2. Now, the essence of a Purchasers' Association, whether it is formed of the consumers of finished goods or of producers who will utilise their purchases in further production, is that its policy is directed to maximise aggregate purchaser's benefit *minus* aggregate costs. It must, therefore, call out just that quantity of output, which, except where others besides the purchasers of the commodity are affected by its production, will make the value of the marginal social net product of resources devoted to it equal to the value of the marginal social net product of resources in general. That is to say, other things being equal, it must eliminate, in great measure, the disharmonies belonging alike to monopoly and to simple competition. This preliminary abstract statement does not, however, solve our problem. It is not enough to know that, *if other things are equal*, Purchasers' Associations will advantage the national dividend. Before we can infer anything from this about the effect of these Associations in actual life, we need to inquire how they compare with ordinary commercial businesses in crude economic efficiency; for it is clear that any advantages, which a Purchasers' Association may possess in price policy, and, therefore, in respect of the distribution of resources among different occupations, are liable to be outweighed if it is inefficient on the productive side.

§ 3. As a prelude to this task, it is desirable to guard against certain confusions. First and most obviously, we need to rule out all appeals to the superior efficiency, in certain fields, of Purchasers' Associations, as compared with the members of these Associations operating as isolated individuals. It is easy to point to services, which many persons need in small individual lots, but which can be produced much more economically in large lots. A good example is the service of marketing agricultural products of variable quality produced in small quantities by small farmers. For economical selling requires careful grading of qualities and a fairly continuous supply of each grade ; and small farmers, who attempt individually to market their butter or their eggs, are not operating on a large enough scale to meet these requirements satisfactorily. Thus Mr. Rider Haggard writes of Denmark : " In 1882 what was called ' peasant butter ' fetched 33 per cent less than first-class butter made on the big farms, but in 1894 the co-operative butter, which, of course, for the most part comes from the peasant farms, took more medals and prizes than that from the great farms, and what used to be called second and third class butter ceased to exist as a Danish commodity of commerce." [1]   The fact, however, that, for this kind of reason, the manufacture of butter, the curing of bacon, and the marketing of eggs " afford a splendid opening for the application of co-operative principles," is irrelevant to the present issue, since these things also afford a splendid opening for the

[1] *Rural Denmark*, pp. 195-6.

application of commercial principles.[1] It is true that a Purchasers' Association can work in this field much more cheaply than a single small farmer; but, exactly the same thing is true of an ordinary commercial firm, undertaking to sell the service of marketing to these farmers. Two examples are given by Sir R. H. Rew. " One is the French butter trade. This has been built up by the merchants in Normandy and Brittany—some of whom are Englishmen—who purchase the butter at the local markets from the individual farmers, and work it up in their blending houses. Another instance is the poultry trade in the Heathfield district of Sussex. There the system is that the fatteners, or 'higglers' as they are termed, purchase and collect the chickens from those who rear them; they are then duly fattened, killed, and prepared for market, and again collected by the carrier or railway agent, by whom they are forwarded to London and other markets. Both these are instances of complete organisation without co-operation." [2] Secondly, we must refrain from stressing unduly the history of English Co-operative Stores. The reason is that, when the device of Purchasers' Associations was introduced into retail trading, it is very doubtful if the rival method was fairly represented. Partly in consequence of the imperfect competition between different shops, not all the economies that were available had been taken up.[3] Even from their own point of view, " retailers

---

[1] In like manner, the charge that the development of Purchasers' Associations on the part of groups of persons other than ultimate consumers may make possible monopolistic action against these consumers is irrelevant; for, so also may the development of commercial firms.

[2] Rew, *An Agricultural Faggot*, p. 120.

[3] Care must be taken, however, not to treat as waste in the work of retailing those costs that are necessarily involved in the kind of retailing that the public chooses to ask for. " Imagine that every one intending to buy a pair of shoes or a suit of clothes was called on to send notice of his proposed purchase a week or two in advance, to give a preliminary account of the thing wanted, and then to accept an appointment for a stated place or time at which the purchases must be made. It is easy to see how the work of retailing could be systematised, how the selling force would be kept constantly employed, how stocks would be kept to the minimum. As things now stand, we pay heavily for the privilege of freedom in the use of our time, for vacillation and choice, for the maintenance of a stock and a staff adequate for all tastes and all emergencies. It is common to speak of the waste of competition; much of it is in reality the waste necessarily involved in liberty " (Taussig, *American Economic Review*, vol. vi. No. 1 Supplement, 1916, p. 182).

as a body kept far more shops than was necessary, spent far too much trouble and money in attracting a few customers, and then in taking care that those few customers paid them in the long run—the very long run—for those goods which they had bought on credit, or, in other words, had borrowed; and for all this they had to charge. . . . Retail trade was the one accessible business—Marshall was probably not thinking of house-keeping and domestic cooking as a business—in which there were great economies to be effected."[1] This view of the matter is fortified by Pareto's observation, that retail shops were easily ousted by the competition, not only of *sociétés co-opératives*, but also of *les grands magasins*[2]—to which should be added, in England, the very important multiple shops. A comparison between retail trading, as it stood when our consumers' stores came into being, and these stores cannot, therefore, be accepted as a conclusive test of the relative merits of the industrial forms they represent. It is like a comparison between a member of one race whom there is some reason to suspect of being less healthy than the average of his compatriots and a thoroughly sound member of another. No great weight, therefore, can be attached to historical examples, and we are driven forward to an analytical study.[3]

§ 4. In attempting, from this point of view, to estimate the economic efficiency of Purchasers' Associations, we may observe, first, that these Associations are, in structure, a form of Joint Stock Company. Like any other Joint Stock Company, a Purchasers' Association is owned by shareholders, and is controlled by a manager under the supervision of a committee elected from among the shareholders. The alternatives to it are the private business and the ordinary commercial company. In attempting to compare its economic efficiency with theirs, we naturally look to the organisation

---

[1] Marshall, *Inaugural Address to the Co-operative Congress*, 1889, p. 8.

[2] Cf. *Cours d'économie politique*, p. 274.

[3] It should be added that, *even if other things were equal*, the payment of a dividend by a co-operative society trading at the same price as another concern would not prove greater efficiency of management; for, if, as is common, the society proceeded to a greater extent on a system of cash sales, the dividend would *pro tanto* be simply payment to purchasers of interest on their earlier discharge of indebtedness.

of the management. Under this head the Purchasers'
Association and the commercial company alike are inferior
to the private business, just in so far as Boards of officials
lack the opportunities for quick action and the stimulus of
personal possession belonging to the private business.[1] But
the Purchasers' Association is likely, in some degree, to make
up for this deficiency through the ardour instilled into the
manager and the committee by the fact that they are engaged
in a service suited to evoke public spirit. The Purchasers'
Association may, in fact, utilise the altruistic motives, alongside of the egoistic, as a spur to industrial efficiency. Against
this consideration, however, there has to be set a second.
In so far as Purchasers' Associations consist of poor persons,
unaccustomed to large business, there is a danger that they
may grudge adequate freedom to their managers and may
discourage them by illiberal treatment in the matter of
salaries. Furthermore, their committee-men are drawn from
a more limited area, and are apt to possess less business
experience than the directors of commercial companies. These
conflicting influences will, of course, have different weights in
different circumstances.

Secondly, when any section of a country's industry is given
over to monopolistic competition, ordinary commercial businesses
are bound to engage in much wasteful expenditure on advertising, in the manner described in Chapter IX. § 14. In this
respect Purchasers' Associations are in a much more favourable
position. When the services they provide consist of such
things as the purchase of agricultural feeding stuffs or manures,
or the work of wholesale trading, they are practically assured,
without any direct effort on their part, of the whole demand
of their members. When they provide the service of packing
eggs, or curing bacon, or converting milk and cream into
cheese and butter, their members may, indeed, sometimes be
tempted by an offer of better terms to go elsewhere, but it is

---

[1] In the United States, where the President of a company often holds a very
large individual interest, it appears that he sometimes acts on behalf of the
company, just as a private owner would do. "Generally speaking, the
President of an American Corporation acts just as freely and energetically on
behalf of his company as he would on his own behalf" (Knoop, *American
Business Enterprise*, p. 26). He only consults the directors when he wishes
to do so.

possible for the Societies, by making "loyalty," within limits, a condition of membership, in great measure to restrain such action without resort to advertisement. When they provide the service of retailing or of granting credit, the enforcement of loyalty by rule is, indeed, impracticable, and is not attempted ; but even here loyalty will in fact be largely maintained through the members' sense of proprietary interest in their own shop. Among non-members, no doubt, when it is desired to extend the range of any Association's business, advertisement of one sort or another may be necessary. The Purchasers' Association, however, has a considerable advantage over an ordinary Joint Stock Company, because it is able to offer to those who join it, not only cheap goods, but also a certain sense of part ownership in an important corporate institution. Such advertisement as it does undertake, therefore, is likely to prove more effective, and less of it is needed to achieve a given result. By so much its efficiency is, *ceteris paribus,* greater than that of its rivals.

Thirdly, there is another way, besides the saving of advertisement costs, in which "loyalty" makes for economy. As was pointed out in Chapter XIV. § 3, it enables the work of a co-operative concern to be conducted steadily without those large fluctuations, to which private concerns are often subject and the presence of which inevitably involves cost. Thus the rule insisting upon loyalty as a condition of membership of co-operative bacon factories and creameries enables these establishments to count on a constant supply of raw material with greater confidence than private firms can do ;[1] and, in like manner, the practice of the English and Scotch

[1] In the Danish co-operative bacon factories loyalty is generally enforced by a provision to the effect that members shall deliver all their saleable pigs (with certain specified exceptions) to the factory for a period of seven years, unless in the meantime they remove from the district (Rew, *An Agricultural Faggot,* pp. 123-4). In like manner many Irish dairying societies provide that "any member who shall supply milk to any creamery other than that owned by the society for the space of three years from the date of his admission to membership, without the consent in writing of the Committee, shall forfeit his shares together with all the money credited thereon" (*Report on Co-operative Societies* [Cd. 6045], 1912, p. xxxix). It will be noticed that in these classes of societies—and it·is only in them that loyalty is enforced in the rules—the use of a considerable plant makes the maintenance of a steady demand a more important influence in eliminating cost than it would be in, say, an agricultural purchasing society.

Wholesale Societies and of local Retail Associations, in concentrating the constant part of their demand upon their own
productive departments and throwing the variable part upon
outside traders, greatly lessens the fluctuations to which these
productive departments are exposed. No doubt, the economies
which co-operative concerns secure in this way have, from a
national point of view, to be balanced against any diseconomies
that may be caused to outside concerns by increased fluctuations thrown upon them; and so are not a net gain to the
nation. To the co-operative concerns themselves, however,
they are a net gain. Moreover, in so far as the aggregate
demand or supply of a market is constant, and fluctuations in
the parts are due to other causes than fluctuations in the
whole, the introduction of steadiness in one part cannot
increase, but necessarily diminishes, the fluctuations of other
parts. Hence it is probable that a considerable part of the
economies which co-operative concerns derive from loyalty
represent a net increase in efficiency for the community as a
whole as well as for themselves.

Fourthly, the relation that is set up between the various
members of a Co-operative Society greatly facilitates the dis-
semination among them of knowledge about the best methods
of production. Thus Sir Horace Plunkett observes of the work
of the Irish Department of Agriculture : " It was only where
the farmers were organised in properly representative societies
that many of the lessons the Department had to teach could
effectually reach the farming classes, or that many of the agricultural experiments intended for their guidance could be
profitably carried out." [1] The root of the matter is reached by
Mr. Fay when he writes : " Both the co-operative society and the
firm are trading bodies, and they will not pay the farmers more
than their milk is worth. But, whereas the firm's remedy is to
punish the farmer by the payment of low prices, the society's
remedy is to educate him so that he may command high ones." [2]

Fifthly, when in any field of industry there is an element
of bilateral monopoly, ordinary commercial businesses and their
customers, respectively, are driven to expend energy, if not

---

[1] *Ireland in the New Century*, p. 241.
[2] *Co-operation at Home and Abroad*, p. 164.

money, after the manner described in Chapter IX. §§ 15-17, in attempts to get the better of one another. Where a Purchasers' Association exists, this class of expenditure is likely to be reduced. In co-operative retail stores, as Marshall has observed, the proprietors, since they are also the customers, have no inducement to adulterate their goods, and costly precautions to prevent such adulteration are, therefore, unnecessary.[1] The gain is no less clear in societies providing for their members the services of insurance and the retailing of loans. The insurance contract is conditional on some event happening to the buyer; the loan contract is conditional on the buyer's promise to repay. In the one case the buyer may gain at the seller's expense by simulating, or even by voluntarily bringing about, the event provided against; in the other he may gain by deliberately breaking, or by so acting as to render himself unable to perform, his promise. Now, it is, of course, true that individual buyers are able to gain by this class of conduct, not only when the relation of identity between buyers and sellers collectively does not exist, but also when it does exist. The point, however, is this. Under the Joint Stock form of industrial organisation the fraudulent or quasi-fraudulent conduct of one buyer does not matter to the other buyers, and can, therefore, only be guarded against by an elaborate and continuous system of inspection. Under the Purchasers' Association form, however, the other buyers are directly injured by such conduct, and are, therefore, interested to prevent it. If, then, the Purchasers' Association consists of neighbours, all will, incidentally and in the course of the ordinary conduct of life, constitute themselves voluntary and unpaid inspectors of each. In this way small local Purchasers' Associations for the supply of insurance or the retailing of loans are, in effect, free from a substantial part, not merely of the nominal, but also of the real, costs that Joint Stock Companies attempting to furnish these services would be compelled to bear. In so far as people are less willing—apart altogether from the prospect of success—to try to defraud a Mutual Association than a commercial company, the gain under this head is increased.

§ 5. The various advantages that have been enumerated above

[1] Cf. Inaugural Address to the Co-operative Congress, 1889, p. 7.

suggest that there is a wide field over which Purchasers' Associations are likely to prove at least as efficient as any other form of business organisation : and in many important departments of industry they have proved their fitness by prosperous survival. This is true of the so-called supply associations often formed by farmers—associations, that is to say, which supply to their members the service of marketing from manufacturing firms such things as manure, seeds and agricultural machinery. It is true of the agricultural selling societies, which provide such services as the sorting, grading, selling and packing of eggs or of butter. It is true of the Co-operative Creameries, which play so important a part in Denmark and in Ireland, and whose services include a manufacturing as well as a marketing operation. Last but not least, it is true of that widespread organisation based on consumers' stores, which provides for the retailing, wholesaling, and sometimes even the manufacturing, of staple household goods (including houses themselves) for large agglomerations of working people with fixed homes.

§ 6. Even, however, in departments of work where experience gives good hope of efficiency and success, it does not follow that Purchasers' Associations will always come into being. Very poor people may lack the initiative and understanding needed to form one. Where the population is migratory, attempts are especially unlikely to be made — a circumstance which explains why co-operative stores " have seemed to shun capital and seafaring towns." Better-to-do persons, while fully competent to develop Purchasers' Associations, if they had the wish, may, in fact, not have the wish. With commodities on which they only spend a very small part of their income at rare intervals—commodities that are luxuries to the main body of purchasers—the possible savings may be too small to be worth while. Or again, even when they are worth while, it may be possible to get an equivalent advantage in some other less troublesome way. British tenant farmers, for example, with their traditional right to appeal to the squire in times of difficulty for a reduction of rent, are slow to overcome their native individualism for the (to them) relatively small advantages of co-operation with their neighbours. No doubt, encouragement may be given to them

by State action. Thus in Canada "in 1897 the Dominion
Department of Agriculture established a system by means of
which loans were made to farmers who undertook to organise
themselves into Butter and Cheese Manufacturing Associations
and to send their produce to Co-operative Creameries equipped
by means of the loans.   The Department undertook to
organise the management of these creameries, and to manufacture and sell the butter for a fixed charge of four cents
(2d.) per lb., an additional charge of one cent per lb. being
made for the amortisation of the loans."[1]   But this device is
obviously of limited scope.   Moreover, there are a number
of very important sorts of work to which the Purchasers'
Association form of organisation is not well suited.   Whenever a large speculative element is present, whenever, in other
words, much uncertainty has to be borne, this factor of production will not be readily forthcoming from organised
purchasers.   For, if capital has to be ventured at a hazard, the
people who venture it will expect to exercise control, and to
harvest the profits, more or less in proportion to their venture.
Associations that raise capital at fixed interest and distribute
surplus in accordance, not with investment, but with purchases,
do not enable them to do this.   The graded machinery of
debentures, preference shares and ordinary shares furnished by
Joint Stock Companies is much more satisfactory.   In risky
undertakings, therefore, Purchasers' Associations will not work.
Nor will they work as regards commodities and services for
which economy demands centralised production, but of which
the purchasers are spread over wide areas and make their
purchases at irregular intervals.   The idea, for instance, that
the services now rendered by the cotton industry could be
provided satisfactorily by any arrangement of Purchasers'
Associations is plainly fantastic.   " In many cases the users or
consumers of the service do not form a practicable constituency,
apart from that of themselves as citizens, which could control
the administration.   The national railway service could hardly
be governed by the votes of the incoherent mob of passengers
who pour out of the termini of our great cities ; or the
characteristic municipal services by any other membership

[1] Mavor, *Report on the Canadian North-West*, p. 44.

than that of all the municipal electors."[1]   We conclude, therefore, that, though the Purchasers' Association, as a means of overcoming the evils of ordinary competitive and ordinary monopolistic industry, has, undoubtedly, an important part to play, the field open to it is limited in extent, and the study of further remedies is, therefore, still required.[2]

[1] Webb, *A Constitution for the Socialistic Commonwealth*, p. 252.

[2] For a full discussion of the various forms of co-operative activity, *vide* Fay, *Co-operation at Home and Abroad*.   I am also indebted to Mr. Fay for useful criticism and suggestion in connection with this chapter.

CHAPTER XX

§ 1. OVER the large field of industry, where voluntary Purchasers' Associations are not an adequate means of overcoming those failures in industrial adjustment which occur under the more ordinary business forms, the question arises whether the magnitude of the national dividend might not be increased by some kind of public intervention, either by the exercise of control over concerns left in private hands or by direct public management. In the present chapter we are concerned, not with the comparative merits of these two sorts of intervention, but with the broadest aspects of intervention generally.

§ 2. It is natural at first sight to look for light on this question from the experience of the war. The urgent national need for enlarged supplies of munitions, home-grown food, ships, and certain other articles, led to extensive State intervention in production. National productive establishments were set up, and private establishments were controlled and sometimes accorded special grants to enable them to expand their operations; while the Board of Agriculture took powers to encourage, and, if need be, to compel, increased cultivation of land, and also provided a number of facilities in the way of soldiers' and prisoners' labour and specially imported machinery to assist farmers. A study of what was accomplished under these and other heads would, indeed, be of great interest. But it would not really do much to help our present inquiry. The difference between war and peace conditions is too great. In those four years of strain the underlying motive of the main part of the Government's industrial action was to force capital, enterprise and labour, forthwith and at no matter what cost, into the production of particular urgently needed things. Nobody denies that, when there is a shortage of anything relatively to the demand for it, this fact by itself always tends to stimulate people to direct their efforts towards producing that thing rather than other things. But this reaction is usually a slow one ; and in the Great War the essential requirement was always speed. The principal purpose of government assistance and coercion was to secure this ; to surmount at once by direct attack obstacles that, in the ordinary course, could only be turned by a slow and gradual movement. The need for such action was, of course, intensified in industries where the Government itself, by artificially keeping down prices, had removed what would normally have been the main stimulus to private efforts after increased production. With the end of the war all this has been changed. The problem of national economy is no longer to effect an instantaneous transformation from one scheme of production to another, but to maintain permanently the best scheme. To show that Government is fit (or unfit) to accomplish the former of these tasks is not to show that it is fit (or unfit) to accomplish the latter. Moreover, the scheme of production called for in the Great War involved an enormous output of things of uniform types for the direct use of Government itself. To show that Government is fit (or unfit) to control or operate industries devoted to a scheme of this kind is not to show that it is fit (or unfit) to control or operate industries devoted to the more variegated scheme called for in normal times. Yet again, in the Great War, the various controls set up by Government were necessarily improvised in a great hurry in a time of abnormal difficulty and pressure. No evidence that intervention in these conditions was wasteful or ineffective could prove that it would display the same defects in the more favourable conditions of normal life. For these reasons war experience can afford very little real guidance, and our problem must be attacked by other means.

§ 3. For some persons the obvious approach towards it is blocked by the supposition that certain industries, those,

namely, that make use of the right of eminent domain, such
as railway service (national and street), gas-lighting, electricity
supply, water supply and so forth, are, for that reason, suitable
for public intervention, while other industries, because they
do not make use of the right of eminent domain, are not
suitable.   This supposition is erroneous.   It is true that the
exercise of eminent domain practically implies monopoly, since
neither State nor municipal authorities are at all likely to allow
double parallel interference with streets and highways.   But
this circumstance only puts these public utility services into
the general class of monopolistic services : it does not render
them different, in any essential respect, from services that
have come into that class—like the oil and tobacco industries
in America—in quite other ways.   Thus eminent domain
is in no way a condition precedent either to governmental
management or to governmental control through a licence.
Public slaughter-houses, licensed premises for the sale of
intoxicants, and the system of licensed cabs in London are
practical illustrations of this fact.   The broad question of
policy is different according as we are concerned with monopolistic or with non-monopolistic industries ; it is different
again, within monopolistic industries, according as discriminating prices are, or are not, practicable ; but it is the
same, *ceteris paribus*, whether the industry concerned does or
does not require to exercise the right of eminent domain.
No doubt, as will appear presently, undertakings at the
start of which this right has to be exercised, since they
necessarily come into contact with the public authorities in
their first beginnings, and, therefore, can be brought under
control at once before any vested interests have grown up,
can be subjected to public intervention much more easily
than others.   This distinction of practice is very important,
but it is not, and should not be treated as, a distinction of
principle.

§ 4. In any industry, where there is reason to believe
that the free play of self-interest will cause an amount of resources to be invested different from the amount that is required in the best interest of the national dividend, there is a
prima facie case for public intervention.   The case, however,

cannot become more than a *prima facie* one, until we have
considered the qualifications, which governmental agencies
may be expected to possess for intervening advantageously.
It is not sufficient to contrast the imperfect adjustments
of unfettered private enterprise with the best adjustment
that economists in their studies can imagine. For we
cannot expect that any public authority will attain, or will
even whole-heartedly seek, that ideal. Such authorities
are liable alike to ignorance, to sectional pressure and to
personal corruption by private interest. A loud-voiced part
of their constituents, if organised for votes, may easily
outweigh the whole. This objection to public intervention
in industry applies both to intervention through control of
private companies and to intervention through direct public
operation. On the one side, companies, particularly when
there is continuing regulation, may employ corruption, not
only in the getting of their franchise, but also in the execution
of it. "Regulation does not end with the formulation and
adoption of a satisfactory contract, itself a considerable task.
. . . As with a constitution, a statute, or a charter, so with
a franchise. It has been proved that such an agreement
is not self-enforcing, but must be fought for, through a term
of years, as vigorously as at the time of formulation and
adoption. A hostile, lax, or ignorant city council, or even
a State legislature, may vary the terms of the agreement
in such a manner as totally to destroy or seriously to impair
its value." [1] For this the companies maintain a *continuing
lobby*. "It is from them that the politicians get their
campaign funds." [2] This evil has a cumulative effect; for
it checks the entry of upright men into government, and
so makes the corrupting influence more free. On the other
side, when public authorities themselves work enterprises, the
possibilities of corruption are changed only in form. "The
new undertakings proposed by the municipalisers would lead
to dealings to the extent of many million dollars with tradesmen, builders, architects, etc., to the increase, by hundreds, of

---

[1] *Municipal and Private Operation of Public Utilities* (Report to the National Civic Federation, U.S.A.), vol. i. p. 39.

[2] Bemis, *Municipal Monopolies*, p. 174.

important offices, and to the employment of tens of thousands of additional public servants. Party leaders would have their proportion of increased patronage. Every public official is a potential opportunity for some form of self-interest arrayed against the common interest." [1]

§ 5. The force of this argument for non-interference by public authorities is, clearly, not the same at all times and places; for any given kind of public authority will vary, alike in efficiency and in sense of public duty, with the general tone of the time. Thus, during the past century in England, there has been " a vast increase in the probity, the strength, the unselfishness, and the resources of government. . . . And the people are now able to rule their rulers, and to check class abuse of power and privilege, in a way which was impossible before the days of general education and a general surplus of energy over that required for earning a living." [2] This important fact implies that there is now a greater likelihood that any given piece of interference, by any given public authority, will prove beneficial than there was in former times. Nor is this all. Besides improvement in the working of existing forms of public authority, we have also to reckon with the invention of improved forms. This point may be put thus. The principal disadvantages of municipal and national representative assemblies, as organs for the control or the operation of business, are four in number. First, in the United Kingdom—though this statement is hardly true of Germany—these bodies are primarily chosen for purposes quite other than that of intervention in industry. Consequently, there is little reason to expect in their members any special competence for such a task. Secondly, the fluctuating make-up of a national government or of a town council is a serious handicap. Sir W. Preece wrote : " I have the experience of electric lighting in my mind. Large municipalities overcome the difficulty by forming small and strong committees and selecting the same chairman, and thus maintain a kind of continuity of policy. Small corporations start with very large committees ; they

---

[1] *Municipal and Private Operation of Public Utilities*, vol. i. p. 429.

[2] Marshall, " Economic Chivalry," *Economic Journal*, 1907, pp. 18-19.

are constantly changing, and the result is that you find, sometimes inability to agree upon the system to be used, sometimes inability to agree upon the means to be employed to
conduct the service; and it is incessant trouble and
squabble." [1]　Moreover, this incident of fluctuating membership may lead to action based on short views—views
bounded by the next election, not extending to the permanent
interests of the community.　Thirdly, the areas, to which
public authorities are normally allocated, are determined by
non-commercial considerations, and, consequently, are often
likely to prove unsuitable for any form of intervention with
the working of an industry.　It is well known, for example,
that attempts, on the part of some municipalities to regulate,
and of others to operate, the service of, street-traction and the
supply of electrical power have suffered greatly from the
fact that these services, since the development of modern
inventions, can be organised most economically on a scale
much in excess of the requirements of any one municipality.
Finally, as indicated above, regular governmental agencies,
in so far as they are elective bodies, are liable to
injurious forms of electoral pressure.　These four disadvantages are all serious.　But all of them can be, in great
measure, obviated.　The first, second and fourth are practically
done away with under a system of municipal government
such as prevails in Germany, where the burgomasters and
aldermen, corresponding to the English chairmen of committees, are whole-time paid experts with practically permanent
tenure of office.　All four disadvantages can be overcome,
perhaps even more effectively, by the recently developed
device of Commissions or *ad hoc* Boards, that is to say, bodies of
men appointed for the express purpose of industrial operation
or control.　An example of a Commission for operation is
afforded by the Railway Department of New South Wales
or the Port of London Authority in this country, and one of a
Commission for control by the Interstate Railway Commission
of the United States.　The members of such Commissions can be
specially chosen for their fitness for their task, their appointment can be for long periods, the area allotted to them can

[1] H. Meyer, *Municipal Ownership in Great Britain*, p. 258.

be suitably adjusted, and their terms of appointment can be such as to free them, in the main, from electoral pressure. The system of Commissions or *ad hoc* Boards also, in great part, escapes a further important objection to intervention in industry by such bodies as municipal councils. This objection, as stated by Major Darwin, is that such intervention "lessens the time which these bodies can devote to their primary and essential duties, and, by increasing the unwillingness of busy men to devote their time to public affairs, it lowers the average administrative capacity of the Local Authorities."[1] When industries are operated or controlled by special public Commissions, this objection is inapplicable. The broad result is that modern developments in the structure and methods of governmental agencies have fitted these agencies for beneficial intervention in industry under conditions which would not have justified intervention in earlier times.

[1] Darwin, *Municipal Trade*, 102.

CHAPTER XXI

PUBLIC CONTROL OF MONOPOLY

§ 1. In the course of Chapters IX., X. and XI., reference was frequently made to devices, by which the State could interfere, where self-interest, acting through simple competition, failed to make the national dividend as large as it might be made. Apart from governmental operation of industries into which the right amount of resources would not otherwise be turned, and apart also from penal legislation in extreme cases, these devices were fiscal in character and consisted in the concession of bounties or the imposition of taxes. Where self-interest works, not through simple competition, but through monopoly, fiscal intervention evidently ceases to be effective. A bounty might, indeed, be so contrived as to prevent restrictions of output below what is socially desirable, but only at the cost of enabling the monopolist to add to his already excessive profits a large ransom from the State. In the present chapter, therefore, I propose to consider what methods are available under conditions of monopoly. For simplicity of exposition, I shall ignore the qualifications set out in Chapter XI. and proceed as though simple competition might still be believed, as it was believed by some of the more rigid followers of the classical economists, to make the national dividend a maximum. The State, then, contemplating a monopoly or the possibility of a monopoly in some industry, may be supposed to contrast the dividend under it with the dividend under simple competition. Its problem will be, not to make things perfect, but to make them as good as they would be if monopolistic power were not at work.

§ 2. In industries where monopolistic power is liable to be introduced through the development of combinations, it is open to the State, if it chooses, to aim at preventing monopoly power from arising, or, if it has arisen, at destroying it. The original Federal Anti-Trust Law (1890) of the United States, commonly known as the Sherman Act, was overtly directed against actions " in restraint of trade or commerce among the several States," but was interpreted in the earlier decisions of the Supreme Court as an Act banning all combinations large enough to possess a substantial element of monopolistic power. Thus Justice Harlan's judgment in the Northern Securities Case, 1904, asserted that " to vitiate a combination, such as the Act of Congress condemns, it need not be shown that the combination in fact results, or will result, in a total suppression of trade or in a complete monopoly, but it is only essential to show that by its necessary operation it tends to restrain interstate or international trade or commerce, or tends to create a monopoly in such trade or commerce and to deprive the public of the advantages that flow from free competition." [1]   The Clayton Law of 1914, while making no further provision as regards combinations that had already been formed, follows the line of this interpretation as regards the formation of new combinations in the future.   It lays it down, not only that no person shall be a director of more than one large bank or large corporation, but also that no corporation shall acquire—acquirements already made are not affected—the whole or part of the stock of any other corporation, when the effect of such acquisition may be substantially to lessen competition, or to restrain commerce in any section of the community, or to tend to the creation of a monopoly in any line of commerce. This general policy—trust prohibition and trust breaking— seems, however, to be open to three serious objections.

First, it is a policy exceedingly difficult to enforce in an effective manner. The legislature and the courts may succeed in getting rid of certain forms of combination, but the result will often be merely the appearance of other forms—possibly of forms, which, as would happen if an

[1] Jenks and Clark, *The Trust Problem*, p. 295.

informal price-fixing agreement took the place of a complete amalgamation, sacrifice the merits, without getting rid of the demerits, of those which preceded them. The declaration of the Supreme Court of the United States, that the granting of a power of attorney to common trustees by a number of companies was *ultra vires*, led, in some industries, to the purchase of a majority of stock in each of the companies by the said trustees, and, in others, to the substitution of a holding company for a trust. Governmental attacks on holding companies can easily be met either by complete consolidation, if this is not also made illegal, or by dissolution into separate companies, each subject to the same controlling interest. The Austrian law against Kartels likely to injure the revenue abolished Kartels possessed of a central office; but only with the result of substituting informal understandings. The British Committee on Railway Agreements and Amalgamations (1911) summed up the situation thus : " While Parliament may enact that this must be done and that must be prohibited, past experience shows that even Parliament appears to be powerless to prevent two parties, either by agreement or without formal agreement, from abstaining from a course of action, namely, active competition, that neither party desires to take. Parliament can, of course, refuse to sanction Bills authorising the amalgamation or working union of two or more railway companies, and may provide that certain classes of agreement shall be invalid or even illegal. But it cannot prevent railway companies [and, of course, the same thing is true of industrial companies] coming to understandings with each other to adopt a common course of action, or to cease from active competition." [1] The recent policy of the United States Government and Courts, in forcing the dissolution of monopolistic companies into their constituent parts and providing at the same time various regulations to prevent these from becoming subject to a common control, may, indeed, for a time be more effective, and, even though it does not succeed in stimulating real competition among men formerly colleagues, yet may, by its harassing

[1] *Departmental Committee on Railway Agreements and Amalgamations*, 1911, p. 18.

effect, make the task of forming new combinations less attractive. It was stated, for example, by Professor Durand in 1914, that no new combinations had been formed since the Government began to bring suits under the Sherman Act.[1] This, however, is no longer true. In the Memorandum on American Combinations furnished by the Board of Trade to the Committee on Industry and Trade in 1927, the following conclusion is reached. " Only a very partial success has been achieved in preventing the growth of combination or the lessening of competition. The experience of the administration of the Sherman Act between 1890 and 1914 seems to have been repeated. When one form of combination is attacked and declared illegal, the lawyers advising the corporation evolve a new form, which, even if an objection by the Federal Trade Commission is eventually upheld, takes a considerable period to upset." [2] Thus it may still be claimed, as the teaching of experience as a whole, that laws aimed directly at " maintaining competition " have very small prospect of succeeding in their purpose.

There is a second serious objection to this policy. The root idea lying behind it is that competition implies a condition of things in which the value of the marginal social net product of investment in the businesses affected is about equal to the value of the marginal social net product elsewhere. But, passing by the qualifications to this view set out in Chapters IX. and XI., we have to note that the competition, from which the above good result may be expected, is " simple competition," whereas the competition, to which laws against combination lead, will very probably be monopolistic competition, namely, competition among a *few* competitors. With railway combinations this result is certain ; for the number of railways plying between any two given centres is necessarily very small. With industrial combinations the issue at first sight seems more doubtful, since there is no such necessary limitation in the number of industrial concerns of any given type. When,

[1] Cf. *American Economic Review Supplement*, March 1914, p. 176. For a full account of American Anti-Trust Laws and Cases, cf. Davies, *Trust Laws and Unfair Competition*.

[2] *Factors in Industrial and Commercial Efficiency*, 1927, p. 107.

however, we reflect that combinations can rarely be organised
except in industries where, as a matter of fact, the number
of leading firms is small, the force of this objection is much
reduced.   Among industrial combinations, as well as among
railway combinations, dissolution is much more likely to
lead to monopolistic than to simple competition.   It has
been shown, however, in Chapter XV., that monopolistic
competition does not tend to bring about an output of such
a magnitude that the value of the marginal social net
product of investment in the industry affected is equal to
that prevailing elsewhere.   On the contrary, the output is
indeterminate.   When the competitors hope to destroy or to
absorb one another, we may get " cut-throat competition,"
under which production is carried so far as to involve absolute
loss ; and the chance of this is made greater by the desire of
one giant business to win even a barren victory over another.
In short, even if the conditions were such that laws for " maintaining competition " could really prevent combination, they
would still be unable to secure the establishment of competition in that sense in which alone it can be expected to evolve
the level of prices and the rate of output which is most
advantageous from the standpoint of the national dividend.

Even now, however, the case against the policy we are
considering is not exhausted.   There remains a third objection.
Combination is not the parent of monopoly only, but also,
very often, of incidental benefits.   Thus, as was observed in
Chapter XIV., a combination, which is large relatively to the
market in which it trades, has more inducement than a small
single seller to adopt a policy of developing demand among
potential customers, since it may reckon on receiving a larger
proportion of the gain resulting from any investments which
it may make with this object.   In addition to this, a large
combination will often enjoy certain economies of production,
which, if the Government were to adopt a policy of maintaining active competition, would fail to emerge.   No doubt,
some of those forms of Kartel agreement, under which a proportion of the market is guaranteed to the several members,
since they tend to conserve weak firms, which competition
would " naturally " destroy, not only fail to yield economies,

but actually yield diseconomies.[1]   It should be observed, however, that pooling agreements do not necessarily act in this way.
The British Committee on Trusts (1919), for example, reports
that in a great many associations there is an arrangement
under which firms, on producing less than their quota, receive
from the pool 5 per cent in value upon the amount of
their deficiency.   It was urged by some witnesses that this
arrangement had the effect of driving weak firms out of the
industry by the economical method of pensioning, instead of
the more costly method of fighting them.[2]   Against this, indeed,
we have to set the fact that the money to provide the
pensions has to be obtained by some kind of tax on firms
that exceed their quota—a necessary discouragement to them.
Moreover, some forms of pool, by making the profits of each
member severally depend on the efficiency of all collectively, may
lead to relaxed energy and enterprise.   But, on the other hand,
in all combinations that involve any measure of common
management, savings of the kind referred to in Chapter XIV.
are bound to accrue in greater or less degree.[3]   In a
peculiar industry like the telephones, where the actual thing
supplied to A is improved if B draws his supply from the
same agency, the advantage is especially great.   It may also
be considerable in more ordinary industries.   *Inter alia,*
weak or badly situated plants are apt to be shut down

[1] Cf. Walker, *Combinations in the German Coal Industry,* p. 322. Mr. Walker
points out, however, that this tendency, at all events in the Ruhr Kartel, is
smaller than appears at first sight, since the large mines, by sinking more
shafts and by buying up small mines, can increase their "participation"
(*ibid.* p. 94). Morgenroth, in his *Exportpolitik der Kartelle,* emphasises this point
in regard to Kartels generally. He points out further that the anti-economic
effects of Kartels are mitigated by their tendency to lead to the development
of "mixed works," which refuse to admit any limitation in their output of
raw stuff to be worked up in their own further products. Thus among these
important mixed works the selective influence of competition is not restrained
by agreements (*loc. cit.* p. 72).

[2] Report of the Committee on Trusts, 1919, p. 3.

[3] Cf. Liefmann's statement : " Verschiedene grosse Unternehmungen erwarben
nämlich diese kleinen Zechen nur um ihrer Beteiligungsziffer im Syndikat
willen, legten sie aber dann still und förderten deren Absatzquote auf ihren
eigenen Schächten billiger. War dies auch natürlich für die betroffenen Arbeiter
und Gemeinden sehr nachteilig, so ist doch zu berücksichtigen, dass diese
kleinen Zechen bei freier Konkurrenz längst zugrunde gegangen wären. Höch-
stens kann man sagen, dass dann die Still-legung und die Entlassung der
Arbeiter sich weniger plötzlich vollzogen hätte und länger voraussehbar gewesen
wäre " (*Kartelle und Trusts,* pp. 61-2).

much more quickly than they would be under competition ; while, among those that remain, the purposive force of " comparative cost accounting" may be expected to stimulate the energy of managers more strongly than the blind force of market rivalry could ever do.[1]

We must, indeed, be on our guard against exaggerating the importance of these economies. For, if by combination we mean existing combinations, it is necessary to recollect that, since the magnitude of the unit of control is determined by monopolistic considerations as well as by considerations of structural and other economies, this unit is often larger than the unit of maximum efficiency. If we mean only such combinations as it would be profitable to form *de novo*, were the exercise of monopolistic power wholly excluded, combination will, indeed, evolve the unit of maximum *immediate* efficiency, but that unit will very likely prove too large when ultimate indirect effects, as well as immediate effects, are taken into account. For this there are two reasons. The first is that a producer controlling the main part of any industry, in considering the wisdom of adopting any mechanical improvement, is tempted to take account, not merely of the direct positive yield to be expected from capital invested in that improvement, but also of the indirect negative yield in lessening the returns to his existing plant. But, if he does this, he will, as was shown on pp. 190-92, be holding back from improvements which it is to the interest of the national dividend that he should adopt. A monopoly makes no proper use—at all events is under temptation to make insufficient use—of that invaluable agent of progress, the scrap heap.[2] The second reason is that indicated in Chapter X., namely, that large combinations, by lessening the opportunities for training in the entrepreneur function, which are available when men who have done well in one company can be passed on to more responsible work in another, and by weakening the stimulus to keenness and efficiency, which is afforded by the rivalry of

[1] Cf. Macgregor, *Industrial Combination*, p. 34. This device rules prominently in the United States Steel Corporation (Van Hise, *Concentration and Control*, p. 136). An elaborate account of it is given by Jenks in the *U.S.A. Bulletin of Labour*, 1900, p. 675.

[2] Clark, *The Control of Trusts* (revised edition), p. 14.

competing concerns, tend indirectly to prevent the average
level of business ability from rising as high as it might
otherwise do.

The qualifications which these considerations suggest are
of great importance. They tell strongly against the claim
made by Professor Clark, when he writes: " A nearly ideal
condition would be that in which, in every department
of industry, there should be one great corporation, working
without friction and with enormous economy, and *compelled to
give to the public the full benefit of that economy.*" [1] Nevertheless, there can be little doubt that, *in some circumstances*, the
combination of competing institutions into "Trusts" and con-
solidations that dominate the market does involve, even from
a long-period point of view, considerable net economies.[2]
These economies *may* be so great that the favourable effect
produced by them on the output of the monopolised commodity
exceeds the unfavourable effect produced on this output by
the exercise of monopolistic power. Attempts to determine,
by a comparison of prices, or of " margins " between prices and
the cost of materials, before and after the formation of any
combination, whether or not this has actually been so, are
inevitably baffled by our inability to allow for changes in
manufacturing methods and in the utilisation of by-products, or
to gauge accurately the—probably abnormal—price conditions
that ruled immediately before the combination was formed.[3]
Analysis, however, enables us to say that combination is likely,
on the whole, to diminish the output of the commodity affected
by it and to raise its price, unless the associated economies are

[1] *The Control of Trusts*, p. 29.

[2] Professor Durand argues in favour of a policy of trust-breaking that,
in general, the business units evolved apart from combination would be large
enough to secure practically all the structural and other economies of production available to trusts (*Quarterly Journal of Economics*, 1914, p. 677
et seq.). It should be observed, however, that, even if this were true, the
policy of trust-breaking would not be shown to be superior to one of depriving
trusts of monopolistic power : for *both* policies would then lead to the
establishment of business units of a size yielding maximum efficiency.   In
fact, however, it is plainly not true in all industries ; and, when it is not true,
trust-breaking leads to the establishment of units too small to yield maximum
efficiency.

[3] For these reasons the admirable price studies in Jenks's *Trust Problem* are
hardly adequate to support the favourable judgment as to the effect of combinations that he rests on them.

so large that, had they been introduced without monopolisation, they would have raised output to about double its former amount.[1] Economies so large as this are improbable, and I do not, therefore, claim that to prevent combination in any department of industry would often make the output of that department smaller than it might have been. But—and this is the essential point—the effect of combination on the output of the commodity affected by it is not the same thing as its effect on the national dividend. For suppose combination to bring about economies which enable the same output as before to be produced by the use of half the former quantity of productive resources, and suppose that, in consequence of monopolistic action, no more than this output is in fact produced. The released productive resources will not, in general, be idle, but will be occupied in adding to the output of other commodities. Hence, in this case, the output of no commodity is diminished and the output of some commodities is increased, which obviously implies that the size of the national dividend is increased. It follows that to prevent combination would sometimes injure the dividend, even though it enabled the output of the commodity immediately affected to be larger than it would have been. This point need not, however, be laboured further. For it is in any event certain that to prevent combination, when combination carries with it any net economies, must be more injurious to the dividend than to allow combination and to prevent the exercise of monopolistic power.

§ 3. A second line of policy which it is open to the State to pursue is as follows. Instead of endeavouring, by obstructing combination, to prevent industrial concerns from becoming possessed of monopolistic power, it may seek, by conserving *potential* rather than actual competition, to make it to their interest to leave that power unexercised; the idea, of course, being that, if they expect new competitors to come into the field, should output be restricted and prices be raised high enough to yield abnormal profits, they will have no inducement to charge more than " reasonable " prices. The policy,

---

[1] This proposition is exactly true on the hypothesis that the curves of demand and supply are straight lines.

to which this line of thought leads, is that of penalising the use of "clubbing" devices, whose repute might otherwise drive potential competitors away. Among these devices the two principal are cut-throat competition, as described in Chapter XV., and various forms of boycott, namely, the exercise of pressure upon third parties not to purchase services from, or sell services to, a rival seller on terms as favourable as they would have offered to him if left to themselves.[1]

§ 4. It is obvious that the weapon of cut-throat competition, or, as it is sometimes called, "destructive dumping," when practised by a business already large enough to monopolise any department of industry, must prove overwhelmingly powerful against newcomers. The monopolist necessarily possesses immense resources, and these can be poured out, in almost unlimited quantities, for the destruction of a new, and presumably much less wealthy, intruder. This is especially clear when a monopolist, dealing in many markets or in many lines of goods, has to do with a competitor dealing only in a few; for in these conditions the competitor can be destroyed by a cut, made either openly or through a bogus independent company,[2] that affects only a small part of the monopolist's business. An extreme example of this kind of cut is given in the statement of certain opponents of the Standard Oil Trust, "that persons are engaged to follow the waggons of competitors to learn who their customers are, and that then they make lower offers to those customers; and it is still further asserted that at times the employés in the offices of rivals are bribed to disclose their business to the Standard Oil Company."[3]   It is needless to emphasise

---

[1] The weapon of boycott can also be used to force upon retailers an agreement to maintain the prices of particular goods sold by them at a level dictated by the manufacturers of the goods. It would seem that manufacturers do not wish quality-articles to be sold too cheap to consumers, lest they should "lose caste" with them. But probably their main motive is the knowledge that, if the goods are made into "leaders," on which the retailers make scarcely any direct profit, and which serve merely to advertise other wares, the retailers will tend not to push their sale (Taussig, *American Economic Review*, vol. vi. No. 1 Supplement, 1916, pp. 172-3).

[2] This method is alleged to have been practised by the Standard Oil Company. The object, of course, is to obviate a clamour from customers in other markets for a similar cut on their purchases. (Cf. Davies, *Trust Laws and Unfair Competition*, p. 319.)

[3] *U.S.A. Industrial Commission*, I. i. p. 20.

the immense power of this weapon. "After two or three attempts to compete with Jay Gould's telegraph line from New York to Philadelphia had been frustrated by a lowering of rates to a merely nominal price, the notoriety of this terrible weapon sufficed to check further attempts at competition."[1]

§ 5. The weapon of boycott has a narrower range than that of cut-throat competition. It is worked through a refusal to deal, except on specially onerous terms, with any one who also deals elsewhere. When the worsened terms attached by a dominating seller to dealings with himself are more injurious to the client than the loss of that client's other dealings, the monopolist can force the client to boycott his rivals. In order that he may be able to do this, the goods or services that he offers for sale must be rendered, by nature or by art, non-transferable;[2] for it is impossible to hurt a customer by refusing to sell to him, if he is able to purchase through a middleman the goods which are refused to him by the monopolist. Hence, when nature does not cause non-transferability, there must be stringent conditions about re-sales in the contracts between the monopolist and any intermediary agents, if such there are, who intervene between him and the ultimate consumers. But non-transferability is not sufficient by itself. It is necessary, further, that the rival producer's possible supply *to one recalcitrant consumer* at current prices shall be very small. Usually, of course, though any one seller's output is likely to be small relatively to the total consumption of the market, it is many times as large as that of any representative single consumer. Where this is so, recalcitrant consumers can successfully counter a refusal to sell on the part of the monopolist by purchasing all that they want from outside competitors and leaving to non-recalcitrants the whole output of the monopolist. This consideration is not, however, entirely fatal to the weapon of boycott, because in many industries, though by no means in all,[3] producers deal with their customers

---

[1] Hobson, *Evolution of Modern Capitalism*, p. 219.

[2] Cf. my paper, "Monopoly and Consumers' Surplus," *Economic Journal*, September 1904, p. 392.

[3] Thus Jenks (*U.S.A. Bulletin of Labour*, 1900, p. 679) states that "about half the combinations reporting sell direct to consumers."

indirectly through wholesalers or further manufacturers or transporters, who purchase individually a considerable mass of products. When intermediaries of this kind are present, effective boycott may become practicable.

First, a boycott can be forced when the commodities or services supplied by the monopolist consist, not in a single kind of good, but in several goods, and when, among these several goods, there are one or more for which the demand is very urgent, and of which the monopolist has, through patents or reputation (*e.g.* brands of tobacco) or otherwise, exclusive control. A good example is furnished by the boot and shoe trade, in which certain firms control important patents. The patented machines are not sold, but are let out on lease, under "conditions which debar manufacturers from employing these machines save and except in conjunction with other machines supplied by the same controlling owners . . . one of the conditions being that the latest machines must not be used for goods which have, in any other process of manufacturing, been touched by machines supplied by other makers." [1] This kind of boycott is also illustrated by the "factors' agreement," which makers of popular proprietary goods sometimes secure from retailers.

Secondly, a boycott can be forced where it is important for purchasers—here, as before, the purchasers are, in general, manufacturers—to be able to get the service that they need immediately the need arises, and where an ordinary supplier, though producing much more service in the aggregate than any single purchaser wants, may not be producing more than such a purchaser wants at some definite single moment. This condition is realised in the transport of goods which are so perishable, or for which the demand is so instant, that transport, to be of use, must be available at the moment when it is asked for. It is in the transport by sea of goods of this kind that the method of boycott has been most fully elaborated.

---

[1] *Times*, 8th February 1903. Cf. Appendix to the Report of the (British) Committee on Trusts, 1919, p. 27. Action of this kind is directly prohibited in Australia under the Patents Act of 1903. (Cf. Davies, *Trust Laws and Unfair Competition*, p. 247.) The British Patents Act of 1907 permits it only provided that the lessee is given an opportunity of hiring the patented machine without the tying clauses on "reasonable," though not, of course, equal terms.

The transport of goods, which are in fairly steady demand
and which have no need of speedy delivery, can be arranged
for by purchasers, if they wish, wholly through tramp
steamers; but the transport of urgent goods cannot be so
arranged for, because tramps and small lines cannot guarantee
regular sailings.[1] Hence it comes to be practicable for shipping
rings to force a boycott against independent lines. They
usually accomplish this through "deferred rebates."[2] Of these
there are two degrees. When the Royal Commission on
Shipping Rings published their report (1909), in the West

---

[1] Cf. *Royal Commission on Shipping Rings*, 1909, Report, p. 13. The Commissioners suggest that it is for this reason that the deferred rebate system is not
applied to our outward trade in coal or to the greater part of our inward trade,
which consists of rough goods, but only to those cargoes for which a regular service
of high-class steamers is essential. (Cf. *ibid.* p. 77.)

[2] This method was described by the Royal Commissioners on Shipping Rings,
1909, thus: "The Companies issue a notice or circular to shippers informing
them that, if at the end of a certain period (usually four or six months) they
have not shipped goods by any vessels other than those despatched by members
of the Conference, they will be credited with a sum equivalent to a certain part
(usually 10 per cent) of the aggregate freights paid on their shipments during
that period, and that this sum will be paid over to them, if at the end of a
further period (usually four or six months) they have continued to confine their
shipments to vessels belonging to members of the Conference. The sum so paid is
known as a deferred rebate. Thus in the South African trade at the present day
the amount of the rebate payable is 5 per cent of the freight paid by the shipper.
The rebates are calculated in respect of two six-monthly periods ending with the
30th June and 31st December respectively, but their payment to the shipper is not
due until a further period of six months has elapsed; that is to say, that, as to
shipments made between the 1st January and the following 30th June, the rebates
are payable on the 1st January following, and, as to shipments made between the
1st July and the 31st December, the rebates are payable on the following 1st July.
It follows that in this instance the payment of the rebate on any particular
item of cargo is withheld by the shipowners for at least six months and that, in
the case of cargo shipped on the 1st January or 1st July, it is withheld for a period
of twelve months. If during any period a shipper sends any quantity of goods,
however small, by a vessel other than those despatched by the Conference Lines,
he becomes disentitled to rebates on any of his shipments by Conference vessels
during that period and the preceding one" (Report, pp. 9-10). Since the issue
of the Royal Commission's Report a new method of tying shippers, known as
the agreement system, has come into operation. When South African legislation in 1911 "forced the liner companies trading with South Africa to relinquish
the rebate system, an agreement was drawn up after negotiations between the
South African Trade Association and the South African Shipping Conference. . . .
The shippers who sign agree to give their active support to the regular lines in
the Conference. In return the lines undertake to maintain regular berth
sailings at advertised dates, the ships to sail full or not full, and to provide
sufficient tonnage for the ordinary requirements of the trade; and, further, to
maintain stability of freights, which are definitely prescribed in the agreement,
and equality of rates to large and small shippers alike" (*Report of the Imperial
Shipping Committee*, 1923, Cmd. 1802, pp. 20-21).

African Shipping Conference and in all the Conferences engaged in the trade with India and the Far East, the rebates were paid to exporting merchants only, on condition that these merchants had not been interested in any shipment by rival carriers, but there was no requirement that the forwarding agent, through whom the merchant might have acted, should have dealt exclusively with the Conference in respect of the goods of his other clients.[1]   In the South American Conferences, however, " the form of claim for rebates has, in the case of goods shipped through a forwarding agent, to be signed by such agent as well as by the principal, and, if the forwarding agent has not conformed to the conditions of the rebate circular in all his shipments for all his clients, claims to rebates are invalidated." [2]

Thirdly, a boycott can be forced when the intermediary, whom a monopolist wishes to use as his instrument, is, not a manufacturer or a wholesaler purchasing that rival's goods, but a railway company conveying them.   When an alternative route for his own goods is available, the monopolist, by threatening the railway with the withdrawal of his custom, is sometimes in a position to compel it to charge differential rates against his rival.   In a boycott engineered by the Oil Trust it is even asserted that the railways were compelled to hand over a part of the extra charges levied on their rivals to the executive of the Trust.[3]   When the boycotting concern actually owns the agency of transport, its power in this matter is, of course, still greater.[4]   A boycott of this kind

---

[1] *Royal Commission on Shipping Rings*, Report, pp. 29-30.

[2] *Ibid.* p. 30.   The decision of the House of Lords in the Mogul Steamship Co. case, 1892, was to the effect that the party injured by an arrangement of this kind had no ground of action for damages, but it did not, it would seem, necessarily imply that the combination against which action was brought was itself lawful (Davies, *Trust Laws and Unfair Competition*, p. 234).   In a similar case in the German Imperial Court (1901), an injunction against discrimination was granted (*ibid.* p. 262).

[3] Cf. *The Great Oil Octopus*, p. 40 ; Ripley, *Railroads, Rates and Regulation*, p. 200.

[4] The same thing is true when the boycotting concern owns, as the Big Five meat-packers do, stockyards and cold-storage warehouses which their rivals must use and in respect of which they can make discriminating charges against them.   The Federal Trade Commission, in their report on the meat-packing industry in 1919, urged that, to obviate this, the State should itself acquire these stockyards and cold-storage plants.

may also be operated through banks, pressure being exerted upon them to refuse loans to a rival producer.

§ 6. Attempts to prevent the use of cut-throat competition, *i.e.* destructive dumping, by legal enactment are confronted with the difficulty of evasion. The American Industrial Commission recommended that "cutting prices in any locality below those which prevail generally, for the purpose of destroying local competition," should be made an offence. Any person damaged was to have the right to sue for penalties, and officers were required to prosecute offenders.[1] It is plain, however, that, even when it is possible, as it is with public service corporations, to insist that tariff rates shall be regularly published, evasion may be practised through unpublished discounts and rebates to particular customers; nor, since discovery is unlikely, will the enactment of heavy penalties against breaches of the law necessarily secure obedience thereto.[2] Where destructive dumping is threatened, not by public service corporations, but by industrialists engaged in the manufacture of many commodities at different places, the enforcement of regular published rates is impracticable. Hence the problem confronting the legislator demands the unravelling of still more tangled knots. Where the form of destructive dumping which is employed is that of price-cutting limited to the local market of a particular competitor or group of competitors, the offence is at least definite, though, especially when worked through a bogus independent company, it may be extraordinarily difficult to detect. Against destructive dumping of this kind *operated by foreigners* the Governments of Canada (1904) and South Africa (1914) have endeavoured to guard their citizens by anti-dumping legislation, providing that, when goods are exported to them at prices, which, exclusive of freight charges and so on, are substantially below

---

[1] *United States Industrial Commission*, vol. xviii. p. 154.

[2] It is instructive to read in M. Colson's great work (*Cours d'économie politique*, vol. vi. p. 398) that abusive discriminations "semblent être devenus bien plus rares en Angleterre qu'en Amérique, bien que l'Administration y ait des pouvoirs beaucoup moins étendus et que les pénalités y soient moins sévères, parce que l'entente entre Compagnies y est admise par la loi ; au contraire en Amérique, les pouvoirs publics s'efforcent d'empêcher les accords qui mettraient fin à la concurrence, cause essentielle des inégalités de traitement, et par suite ne sont pas arrivés, jusqu'ici, à déraciner celles-ci."

the contemporary prices ruling at home, these goods shall be subjected to a special import duty equivalent to the difference between the home and foreign prices.[1] This legislation, however, hits, not merely destructive dumping in the sense here defined, but also (1) the clearing of surplus stock on a foreign market at less than home prices in periods of depression and (2) the permanent selling abroad at the world price, by a foreign monopolistic producer, of goods for which at home he is able to charge monopoly prices. The policy of discouraging the former of these two practices is one whose merits are open to debate, but clearly there is nothing to be said for discouraging the second—except, indeed, the least tenable of the things that can be said in favour of all-round protection. The United States Government, wishing to direct its legislative blows against destructive dumping exclusively, included in the Federal Revenue Act of 1916 the following modified version of the Canadian anti-dumping law. In Section 801 of the Act it is enacted: "That it shall be unlawful, for any person importing or assisting in importing any articles from any foreign country into the United States, commonly and systematically to import, sell or cause to be imported or sold such articles within the United States at a price substantially less than the actual market value or wholesale price of such articles, at the time of exporting to the United States, in the principal market of the country of their production, or of other foreign countries to which they are commonly exported, after adding to such market value or wholesale price freight, duty and other charges and expenses necessarily incident to the importation and sale thereof in the United States. Provided, that such act or acts be done with the intent of destroying or injuring an industry in the United States or of preventing the establishment of an industry in the United States or of

[1] For these laws cf. Davies, *Trust Laws and Unfair Competition*, pp. 550-51. Australia (1906) has a more complicated law which condemns dumping in the Canadian sense, along with certain other forms of importation, under the general head of unfair competition, and meets it with a penalty, not a special duty. Cf. for a general discussion of anti-dumping legislation, Viner, *Dumping* (1923), ch. xi.-xiv. For the most recent facts cf. *Memorandum on the Legislation of Different States for the Prevention of Dumping*, Economic and Financial Section of the League of Nations, C.E., 1.7.1927.

restraining or monopolising any part of the trade or commerce in such articles in the United States." Offences against this clause were penalised, not, as in Canada, by a special duty, but by a fine. Under the Emergency Tariff Act of 1921 and the final Act of 1922 the reference to intention was omitted, and the imposition of a special duty was authorised whenever an efficiently conducted industry of the United States was being, or was likely to be, injured by importation at less than the price ruling in the principal home market of the exporting country *plus* f.o.b. costs. In the United Kingdom the Safeguarding of Industries Act 1921 provided for the imposition of special duties on goods that are being imported from any foreign country and sold in the United Kingdom at a price, *inclusive of freight charges*, less than 95 per cent of the wholesale price at the works charged to consumers in that country; provided that, by reason of the importation, employment in any industry in the United Kingdom is being, or is likely to be, seriously affected. An Act of the same general character was passed in Australia in 1921, though under that Act discretion is allowed to the Executive to refrain from action if it so chooses. We need not concern ourselves here with the difficult problems which legislation of this kind provides for the officials charged with ascertaining the relevant facts— including, as these did under the Federal Revenue Act of 1916, the motive actuating foreign sellers—and for those who have to detect and prevent the evasive use of nominally independent agents, on whose account goods may be imported at full price, thereafter to be sold at less than was paid for them. The main point for our present purpose is that, when, as in the conditions which this legislation contemplates, destructive dumping is attempted by inter-local price discriminations, the task of preventing it is *relatively* easy, because there is something definite to go on. When, however, as often happens in domestic trade, we have to do with cuts made on *all* sales of a particular line of goods, the offence is not definite; for, clearly, not all cuts are destructive dumping, and it is difficult to distinguish among them the innocent from the guilty. One authoritative writer proposes as a test that, " if the price of the particular grade of goods were first put down and then put up again, and if rivals were crushed in the interval, this would be evidence that the purpose of the cut was illegitimate." [1]   Such a test has been attempted in the American Mann-Elkins Railway Law of 1910, which provides that, " when a railway reduces rates between competitive points, it shall not be permitted to increase the rates on the cessation of the competition, unless it can satisfy the Commission that the conditions are changed otherwise than by the mere elimination of water competition." [2]   There is a similar provision in the American Shipping Act of 1916 as regards shipping charges in interstate trade.   But this test cannot be pushed very vigorously ; for, if it were, any firm, which lowered prices in a time of depression or for purposes of experiment, might find itself precluded from afterwards raising them again, should any other firm in the same line meanwhile have failed.

Similar difficulties stand in the way of effective legislation against boycotts.   It is true that such legislation has been widely attempted.   The United States (under the Clayton Law), Australia and New Zealand all prohibit, under penalty, any person from making the act of sale, or the terms of sale, of anything conditional on the buyer not using or dealing in the goods of any competitor.   On similar lines the United States Federal Revenue Law of September 1916 " imposes a double duty upon goods imported under agreement that the importer or others shall use those goods exclusively." [3]   Yet again, the American Shipping Act of 1916 makes deferred rebates illegal.   It is obvious, however, that, when the condition or agreement is made between a manufacturer and a dealer, both of whom profit by it, the difficulty of preventing evasion must be very great.   When the boycott is worked, not through a wholesaler, but through a railway company, the difficulty is still

[1] Clark, *The Control of Trusts*, p. 69.

[2] *Economist*, 25th Jan. 1910, p. 1412.   Cf. Ripley, *Railroads, Rates and Regulation*, p. 566.

[3] The English Patents and Designs Amendment Act of 1907 prohibits exclusive dealing contracts of this kind, unless the seller, lessor or licensee proves that, when the contract was made, his competitors had the option of obtaining the patented goods on reasonable terms without the exclusive condition (Davies, *Trust Laws and Unfair Competition*, p. 539).

greater. American law has long endeavoured to prevent railway discriminations favourable to the large Trusts. But : "A
partisan of the Trust said to me : ' The Pennsylvania Railroad
could not refuse the cars of a competitor of the Standard Oil
Company, but nothing could hinder it from side-tracking
them.' " [1] " A consignment note acknowledges the receipt of
70 barrels of flour; 65 only are shipped, and the railway company pays damages for the loss of the five non-existent
barrels." Except when long notice of alterations is required
by law, rates may be changed suddenly, secret notice being
given to the favoured shipper and no information to others;
and so forth. It is true that the Attorney-General of the
United States declared in 1903, after the passing of the
Elkins law : " The giving and taking of railroad rebates is now
prohibited by a law capable of effective enforcement against
corporations as well as against individuals." [2] This view, however, appears to have been unduly optimistic. The Interstate
Commerce Commission reported, as to the conditions in 1908,
that many shippers still enjoy illegal advantages. " Thus
the rebate, as an evil in transportation, even since amendment
of the law in 1906–10, while under control, is still far from
being eradicated. Favouritism lurks in every covert, assuming
almost every hue and form. Practices, which outwardly appear
to be necessary and legitimate, have been shown to conceal
special favours of a substantial sort." [3] The boycott engineered
through railway companies thus dies hard. It is said, however,
that, in the United States, the Transportation Act of 1920,
which created a system of Federal supervision over railways,
has finally put an end to it. [4]

These considerations make it clear that a policy of legal
prohibition against the exercise of clubbing methods cannot
easily be rendered proof against evasion. It should not be
forgotten, however, that laws, which *could* be evaded if people
took sufficient pains, as a matter of fact are often not evaded.
For the mere passage of a law reacts on public opinion and

---

[1] Quoted by Ely, *Monopolies and Trusts*, p. 97.

[2] *Economist*, 28th Feb. 1903.

[3] Ripley, *Railroads, Rates and Regulation*, p. 209.

[4] P. de Roussiers, *Cartels and Trusts and their Development* (Economic and
Financial Section of the League of Nations, 1927, II. 21), p. 9.

throws on the side of the practice upheld by law the strong forces of respectability and inertia. Hence we may reasonably expect that laws of this character, if carefully prepared, would, at all events, partially succeed in their immediate purpose. It is, therefore, of great interest to observe that Section 5 of the United States Federal Trade Commission Act of 1914 declares " that unfair methods of competitive commerce are hereby declared unlawful," and establishes a Federal Trade Commission to take proceedings to enforce this declaration whenever it appears to it to be in the public interest to do so. Section 14 of the Clayton Act provides further that, whenever a corporation violates any of the penal provisions of any of the anti-trust laws, " such violation shall be deemed to be also that of the individual directors, officers, or agents of such corporation as shall have authorised, ordered, or done any of the acts constituting in whole or in part such violation." Upon conviction any director, officer or agent is subject to a fine not exceeding 5000 dollars, or to imprisonment not exceeding one year, or to both, in the discretion of the Court.

§ 7. Granted that clubbing methods can be, in some measure, prevented, we turn to the further question, how far their prevention would avail to maintain potential competition. Professor Clark appears to hold that it would avail completely for this purpose. " In so far," he writes, " as legitimate rivalry in production is concerned, it is safe enough to build a new mill." In reality, however, even when clubbing methods are excluded, other obstacles to the full maintenance of competition are still present. First, when the unit firm normal to any industry is very large, the heavy capital expenditure required to start a new firm will check the ardour of aspirants. Furthermore, it should be noticed, in this connection, that in many industries the size of the normal unit firm has recently been increasing. For example, the output of the English paper industry between 1841 and 1903 rose from 43,000 to 773,080 tons, but the number of firms fell from 500 to 282;[1] and a like development has taken place in the raw iron industry. Secondly, the inducement

[1] Levy, *Monopole, Kartelle und Trusts*, p. 197.

to new competitors to spring up is smaller, the greater are
the productive economies which concentration on the part of
the monopolistic seller has involved. For, if great economy has
been brought about by concentration, a potential competitor
will know that the monopolistic seller, by simply abandoning
some of his monopoly revenue, can, without suffering any
positive loss, easily undersell him. Thirdly, the obstacles
in the way of new competition are further enlarged, when
a policy of secrecy as to costs and profits makes it difficult for
outsiders to guess at what rate the monopolistic seller *could*
sell, if he were to content himself with the normal gains of
competitive industry. Fourthly, a combination, by extensive
advertising or a distinctive trade mark, may have established
a sort of monopoly of reputation, which it would require heavy
advertising expenditure on the part of any would-be rival to
break down. It may, indeed, be suggested that, even so, the
combination would be kept in check by fear of a rival concern
being started with a view to forcing the combination to buy it
out. But there is less in this than there might appear to be
at first sight. For, if a rival did succeed in this policy, the
increase in the combination's capital might well be so large
that the rate of profit available per unit of capital would
turn out too small to make the venture worth the rival's
while.[1] This consideration would, of course, tend strongly to
hold him back. Thus attempts to maintain potential competition by preventing the employment of clubbing devices
can at best be only partially successful, and are, therefore,
very imperfect means of restraining bodies that possess monopolistic power from making use of that power. This is true
even of industry proper. In some departments of production—
roughly those covered by public utility concerns—the evident
wastefulness of competition makes it practically certain that
the public authorities will not permit it, and so exempts
monopolists from any check which the fear of it might otherwise exercise upon them.

§ 8. The inadequacy, as a method of control, of preventing
combination, which means maintaining actual competition,
and of anti-clubbing legislation, which means maintaining

---

[1] Cf. Jenks and Clark, *The Trust Problem*, pp. 69-70.

potential competition, leads forward naturally to the suggestion of direct methods. The position, which is relevant to industrial, no less than to railway, monopolies, is well put by the Departmental Committee on Railway Agreements and Amalgamations (1911) with special reference to the latter class. They write : " To sum up, we are strongly of opinion that, in so far as protection is required from any of the consequences which may be associated with railway co-operation, such protection should, in the main, be afforded by general legislation dealing with the consequences as such, independently of whether they occur as the result of agreement or not. Such a method would afford a much more extensive protection than the regulation of agreements. It would protect the public in the case of understandings as well as agreements. . . . It would not tend to introduce a confusing distinction between what a company might reasonably do under an agreement and what it might reasonably do if no agreement existed." [1] If this method could be employed with perfect accuracy, there would, of course, be no need for *any* accompanying indirect methods of the kind we have so far been discussing. In practice, however, the policy of dealing directly with the consequences of monopolistic power is, as will presently appear, exposed to very great difficulties. Furthermore, since in most forms it must almost necessarily work on the basis of some standard of reasonable earnings, deduced from the circumstances of other industries in which competition is available, these difficulties would become enormous, if attempts to maintain potential competition were abandoned altogether and resort had universally to direct methods. Consequently, it would seem that the policy of maintaining potential competition should be pursued everywhere vigorously, and that direct methods of dealing with the consequences should be employed, not instead of, but in addition to it.

§ 9. At first sight it seems obvious that direct dealing with the consequences of monopolistic power means, and can only mean, some kind of direct interference on the part of the public authority. In the main, of course, this

---

[1] *Report of the Departmental Committee on Railway Agreements and Amalgamations*, p. 21.

is what it does mean. But it is of some theoretical interest to
note a possible alternative line of policy which was advocated,
as regards shipping, by the Royal Commission on Shipping
Rings. The Commission recommended, in effect, that the
State should encourage the formation, over against a
monopolistic seller, of a combination of buyers possessing also
monopolistic powers. It was hoped that the combination
of buyers might be able to neutralise attempts on the part
of the seller to charge monopoly prices. This plan was
advocated as a partial remedy for the evils that have
arisen out of the conference system. Analytically, the plan
is a weak one, because what the creation of the second
monopolist does is, not to bring prices to the natural, or
competitive, point, but to render them indeterminate over a
considerable range, within which that point lies. No doubt,
the position of the purchasers is made better than it would
be if combination among them were absent; and there is
reason to hope that prices and output will approach more
nearly to what, from the standpoint of the national
dividend, is desirable than they would do under those
conditions. But the chance that the bargain between the
two combinations will lie in the near neighbourhood of that
proper to simple competition is not very large. This
difficulty would exist even though the monopoly created
to stand against the sellers were a monopoly of ultimate
consumers. In practice, however, ultimate consumers are
scarcely ever in a position to combine in this way. The only
persons who can so combine are middlemen between the
ultimate consumers and the monopolistic seller,—middlemen
who are not particularly concerned to fight for the consumers'
interests.[1] If they combine, the goods in which they deal will
have to pass through the hands of two monopolistic combinations, instead of one, before they reach the ultimate consumers.
The effect upon the price which those people will then have
to pay is economically indeterminate. The price may be less
than it would have been if the middlemen had not combined,
but it may, on the other hand, be greater. In any event,
it and, with it, the quantity of service accessible to the

[1] Cf. Marshall, *Industry and Trade*, p. 625.

ultimate consumers, are likely to be exceedingly unstable.[1] These considerations show that there is a serious flaw in the Commissioners' policy.[2]

§ 10. Interference on the part of the public authority does not necessarily mean orders about the terms of sale. It may well be that anti-social practices by powerful corporations might be substantially restrained by publicity alone. An important part of the task assigned to the Federal Trade Commission of the United States is to make investigations and to publish reports. The British *Committee on Trusts* (1919) recommended that the Board of Trade should obtain and publish in an annual report information about the development of organisations having for their purpose the regulation of prices or output so far as they tended to the creation of monopolies or to the restraint of trade ; and should investigate complaints regarding the action of such organisations. Powers would, of course, need to be taken to compel the officers of the organisations affected to produce their books and to answer questions. The fear of an adverse report issued by an investigating body in which public opinion had confidence might often turn the scale against gross abuses of monopoly power. There is, in short, little doubt that the weapon of publicity can accomplish something of importance : but it can hardly accomplish all that is required.

§ 11. We turn, therefore, to interference by the public authority with the terms of sale—a method which *may* be necessary even in industrial enterprises, when the " remedies " considered so far prove inadequate, and which, apart from public operation, is certainly necessary in public utility concerns. Analytically, the problem may be stated as follows. Assuming that the output proper to simple competition (allowing, of course, for any economies in production which a combination may have introduced) is also the output most advantageous to the national dividend, we need so to regulate things that that output will be forthcoming. In industries operating under

---

[1] Cf. Marshall, *Principles of Economics*, Bk. v. ch. xiv. § 9.

[2] The Imperial Shipping Committee 1923, while endorsing that policy, observe that (so far as shipping is concerned) " only two bodies of importance formed on the lines recommended by the Commission and since its appointment have come to their notice " (Cmd. 1802, p. 23).

conditions of increasing supply price, this type of regulation cannot be accomplished by the machinery of price control alone. For, if the price be fixed by the State at the level proper to competitive conditions, *i.e.* at such a level that, if competitive conditions prevailed, the output would be adjusted to yield normal profits, it will pay a monopolist to produce less than this output. By reducing output he will, under conditions of increasing supply price, also diminish the supply price, thus obtaining a monopoly gain measured by the difference between the regulated selling price multiplied by the output and the supply price multiplied by the output. It will be to his interest to control his output in such a way as to make this monopoly gain as large as possible. According to the form of the demand and supply schedules, the resultant output may be greater or less than it would have been under unregulated monopoly; but, in any event, it is certain to be less than the output proper to competition, at which the Government is aiming. This difficulty, however, is only present in industries operating under conditions of the increasing supply price. When constant supply price or decreasing supply price prevails, it will not pay a monopolist, when price is fixed at the competitive level, to reduce output below the competitive output; for he would not secure any diminution in his costs by doing this. Consequently, if the Government can succeed in fixing prices at the competitive level, it will also indirectly secure competitive output.[1] As a matter of practice, concerns (whether industrial combinations or public utility corporations), which it is necessary to regulate because they tend towards monopoly, are rarely of a kind which we should expect to be subject to increasing supply price. In the main, therefore, control means control over price.

§ 12. When this has been said, there inevitably comes to mind the sort of control over price which was exercised during the Great War, and some account of which was given in Chapter XII. It is very important, however, to realise that what we are now concerned with is fundamentally different from that. In controlling monopoly, it is required to prevent the monopolist from charging high prices, because, by so doing, he will

[1] Cf. Appendix III. § 23.

reduce output below the level at which he could put it with normal profits to himself. As explained above, under conditions of constant supply price or decreasing supply price, the fixing of maximum prices at the rate corresponding to the "competitive" output will in fact cause that output to be forthcoming. There is no question of the maximum price being associated with an output for which the demand price that the public are prepared to pay exceeds that price.[1] But in the war problem, as was clearly brought out in Chapter XII., the whole point of intervention was to fix a maximum price below the demand price that the public would be prepared, at need, to pay for such quantity of the commodity as was forthcoming. This is the reason why, at the maximum price, there was always a greater quantity demanded than could be supplied, and why, therefore, it was necessary to prevent accidental inequities in distribution by rationing all consumers to purchases smaller than many of them would have wished to make. This, too, is the reason why it was not sufficient to fix prices as from the producer only. Because the demand price was bigger than the price which the Government wished to allow, to have limited, *e.g.*, shipping freights, without also limiting the price of the things brought in at the limited freights, would merely have enabled the intermediaries between the ship and the consumer to take the whole benefit for themselves. It was necessary, therefore, not merely to fix maximum prices to the original producer, but also to fix maximum additions that might be put on to these prices by the various persons through whose hands (whether as further manufacturers or as retailers) the controlled commodities would afterwards pass. In the regulation of monopoly charges there is, of course, no need for any of these secondary arrangements.

§ 13. We may now proceed to investigate this form of price control directly. One way in which it may be exercised is, as it were, negative. It may take the form of general provisions against "unreasonable" conduct, leaving the definition of what is, in fact, unreasonable to the decision of a

---

[1] In technical language, the limitation of monopoly prices moves the exchange index along the demand curve towards the right ; the limitation of competitive prices pushes the exchange index below the demand curve.

Commission or of the Courts. This way was, in substance, followed, for proposed *changes* of rates, in the work of the English Railway Commissioners prior to 1921, and of the American Railway Commissioners prior to the passage of the Hepburn law. The Commissioners had to decide whether any proposed increase of rates was reasonable, and to permit or forbid it accordingly. Thus their task was *comparatively* light. They had not to regulate all prices always, but only to intervene against specially unreasonable prices ; and, furthermore, the knowledge of their existence was likely to serve indirectly as a check against the setting-up of unreasonable prices.[1] The negative way is also followed in certain franchises, which permit municipalities to take over the business of a licensed corporation *at a proper price*—an ambiguous phrase—should the corporation fail to " operate and develop it in compliance with reasonable public requirements."[2] It is followed again in the Canadian Industrial Combines Investigation Act (1910). Provision is made for determining whether, with regard to any article, on the subject of which complaint has been made, "there exists any combine to promote unduly the advantage of the manufacturers or dealers at the expense of the consumers by fixing the price higher than is proper "; and, if the charge is established, penalties are provided. In New Zealand the Act of 1910 applies the same test. " Any person commits an offence, who, either as principal or agent, sells or supplies, or offers for sale or supply, any goods at a price which is unreasonably high, if that price has been in any manner, directly or indirectly, determined, controlled, or influenced by any commercial trust, of which that person or his principal (if any) is or has been a member." The Russian Criminal Code of 1903 had a similar proviso : " A merchant or manufacturer, who increases the price of victuals or other articles of prime necessity in an extraordinary degree in accord with other merchants or manufacturers dealing in the same articles, shall be punished with imprisonment."[3] In all these

---

[1] Cf. Van Hise, *Concentration and Control*, p. 261.

[2] National Civic Federation, *Municipal and Private Operation of Public Utilities*, vol. i. p. 41.

[3] The text of these laws is printed in Appendix G to Jenks and Clark, *The Trust Problem*.

rules excessive prices are forbidden, but no attempt is made actually to fix prices by decree. The other, positive, way, in which control may be exercised, consists in the authoritative determination of definite maximum rates of charge or minimum provision of service. This way is illustrated by the terms of the charters usually accorded to companies operating public utility services under lease from city governments and by the power, conferred on the Interstate Commerce Commission by the Hepburn law of 1906, to "determine and prescribe" maximum rates for railway, telephone, and other services of communication.

§ 14. Whether the negative or the positive way of regulation is followed, some sort of sanction to make the law effective must be provided. This can be done in a variety of ways. Sometimes the penalty for breach is a direct money fine. Sometimes, in protected countries, for example in Brazil,[1] it consists in the withdrawal of duties on competing foreign goods. The Canadian Industrial Combines Investigation Act of 1910 provides for both sorts of penalty. If a statutory Commission "finds that there is a Combine, the Government may either lower or repeal the duties, and, in addition, impose a fine of 1000 dollars a day on those who continue in their evil courses after the judgment of the Board has been officially published."[2] Another interesting form of sanction is provided, as against the owners of vessels which violate any of the American anti-trust laws, by a clause in the Panama Canal Act of 1912 forbidding the use of the canal to their ships.[3] Sometimes the sanction consists in the threat of governmental competition. Thus, in connection with the 1892 agreement, by which the Post-Office took over the National Telephone Company's trunk lines, the Chancellor of the Exchequer hinted that the State, while securing its right to compete, would not be likely to exercise that right if the Company acted reasonably.[4] Sometimes, again, the sanction consists in the threat of State purchase, on terms either fixed beforehand or to be decided by arbitration, of the whole

---

[1] Cf. Davies, *Trust Laws and Unfair Competition*, p. 294.

[2] *Economist*, March 26, 1910, p. 665. Cf. *Annals of the American Academy*, July 1912, p. 152.

[3] Cf. Johnson and Huebner, *Principles of Ocean Transportation*, p. 386.

[4] H. Meyer, *Public Ownership and the Telephones*, pp. 56, 199.

of the plant of the regulated business.   Sometimes, finally,—
and this, in effect, is what seems to be contemplated under the
authoritative interpretation of the Sherman Act, as given by
the United States Supreme Court in the Standard Oil Case
(1911)—combinations, whose price (and other) policy is found
to be reasonable, may be left undisturbed, but combinations
which use their power to the injury of the public may be
dissolved by order of the Court.[1]

§ 15. Though, however, many sanctions, some of them
of great force, are available when breaches of the law
are detected, it is necessary to add that, whether the
negative or the positive method of control is adopted,
it is exceedingly difficult to prevent people from escaping
these sanctions by evasion.   Thus in the pre-war period our
railway companies, in effect, raised their rates without applying for the consent of the railway commissioners.   Charges
for rent of sidings and so forth were created; the
number of articles which the companies refuse to carry
at owner's risk, unless packed to their satisfaction, was
increased; rebates were withdrawn; and other such devices
were employed.[2]   But the kind of evasion which it is hardest
to deal with is that which meets price regulation by manipulating quality.   To prevent this it is essential to couple
with rules about maximum price further rules about minimum quality.   But in some things, such as the comfort and
punctuality of a tramway service, or the sanitary condition of
slaughter-houses and sewers, it is difficult to *define* a minimum
of quality.   When there are a number of different grades of
quality, all of which have to be distinguished from one another
and subjected to a separate maximum price—different grades,
even of simple things like tea, and, still more, of complicated
things like hats—the difficulty of effective definition is
enormous.   It is easy to sell a lower-grade thing at a higher-
grade price.   In other things, such as water supply, gas
supply, milk supply and house accommodation, where tests
of quality are available to give a basis for definition, it may

[1] Cf. the judgment of Chief-Justice White, laying down in this case what
has now become known as "the rule of reason" in interpreting the Act (quoted
by Jenks and Clark, *The Trust Problem*, p. 299).

[2] Cf. *Railway Conference Report*, p. 57.

be difficult to *detect* departures from the stipulated minimum. Something can, no doubt, be done by an elaborate system of inspection, like that developed in support of the Adulteration of Food and Drugs Act, but the openings for evasion are, in any event, likely to be considerable.

§ 16. Even, however, if this difficulty could be completely overcome, the most formidable obstacle in the way of direct control would still remain. It is necessary to determine what prices shall be regarded as unreasonable, and, when the positive method of fixing maxima is adopted, what the maxima shall be. As was explained at the beginning of this chapter, the goal aimed at is the competitive price, *i.e.* the price which would have been arrived at if other things had been the same but the output had been that proper to simple competition instead of that proper to monopoly. In what way is this price to be ascertained by the controlling authority ? It is conceivable that some reader, thinking loosely upon recent experience, may claim that competitive prices could be determined directly from the recorded expenses of converting the raw material used into finished goods. Plainly, however, in order to get the *full* conversion costs, we need to know how much should be added to the cost of material and labour for the share due, for the article we are studying, to the standing charges of the business. Given a decision about that, we can, indeed, by conversion cost accounting—the technique of which was greatly developed during the war—determine the proper price for any particular product or group of joint products;[1] but to proceed in the reverse direction is impossible. The calculation of conversion costs is a necessary step towards any practical scheme of price regulation. But it is a subordinate step.

§ 17. It seems clear that our problem can only be solved by some reference to a " normal " rate of return on investment. We know that, had the investment proper to competition been made, a price, which, on the then profitable output, would

---

[1] With joint products, of course, it is impossible to isolate separate costs of production, and the " proper " price for each of them will depend on the comparative demands for them severally as well as upon their cost of production jointly : a fact which still further complicates the task of any would-be price-fixer.

have yielded a normal return on this investment, would be the price we require. Unfortunately, however, the investment that actually has been made is not likely to be equal to that proper to competition. If the monopoly has been started *ab initio*, so to speak, it will be less than that proper to competition, and, if the monopoly is a result of a combination of unduly numerous concerns engaged in cut-throat competition, it will be greater than this. Clearly then the price we require is not the price that, with the output profitable in respect of the actual investment, would yield a normal return, unless it so happens that that price is equal to the price which would have yielded a normal return on the amount of investment proper to competition, had that amount been provided. This condition implies that the commodity with whose production we are concerned is one that, from a long period point of view, is produced under conditions of constant supply price. With a monopoly that has been started *ab initio*, if the commodity is produced under conditions of increasing supply price, the price that yields a normal return on actual investment will be too high; if it is produced under conditions of decreasing supply price, too low. In fact, as has already been observed, there is little likelihood of commodities subject to increasing supply price coming under monopolistic control. If then we calculate our "proper price," for control purposes, by reckoning what price would yield a normal return were the output most profitable at that price produced,[1] the figure we reach will, with a monopoly that has been started *ab initio*, probably be somewhat too high. With a monopoly that is the aftermath of excessive investment and cut-throat competition, it will, on the other hand, probably be too low. There is not, however, so far as I can see, any other way in which a figure can be calculated at all.[2]

[1] The careful reader will have noticed that, should the equipment possessed by the monopolist be larger than that proper to competition, it will not in fact be possible, at a price determined as above, to find a market for the whole of the output that it would be profitable to produce at that price. This fact, however, does not in any way impair the analysis of the text.

[2] The difficulty dealt with in the above section, which in earlier editions I had not noticed, was brought out in an illuminating article on "Control of Investment versus Control of Return" by Professor Knight in the *Quarterly Journal of Economics* for February 1930.

§ 18. If then, *faute de mieux*, we decide to make use of this way, it becomes necessary to determine what rate of profit, in any particular enterprise, the price of whose product has to be regulated, may rightly be considered normal. At first sight it might be thought that this issue can be settled fairly easily. Will not normal profit be such profit that, when allowance is made for earnings of management (as in joint stock companies is done automatically), what is left provides interest at the ordinary rate on the capital of the concern ? This plausible suggestion is, however, easily shown to be very far from adequate. Let us, to begin with, suppose that the ordinary rate of interest really does correspond in all businesses to normal profits. We have still to determine what the capital is on which this ordinary rate is to be paid. Clearly we cannot interpret it as the market value of the concern, because, the market value of a business being simply the present value of its anticipated earnings, these earnings *must* yield the ordinary rate of interest on it, allowing for the particular risks involved, whatever sum they amount to. Indeed, if we were to take existing market value as our basis, since this depends on what people believe that the system of rate regulation will be, we should come perilously near to circular reasoning. Capital value, therefore, for rate control purposes, is something quite different from capital value for, say, taxation purposes. It must mean, in some sense, that capital which has in fact been invested in the business in the past. But this is not at all easy to calculate. When the sums of money invested in any concern include commission paid to a promoter for accomplishing a fusion, the advantage of which is expected to consist in the power to exact monopoly charges from the public, this commission ought not, it would seem, to be counted, except in so far as the fusion has also brought about increased productive efficiency. That this is an exceedingly important point becomes apparent when we learn that, according to high officials in some of the industrial combinations of the United States, " the cost of organisation, including the pay of the promoter and financier, amounts often to from 20 to 40 per cent of the total amount of stock issued." [1]

[1] Jenks and Clark, *The Trust Problem*, p. 90.

The same difficulty has to be faced as regards that part of the capital expenditure which has been employed in buying up existing concerns at a price enhanced by the hope that combination will make monopolistic action practicable. Apart from these difficult items, what we want to ascertain is the original capital expenditure, whether employed in physical construction, parliamentary costs, the purchase of patent rights or the upbuilding of a connection by advertisement, together with such later expenditure, in excess of the repairs and renewals required to keep the original capital intact, as has not been taken out again in earnings, allowance being made for the different dates of the various investments.[1] For new businesses, to be established in the future, it would be easy enough to secure by law that information about all these items should be made available. But for businesses already long established it may be impossible to get this information. For example, similar expenditures on good-will and so forth, which one concern may have charged to capital, another will have treated as current expenditure, in such a way that it cannot practically be distinguished. In view of these difficulties some roundabout way of approximating to the truth may have to be employed. Obviously the nominal capital is quite useless for this purpose. It may have been watered and manipulated in ways that completely disguise the real facts. The market value of the capital we have already shown to be inappropriate. It is usual, therefore, to make use either of the estimated " cost of reproduction " of the concern's plant—which may be very misleading if the relevant prices have changed substantially since the original investment was made—or of a value ascertained by direct physical valuation of the plant—the amount of which will, of course, depend on the principles in accordance with which the valuation is made—; and then to make some more or less arbitrary allowance for costs of promotion, investments to build up good-will, patent rights, and so on. These *data* are not wanted for themselves, but are supposed to enable a rough estimate to be made of the actual capital investment, when this is not directly ascer-

[1] Cf. Heilman, " Principles of Public Utility Valuation," *Quarterly Journal of Economics*, Feb. 1914, pp. 281-90.

tainable. To develop the difficulties of this process is outside my present purpose.[1]

§ 19. There remains a more fundamental complication. Up to this point it has been tacitly assumed that the capital invested in any concern is properly and unambiguously represented by the money invested in it. In actual fact, however, a real investment of 1000 days' labour may be measured by £200 if it happens to be made in one year, and by £400 or, in conceivable circumstances, by £400,000 if it happens to be made in another. In periods during which currencies are violently unstable, as in Russia and Germany after the war, this sort of difficulty inevitably becomes prominent. It is plain that real investment, and not money investment, is the fundamental thing, and that, therefore, in strictness, when general prices have changed, money investments ought, for our present purpose, to be written up or down so as to allow for this fact. This means revising all the records of past years and multiplying the money investment of each year by the ratio between the index number of general prices for that year and for the present time. In view of the acknowledged imperfections of existing index numbers, a device of this kind could hardly hope to win sufficient acceptance to make it practicable. When, as often happens, a substantial part of the investment in a concern has been made in the form of bonds or debentures, on which a fixed money interest is contracted for whatever happens to prices, it is open to a further serious objection. To allow a doubled gross money return to offset a doubling of prices would involve compensating the stockholders for the bondholders' losses as well as for their own and leaving the bondholders to bear their fate unaided.[2] None the less, to ignore altogether large and rapid changes in general prices, such as have resulted from the Great War, would be to accept and act upon a serious falsification of the facts. These considerations, taken in conjunction with those set out in the preceding paragraph, suffice to show that to determine what the capital of a concern

[1] Cf. Barker, *Public Utility Rates*, chapters v. and vi.

[2] Cf. Bauer, " Fair Value for Effective Rate Control," *American Economic Review*, December 1924, pp. 664-6.

is, on which "ordinary" interest is to be allowed, is not an easy task.

§ 20. But this is not all. It is not true that the normal "competitive" profits of any enterprise are the profits that would yield the "ordinary" rate of interest on the capital that has actually been invested in that enterprise. For the establishment of different enterprises involves both different degrees of risk and different initial periods of development, during which no return at all is likely to be obtained; and appropriate compensation under these heads must be made to those investors—the only ones with whom the State can deal —whose enterprises turn out successfully, and who, therefore, must be paid enough to balance the losses of those who have failed.[1] This circumstance need not, indeed, be responsible for large practical difficulties in industries in which production has attained more or less of a routine character, but in all industries in an experimental stage it is of dominant import-ance.[2] Furthermore, even if there were no risks, we could not regard as proper prices which would yield the ordinary rate of interest in all circumstances, but only prices which would yield that rate, if the management, and, indeed, the actual organisation of the original investment also, were conducted with "ordinary" ability; and this is a vague and difficult con-ception. As Professor Taussig pertinently observes: "Every one knows that fortunes are made in industries strictly com-petitive, and are to be ascribed to unusual business capacity. . . . When a monopoly or quasi-monopoly secures high returns, how are we to separate the part attributable to monopoly from the part attributable to excellence in management?"[3] To allow the same rate of return to companies which invest their

---

[1] Cf. Greene, *Corporation Finance*, p. 134.

[2] If a concern has been taken over by a company after the first stage of speculative adventure has been successfully passed, the purchase price will probably include a large sum above cost. This may be a fair remuneration for the risk taken and uncertainty borne. But clearly, after it has been paid, to allow the new company to reap profits which are both adjusted to the risks of the occupa-tion and also calculated upon a capital which includes the above sum, would be to compel the public to reward it for risk-taking for which it has not been re-sponsible, and recompense for which has already been made. For an excellent general discussion of good-will cf. Leake, *Good-will, its nature and how to value it*.

[3] *American Economy Review Supplement*, March 1913, p. 132.

capital wastefully as to those which invest it well plainly makes against economical production. Incidentally, if there were two competing combinations to be dealt with, it would logically require forcing the better managed one to charge lower prices than the other, an arrangement which would not only have awkward consequences at the moment but would effectively discourage good management. In this connection it should be noted that to extend combination further, so long as extension involves economies, is a form of good management, and a form that would be discouraged if prices were so regulated that no advantage were allowed to accrue to those who had brought it about. Finally, when a plant has been built to fit an expected future demand much in excess of the present demand, it would plainly be unreasonable to sanction rates high enough to yield a full return on the whole investment before that future demand has developed.[1] In view of these complications, and of the necessary limitations of its knowledge—for, as a rule, the controllers are bound to be much behind the controlled in technical experience—a public authority is almost certain either to exact too easy terms from the concerns it is seeking to control, and so to leave them with the power of simple monopoly, or to exact too hard terms, and so, though not permitting monopoly exaction to them, nevertheless to prevent the development of their industry to the point proper to simple competition. The British Tramways Act of 1870 appears to have failed in the latter way, and to have been responsible for prolonged delay in the development of electric traction in this country.

§ 21. It is evident that the difficulties, which are involved in determining what scale of return should be regarded as normal in any particular productive enterprise, complicate alike the negative way of control, under which the Legislature simply condemns unreasonable prices, leaving the Courts to decide whether any given price scheme is in fact unreasonable, and the positive way, which lays down definite price maxima. Plainly, however, they complicate the positive way more seriously than the other. An ordinary industrial concern produces a great number of different varieties of goods, the raw materials

---

[1] Cf. Hartman, *Fair Values*, p. 130 *et seq.*

for which are continually altering in cost, and the distinctive character of the finished product continually being modified. For any outside authority to draw up a schedule of permitted charges for a concern of this sort would be a hopeless task. On the other hand, for a trained Commission or judicial body equipped, like the American Federal Trade Commission, to make full inquiries, it would not be impossible to decide in a broad way whether, taking one product with another and one time with another, some selected large combination—the Standard Oil Company, the United Steel Corporation, or another—was charging prices calculated to yield to it more than the return deemed in the circumstances to be reasonable. For industrial concerns in normal times no attempt has ever been made to go beyond this negative way, and it does not seem, at all events in the present condition of economic knowledge and governmental competence, that any such attempt either can, or should, be made. Imperfect as the results to be hoped for from the negative way are, they are better than would be got from a blundering struggle after the other. In public utility concerns, on the other hand, the excess difficulty of the positive over the negative way is slight. As a general rule, the service provided by these concerns is single and relatively simple—gas, water, electricity, transport of passengers. Not many separate prices —railway freight rates are, of course, a very important exception—have, therefore, to be fixed. Further, the demand is generally unaffected by fashion, and equipment plays so large a part in the cost that changes in the price of raw material do not very greatly matter. Finally, even if these things were otherwise, the nature of the goods sold and the convenience of customers make it very desirable that the prices charged should not undergo frequent change. In these concerns, therefore, the positive way of control by fixing maximum prices has generally been adopted.

§ 22. When this is done, it becomes imperative to seek out the best means of guarding against the two opposite sorts of error, undue laxness and undue harshness, to which, as was shown in § 20, all forms of regulation are in practice inclined. For this purpose one device sometimes recommended is to put up the licence to operate certain public utility services to a kind of auction. This plan allows the persons most interested themselves to present estimates of terms which they would reckon profitable. It has been described thus: " According to the best plan now in vogue, the City sells the franchise for constructing the works to the company, which bids to furnish water at the lowest rates under definitely specified conditions, the franchise being sometimes perpetual, but often granting to the City at some future date an option for the purchase of the works." Since, however, in many cities, the companies capable of making tenders will be very few in number, and since, furthermore, their own estimates must be largely tentative, the adoption of this device is not incompatible with large errors. The likelihood of error is made greater by the fact that the conditions of most industries are continually changing, in such wise that the scheme of price-regulation, which is proper at one time, necessarily becomes improper at another.

§ 23. A further effort at limiting the range of error can be made through arrangements under which the regulations imposed are submitted to periodical revision. Franchises " cannot be fixed, or justly fixed, for all time, owing to rapidly changing conditions." [1] With the growth of improvements and so on, it may well happen that a maximum price designed to imitate competitive conditions will, after a while, stand above the price that an unrestricted monopolist would find it profitable to charge, and will, therefore, be altogether ineffective. " The public should retain in all cases an interest in the growth and profits of the future." [2] A provision for periodic revision in a franchise may, however, by creating uncertainty, restrict investment in the industry concerned to an extent that is injurious to the national dividend. Further, if the revision is to occur at fixed intervals, it may tempt companies, shortly before the close of one of these intervals, to hold back important developments till after the revision has taken place, lest a large part of their fruits

[1] Bemis, *Municipal Monopolies*, p. 32.
[2] *Municipal and Private Operation of Public Utilities*, vol. i. p. 24.

should be taken away in the form of lowered prices;[1] and this difficulty cannot be wholly overcome by clauses stipulating for the introduction of such technical improvements as are, from time to time, invented elsewhere. One way of meeting these dangers is to hedge round the revising body with conditions designed to defend the company's interest. For example, the Railway Act of 1844 provided that, if dividends exceeded 10 per cent on the paid-up capital after twenty-one years from the sanctioning of the lines, the Lords of the Treasury might revise tolls, fares, etc., on the condition that they guaranteed a 10 per cent dividend for the next twenty-one years. Another way is to make the revision period so far distant from the date at which an undertaking is initiated that the effect upon investment due to the anticipation of it will be very small. It is evident that, just in so far as either of these lines of defence is adopted, the efficacy of revision, as a means of lessening the gap between actual regulation and ideal regulation, is diminished. But, if regulation is to be attempted at all, the retention by the State of revising powers in some form is absolutely essential. It would seem that this could be provided for without imposing a serious check either on investment or on enterprise, if the principles on which the revision would proceed were clearly laid down and understood. The revisers might be instructed at each revision period to fix a price—or, when they have to do with joint products, several adjusted prices—sufficiently high to continue to the company a fair rate on their total real investment, account being taken of the fact that the capital turned into it in the first instance was probably subject to great risk, while that added subsequently needs a less reward under this head. They might be instructed further, in deciding what constitutes a fair return, to consider generally the quality of management that has been displayed, fixing prices to yield higher returns when the management has been good than when it has been indifferent or bad. No doubt, the technical difficulty of this kind of revision would be exceedingly great, but it

[1] Cf. Whitten, *Regulation of Public Service Companies in Great Britain*, p. 224.

would not be nearly so great as that of the initial regulation. It is not unreasonable to suppose that a class of official might eventually be evolved whose decision on such matters, when founded on adequate comparative statistics, would at once deserve and command the confidence of would-be investors. Such investors would have the consolation of knowing that, while, on the one hand, the price of their product was liable to enforced reduction, on the other hand, if costs of material and labour went against them, it might be raised in their favour.

§ 24. Yet another device designed to limit the range of error remains. In all ordinary industries many variations in the costs of material and so forth occur *within* the successive revision periods. If the guidance of simple competition is to be followed, such variations should be accompanied by variations in the prices charged to consumers. No doubt, where, as in railway service, the technical inconvenience of constantly changing prices would be very great, it may, on the whole, be best not to follow this guidance for short-period movements; but such cases are probably rare. Attempts are sometimes made by controlling authorities to organise the required price variations by some sort of self-adjusting arrangement. A crude method, which has been applied to some gas companies in this country, is to fix a *maximum* dividend. If the competence of the management remains constant, this implies that, when costs fall beyond a certain point, the prices charged to consumers must also fall. This method, however, has the grave disadvantage that it is likely, so soon as it becomes operative, to cut away the normal motives for skill and care in management and for avoidance of waste. A less crude method is to lay down a standard of earnings, always to allow prices to be charged high enough to yield this standard, and to provide further that, when this standard is passed, a defined proportion of the balance shall be used to reduce prices, while the remainder is left to augment earnings. In the South Metropolitan Gas Company's Act of 1920 there is an arrangement of this kind, three-quarters of whatever balance there may be over standard earnings being allotted to consumers. Railway rates in this country are now governed on a somewhat similar plan. The Railways Act, 1921, lays down for each amalgamated company a *standard income*, based on the earnings of 1913 with allowances for new investments, and so forth. If experience shows that the rates of charge fixed by the Rates Tribunal yield, or could, with efficient and economical management, have yielded, an income greater than the standard income, the Rates Tribunal are instructed to reduce the rates of charge " so as to effect the reduction of the net income of the company in subsequent years to an extent equivalent to 80 per cent of such excess "; and, if the net income actually yielded turns out to be less than the standard income together with appropriate allowances for new capital, the tribunal shall increase the rates of charge to bring it up to this amount, provided that the deficiency is not due to lack of efficiency or economy in the management. Plainly, under this arrangement the discouragement to skill and economy will be smaller than it would be under a maximum dividend plan *after* the maximum has been reached; but, in view of the extreme difficulty that any tribunal must find in adjudicating as to efficiency and economy in management, it is bound to be greater than it would be under that plan *before* the maximum has been reached. Yet a third method is that of connecting changes in the dividend paid to shareholders during any licence period with changes in selling price by means of a sliding scale. Illustrations of this method are furnished in a number of English Acts of Parliament dealing with gas companies. One pre-war Act, for example, fixed a standard price of 3s. 9d. per thousand cubic feet, and provided that, for every penny put on or off that price, the company might, when there are reductions, and must, when there were increases, move the dividend up or down a quarter per cent. Another illustration is furnished by the Act governing the Lancashire Power Company, which furnishes electricity in bulk. This Act " provides for a dividend of 8 per cent and an additional 1·25 per cent reduction in price for every 0·25 per cent increase of dividend above 8 per cent, in respect of every 5 per cent charged below the maximum price allowed by the Act." [1] Sliding scales of this kind—.

[1] H. Meyer, *Municipal Ownership in Great Britain*, p. 281.

which, if they are to be effective, must, of course, be combined with Government control over the issue of new capital by the companies concerned—are, like sliding scales of wages, not substitutes for, but complements to, a system of periodic revision of the licence terms; for, if they were treated as permanent arrangements, all improvements and discoveries that reduced cost of production, whether made by the concerns themselves or by others, would steadily and continuously enhance profits.   They are not easily organised for new companies, because the appropriate standards of price and dividend cannot be determined till some experience has been gained of the working of a concern.   But it is feasible, and before the war it was the practice of the Board of Trade in dealing with gas companies, to fix a simple maximum price at first and to reserve power to substitute a sliding scale after the lapse of a certain interval.[1]   These scale arrangements, like the other methods discussed above, are open to the objection that they push prices up, not only when the costs of raw materials and labour rise, but equally when the profits of a company are reduced by incompetent management. In spite, however, of these difficulties, sliding scales—and the same thing may be said of the standard earnings plan —may be expected, when carefully constructed, to make possible a nearer approach to the system of prices proper to simple competition than would be possible under any plan that, over the intervals between revision periods, fixed prices rigidly.   Moreover, the danger of discouraging competent management may be met to some extent by provisions, such as those embodied in the British railway law, under which the controlling authority is allowed to veto an increase of charges when falling earnings appear to be the result, not of natural causes, but of incompetence.

§ 25. It should be added that arrangements of the kind I have been describing, though they may make fair provision for adjusting charges within the revision periods to variations in the cost of raw materials, and so forth, are extremely ill-fitted to cope with variations in demand; for, whereas, if simple

[1] Cf. Whitten, *Regulation of Public Service Companies in Great Britain*, p. 129.

competition is to be followed, upward movements of demand
—we are here, of course, only concerned with short-period
fluctuations—should be associated with upward movements of
price, under these arrangements they will be associated with
downward movements of price.   Demand variations, moreover,
may be very important, and may call for large associated price
variations.   With given demand variations, the extent of
these should be especially great in industries where the part
played by supplementary costs—which are not reduced proportionately when output is reduced—is large relatively to
the part played by prime costs: and supplementary costs
are, in fact, very important in the generality of industries.
It might be possible to take account of variations in demand,
as well as of variations in cost, by a scale system that
should link up permitted changes in price with changes in
the volume of service supplied, instead of with changes in
earnings.   So far as I am aware, however, no self-acting
system of this kind is as yet anywhere in operation.

§ 26. There remains another difficulty of a different
order.   The main part of what has been said so far has
tacitly assumed that, in framing our control policy, we start
with a clear table.   For industrial monopolies that come into
being after the general lines of our policy have been fixed, and
for public utility corporations upon which conditions are
imposed at the time when the original franchise is granted, this
is, of course, true.   But, in so far as we have to do with
monopolistic concerns over which at present control is either
not exercised at all or exercised in a very imperfect manner,
the case is different.   To bring these concerns now under a
system of price regulation of the type that we are contemplating would, in many instances, involve a large reduction in their
income and in the capital value of their shares.   So far as original
shareholders or persons who have inherited from them are
concerned, this does not greatly matter.   The fact that these
persons have made abnormal profits in the past is no reason
why they should be allowed to do so in the future.   But the
position is different with recent purchasers of shares, whose
purchase price has been regulated by the conditions ruling
before control, or the strict form of control here contemplated,

was seriously thought about. Such persons may perhaps be getting now, say 8 per cent on their money, and control may knock this down to 5 per cent, reducing the value of their capital by one-third or even one-half. To make regulations that will strike with cruel severity on arbitrarily selected groups of perfectly innocent persons is not a thing to be lightly undertaken. There are limits to the right of the State to ride rough-shod over legitimate expectations. And yet to refrain from control that ought to be imposed, because we neglected our duty in not imposing it before, is to enslave ourselves to past mistakes. Surrender to the " widows and orphans " argument means, in substance, abandonment of reform. No perfect solution of this conflict can be hoped for. But it would seem a reasonable compromise, and one adequately careful of vested interests, to provide that, when the sudden introduction of a full measure of price control on the principles indicated above would greatly depress values, this control should only be introduced after an interval of notice, and then by gradual steps.

§ 27. Even, however, if this somewhat special difficulty be left out of account, the preceding general review makes it evident that, under any form of State control over private monopoly—and it should be noticed that, though the examples cited have to do only with special kinds of private monopoly, the argument refers to all kinds—a considerable gap between the ideal and the actual is likely to remain. The method of control, whether positive or negative, is, in short, an exceedingly imperfect means of approximating industry towards the price level and output proper to simple competition. Moreover, it is apt to prove a costly method. As Professor Durand observes : " Government regulation of prices and profits of private concerns always involves a large element of waste, of duplication of energy and cost. It means that two sets of persons are concerning themselves with the same work. The managers and employees of the corporation must study cost accounting and conditions of demand in determining price policy. The officers and employees of the Government must follow and do it all over again. Moreover, the fact that these two sets of persons have different motives in approaching their work means friction and litigation, and these spell further expense. To superimpose a vast governmental machinery upon the vast machinery of private business is an extravagance, which should be avoided if it is possible to do so." [1] This consideration is one that ought not to be ignored. The expense involved in public supervision should be debited against the system of private enterprise in monopolistic industries before the real efficiency of this system is brought into comparison with the rival system of public enterprise.

[1] *Quarterly Journal of Economics*, 1914, pp. 674-5 ; and *The Trust Problem*, p. 57.

CHAPTER XXII

PUBLIC OPERATION OF INDUSTRIES

§ 1. IN earlier chapters of this book it has been shown that private enterprise left to itself, even when it operates under conditions of simple competition, often leads to a distribution of resources less favourable to the national dividend than some other possible distributions. In some occupations the value of the marginal private net product of the resources employed is less than the value of the marginal social net product, with the result that too little is invested; in other industries the value of the marginal private net product is the larger, and too much is invested; in yet others the exercise of monopoly power contracts output, and investment falls much below what the public interest requires. When competition rules and social and private net product at the margin diverge, it is theoretically possible to put matters right by the imposition of a tax or the grant of a subsidy; when monopoly rules, it is theoretically possible to render it innocuous by the regulation of price,—in conjunction, in some circumstances, with the regulation of output. The preceding discussion, however, has made it plain that to counter the bias of private interest in these ways must prove in practice an extraordinarily difficult task, and one which cannot be carried through completely. Hence the question arises whether, other things being equal, it would not be better for public authorities themselves to operate certain classes of undertaking instead of trying to control their operation by private enterprise.

§ 2. It must be clearly understood that the issue here raised concerns public operation, not public ownership.

Public ownership by itself, and apart from any distributional change that may have come about if the ownership has been acquired without the payment of full compensation, means very little. Suppose, for example, that a municipality raises a loan of a million pounds in order to establish an electric supply works, interest to be paid at 5 per cent and the principal to be paid off in fifty years through a sinking fund. The legal position will be that the municipality owns the works from the moment they are built, subject to what is, in effect, a mortgage to the fundholders. If a private syndicate had put up money, built the works, and loaned them to the municipality on terms involving exactly the same charges to the municipality and providing for the works to pass into its possession after fifty years, the syndicate would, during those fifty years, be the owner. But, granted that the municipality was free to do what it chose with the works, whether by altering them or adding to them, the real position would be exactly the same on this as on the other plan. The distinction between public ownership and private ownership would be a mere technicality of no practical effect. In like manner, if a public authority lends a million pounds to a private concern at 5 per cent perpetual interest to enable it to build an electric works, the real position is exactly the same as if it built the works itself and let them to a private concern at a perpetual interest of equal amount: but under the former plan the private concern, and under the latter the public body, is technically owner. There is a difference in form, but identity in substance. Between public operation and private operation, on the other hand, there is always and necessarily a fundamental difference of substance.

§ 3. In view of the many technical difficulties, to which attention has been called in the preceding chapter, in the way of the effective exercise of public control over private industry, the case for public operation, at all events in industries with a tendency towards monopoly, is, from the point of view of a right distribution of national resources among different occupations, a very strong one. It remains very strong in spite of the fact that, as is alleged to have happened with Government railways in certain democratically governed States,

CH. XXII PUBLIC OPERATION OF INDUSTRIES 383

it may be perverted to satisfy local and sectional, or even personal, ends;[1] for this danger has been substantially lessened by the invention of extra-parliamentary "commissions," as described in Chapter XX., for working public enterprises. But the comparative effect of public control and public operation upon the right distribution of national resources among different occupations is not the only thing we have to consider in making our choice between them. Other things besides this are involved, just as other things were involved in our comparison between voluntary Purchasers' Associations and ordinary commercial businesses. We are not entitled to assume without argument that the economies of production will be the same under public operation and private operation. It may be that public operation is less economical than private operation, even when private firms are subject to public control. If this is so, the disadvantages of public operation as regards economical production have to be balanced against its advantages as regards the distribution of resources among different occupations. Hence, before any real answer to our question can be attempted, it is necessary to undertake some comparison of public with private operation from the standpoint of productive efficiency.

§ 4. It will be well at the outset to clear out of the way two arguments drawn from the experience of the war, which are based on a loose use of the term efficiency and are not really relevant.

First, it has been argued as follows : " If the individualist principle is the right thing, then it was manifestly absurd in war time to do what the Government did, for example, in taking over the railways. If divided railway control was efficient, why interfere with it; why not carry on as usual ? What was there in the way of moving trains and men that was not the proper business of railway companies, and why, then, were they 'interfered with' ? If it becomes obviously necessary to mobilise railways in war to move some hundreds of thousands or millions of men, why is it not necessary to mobilise railways in peace to move to the best advantage nearly three hundred million tons of coal in a year—the

---

[1] Cf. Acworth, *State Railway Ownership*, p. 103.

coal which is the very life-blood of British industry ? " [1] This reasoning assumes that the State took over the railways in war time in order to render them technically more efficient. In fact it took them over in order to ensure that the Government should have full command over their lines and equipment, and should not have to do without services it needed on account of conflicting claims from private persons. Normally railways, like all other concerns that sell their output for money, allocate that output in accordance with the effective monetary demand of their various customers. In war time it was obviously necessary to scrap effective monetary demand as the directing factor in the distribution of railway services among rival customers. The fact that this was done with general agreement is no proof that any one considered railways to be technically less efficient, *i.e.* to require a greater real cost to obtain a given result, under private than under public management.

Secondly, an analogous argument has been built up to prove that the establishment of national munition factories enabled the Government to obtain its supplies enormously more cheaply than it could have done, and was in fact doing, from private firms. But the circumstances of the war were such that the private sellers of munitions, faced with an unlimited Government demand, were able to exact prices very greatly in excess of their own cost of production. Such a state of affairs does, indeed, provide a strong argument for national action, but the fact that a national shell-works can produce shells at a less cost than the price that a private works can force the Government to pay is no proof that it is technically more efficient. Technical efficiency concerns real costs of production, not sale prices fixed under conditions of shortage or conditions of monopoly. I do not here raise the question whether, in fact, cost of production was less in Government than in private shell factories. Whether it was so or not, it certainly cannot be proved to have been so by a comparison of the costs of production in Government factories with the selling price of private factories. This argument, like the preceding, therefore, falls to the ground.

[1] Chiozza Money, *The Triumph of Nationalization*, pp. 86-7.

§ 5. Another negative proposition of a general character may be set down. This is that attempts to conduct such a comparison by reference to statistics are foredoomed to failure. No doubt, if it could be shown that, *other conditions being the same*, a given output was, in general, obtained at greater, or at less, real cost under public than under private management, genuine evidence about the relative efficiency of the two forms of organisation would be obtained. But in real life this is impracticable. In the first place, the quality of services, which are called by the same name, varies enormously in different places, and it is almost impossible properly to allow for these variations. " Our street cars," say the Reporters of the American Civic Federation, " run faster, carry more strap passengers, and kill and injure more people than the street cars, public or private, of any other country. Our people seem to like this, but the English would not." [1] How can differences of this sort possibly be taken into account ? Again, the conditions of production in different places are utterly different. " In Syracuse (U.S.A.) the water flows to the city by gravity ; in Indianapolis it must be pumped." [2] " To compare a private corporation within the limits of a great city, where an immense supply is furnished, and where special conditions of non-interference with adjoining property rights are to be met, with some municipal plant in a suburban town, upon a basis of the relative amount of supplies and labour required per unit of electrical energy, would obviously be unfair to both contestants. Nor is it possible to compare in this manner two lighting-stations having approximately the same yearly output, and which are similarly located with reference to adjoining interests, but are situated, the one in the North and the other in the South, for the reason that the daily period of service will vary in these two localities on account of variation in the hours of darkness. For the same reason we cannot compare the summer service of one station with the winter service of another, even though we should attempt to reduce them both to a common basis by obtaining the amount of human effort employed per unit of electrical

[1] *Municipal and Private Operation of Public Utilities*, vol. i. p. 287.
[2] *Ibid.* vol. i. p. 21.

energy." [1] In short, arguments from statistics, even apart from the pitfalls with which unwary inquirers are confronted in the interpretation of municipal accounts,[2] are, in this field, almost entirely valueless. This remark is of general application. But, in view of the exceptional psychological conditions of war time and the temporary use by government of a large number of able men normally engaged in private business, as well as of the fact that the commodities produced in government factories during the war were for State use and not for the market, it has very special relevance to arguments drawn from the experiences of the war period.

§ 6. Statistical evidence being thus inadequate, it is necessary to proceed—again as in our study of voluntary Purchasers' Associations—by way of general considerations. Let us begin by comparing public operation with *uncontrolled* private operation. There is general agreement that, when conditions are such as to allow of small scale production by private businesses, the personal interest of the head of the business in its success provides a stimulus to efficiency that is lacking in both joint stock private concerns and in public concerns. Over a large field of industry, however, the practical choice is, not between private businesses and public concerns, but between joint stock companies and public concerns. Here the initiative, freedom and interest of the captain of industry working his own comparatively small business cannot be had in any event. The issue is a different and more evenly balanced one. The discussion of it may well be started with an observation of the Committee of the American Civic Federation: "There are no particular reasons why the financial results from private or public operation should be different if the conditions are the same." [3] The reason for this remark, of course, is that, whether a service is provided by a private company or by a public governmental authority, the actual running of the business must be similar. An expert staff must be appointed, controlled in a general way, in the one case by a committee of

[1] Bemis, *Municipal Monopolies*, pp. 289-90.

[2] Cf., *inter alia*, Knoop, *Principles and Methods of Municipal Trading*, chap. v.

[3] *Municipal and Private Operation of Public Utilities*, vol. i. p. 23.

directors chosen by the shareholders, in the other case by a committee, a commission, a council, a ministerial department, or an *ad hoc* body like the Port of London Authority, to represent the public. Managing power, as a whole, may be conceived as distributed among electors, directors—or committee, or whatever the controlling authority is—and staff. There seem no general *a priori* grounds for holding, without reference to the special nature of the controlling organisations evolved under them, that either public or private management is likely to prove technically the more efficient.

§ 7. In some matters of slight, but not negligible, importance experience suggests that the public authority has an advantage. This advantage is analogous to one found in productive co-operation. It is that, for a given sum of money, a more efficient engineer or manager can be obtained than will be forthcoming under private management, for the reason that the position of a public servant is at once attractive in itself and also makes appeal to altruistic motives; or, alternatively, that an engineer or manager of given efficiency can be obtained for a smaller sum of money. This advantage, it must be clearly understood, is a real advantage, and not a kind of bounty obtained at the expense of the engineer or manager; for there is created a new value in the extra satisfaction which the said engineer or manager derives from the fact of serving the public. The difference between what a man of given ability would have been willing to work for in a private company and what he does work for in a State department is, in effect, extra product due to the adoption of the public form of industrial organisation. This difference is not, of course, equivalent to the difference between the earnings of the head of a State department and those of the head of a private business, because in the earnings of the latter there is generally included a return for " waiting " and " uncertainty-bearing,"—services which in the public departments are provided by the tax-payer. It is fallacious to take the excess of the income of an American railway king over that of the administrator of the Prussian State railways in pre-war days as a measure of the comparative wastefulness of private enterprise. Still there is, *pro tanto*, an advantage on the side of public operation in the fact that good technical experts under it cost less.

§ 8. A more important matter is the business capacity of the authority above the technical managers which determines general policy. In municipal undertakings this authority is generally a committee of the town council—a body whose members are elected for their political, rather than for their commercial, qualifications, and are also more liable than the directors of a company to lose their seats at short intervals. There is the further difficulty that the employees of a municipal enterprise may play an important part in electing councillors. This may lead some councillors to interfere for political reasons with the disciplinary and other discretionary powers of the higher officials. It has even been suggested that in some towns city engineers have been hindered by the council from introducing labour-saving devices, by which the employment of some of the councillors' electors would be threatened.[1]

In national undertakings run by a government department the higher authority is a body of civil servants technically subordinate to a political head responsible to Parliament. Through this political head, pressure of various sorts, some of it probably anti-social in character, can be exercised on the running of the undertaking. But, even if this does not happen, the civil service organisation, no doubt excellent for the purposes for which it is primarily designed, is apt to cramp efficiency. When important decisions have to be taken there is a tradition of method in government offices that makes for delay, hesitancy and immobility.[2] Thus Mr. Justice

---

[1] *Municipal and Private Operation of Public Utilities*, vol. i. p. 23.

[2] Mr. Hawtrey writes: "Substitute a functionary for an independent trader, and he finds himself precluded from doing anything which he cannot explain and defend if called upon, to his official superior. . . . The practical judgment is partly sub-conscious, and, in so far as it is conscious, its mental processes are not *linguistic*. To express in language even the decision itself is an effort; to express the grounds on which it is taken would often be a formidable exercise in both psychology and literary composition. . . . There is a tendency for any official hierarchy to be limited to those decisions that can be readily communicated in language from one functionary to another. . . . An enlightened bureaucracy would try by every available means to escape from this paralysing limitation, and to devolve and decentralise whenever possible. But the limitation is inherent in the system and cannot be avoided altogether" (*The Economic Problem*, pp. 339-40).

Sankey, in his report on the coal mining industry, speaks of
"the present Civil Service system of selection and promotion
by length of service, of grades of servants, of minuting copies
and reports from one servant to another, and of salaries and
pensions." In pure routine work this system may do no
harm, but, when enterprise and quick decisions are necessary,
it cannot fail to prove hampering both in the choice of the
most suitable man for a given work and in the actual carrying
on of work. It should be noted that this consideration is
very much less important in concerns producing exclusively,
as, in war time especially, certain concerns do, for government;
for work of this kind must be done on order, and there is no
scope for that forecasting of the market in which government
departments are commonly supposed to be inferior to private
businesses or joint stock companies. Thus Professor Lehfeldt
has well observed: "Anyone—government, company or individual—who can take over the whole output of a factory
may well be justified in setting one up for himself; but the
ordinary factory has to sell its products and to find customers:
that is quite a different matter."[1] In this connection the
early history of telegraphic communication is interesting.
The semaphore system of optical telegraphy invented at the
end of the eighteenth century was taken up by the French
Government for military use, confined to that use, and worked
by the government exclusively. In 1845 the French Government, in a like spirit and for a like purpose, started an electric
telegraph. "The public authorities felt a need of their own,
and, finding no one else to supply it for them, set to work
to supply it for themselves. . . . Public ownership of
telegraphs in the beginning was not, strictly speaking, a
manifestation of the spirit of business enterprise. It was
simply a branch of the public administration, forced upon the
government by the lack of private enterprise."[2] When an
industry is chiefly engaged in producing things for the consumption of the general public, the call for prevision and constructive
speculation is, of course, much greater, and, therefore, the defects
of civil service methods correspondingly more marked.

[1] *Economics in the Light of War*, p. 26.
[2] Holcombe, *Public Ownership of Telephones on the Continent of Europe*, p. 21.

It is coming, however, more and more to be realised that the public operation of national undertakings does not necessarily imply that these undertakings are run by a government department organised on civil service principles. The Port of London Authority is a special authority working quite differently from a government department. Canada has created the Canadian National Railways Company, with the government as the only shareholder, but with business directors appointed like ordinary directors and endowed with complete freedom of management.[1] The proposals of the Sankey Commission also aimed at setting up an authority for coal mining, which, though national, should nevertheless be run in the main on non-bureaucratic and non-political lines. Consumers' representatives were to be associated with the management, as is already done in the national telephone service of Switzerland.[2] A comparison of a body of this type with the directorate of a joint stock company might well work out more favourably than a comparison of, say, the body ruling the Post Office with such a directorate. Plainly, it is impossible to generalise on this matter of business competence, apart from a knowledge of the detailed organisation under which it is proposed that particular public undertakings should be run.

§ 9. So far governmental operation has been set against *uncontrolled* private or joint stock operation. In practice, however, as has already been made clear, where public operation is a live issue, the alternative is *controlled* private or joint stock operation. Control must hamper that initiative which is the chief merit of private enterprise, and the extent to which it hampers it will be greater the more far-reaching is the control. If it goes so far as to settle the things to be produced and the method of production, it will hamper initiative greatly. If, on the other hand, it does not extend beyond fixing a maximum price with a liberal margin, or even

[1] Acworth, *State Railway Ownership*, p. 12. The directors are, however, only appointed for one year, and it is, therefore, in the power of the government at any time to make the management, in effect, political by choosing directors subservient to itself.

[2] Cf. Holcombe, *Public Ownership of Telephones on the Continent of Europe*, p. 252.

fixing a sliding scale of profits and prices in combination, as under some gas company charters, it will, of course, hamper initiative much less. It is, thus, not possible to compare the technical efficiency of government operation and of controlled private operation in general terms, because controlled private operation may mean any one of a great number of different things—just, indeed, as, on the showing of preceding sections, government operation itself may also do. The only broad inference to which we are entitled is that, as between government operation and controlled private operation, a comparison of technical efficiency is likely to be somewhat more favourable to government operation than it would be as against uncontrolled private operation.

§ 10. This somewhat impotent conclusion does not, however, exhaust the discussion. There remain three important groups of considerations which, when we look beyond mere technical competence, tend to suggest that public operation is likely—not, of course, always, but as a general rule—to be inferior, from the standpoint of the dividend, to public control. The first of these has to do with the fact that, not only different producers within the same industry, but also different producers in apparently disconnected industries, are often, in reality, rivals. No doubt, an industry can be imagined which is monopolistic in the widest possible sense, in such wise that not only are there no competing firms within it, but also there are no competing industries outside it. There is some reason to believe that the service of supplying a modern city with water is monopolistic in this sense. It would be possible, by combining together a number of industries that are now separate, to create other monopolies of the same sort. For example, the various means of communication, such as omnibuses, trams, motor cars and carriages, might all conceivably be brought together under one hand. The same thing might conceivably be done with all the means of providing artificial light or all the means of providing power. But such arrangements are quite out of relation to actual facts. As things are at present, I should doubt if any industry, except that of water supply, can properly be regarded as monopolistic in the wide sense here taken. Now, the interest of the national dividend requires that, where a number of establishments, whether in the same industry or in different industries, are competing for the supply of some public need, that one which can supply it most efficiently shall oust the others. But, when any enterprise is operated by a public authority, it is likely to be maintained by artificial support, even though it is less efficient than its rivals. The reason is that persons in control of such an enterprise, being naturally anxious to make that enterprise a success, tend to identify the good of the whole with the good of their own department. Hence a government authority embarked on a business is almost certain, if it prove commercially weak, to employ unfair weapons from its non-commercial armoury, the use of which will maintain it more or less permanently in being, despite the fact that its productive methods are more costly than those of its rivals. These unfair methods are of two sorts, according as they are directed primarily to defend the government enterprise or to obstruct its competitors.

Defensive non-commercial methods consist, in the main, in the conscious or unconscious practice of devices for securing a differential bounty from the general public. A government authority, which is engaged partly in business and partly in rendering general unremunerated services, may charge expenses that really belong to the business against the other part of its work. A very glaring example is the practice of the London County Council in writing down the value of land purchased for workmen's dwellings to the value which it has, not in the general market, but as ear-marked for this particular purpose. Again, municipal tramway accounts may be given a false appearance of prosperity by the device of charging expenditure upon roads, which is properly attributable to them, to the general road account.[1] A like device is adopted in a milder form when a municipality fails to set aside a special fund to balance the advantage it possesses over private enterprise in being able to borrow money on easier terms. " A municipality can float bonds at a lower rate of interest than a private company, since the whole assessable

---

[1] *Municipal and Private Operation of Public Utilities,* vol. i. p. 469.

property of the town is generally liable for the payment of interest and principal, while the company can give security only on the works."[1] This ability on the part of a municipality is thus due, in the main, simply to the fact that it is able to force upon the ratepayers an obligation to pay its bondholders even if the enterprise fails, while a private company has, by the offer of higher pay, to obtain debenture holders who are prepared, in the event of failure, to lose their money. Except in so far as the fear of failure, and, therefore, the extra compensation asked for by debenture holders, is due to public ignorance of facts which are more readily ascertainable in connection with municipalities than with companies[2]—to that extent municipal operation effects a small real saving—the social cost of the municipality's cheap loan is the same as that of the company's relatively dear loan. If the two enterprises are to compete fairly, the municipality ought to transfer to the rates the bulk of its gain from better credit, before balancing the accounts of its business. If it does not do this, it is, in effect, assisting that business by a contribution from the general public. In so far as the lower terms on which it can engage managers and engineers are due to the fact that the shouldering of risks by the ratepayers safeguards them against the possibility of their employers going bankrupt, it is doing the same thing a second time, unless it transfers the gain made under this head also to the rates. Of course, if a municipally managed undertaking, *on account of superior efficiency*, is less likely to make a loss than a corresponding private concern, there is a real gain. But, since, in any event, there is the gilt-edged guarantee of the ratepayers, that gain is not reflected in the better terms on which the municipality can borrow.

Aggressive non-commercial methods are made possible by the fact that public authorities, besides operating their own

---

[1] Bemis, *Municipal Monopolies*, p. 45.

[2] The advantage available for municipal enterprise, thus hinted at, turns upon the fact that, when people invest in any undertaking through an intermediary, they always face the possibility that this intermediary may prove to be dishonest and unwilling to fulfil his obligations. The uncertainty-bearing undertaken in this way is a real element in the cost of production. When the State is the intermediary, its honesty and financial strength are, in general, so well known that this element is practically eliminated.

enterprises, are often also endowed with powers of control over other enterprises. When they are in this position, there is a grave danger that the public authorities may be tempted to use their powers of control in such a way as to obstruct and injure rivals. An Education Authority, for example, which both runs schools of its own and makes regulations for the running of rival schools, is under strong temptation. So is an authority which at once builds houses and frames building bye-laws; and so also are municipalities operating gas-lighting or tramways and controlling electric-lighting or motor omnibuses. Among the methods of aggression open to them perhaps the simplest is that of making the conditions about sinking funds, under which their own establishments work, more favourable than the conditions about purchase at the end of the lease, which are imposed upon private companies. A public authority, which provides a sinking fund to extinguish the capital debt of its enterprise, as well as a fund to cover depreciation and obsolescence, is, in effect, taxing its present citizens for the benefit of posterity.[1] In like manner, a public authority, which confers a franchise on a private company upon condition that the company's plant shall pass to itself at the end of the lease, either free of charge or at "cost of replacement," is imposing a similar tax. It is readily seen that the terms of sinking funds and franchises respectively *can* be so arranged that the burden under the sinking fund is the smaller, and, therefore, that private operation suffers, as against the rival system, a differential injury.

There are, however, grosser forms of aggression than the above. It is notorious that those municipalities which operated their own gas-plant vigorously obstructed, by the exercise of their veto and in other ways, the development of electric-lighting companies. Again: "Since 1898 the desire to protect the local municipal electric light plants has been permitted to impede the spread of the so-called electricity-in-bulk generating and distributing companies."[2] In like manner,

---

[1] The Board of Agriculture has made a new departure in not requiring the County Councils to charge small holders, who hire land from them, rents high enough to provide this kind of sinking fund.—[Cd. 4245], p. 12.

[2] H. Meyer, *Public Ownership and the Telephones*, p. 351.

the central government, in order to protect its telegraph monopoly, has placed administrative obstacles in the way of other means of electrical communication. In 1884 the Postmaster-General declined to allow the National Telephone Company to receive or deliver a written message at any of its offices, and, in defending this course, said : " It would make, I am afraid, a serious hole in the telegraph revenue, if written messages were allowed to be sent." [1] In like manner, in Norway, when (in 1881) a company sought a licence to establish a long-distance telephone between Drammen and Christiania, the Government made it a condition that the company should guarantee to make good " all losses occasioned to its (the Government's) telegraph lines between the two cities "; and similar compensations were required of other telephone promoters. [2] Finally, in the charter granted to the Marconi Wireless Company in 1906, permitting the transmission of wireless messages between the United Kingdom and North America, it was specially provided that permission would not be granted for messages to or from any European country except Italy, the purpose being to safeguard the interests of the cables owned by the British and Continental governments. [3]

The use of defensive and aggressive weapons of an " unfair " uncommercial character by public authorities operating enterprises brings it about, as already explained, that an enterprise run by them is often maintained in existence, despite the fact that the end served by it would be served more cheaply by a rival enterprise. It is necessary to note, in conclusion, that the use of these methods tends to extrude economically superior rivals even more effectively than it appears to do at first sight. For it acts, not only directly, but also indirectly through anticipation. It not only drives out of the market existing competitors, but checks the entry of new ones. When a man contemplating a philanthropic enterprise is given to understand that, should his experiment succeed, a public authority will enter the field he has proved fruitful, he

---

[1] H. Meyer, *Public Ownership and the Telephones*, p. 18.

[2] Cf. Holcombe, *Public Ownership of Telephones on the Continent of Europe*, pp. 375 and 377.

[3] H. Meyer, *Public Ownership and the Telephones*, pp. 341-2.

does—or should—rejoice. But, when a man engaged in a
business enterprise is given to understand this, the end he is
pursuing is not, like the philanthropist's, furthered. It is, on
the contrary, thwarted, and his energies are, therefore, diverted
from the undertaking. An effect of this kind is claimed to
have resulted from municipal experiments in house-building.
These considerations, when they have relevance, evidently
strengthen the probability that the operation of industries
by public authorities will be injurious to productive efficiency ;
and they are bound to have some degree of relevance except
in industries that are monopolistic in the widest possible
sense.

§ 11. I pass to a second consideration. This has to do with
the fact that the working of any industrial enterprise involves
some degree of uncertainty. As will be explained at length in
Appendix I., the exposing of money to uncertainty is a definite
factor of production, which makes output larger than it would
become without it. In the long run willingness to expose
£100 to an equal chance of becoming £160 or of becoming
£50 is bound to increase the national dividend. If willingness to expose money to uncertainty on the part of people in
control of industry is " artificially " restricted, enterprise and
adventure that make for industrial progress, and, therewith, for
production, will be hampered. Furthermore, the injury thus
wrought is very much larger than appears at first sight. For,
since any experiment with an untried process *may* fail, a
diminished willingness to expose money to uncertainty implies
a restriction of experiment, and, hence, a diminution in the
inducement to enterprising persons to make useful inventions.
No doubt, there is reason to believe that, with the growing
dependence of industry upon non-commercial science, this
consideration has become less important than it used to be.
Dr. Mertz has well observed : " The great inventions of former
ages were made in countries whose practical life, industry and
commerce were most advanced ; but the great inventions of
the last fifty years in chemistry, electricity and the science of
heat have been made in the scientific laboratory ; the former
were stimulated by practical wants ; the latter themselves
produced new functional requirements, and created new spheres

of labour, industry and commerce."[1]   It still remains true, however, that, though the fundamental discoveries are often non-commercial, yet the application of them through "inventions," in the earlier stages before the inventions have been proved by experience, generally requires a commercial stimulus.   Anything which restricts unduly willingness to make ventures in any industry must still, therefore, threaten heavy loss.   The point I have to urge is that a public body engaged in industrial operations is *likely* to restrict unduly this willingness.

The defence of this proposition rests on the following reasons.   First, public authorities recognise that hostility to government on the part of the people is an evil, and they also recognise that an unsuccessful State speculation, "if it involves repudiation or oppressive taxation for years to come, produces a popular revulsion and deep-seated distrust of government itself in all its branches."   Secondly, the persons at any time in control of a public authority, when that authority is dependent on the party system, cannot but know that "failure would give their political opponents too good an opportunity to ride into power."[2]   Thirdly, these persons are partly able to perceive that, if people are *compelled* to expose resources to uncertainty in proportion to the rateable value of their houses, more real sacrifice will be involved than if the same aggregate of resources to be exposed to the same scheme of uncertainty were obtained, by way of voluntary contributions, in proportion to the attractive force exercised upon the several contributors by the prospective profits.   Finally, and this is really the most fundamental point, if inventors must appeal to government officials, they are confronted, as it were, with the average daring of the community, whereas, if they are free to appeal to private enterprise, they can select a group of supporters from persons above this average.   As Leroy Beaulieu well wrote : "A man of initiative will always find, among the forty million inhabitants of a country, *some* audacious persons who will believe in him, will follow him, will make their fortunes with him or will ruin themselves with him.   He would waste

---

[1] Mertz, *History of European Thought*, vol. i. p. 92.
[2] H. Meyer, *Public Ownership and the Telephones in Great Britain*, p. 349.

his time in trying to convince those hierarchical bureaus which are the heavy and necessary thought-organs and action-organs of a State."[1] It follows that, in general, while the hope of gain operates more strongly on private enterprise than on the public authority, the fear of loss operates more strongly on the public authority. Of course, this is not true in war time. Then, as recent experience has shown, governments will authorise experiments in new types of destructive apparatus regardless of cost. But the fact that it is not true in war time is no argument against its truth in times of peace. Just as experience shows it to be untrue in war, so also it shows it to be true in normal conditions. Public authorities are, in general, less willing than private concerns to take risks, or, to put it technically, to provide the factor uncertainty-bearing. A good illustration of this tendency is afforded by the conduct of the British Government in regard to the working of the telephone trunk lines after they had been taken over by the Post Office in 1892. "The Treasury compelled the Post Office to adopt the policy of refusing to make any extensions of doubtful prospect, unless private persons, or the local authority interested, should guarantee 'a specific revenue per year, fixed with reference to the estimated cost of working and maintaining a given mileage of trunk-line wire.'"[2] The opinion of Sir George Gibb may be cited in evidence that this proceeding is representative of the general attitude of public authorities. He wrote: "Whatever may be thought as to the respective merits of private and public ownership, it cannot be denied that private enterprise does take more risk than any government is likely to do except under pressure of military necessities."[3] Marshall brings out very clearly the effect upon inventions implied in this unwillingness of public bodies to bear uncertainty: "It is notorious that, though departments of central and municipal governments employ many thousands of highly-paid servants in engineering and other progressive industries, very few inventions of any importance are made by them; and nearly all of these few are the work of men like

[1] *L'État moderne*, pp. 55, 208.

[2] H. Meyer, *Public Ownership and the Telephones in Great Britain*, p. 65.

[3] *Railway Nationalisation*, p. 9.

Sir W. H. Preece, who had been thoroughly trained in free enterprise before they entered Government service. Government creates scarcely anything. . . . A Government could print a good edition of Shakespeare's works, but it could not have got them written. . . . The carcase of municipal electric works belongs to the officials, the genius belongs to free enterprise." [1] Again, the Reporter of the American Civic Federation writes: " The Assistant Secretary of the Board of Trade, Mr. Pelham, told the Committee [of the Civic Federation] that they did not encourage the trying of new inventions, or the trying of systems in any way experimental, by municipalities. They waited for these to be proven out by private companies. Progress is all with the companies." [2] Moreover, at present, the comparatively small number of undertakings which are operated by public authorities stand in a *milieu* where private enterprise is dominant, and where most of the constituents of governing persons are working under private enterprise. In these circumstances public enterprise may be keyed up to a degree of daring which it would not attain if, instead of being the exception, it became the rule.[3]

Now, it is evident that the effect of a restriction of the willingness to take risks, and, therewith, of the stimulus to invention, upon the economies of production will vary in importance in different industries, according to the extent of the speculative element involved in them. Hence it follows that the relative inefficiency of public operation, as compared with private operation, is very large in highly speculative undertakings, and dwindles to nothing in respect of those where the speculative element is practically non-existent. This idea is sometimes crystallised in an attempt to group industries into two divisions, the speculative and the non-speculative, after the manner in which trustees distinguish between speculative securities and investment securities. This grouping, it is sometimes suggested, can be adequately worked out by setting on the one side new industries in an experimental stage, and on the other industries that are

[1] *Economic Journal*, 1907, pp. 21-2. Cf. also Ryan, *Distributive Justice*, p. 165.
[2] *Municipal and Private Operation of Public Utilities*, vol. i. p. 437.
[3] Cf. Aftalion, *Les Fondements du Socialisme*, pp. 233-4.

already tried and known.   Thus a recent writer has put in
the former category " airship construction, wireless telegraphy,
ornamental and luxury trades, the production of single special
machines and special transport arrangements, the erection of
big and difficult buildings and the like," and in the latter
" coal mines, the manufacture of steel, cement, locomotives,
telephones, electric cables, motors, and so forth." [1]   Again,
Sir George Gibb distinguishes, from this point of view, the
railway industry at an early, and at a mature, age.   " As
regards the age of construction, at all events, England has
derived incalculable benefit from the fact that the railway
system has been made by private enterprise.   But the problem
of working the railway system after it has been constructed
is, I admit, essentially different from the problem of securing
its construction." [2]   In like manner, Professor Commons, writing
in 1904, while he approved of the establishment of city electric-
lighting plants at that time, considered that " those cities which
entered upon municipal electric lighting eight or ten years ago
are open to criticism."   " Private parties," he holds, " should be
encouraged to push forward in all the untrod fields." [3]   The
distinction thus insisted on has, no doubt, considerable importance.   Two points, however, should be noticed.   First,
an industry, which is old-established at one place, may need
new construction at another, and the conditions of construction
there may be such that a large speculative element remains.
For example, though the industry of water supply is an old
one, different towns have to be supplied from sources situated
so differently, and along routes of such varying character, that
little guidance for one town can be drawn from the experience
of others.   Secondly, no industry is likely to be so far established that experimentation—which involves speculation—as
to improved methods is undesirable.   In some measure all
industries, in which possibilities of development remain, demand
readiness to take risks if further inventions are to be made,
and are, therefore, liable to be hampered by anything that
obstructs this readiness.   It would, therefore, be an error to

[1] Strobel, *Socialisation in Theory and Practice*, p. 281.
[2] *Railway Nationalisation*, p. 11.
[3] Bemis, *Municipal Monopolies*, p. 56.

suppose that the relatively uneconomic character of public operation, due to the circumstances discussed in this section, is significant only for new industries. It probably has some appreciable significance in regard to nearly all industries, though, of course, its importance is greatest in regard to those in an experimental stage.

§ 12. I pass to a third consideration. The relative inferiority of public operation, due to the interference which it causes with the most economical combination of the different factors of production—for that is, in effect, what obstacles in the way of people's readiness to take risks, or to brave uncertainty, implies—is paralleled, in many industries, by a further inferiority due to interference with the most economical size of business unit. Practically speaking, public undertakings can only be operated by groups of people united into some form of political organisation. But it is highly improbable that the areas of control most economical for the working of any industry will correspond in size with the areas covered by the public authorities existing in a modern State, since these are set up with regard to quite other considerations than the efficient running of industries. Consequently, in general, it must happen either that special public authorities are created for the express purpose of running certain industries or that the size of the units of control in these industries is altered to fit the scope of existing public authorities. For very large enterprises having a scope midway between that of the central government and that of the relevant local authority, experience shows that special public bodies, adapted to this scope, can be, and have been, created. We are familiar, for example, with the various harbour trusts and dock trusts, with the London Water Board and the Port of London Authority. Another device is that of joint boards of management representing two or more local authorities. "In England and Wales, during the year 1907–8, there were twenty-five joint boards or committees for the supply of water, two for the supply of water and gas, and one for the supply of electricity and the management of a tramway undertaking."[1] Though, however, for very

[1] Knoop, *Principles and Methods of Municipal Trading*, p. 117. As Prof. Knoop further points out, it not infrequently happens that a municipality enters into

large businesses, the creation of special public bodies is admittedly a practicable policy, it is not always likely to be
adopted.   The danger, that, under public operation, local
authorities inadequate in area will become the agents of that
operation, is especially great in industries originally adapted
to the area covered by these agents, but afterwards fitted, as a
result of new inventions, for larger areas.   In former times the
areas of management most suitable for the industries of water
supply, gas lighting and electric power supply were approximately coincident with the several municipal areas.   But, since
the advent of certain modern discoveries, the areas, which might
be expected to prove economically most efficient, are often
much larger than municipal areas.   Thus, " with horse traction
the limit of each local authority was, roughly, the limit of
commercial working.   With electric traction the parish became
a mere item in a comprehensive system, which might extend
over a whole county." [1]   Again, with the improvement in
methods of distribution for electricity in bulk, the most
economical area for the supply of electricity has come to
extend over thousands of square miles.   Even in the supply
of water, now that the needs of large towns are satisfied by
the tapping of distant lakes, there may be economy in a
joint organisation for supplying a number of towns along the
route that the pipes must follow.   Indeed, it would seem that
gas lighting is the only one of the public utility industries
for which the most economical area of management at the
present time does not exceed the municipal area.   These
changes in the area proper to management have not, however,
in general, been followed by the transference of the public
utility industries to new public authorities created *ad hoc*;
for the task of ousting the municipalities is opposed by an
immense amount of friction, and is, therefore, little likely to
be successfully undertaken.   Hence, in practice, public operation often implies that industries, whose most economical area
of management is intermediate between the areas representative
of the central authority and of local authorities respectively,

---

an arrangement with smaller authorities to extend its tramway, water, or gas
system beyond its own boundaries so as to include adjacent areas also.
    [1] Porter, *Dangers of Municipal Ownership*, p. 245.

will, in fact, be worked by local authorities; and this, of course, implies a reduction of the unit of management below what is economically best.[1]   In enterprises whose most economical area of management is smaller than that covered by the smallest existing type of public authority, the creation of new authorities for the special purpose of running them cannot even be said to be practicable.   If such industries are to be taken over by any public authority, this authority can hardly be other than one of the authorities that already exist for other purposes. Consequently, in these industries public operation, not merely in general, but practically always, implies the introduction of a scale of management larger than is economically most efficient.

§ 13. Now, if it were the fact that under private enterprise all industries would always evolve the most economical unit of management, it would follow that public operation could not, in this respect, be superior, and would, in general, be greatly inferior, to private operation.   In industries normally conducted under conditions of simple competition, such as the industries of baking, milk-supply, house-building or farming, we may fairly presume that private enterprise will, for the most part, evolve the most efficient size of unit.   But, where any element of monopoly is present, we may by no means presume this.   The most economical unit may be prevented from realising itself through friction, or through the hindrance imposed by popular dislike of large amalgamations, or in other ways.   The probability that it will be so prevented is especially great in an industry whose normal condition is, not that of simple monopoly, but that of monopolistic competition. Here, as was pointed out in Chapter IX., there are large wastes due to competitive advertisement and so forth, which

[1] It may be objected that the alternative to municipal operation is usually municipal control, and that this control, when the area of the municipality is too small, may render private undertakings as inefficient as municipal under- takings would be.   But it is easier to transfer control than it is to transfer operation to an authority of wider scope than the municipalities.   The British Light Railways Act of 1906 establishes such a wider authority in the shape of the Light Railway Commissioners.   (Cf. H. Meyer, *Municipal Ownership in Great Britain*, p. 69.)   Again : " When, as in Massachusetts, it is not uncommon for a street railway company to operate franchises from ten, and, in one case, from nineteen different towns, independent municipal control is out of the question. The State railroad commission is the recognition in law of this condition of fact " (Rowe, *Annals of the American Academy*, 1900, p. 19).

centralisation under a single management might remove. Of railways, for example, Sir George Gibb wrote some years ago: "Each railway company works for its own route. The result is that unnecessary mileage is run, and train loads are lessened. . . . If those responsible for the handling and carriage of railway traffic could work with a single eye to economical results, and in all cases forward traffic by the routes which yielded the best working results, great economies could undoubtedly be effected."[1] This statement was borne out by the experience of the joint working of British railways during the war; though it must be remembered that the character of war-time traffic, with its large train loads of munitions and troops, was exceptionally favourable to economical working. Like economies are sometimes obtainable from the combination, not of different firms engaged in the same occupation, but of different occupations. There is probably an economy in the co-ordination under one hand of the various industries that utilise the public streets. "Water mains may be laid before streets are paved, thus saving the damage and expense of tearing up good pavement to lay water pipes."[2] In like manner, it may well be held that important economies would result if the work of treating disease could be brought, by means of a State medical service, into direct connection with the work of preventing disease that is now undertaken by the Public Health authorities. Though, therefore, indirect evil consequences of the kind discussed in Chapter X. § 4 may emerge, and though also certain vertical combinations, e.g. between a particular coal-mine and a particular ironworks, that would yield structural economies, may be impeded, it is at least possible that, in enterprises of this sort, public operation, instead of hindering, might actually foster the growth of the most economical unit of management.[3]

§ 14. So far of generalities. When the practical issue is

---

[1] *Railway Nationalisation*, p. 21.

[2] Bemis, *Municipal Monopolies*, p. 46.

[3] This conclusion is not, of course, upset by the fact that, as shown in the recent Act for grouping British railways, it is *possible* for the State to further an expansion of the unit of management in an industry, while leaving that industry in private hands.

raised whether a particular class of enterprise could, with greater advantage to the national dividend, be publicly controlled or publicly operated, it will be necessary, in order to reach a satisfactory conclusion, to take into account both the comparative effects which the two forms of management are likely to have on productive efficiency and the comparative ease with which whatever regulation the public interest may require can be applied under them. In industries closely associated with the public health, where reliable quality is essential and where inspection cannot easily be made thorough, public operation may be desirable, even though the probable alternative is competitive, and not monopolistic, production. Thus there is much to be said for the public provision of slaughter-houses, to which, as in Germany, all butchers are compelled to resort, and for the public provision of milk for the use of young children. The Reporters to the American Civic Federation are of opinion that "undertakings in which the sanitary motive largely enters should be operated by the public." [1] On the other hand, industries, in which the typical producing unit is small, and private firms,. rather than joint stock companies, are dominant, are hardly ever suitable for management by public authorities. Apart from a few special exceptions, the proposal for public operation is a live one only in industries in which the typical producing unit is large, and which, therefore, tend towards monopoly. The case for it, as against the case for public control, is strongest in industries which have been reduced more or less to routine and in which there is comparatively little scope for daring adventure. It is relatively weak in industries which are to an important extent rival to other privately operated industries, or in which the normal unit of management covers an area widely different from that covered by existing public authorities. Whether any particular monopolistic industry should be publicly operated or publicly controlled cannot be determined in a general way. Before a decision between these alternative methods is arrived at, a detailed investigation of the industry must be made, and this should be supplemented by an impartial estimate of the quality of the particular

[1] *Municipal and Private Operation of Public Utilities*, vol. i. p. 23.

public authority whose action is involved, as well as of the probable effect of new tasks upon its efficiency for the purpose of its primary non-industrial duties.

§ 15. If, on the strength of the foregoing or other considerations, it is decided that an industry already in existence and operated by private persons shall be taken over by public authority, it is necessary to settle the terms on which this shall be done. Let us, for simplicity, suppose the conditions to be such that under public operation the technical efficiency of production will be unaltered. Public operation is desired because, without it, a monopolistic or partially monopolistic concern is able to force up prices against the public and so to check the development of the industry under its command. If, in these circumstances, a public authority buys up the concern *at its market value*, it will have either itself to charge the same price for its services as the private company was charging, or else to operate the concern at a loss. In other words, if it buys the concern at its market value, the proprietors will have made the public *buy* their right to make monopolistic exactions; for the market value will, of course, be, in part, the result of people's belief in their possession of that right. It is natural, therefore, to say that the price paid ought not to be the market value as it actually is, but the market value as it would be if this anti-social right were eliminated. But here the considerations set out at the end of the last chapter give us pause. Some concession must, it would seem, be made in the interests of recent purchasers who have acquired shares in the concern in good faith at the high existing values. How large this concession should be cannot, of course, be laid down in general terms. In each separate instance a detailed review will have to be made of all relevant circumstances, including "legitimate expectations" that have been created, and on this foundation common sense must be invoked to furnish a "reasonable" compromise. When the purchase price is settled, payment will, of course, in general be made by an issue of government, or municipal, or "public authority" (*e.g.* Port of London Authority) stock bearing fixed interest, and not by an actual transfer of cash.

§ 16. This question of the purchase price leads on to

a very important consideration, with which this Part may suitably close. At first sight it might seem that, if the public has to pay the full market value for a monopolistic concern, which is charging exorbitant prices for its products, no national advantage can possibly result. The monopolist simply takes in a lump sum what otherwise he would have got in an annual tribute. This way of looking at the matter is, however, mistaken. The evil of monopoly is not merely, or even mainly, that it enables one set of people to mulct another set. It is that it causes resources to be held back from a form of investment in which the value of the marginal social net product is larger than it is elsewhere, and thereby contracts the national dividend. To do away with this monopolistic policy will increase the size of the national dividend and augment economic welfare, in spite of the fact that, in order to do away with it, one part of the community has to pay a fine to another part. For this reason it is greatly preferable that the government should pay the ransom demanded by the monopolist, write off part of the purchase price, and then operate the concern on terms that would have yielded normal returns if no ransom had been necessary, than that it should allow the private monopolist to continue, by exorbitant charges, to hold back production and check the flow of resources into the enterprise. It is true that, if it does this, the government will have to borrow the purchase price from the public, and, subsequently, to levy taxation to provide interest upon it, and that the amount of this taxation will be roughly equivalent to the exaction which the monopolist would otherwise have made. We may presume, however, that the taxes imposed will either be direct, or, if indirect, will be spread over several commodities, and, therefore, will not shift industrial effort out of its normal channels nearly so far as the monopolist's exaction would have done. This consideration must not, of course, be allowed to make those persons who have to bargain on the public's behalf unduly pliant to the pressure of interested sellers. But it is, none the less, an important consideration. When the vested interests of new shareholders in monopolistic concerns make the government unwilling to force prices down to the proper level through a policy of control, it constitutes a very powerful argument for a policy of purchase. If purchase is made, the natural consequence would be for the government to operate the industry itself. But, if, for any reason, it does not wish to do this, and prefers to sell or lease it to private persons, on terms which involve a money loss to itself but provide for the establishment of a proper price level, it will still have eliminated the evil of monopolistic restriction of output and indirectly benefited the national dividend.

COSIMO is an innovative publisher of books and publications that inspire, inform and engage readers worldwide. Our titles are drawn from a range of subjects including health, business, philosophy, history, science and sacred texts. We specialize in using print-on-demand technology (POD), making it possible to publish books for both general and specialized audiences and to keep books in print indefinitely. With POD technology new titles can reach their audiences faster and more efficiently than with traditional publishing.

> **Permanent Availability:** Our books & publications never go out-of-print.

> **Global Availability:** Our books are always available online at popular retailers and can be ordered from your favorite local bookstore.

COSIMO CLASSICS brings to life unique, rare, out-of-print classics representing subjects as diverse as *Alternative Health, Business and Economics, Eastern Philosophy, Personal Growth, Mythology, Philosophy, Sacred Texts, Science, Spirituality* and much more!

COSIMO-on-DEMAND publishes your books, publications and reports. If you are an Author, part of an Organization, or a Benefactor with a publishing project and would like to bring books back into print, publish new books fast and effectively, would like your publications, books, training guides, and conference reports to be made available to your members and wider audiences around the world, we can assist you with your publishing needs.

Visit our website at www.cosimobooks.com to learn more about Cosimo, browse our catalog, take part in surveys or campaigns, and sign-up for our newsletter.

And if you wish please drop us a line at info@cosimobooks.com. We look forward to hearing from you.

CPSIA information can be obtained
at www.ICGtesting.com
Printed in the USA
BVOW03s0322011017
496384BV00001B/2/P